D1092711

NEW FACES OF THE FUR TRADE

NEW FACES OF THE FUR TRADE

Selected Papers of the Seventh

North American Fur Trade Conference,

Halifax, Nova Scotia, 1995

Edited by
Jo-Anne Fiske
Susan Sleeper-Smith
William Wicken

Michigan State University
East Lansing

Copyright© 1998 Michigan State University Press

All Michigan State University Press books are produced on paper which meets the requirements of American National Standard of Information Science—Permanence of paper for printed materials ANSI Z39.48-1984.

Michigan State University Press
East Lansing, Michigan 48823-5202

03 02 01 00 99 98 2 3 4 5 6 7 8 9

Library of Congress Cataloging-in-Publication Data

North American Fur Trade Conference (7th: 1995: Halifax, N. S.)
    New Faces in the fur trade: selected papers of the Seventh North American Fur Trade Conference, Halifax, Nova Scotia, 1995/Jo-Anne Fiske, Susan Sleeper-Smith, and Bill Wicken, editors.
        p.   cm.
    Includes bibliographical references and index.
    ISBN 0-87013-434-5 (alk. paper)
    1. Fur trade—North America—Congresses.   2. Fur trade—North America—History—Congresses.   I. Fiske, Jo-Anne, 1946-   II. Sleeper-Smith, Susan.   III, Wicken, William.   IV. Title.
HD9944.N6N67   1995
380.1'456753'097—dc21   97-51510
                                                                                              CIP

⚛ Contents

Section III
New Versions of Old Tales

Section IV
Enduring Issues, New Perspectives

Section V
Old Faces, New Voices

☙ | Preface

THIS VOLUME comprises a selection of papers initially presented at the Seventh North American Fur Trade Conference held in Halifax, Nova Scotia, in May of 1995.

The Halifax conference constituted a critical moment in the historiography of the North American fur trade. This conference drew together a community of scholars long fascinated with the trade and attracted a range of new faces, many of whom brought fresh perspectives on fur trade scholarship that incorporated relevant issues in history, anthropology, women's studies, and historic preservation. The conference also included members of the fur industry. The Halifax location shifted the meeting itself from the historic sites of the trade to the margins of commercial support. Although maritime historians and cultural anthropologists have granted considerable attention to the historic trade triangle, which found furs taken from North America to London, trade goods shipped from London to the Caribbean, and rum, in turn, shipped to Halifax, the role of maritime merchants, traders, and shippers has not been integrated into the body of fur trade studies. Thus, this conference offered us a moment in which to reconsider the place of cities and merchants on the margins of the fur trade and to reevaluate the direction of fur trade scholarship.

This collection of selected conference papers brings together varied views, experiences, and perspectives. These papers represent a small portion of the conference itself, which drew historians, economists, anthropologists, archaeologists, geographers, literary critics, librarians, archivists, and fur traders. A limited number of the presented papers were reviewed for inclusion in this volume, and of the forty papers selected for review only fifteen were chosen for final publication. This volume is thus not intended to be an inclusive portrait of fur trade scholarship but, instead, is meant to represent new directions in that scholarship. We regret that many fine papers could not be included in this volume. Limited publication space dictated a narrowing of perspective and the editors chose to focus on emerging perspectives in the mainstream historiography. There remain many current issues in the trade that are of considerable significance that are not represented in this volume: the antifur movement of urban environmentalists is perhaps the most obvious of these critical issues. We hope that in the future, these issues will be represented both at the conferences themselves and in the conference proceedings.

We thank all the presenters who submitted their papers and praise the patience of our contributors as they received our requests for revisions and editorial changes.

The fifteen papers that follow provide a balance between subjects and themes that have acquired prominence in North American fur trade studies and those that have either been formerly overlooked or, as in the case of gender relations, have been introduced and then neglected. Indeed, despite the wealth of issues covered in fur trade studies by conference presenters over the past thirty years, and despite the rich diversity of genres and theoretical analyses that have appeared in published studies, the trade and its historical impact on North American societies remains vastly understudied. The field of fur trade studies has been criticized for paying scant attention to the rich insights revealed by the fields of social history and feminist anthropology. This collection of selected conference proceedings partially addresses these concerns and has allowed us to focus on the interdependence and mutuality of the diverse communities within the fur trade.

New Faces of the Fur Trade would not have been possible without the support and assistance of a diverse and large number of people. Saint Mary's University opened its doors to warmly welcome scholars from around the world. They housed us, fed us, and provided us rooms in which to listen to the papers and engage in discussion. The Gorsebrook Institute organized and arranged the entire conference. They also provided us with their own human dynamo: Jackie Logan. We called her our Dennis Au of the Seventh Fur Trade Conference. Jackie's organizational skills and warm, welcoming presence made all of us feel welcome in Halifax. It is she who mailed papers and arranged preliminary conference calls. Jackie also reminded us of Dennis's help and advice in making this conference work as well as the previous one, for which Dennis bore administrative responsibility.

There were many people who made this conference especially memorable. Dr. Allen Robertson took us on a walking tour of Halifax, providing insight and information about this fascinating city. Jim Meyerle and Dave Whitaker of Project Lakewell in Lansing, Michigan, came all the way to Halifax with a trade transport canoe and French bateau, taking the more adventuresome of us on a journey into North Atlantic waters. Finally, no conference would be complete without a thank you to Vicky Stewart, whose involvement has facilitated many fur trade conferences.

This conference would not have been possible without a hard-working and dedicated Steering Committee. One person merits special mention for her hard work: Madine VanderPlaat, the executive director of the Gorsebrook Research Institute, who chaired the committee. Without her tireless efforts and the help of the institute there would have been no conference. Both Bill Moody from the Department of History at Acadia University and Bill Wicken, then a senior research fellow at the Gorsebrook Institute, served as cochairs of the Program Committee on the Steering Committee. Our deepest thanks to the other steering committee members, including: Gillian Allen from the Treaty and Aboriginal Rights Research Center; Carmen Carroll at the Public Archives of Nova Scotia; Brenda Dunn, who is with the Parks Service; and two faculty members from Saint Mary's University, Harold McGee from the Department of Anthropology and John Reid from the Department of History.

Many Thanks,

Jo-Anne Fiske
Susan Sleeper-Smith
Bill Wicken

✍ Introduction

THIS VOLUME questions the traditional focus of fur trade literature. *New Faces of the Fur Trade* contends that there are richer, more diverse narratives that suggest alternative ways to look at the trade. Many of the fifteen papers that follow raise subjects and themes that have either been formerly overlooked or have been introduced and then neglected. Fur trade studies have been criticized for remaining outside the current mainstream of historiography, in particular for paying scant attention to the rich insights revealed by the field of social history. This volume seeks to redress some of those omissions. It also seeks balance by incorporating subjects and themes that have acquired prominence in North American fur trade studies but does so by suggesting that even enduring issues have acquired new perspectives.

Scholars involved in writing histories of Canada and the United States rely on new analytical categories, such as ethnicity or race, class, and gender to broaden the scope of their research. Consequently, increased attention has focused on the historical development of ethnic and national consciousness and this has raised questions about issues of identity. These are complex issues, fraught with political overtones in the contemporary postcolonial world. As we look in turn at different sites and moments in fur trade history we invoke different relations of power and cultural identity, issues that challenge colonial naming practices. Old terms such as *Indian* and *Native* are fraught with new meanings, as evidenced by the diversity of naming practices selected by the contributors to this volume. *Aboriginal, First Nation, Native, Métis, Indian, Native American, indigenous, tribe*, and *band* invoke differences in power relations through time and differences between nation-states. Expressions of identity are not merely a matter of semantics of word choice, but extend to semiotics. The positioning of words, and the use of upper- and lowercase to configure identity as, for example, Canadian as opposed to native are equally significant. While we have struggled to retain the diversity

1

inherent in the interdisciplinarity and transnationality of fur trade studies, we have sought some uniformity in the use of upper/lowercase, recognizing the significance this has in envisioning the mutuality of relations, as well as the superordination/subordination of colonial societies.

Ethnic identities are complex and interwoven with nationality and the history of state formation. These postcolonial aspects of study in themselves constitute a new "frontier," which challenges the conventional historical narrative with multiple stories and shifting conceptual representations. Incorporation of these histories forces us to ask new questions of old and contemporary sources as they bring to the center formerly marginalized or invisible faces. Many of the contributors, whether self-consciously or not, have been influenced by the recent trend toward postcolonial and postnational conceptualizations of history. Social theory, often absent from historical narratives of fur traders and fur trade communities, emerges as a more central consideration as several authors query the manner in which received categories of analysis and narrative genres shape our understanding of the complicated, ever-unfolding entanglements of Native North American and Euro-American societies.

Unseen Faces, Unheard Voices

This volume opens with three chapters that focus on issues of gender and the fur trade, first raised by Sylvia Van Kirk and Jennifer Brown.[1] While Brown and Van Kirk focused on gender within families of the fur traders, our opening contributors, Jo-Anne Fiske and Caroline Mufford, turn to gender relations within the trappers' communities. They quite literally bring new faces to fur trade history as they relate stories of twentieth-century First Nations women who routinely trapped, often alongside their fathers or husbands, but frequently in the absence of male kin. To date, we have no detailed studies of women's trapping lives nor has their trapping been included in ethnographical or ethnohistorical accounts of trapping societies. The overwhelming silence of male ethnographers regarding female trappers leads Fiske and Mufford to question the ways in which contemporary consciousness of masculinity shapes trapping narratives and theories of a feminine consciousness of history. Will women who share nongendered work such as trapping have gender-specific views of their work, and will these appear in gender-specific narrative genres?

The social construction of masculinity is also explored by Caroline Podruchny in "Festivities, Fortitude, and Fraternalism: Masculinity and the Beaver Club, 1785–1827." Like Fiske and Mufford, Podruchny deals with cultural appropriation of the "frontier" in the construction of urban bourgeoisie masculinity. Members of the elite Beaver Club are viewed through their appropriation and exoticization of the fur trader as frontier adventurer. By attaching a male mystique to the frontier, these bourgeois traders constructed their own masculinity by ritually flaunting the social conventions of a newly urban society. Podruchny exposes the contradictions and tensions created by the desire to erect social boundaries in an increasingly class-conscious world. Rituals of the Beaver Club reveal the fluid and contradictory ways in which masculinity is enacted and social and gender relations are reproduced. Within the cultural expressions of the Beaver Club multiple identities are assumed and shifting boundaries are erected and transversed in the creation of a distinct membership with the fledging Montreal bourgeoisie.

Susan Sleeper-Smith examines the issue of gender within fur trade families, the focus first suggested by Canadian historians Van Kirk and Brown but neglected in American scholarship. Her use of marriage and baptismal records at Fort St. Joseph illuminates the social reproductive powers of women as they created and sustained economic networks through marriage and fictive kin networks. Women emerged as the demographic links of fur trade society, as densely constructed female kin networks ensured or denied access to furs. Eighteenth-century matrifocal households, in which Native women held authority, emerged as provisioners of the trade and relied on their indigenous patterns of kinship to facilitate the exchange process. The author draws our attention to the face-to-face nature of women's involvement in the exchange of peltry for trade goods and questions traditional perspectives that have envisioned the fur trade as a masculine universe. Her chapter raises questions about how the fur trade has been constructed to include men and exclude women.

New Visions

The second section of this volume includes chapters that explore theoretical and practical aspects about how we have used the fur trade "as a kind of shorthand" to describe the exchange process. In this section the authors analyze the received categories of knowledge that define this "shorthand" of the fur trade. These chapters question prevailing interpretations of the fur trade and contend that the failure to include an indigenous perspective has encouraged fur trade scholars to retain common sense meanings and has mitigated against a broader perspective.

Peter Cook calls into question these received categories of analysis as he explores how traditionally separate disciplines must be interrelated. He relies on Bourdieu's "concept of habitus, or ways of being that are inculcated in each actor as he or she grows within a community" to refute the oppositional categories of Western thought. Cook suggests that it is in the notion of symbolic capital, of what people perceive as honor, respect, and prestige, that we can best understand the interaction between European and Native peoples.

The postcolonial questioning of the construction of knowledge introduced by Fiske and Mufford provides a thematic link to Peter Cook's chapter, as well as to those by Laura Peers and Bruce Cox. Peers, drawing on premises of a postmodernist reading of history, interrogates the "living history" of cultural sites in order to explicate their messages about the roles of Native people within the fur trade. Cultural sites are meant to displace museums, whose frozen dioramas and isolated artifacts speak in a colonial voice. Living history is seen as having the potential to incorporate a Native voice and to provide reflexive historical narratives. For Peers, however, the spatial arrangements and artifacts of these sites reconstitute the traditional perspective of frontier settlement and Native demise. Although historic sites purport to re-vision the past and to replace conventional notions of Native dependency and hostility with the agency and integrity of the Native past this potential has been lost in spatial and textual representations that reproduce images of marginality and brutality. The sense of the trade as a reciprocal movement of culture and exchange of goods is lost in the static display of European trade goods that mimic official history and leave unquestioned views of dependence. By failing to fully integrate an indigenous perspective, public historians have diminished understanding of cultural and economic autonomy of Native people and thereby reinforce conventional views of domination and subordination.

In a similar vein, in "Whitemen Servants of Greed," Bruce Cox tackles the issues of representation of the "other" to interrogate the nature of urban society. Drawing on the insights of Rabinow, Cox provides an understanding of the turn-of-the-century texts of animal conservation produced by southern bureaucrats seeking to control the animal harvest in the distant Northwest Territories. By moving from what these conservation texts appear to say to what they ultimately talk about, Cox comes to question how the Conservation Committee's alarm over American traders affected the social construction of the Native hunter of the Northwest Territories. The practical activity that underlies this perception is revealed as the author analyzes the southern context of bureaucratic decision making and the southerners' capacity to dominate the animal harvest in a region about which they had little practical knowledge and perhaps even less cultural understanding. Cox teases our imagination with a provocative epigram, "We need to anthropologize the West: show how exotic its constitution of reality has been . . . ," one that speaks as accurately to Peers's contribution as it does to his own.

New Versions of Old Tales

Economic relations and cultural accommodation remain an important theme in fur trade studies. New versions of these issues appear, however, as researchers turn their attention to discussions of the formation and disruption of community relations and leadership in Aboriginal communities. The revisionist history of the past decade has focused on the hardships and the extreme social and economic losses incurred by Native people in both America and Canada following the introduction of scrip grants and homestead allotments. While not disputing their veracity, Gerhard Ens takes a theoretical departure from these tragic tales of poverty and despair. "After the Buffalo: The Reformation of the Turtle Mountain Métis Community, 1879–1905" recounts the ramifications of land loss and simultaneously examines the fortitude and economic strategy that enabled dispersed Métis scrip holders to reunite in the Turtle Mountain region of the North Dakota/Manitoba border. In contradistinction to the more sorrowful tales of dispossession and dispersal, Ens focuses on the way a consciousness of identity allowed scrip to become a trail to social mobility and to Métis cultural endurance, founded within an intriguing adoption of Chippewa tribal affiliations.

Transformations in community identity were inextricably bound to shifts in political and economic leadership as well as to the flux of trading relations with Euro-Americans. Janet Chute explores these issues for the "Cranes" of Sault Ste. Marie, a people frequently described in fur trade narratives. In doing so, Chute revisits an old controversy respecting social organization and leadership among the Ojibwa. Applying herself to understanding the trade as an "exchange of peltry for power," Chute argues against positions that place trade relations as primary social determinants and in favor of a cultural explanation of ideological responses shaped by traditional values, ones that continue to give meaning to the Ojibwa universe today. From an indigenous perspective, Chute demonstrates the relevancy of "symbolic capital," a partial application of the theoretical model proposed by Peter Cook.

Enduring Issues, New Perspectives

The "shorthand" of the fur trade has traditionally evoked concepts of economic relations. Regrettably, this dichotomy of the economic from the political led to the economic determinism of scholars like Harold Innis earlier in the century. As Peter Cook has indicated, researchers have too long relied on opposing theories of universal rationalism and cultural relativism to account for shifting meanings of cultural and economic exchanges. These broader debates, however, do not encompass several pragmatic questions of specific trade relations. In this section we turn to microstudies that view economic questions of specific trade relations from new perspectives, and that chart the movement of particular trade goods in the search for new understandings in the fabric of social relations.

Like Cook, Bruce White reexamines the interconnectedness of trade and diplomacy, but he does so from a very different perspective. In "Balancing the Books: Trader Profits in the British Lake Superior Fur Trade," White examines the veracity of Lord Selkirk's belief that a lack of profit characterized this region by 1800. White subjects the scant business records and account books of small traders and companies to a cost accounting to determine rates of profit, but does so without neglecting the diplomatic context of the trade itself. Repeating a theme raised in different perspectives by Sleeper-Smith, Cook, and Chute, White seeks to disentangle the interdependency of diplomacy and trade, to elucidate the nature of long-term trading relations, and to explore the economic and social investments required of an exchange process rooted in a cultural context.

"The Eighteenth-Century Anglo-Indian Trade in Southeastern North America" examines the assessment, overwhelmingly accepted by most historians and anthropologists, that southeastern Native people were responsible for "a tremendous slaughter of deer, comparable to the great wastage, by a later generation, of the buffalo of the Great Plains." Based on his extensive archaeological explorations at Cherokee and Creek village sites, Gregory Waselkov uses this evidence to propose that "this overhunting hypothesis is equally suspect." The process of assessing archaeological evidence has led Waselkov to provide his readers with an extensive glossary of terms used to describe trade goods. He also tabulates their advent and acceptance among Native people as trade goods evolved into "symbolic capital." By examining the archaeological assemblages recovered at early historic Indian village sites in connection with export figures of several ports, the author demonstrates how archaeological evidence brings older ideas into dispute.

In contrast to the other authors, Ann Harper Fender turns to the modern-day fur trade in order to reconsider prevailing analyses of state-controlled marketing systems. Fender questions whether the Saskatchewan Fur Marketing Service, established by the Cooperative Commonwealth Federation provincial government of Saskatchewan in the early 1940s, achieved its goal of better prices for trappers while simultaneously improving species conservation. Fender discovers, however, that provincial policies had ambiguous goals and consequences, for the international economic conditions overwhelmed legislative efforts to improve the lives of individual trappers.

Old Faces, New Voices

Biographical narratives of key figures remain a strong interest in fur trade studies. In our fifth section, Old Faces, New Voices, we turn from problems of reconciling theoretical explanations to the lives of individuals who shaped and were shaped by fur traders' sodalities. The dramatic personae of these narratives, Miles Macdonell, James Keith, John Clarke, Johan Beetz, and the Haligonian merchants Robert Grant and Robert Hunter, have all made their way into Canadian history. Their particular place in the fur trade, however, has either been the subject of contrary speculations or as yet remains unexplored. By looking again at their lives within the context of the trade, new insights are offered about family relations, traders' interpersonal disputes, and shifting patterns of commerce.

Heather Devine explores the darker side of kin-based communities in social flux. She illuminates the dilemmas individuals and families faced when confronted with changing opportunities. Devine investigates the impact of patriarchal notions of authority on men as their kin networks struggle to sustain harmonious and deferential relations with the more privileged power brokers of fur trade management. Miles Macdonnell emerges as a tragic hero tempted by Lord Selkirk to deviate from community norms. Spurred by Selkirk's visions of settlement and his apparent largesse as a patron, Miles meets his demise as an ill-suited administrator. Ultimately, the disloyalty of this pitied but shamed kinsman disrupted clan ties that spanned the Atlantic Ocean.

"The 'Dried Spider' and the Gadfly: The James Keith-John Clarke Confrontation at Mingan, 1831–32" explores similar issues of conflict and ventures into a small community of men whose self-worth and identity emerge from comradeship and competition. Keith tells a tale whose tragic drama counterpoises the organizational man, James Keith, against the individualistic maverick, John Clarke. The shifting nexus of center and periphery take on diverse social meanings as Clarke, who rose to fame in distant posts, is marginalized and later banished to remoteness as the final symbol of his fall from grace. His resistance to authority and an overwhelming sense of his own self-worth ensnares him in the spider's web. As the life stories of Keith and Clarke unfold, we are invited into the dangerous game of "spiders and flies," which brings respectable wealth to some and humiliating impoverishment to others.

The geographical margins to which the disrespectable Clarke was banished become the innovative stage on which Johan Beetz rises to fame and fortune at the turn of the twentieth century. Unlike Keith's figure of the outcast John Clarke, Gwyneth Hoyle's "The Search for Silver: Johan Beetz and the Birth of the Fox-Breeding Industry" describes a more successful individualist along the Saint Lawrence River seventy years after Clarke's humiliation. Beetz, a bereaved Belgian aristocrat, shuns being an organization man as his loyalties shift from his European homeland to the trappers of Quebec, to whom he pays prices considered excessive by the established trading companies. Beetz rose to prominence as he combined animal husbandry with commerce and established one of the earliest silver fox farms. Breeders shifted profits away from trapping and became an economic mainstay of Canada's maritime provinces. The changing mode of production produced the gentleman fox farmers of Quebec and Prince Edward Island, and with them a changing consciousness of their social role. Beetz, later acclaimed for his intellect and philanthropy, is presented to us as an innovative figure during this time of economic and social transition.

Fittingly, the volume closes with a piece on Halifax. Harry Duckworth, continuing his work on merchants, establishes the role of the Halifax merchant community in influencing commercial relations on the fur trade hinterland. In "Halifax as a Cradle of the Post-Conquest Fur Trade in Canada," he contends that this commercial and military center was not marginal to the continental trade, as it has hitherto appeared. Like the other contributors to this volume, Duckworth also suggests that the fur trade can be understood only within the context of a broader perspective. The Canadian fur trade, at places as remote as Michilimackinac, depended on the capital investments of London commission merchants whose initial involvement and success in the Halifax trade shifted the focus of trade westward.

In closing the volume with Duckworth's study of Haligonian merchants, we hope to capture the mood of this fur trade conference, held at Halifax. Fur trade scholars surely stand poised not only to continue the trend of bringing forth new faces, but to do so by looking beyond the received notions and maps of the vast networks of goods and peoples traditionally known to us as the fur trade, but which has, through decades of scholarship and conferences, revealed itself to be more complex and far-reaching.

Note

1. J. S. H. Brown, *Strangers in Blood: Fur Trade Company Families in Indian Country* (Vancouver: University of British Columbia Press, 1980); Sylvia Van Kirk, *'Many Tender Ties': Women in Fur Trade Society 1670-1870* (Winnipeg: Watson & Dwyer, 1980). Both reprinted by University of Oklahoma Press.

SECTION 1

Unseen Faces, Unheard Voices

Figure 1. Ellie Peters, circa 1970.

Jo-Anne Fiske and
Caroline Mufford
𝕣

Hard Times and Everything Like That: Carrier Women's Tales of Life on the Trapline

ELLIE PETERS slings the thirty-five pound beaver over her back and smiles at the camera. She is in her late teens and has trapped the beaver herself. A young, newly married Carrier woman of Central British Columbia, she has captured the beaver on reserve land belonging to the Red Bluff First Nation. It is not the first beaver she has trapped; in fact, Ellie has been trapping successfully since 1965, when she left the residential school at age thirteen. As the second eldest of twelve children, she often was responsible for snaring and trapping sufficient food for them while her parents, Lashaway and Janet Alec, worked away at the Mica Dam felling trees. Thus by the time this picture was taken, Ellie had had several years of trapping and had already earned the respect of her family and community for her trapping expertise.

In 1995, Ellie, now forty-three and a grandmother, still lives at Red Bluff, a small community lying at the outskirts of Quesnel (see figure 2). While she has not trapped for several years, trapping forms an important part of her identity as a Carrier First Nations woman, so that Ellie is considering a return to it. Her reasons are manifold. Because she was raised in the bush, and hence has knowledge of traditional land use and trapping, she is highly respected by her community. Although life in the bush was hard, she loved it. Her core reason for considering a return to trapping, however, is the three-year-old nephew for whom she is primary caregiver. To a Carrier woman, mothering, trapping, and providing belong together. They are linked in both public and private discourses as "the same routine everyday," and thus form a chain in social memory that ties identity to the land and to mothering.

13

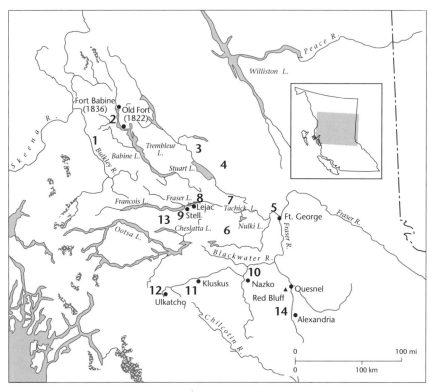

Figure 2. **Carrier Resource Territories and Villages.**
1. Bulkley River (Witsuwit'en); 2. Babine Lake (Ned'u'ten); 3. Stuart-Trembleur Lake (Tl'azt'enne); 4. Stuart Lake: 5. Fort George; 6. Nulki (Sai'kuz'whut'enne); 7. Tachick (Sai'kuz'whut'enne); 8. Fraser Lake; 9. Stellaquo; 10. Nazko; 11. Kluskus; 12. Ulgatcho; 13. Cheslatta; 14. Alexandria (Lhtakot'en)

Source: Margaret Tobey, the Carrier. The Handbook of North American Indians, Volume 6, The Subarctic, vol.ed. June Helm (Washington, D. C.: Smithsonian, 1978), pp.414.

Like other Athapaskan peoples of the North, the Carrier have a long history of trapping and hunting that constitutes the material foundation of their Aboriginal identity and cosmology. Although many cultural and social diversities distinguish the Carrier Nations from each other, similarities in language, resource economy, and religion led Europeans to conceive of them as a cultural/social group. The Carrier do not have a common name by which to refer to themselves as a sociopolitical entity, and many no longer use the term Carrier at all. When Europeans first arrived in 1793, the people called themselves

"Dakelh," and some have resumed use of this term. However, those in the north call themselves collectively "Yinka Dene," or people of the land.[1] When referring to themselves as part of the Athapaskan-speaking peoples, they call themselves part of the Dene Nations. Within these broad categories, Carrier communities identify themselves as distinct First Nations, or, in their language, peoples of specific geographic locations in which their traditional resource territories lie: Sai'kuz'whut'enne (Stoney Creek), Witsuwit'en (Bulkley River), Ned'u'ten (Babine), Lhtakot'en (Red Bluff), and so forth.[2] At this time, Carrier remains the commonly known term that encompasses all these peoples and we use it in this inclusive manner.

In this chapter we shall argue that patriarchy and colonialism have muted Aboriginal women's voices. Our purpose is twofold: first, to add empirical accounts of women's lives on the trapline to the historic and ethnographic literature on Carrier life, and second, to challenge the established genre of ethnographic narrative on Athapaskan trapping cultures. Specifically, we ask: How does an understanding of female narratives alter our perceptions of the lives of the narrators and deepen our understanding of the construction of academic knowledge?

In the first section, Carrier women narrate stories of life on the trapline, telling us when, where, what, how, and why they trapped and what role trapping played in their mothering and identities. They speak to us about their trapping from a common perspective, one that takes their own trapping for granted as a tale of survival and nurture rather than as drama or heroics.

We then turn to our quest to understand more fully how meaning is produced by Aboriginal women and by ethnographic narrators. In this section we contrast the Aboriginal image of woman and mother as trapper with the Western image of trapper as the lone male produced by ethnographers, in order to challenge knowledge construction in the academy. We analyze colonialist appropriation of Aboriginal trapping, and the erasure of Aboriginal women in the production of ethnographic narratives of trapping.[3] Upon examining some theoretical assumptions regarding women's public voice, we are led to contend that women's narrative genre differs in ways others cannot hear. These others, such as Western men, seek accounts of bravery and self-reliance, which impedes their ability to appreciate women's narratives.

Our chapter is woven from two discourses: the women's matter-of-fact narratives and our own theoretical voices.[4] The women's voices are the key. Inclusion of them, we hope, contributes to the understanding and validation of women's non-text-based knowledge.

We base our chapter on a series of interviews with several modern-era Carrier women of varying ages and from several nations. Of the several Carrier women who contributed to our understanding of their lives, Ellie is the youngest. The others are elders, women of senior years whose achievements and character have earned them respect and deference as repositories of cultural knowledge. We spoke to Rose Tom, an elder of Lake Babine Nation. We utilized recent life histories recorded in 1994 with Red Bluff elders Julie George and Catherine Peters. We drew on interviews from 1983 with several elders from Sai'kuz, including Veronica George, Mary John, Mary Thomas, Sophie Thomas, and the late Celina John and Alfonsine Williams.

Mothering on the Trapline

In the seasonal round that the Southern Carrier followed since the early 1800s, families gathered just before autumn to visit, trade, and sometimes to hold a potlatch.[5]

> Division of labor by gender was not rigidly enforced amongst the Carrier Indians. Women trapped beaver and other small animals, and assisted in caribou and mountain goat hunts. . . . In the fall, before snow began staying on the ground, the villages broke up, and individual families dispersed to hunt and trap, living in relative isolation.[6]

Trapping was integrated with other seasonal activities on the vast homelands of the Carrier peoples. The range of animals harvested was enormous. In the winter, Carrier women trapped primarily for commercial pelts, which were tanned and prepared for market throughout the year. During the rest of the year, they trapped and snared to provide food.

Today, Carrier women continue to trap and snare. Just as importantly, they tell stories about these activities, thus continually intertwining Carrier women's identities with trapping. Ellie Peters's life in the bush has followed the time-honored cycle of her ancestors. A member of the Nazkot'en, she grew up west of Quesnel. Her family lived on an isolated part of the reserve, trapping for a living. Of her mother, Ellie says: "She was trapping with her mother and grandfather, like it's been passed on from generation to generation." Ellie describes how her mother would sling the youngest baby over her shoulder, in a traditional Carrier baby basket she had made, and head out to check her trapline. Her mother, Janet Alec, originally trapped and snared on her own lines, independently of her husband. Today, however, her parents hunt and trap together, Ellie tells us, "Because they are getting old."

Just as Janet had learned to trap from her own mother and grandfather, so Ellie's parents took for granted that their daughter would become a skilled trapper. Janet taught Ellie how to set snares for smaller fur bearers. "She taught me her way of skinning and she always told me how to hold your fur bearer and skin it." Beaver, prized as feast meat [7] and for fur, requires a special skill to locate and trap when under the winter ice. Ellie explains:

> My dad taught me how to find the trail from the beaver house, you know, where there is ice on it. You have to listen, you hit it with an axe. You know how you hit something and it sounds empty? Well, if you hit ice and it's solid, it feels kind of hard when you hit it. If it has bubbles and sounds hollow when you hit it, well, the beaver always goes on the same trail, and that keeps the ice thin and it sounds different.

At thirteen years of age, Ellie was well aware of the importance of trapping to the entire family. While her parents went off to fell trees, Ellie was left in charge for months at a time of first several, and finally up to eleven siblings. Because the only commercial food left behind was a little flour for making bannock, Ellie snared and trapped to feed her sisters and brothers. Since she could not leave them alone at the cabin, Ellie often tended her traps with several of the youngsters in tow.

Ellie Peters was not the only young girl for whom trapping ensured nurture and survival. Julie George, now an elder at Red Bluff, was born in 1924 and raised at Nazko by her mother, Justine, and grandmother, Sophie Laurent. Julie grew up on dried fish, rabbit, muskrat, and squirrel. When her mother died her father was unable to support the family and Julie, then twenty, found herself responsible for feeding her eight younger siblings. "My times when I was young were really rough. [We] even had to eat squirrel."[8] In 1950, now twenty-six and married, Julie moved to Red Bluff with her daughters. She and her widowed stepmother, Teresa Palmer, worked together collecting wild foods. "In that time Teresa and I did a lot of hunting and trapping for rabbit and squirrels and picked berries on the reserve."

As the life stories of Julie and Ellie exemplify, at each point in their life cycle, Carrier women trapped to provide for others. In this manner the care of siblings or other kin was a part of a woman's extended mothering work. Just as her mother and grandmother had fed her as a child; so as a young woman Julie trapped to feed her younger siblings.

As mothers Ellie and Julie naturally trapped to feed their own families. As mature women, they quietly convey their remarkable achievements in narratives that lack drama and climactic turning points. The "hard times" are presented as daily routines, their skills and abilities as simple acknowledgment of the way they got their money. The women's pride would go unmarked were it not for their repeated references to particular tasks and routines. In relating her accomplishments to Caroline, for example, Ellie makes several lengthy and unsolicited references to her beaver trapping in the span of four interviews. She also lets us know how important her skills are by contrasting the abilities of her generation with the more recent life pattern of reliance on unearned income accepted by many of her people. When she grew up at Trout Lake during the 1950s and 1960s, she often remarked, they knew nothing of welfare programs.

> Sometimes I wish people would grow up the way I did. Hard times and everything like that, the way I was taught to trap and how to make money from trapping. Even though it was so hard, and I had to go out every day and hunt squirrels and check my traps. I had to get something every day. Every day counts for me, because that's my income. We used to sell our fur and we used to wonder, "How much am I going to get for these?"

Another Red Bluff elder, Catherine Peters, also contrasted her trapping to welfare. Born in the Southern Carrier village of Ulgatcho, she and her husband trapped at White Eye Lake, near Ootsa Lake.

> In those days [1940s] there were no checks. We got our money trapping. That's how we got our food and then we headed back into the mountains. The land was all washed away by Alcan.[9] That's why I'm down here. A lot of hunting land and the traplines are all flooded now.[10]

Trapping establishes the women (and their husbands) in a cultural matrix that places them firmly among their ancestors and as providers for those yet to come. Trapping and narratives of trapping anchor the women in the collective social memory, renewing cultural meanings of women's spiritual and economic relations. A Carrier women on the trapline had to negotiate with the spirits of animals as part of her and her family's survival. Spirituality was interwoven with mothering, and hence with providing. This meant knowing and respecting the diverse spiritual powers of particular animals. Some women did not handle otter, for example, because otter have a "strong power."[11]

Rose Cassam, a Southern Carrier woman in her fifties, currently traps west of Nazko with her husband, Willard. She is a good friend of Ellie's and has shared with her many of her own trapping experiences and her own cultural understandings. Ellie and Rose have different views on some aspects of the power of animals and women. According to Ellie, Rose had been taught to avoid touching an otter and she respected this proscription.

> I heard from Rose that her husband never let her skin an otter. . . . She told me somebody else had to skin it for her because it has such strong power it will do something to you because you are a woman.

However, there is an "antidote," or way to balance the power of women and otter, as Ellie learned as a young woman. She recalls how she skinned and cleaned an otter with no lasting ill effects.

> So far nothing has happened to me because when I did the cleaning and stuff I kind of respected it and everything and after I finish, it had a strong power from my finger up to my shoulder. I was just aching and aching. It felt so bad like burning, that I just wanted to cry.

Her mother cut juniper boughs and built a special fire.

> Then she told me to rub my hands together and get the smoke into my hand because the otter had a strong smell and the smell was in my hand. She had to smoke the stuff into my hand and all over my back. . . . After she done that, everything went away.

In the European cultural sense, a woman was protected from the strong power of the otter, the wolf, or animals similarly dangerous, because she was weak or passive. In Carrier cultures a woman should protect herself from strong animals to maintain her essential ability to trap and hence to sustain her obligations to feed children, the elderly, and even the men. Today, as fewer and fewer women are able to continue trapping, retaining respect for traditional practices adds meaning and significance to women's life stories.

Cultural meanings that link trapping with traditional identity accommodate innovation. The Carrier, a seminomadic people, have survived in the resource-poor interior through placing a high cultural value on knowledge rather than on material wealth.[12] They could transport few goods when traveling from berry picking grounds to salmon fishing areas to trapline and so on, around the seasonal cycle. But knowledge need not be restricted. With knowledge, the Carrier knew where and when to travel, how to make afresh what was needed, how to leave signs for others. In this culture, individuals who could create new knowledge also had a secure place. From the first contact, missionaries and fur traders in the Carrier territory remarked upon their pervasive cultural adaptability, which remains honored among Carrier Nations today.[13] In this cultural context, Ellie devised a way of stretching beaver pelts that used nails on a sheet of plywood rather than the old-style leather lacing. She was proud enough of it to make it her trademark, and to record her achievement with a snapshot. Her ability to create new knowledge gave her further esteem as a mother and provider. Ellie's quiet pride and pragmatic ability are consistent with that found among other women of Northwestern North America. As others have noted, women are esteemed for pragmatic abilities, which have been recorded in variants of narratives known to us as the legends of stolen women, as well as in women's life histories.[14]

In all of these ways, Ellie Peters's life replicates routines and social relations experienced by Carrier women of other generations and other communities. From Witsuwit'en in the west to Tl'azt'enne in the north, Carrier
women quietly relate their trapping tales.[15] Trapping was a lifelong labor,
learned early and given up late. It was, quite simply, women's work and a
labor of love. As an elder of Stoney Creek recalled in 1983,

> All the women, they trap too. Just like the men. They pack their babies with
> them and work their lines next to their husbands'. Sure women worked hard
> then. Poor things, they worked just like men in the bush. . . .
>
> My mother-in-law came here from Cheslatta when she got married. Right
> from then to an old woman she trapped.

Trapping stories mark the rhythm of the seasonal cycle and the developmen-
tal cycle of family and community. In 1927, at the age of fourteen, Mary John
of Stoney Creek left the Lejac Residential School to work the trapline with
her parents and to care for younger siblings. Like Ellie Peters and Julie
George, Mary describes her important role in the family's daily routines.

> I was the housekeeper. I looked after Mark, kept the fires going and, young
> as I was, I helped to prepare the meals. [My stepfather] Johnny would come
> in after a day in the bush and say, "You are a real little mother!" That was
> reward enough for me. . . . Every day was the same. The only changes in our
> lives were the weather and a shortening in the hours of daylight.
>
> . . . it was heavy hard work for my mother and Johnny. Each of them had
> traplines which stretched across the Nechako River to Saxon Lake and beyond.
> Every day, whatever the weather, they had to walk miles . . . to look after their
> traps, and to empty them of coyotes and foxes, or if they were lucky, a lynx.
> That was only the beginning of their labor. The carcasses, often frozen, had to
> be brought back to the cabin, skinned, and the pelts scraped and stretched. Each
> morning, even if the weather was bitter or my parents were tired from their
> work of the day before, they would have to go out on their rounds again.
>
> I never heard them complain. They were young and tough and had been
> accustomed to life on the trapline almost from their infancy.[16]

Mary soon learned to trap and prepare her own pelts.

> I watched my mother and Johnny preparing the pelts of bigger animals, and
> before very long I was able to skin and stretch a pelt of my own. Soon my
> mother showed me how to set out a trapline around our cabin to catch some
> of the smaller animals which came exploring for food.[17]

By watching their adult kin, girls quickly learned trapping skills, as Mary
Thomas of Sai'kuz remembers,

> My mom was an expert trapper and did her share of trapping just like a man.
> I learned how to trap by watching what my Mother and Auntie done. When
> I got married no one had to teach me. . . .

While many women married young and began trapping with their husbands, others could not marry because of family obligations. Veronica
George recalls the dreadful year of 1918 when Stoney Creek was devastated
from the Spanish influenza. Her aunt, faced with responsibility for a family
that included Veronica's grandmother and very young siblings, trapped for
their living.

> Auntie went out on the trapline and she never married until there weren't no
> little kids left . . . . All that time we were there, Granny went out trapping.
> Auntie, too, she trapped all over just like the men. We didn't go home then
> [back to Stoney Creek]. Not until the summer when they were fishing.

Women continued to trap each winter until external circumstances made
it impossible or economically unviable. When a day school was established
on the Stoney Creek reserve in 1948 many women reluctantly left their trapping behind them. Adanas Alexis moved his family to Stoney Creek and his
daughter, Cecile Patrick, recalls,

> I still snared and trapped right here, but most of the time I didn't go far. In
> the fall to fish for char and whitefish sometimes, but not like before. . . .
> Mom stopped trapping then. I don't think she went out after the war. Then
> she leased her line.

Most elders retain a strong attachment to their traplines and to their ancestral territory as a whole. Whether they speak of this land as the "trapline,"
"keyoh," or "homeland," these lands remain the foundation of their identity
as Aboriginal women of the Carrier Nations and as the basis of their people's
economic future. When women are removed from these lines, as were Babine
women in the 1950s, they suffer a psychological stress and cultural loss. In the
1950s, the federal government persuaded residents of Old Fort (now regis-
tered as members of the Lake Babine or Ned'u'ten Nation) to move to
Pendleton Bay, where they would work in small sawmills. With vast distances
separating them from their traplines, many women found returning there difficult. A school was built at Pendleton Bay, which meant women were not
free to trap and travel unless they could leave their older children in a relative's care. For many women, confinement at the sawmill site was painful and
marked the end of the seasonal cycle they had known since infancy. Rose
Tom and her children found the change difficult. Her daughter, Cecile, shares
her sadness,

> We all stopped trapping throughout the winter then. Just some they could go
> out. Mom and I didn't. . . . we were too far away. Then she sent me to Lejac
> and there was no one to help her with the kids.

Disruption of their seasonal cycle meant the Ned'u'ten could no longer trap beaver on clan lands for the feasts as regularly as before. Hereditary chiefs struggled to balance their duties to their land and people with routines of wage labor. They sought to compensate for a loss of traditional wealth items by purchasing commodities for distribution at the feasts.[18] Women continued to teach the children essential knowledge of the trapline, but with a growing awareness that few children would be able to put this knowledge into effect. Today this loss is underscored by knowledge of the environmental damage from clear-cut logging and from mining.[19]

As Ned'u'ten and other First Nations of British Columbia prepare for the modern day treaty process initiated by the British Columbia Treaty Commission, the significance of women's lives on the trapline is made evident.[20] Women eloquently lay claim to the land where they bore their children. As Rose Tom explained in public meetings regarding treaty negotiations, "The Creator put us there. I had my children there and I was born in the bush. How can anyone take away the land where we were born?"

By telling her stories of giving birth on the homeland she substantiates her claim to the ancestral land and her right and obligation to preserve it for her children. "I had my kids there. I stayed out there all the time. It was our home. Even after my husband died that's how we lived." Her daughter, Cecile, recalls with fondness her childhood there and the summers spent upon return from Lejac Residential School. For her, birth on her "mother's homeland" is special: "I was born there, I'm part of that place. My mother had her babies there and then just went on with her work."

The two women worry that they will lose their trapline, and spend considerable time and energy in an effort to secure their names on the provincial registry and to gain legal assurances that their lands will not be lost to forest and mining companies. Arguments that she might not have full resource rights to her line are angrily dismissed. As a "steward" of the line, a trapper must manage all the natural resources in order to preserve the fish and animals that fed her children.

Giving birth in the homelands, far from the security of a hospital or the comfort of midwives, was a common experience for Carrier women before the 1950s, when most found themselves in a more sedentary lifestyle. Mary John captures the feelings shared by many as she recalls giving birth in a tent in 1945:

> We had two tents set up in Wedgwood with a campfire between the two. . . .
> My aunt and I had been working very hard, slicing up meat and scraping
> hides. The men had killed many moose that fall. It was heavy work. . . .

Suddenly, one evening after working hard all day, my labor pains started. . . .
The men built a big fire between the two tents, and with the light of the camp-
fire making my tent as bright as day, Ernie was born after a long, hard labor.
. . . I rested in the tent for a week.[21]

Thus Mary John and other Carrier women continued the ancestral cycle of
life on the trapline, giving birth and killing the animals to provide for their
children.

The Persistence of an Illusion

From the time of earliest European intrusion through to the present, the truth
of women's lives on the trapline has remained hidden from the dominant
society. European patriarchal assumptions shaped early observers' accounts,
which ignored women's provisionary roles and personal autonomy. Christian
missionaries stressed the subordination of women and took for granted that
women were (or should be) less influential than men. With rare exception
traders and priests privileged the male and tended to observe and record
men's lives more fully than women's, marking feminine labors as routine
drudgery of the camp.[22] Nonetheless we now realize that across much of
what is now Canada, as well as in the Carrier region, women supplied the
larger portion of caloric needs, perhaps as much as 80 percent, by gathering,
fishing, and trapping. When not providing food directly, women were transforming the fur harvest into money by production of pelts and handcrafted
commodities.[23]

Often, however, when Aboriginal men speak of "being on the trapline,"
they fail to mention women and all the quotidian chores women performed:
gathering wood, child care, getting and preparing food, and so on; all tasks
that freed men to trap their own lines. In modern times throughout Central
and Northern British Columbia, women maintained the critical traditional
use of the land while men were absent to make railway ties or to take waged
jobs. As late as 1983, Hudson was able to make a similar point with respect
to the Tl'azt'enne of Stuart Lake: "No Tl'azt'enne could afford to become
dependent on wage labour . . . the women and the children fished and ran
small traplines to support the families."[24] Yet the patriarchal illusion persists:
men are trappers, women domestic workers. While men are said to "wrest" a
living from a harsh world, women monotonously toil in the home.[25] Men produce commodities for trade, women do "handicrafts" and care for children.

What accounts for the persistence of this illusion? What allows, for example, an otherwise insightful and sensitive ethnographer of Athapaskan life to
assert the following?

> Men's work is concerned with killing and butchering; women's work is cen-
> tred on distribution and preparation of food and skins. Men hunt very inten-
> sively for short periods; but women work all the time—and have complete
> responsibility for young children. . . . The work of women is concealed; its
> produce is even more difficult to quantify than is men's—with one exception,
> perhaps, of handicrafts.[26]

Anthropologists and social historians have wrestled with the issues of male narrative dominance. Ardener appeared to provide the key when he argued that in many cultures women's voices are "muted"; insofar as they are heard, he argued, women's memories and cultural representations do not appear as a gender-distinct discourse derived from a distinct culture, but as a replication of the motifs and expression of a male culture in which women are embedded.[27] Assumptions that this is so persist and shape the undertaking of oral histories and theorization of social memory. Speculating on the existence of women's historical consciousness, Fentress and Wickham identify apparent problems of method in seeking women's memories:

> One is the objective diversity of women's experience in different societies:
> societies constituted by different family structures, different levels of male
> tolerance of female points of view or of female articulacy, different eco-
> nomic roles for women, different levels of sexual exclusion and difference,
> and different levels of women's mutual cooperation or "complicity" with
> men. Another is the as yet unresolved issue of how far women's separate
> consciousness depends on a diversity of experience from men's rather than
> on something innate in gender. A third is the fact that, despite all the work
> in the field of women studies in recent years, very little has yet been done on
> the specific nature of female perceptions of the past.[28]

Missing from this list of "problems" is a self-conscious inquiry into the gendered nature of their subject, for Fentress and Wickham do not interro-gate assumptions regarding female articulacy or, more significantly, their own association of masculinity with the dramatic, femininity with the undramat-ic: "women's religiosity was much more continuous and undramatic than that of men; their stories lacked the same sort of turning-points."[29] Not only do they fail to ask whether, in fact, women are culturally muted or if the profes-sional narrator chooses to render them as such, Fentress and Wickham also fail to question the manner in which taken-for-granted perceptions of mas-culinity and femininity structure dominant genres. Thus, they reproduce the very context in which masculine myths persist.

Deconstruction of dominant masculine motifs, however, is critical to com-prehending the persistence of the illusion of male drama and heroics. Returning to Brody's account of the Beaver peoples, we see the consequences of masculine hegemony. Trapping narratives project European motifs of masculinity onto trapper and narrator. Both emerge from the page as the European archetypal male hero, an intrepid loner engaged in a transformative quest. From the Medieval pursuit of the Holy Grail to managing the modern trapline, male heroes combat nature in order to create culture. Allowing female images to intrude, indeed subvert male heroics, has far-reaching consequences. Feminine intrusion not only disrupts inequality of gender but unsettles racial identity as well.

Male heroics cannot be sustained if women, too, wrest their living from a harsh world. If women routinely butcher and kill, wherein lies the glamour the male narrator has appropriated for himself? More compelling a threat, if women of a subordinated race/ethnic group provide for others free from male company, whom will men protect? The recognition of women as independent providers upsets the sexual division of labor normalized by the European worldview. No longer can the male stand alone against nature while women huddle together in sheltered domesticity. Dependent female can no longer be deployed in contradistinction to self-reliant male. To accept the ungendered reality of life on the trapline is to destroy a male identity constructed to span ethnic divisions and to rend male heroics universal. Appropriation of the masculine "other" to affirm self-identity is no longer possible, for the vested interest of the male narrator is now exposed.

Men are not the only narrators to construct women's lives as undramatic, however. Carrier women do likewise. Their narratives *are* marked by singular lack of heroics and glamour. As their lives routinely unfold, so do their stories. The distinct, matter-of-fact genre in which women speak conserves social information that constitutes the foundation of ethnic identity. Women's historical consciousness is revealed in the commemoration of self and female ancestors as providers for their children *and their men*.

The symbolic value of women's trapping is captured by repetition. As we noted, Ellie repeatedly referred to trapping beaver in interviews (and other women have related similar stories over many years), thereby signifying cultural meaning by repetition, not by dramatic detail. Ellie's repetition of the beaver story also grows out of her own pride in accomplishing this difficult feat. Her husband's snapshots of her with the large beaver, of her holding another pair of beaver, of her innovative peltmaking preparations make manifest his admiration of her accomplishments. This is not to be interpreted as an individualistic or false pride; it is respect that relates to community dignity and cultural continuity. Among the Carrier, women are esteemed both for their ability to provide for their families as well as for their direct mothering, and Ellie had established herself as a woman who could provide while still an adolescent. By repetition women celebrate the productivity and respect for their ancestors and achieve respect of their communities. Today Ellie is esteemed not just for her trapping past and her knowledge, but for her symbolic value as a successful, hardworking Carrier women who provided for her family by trapping even as a young girl.

In contradistinction to Fentress's and Wickham's perceptions of methodological problems, women's historical consciousness does emerge in the absence of a gendered culture. Carrier women's economic activities are neither spatially nor ideologically distinct from male labors.[30] Unlike the dominant narrators of the trapping culture, Carrier women do not employ contrary images of the other gender to define their individual or collective identity. Insofar as men appear in their narratives they do so as cultural members sharing in the same productive roles as women. Thus wives and daughters recollect the similarity of male and female daily routines. Mothers and fathers, aunts and uncles are pictured in a gender-neutral role: trappers who provide for themselves and others. Yet women derive their identity from their foremothers who were born on the trapline and who in turn bore and reared their children there. Women's identity is expressed in their quiet celebration of their grandmothers' ordinary lives. Gender inclusion, not sexual difference and exclusion, has given rise to a distinct feminine genre that celebrates women's historical consciousness without condescension to the male "other."

Notes

The chapter title and the phrase, "the same routine everyday," are drawn from Caroline Mufford's interviews with Ellie Peters in 1995, as are all other quotes from Ellie. Transcripts are held by Caroline Mufford. These two phrases in particular capture the essence of women's lives on the trapline and were used by Ellie when she explained why she like to trap even though she had hard times.

1. E. Furniss, *Dakelh Keyoh: The Southern Carrier in Earlier Times* (Quesnel, B.C.: Quesnel School District, 1993), 3.

2. The correspondence between divisional names in English and Carrier is awkward, which can lead to some continuing misunderstanding. On our attached map, for example, Red Bluff is the community marked immediately south of modern day Quesnel, yet it has at times been included in the larger category of Alexandria, a term used by Margaret Tobey as it was in the nineteenth century to include several of the communities south of Quesnel.

3. H. Brody, *Maps and Dreams* (New York: Pantheon Books, 1982). D. Hudson, *Traplines and Timber: Social and Economic Changes among the Carrier Indians of Northern British Columbia* (Ph.D. diss., University of Alberta, Edmonton, 1983). This image also prevails in historical narratives which have not pursued women's work as trappers perhaps because of the biases of their primary sources. A. J. Ray, "Men of Property and the Exercise of Title," in *Aboriginal Resource Use in Canada*, ed. K. Abel and J. Friesen (Manitoba: University of Manitoba Press, 1991), 301–15. Athapaskan female trapping is also overlooked in studies dealing specifically with gender and fur trading families. J. S. H. Brown, *Strangers in Blood: Fur Trade Company Families in Indian Country* (Vancouver: University of British Columbia Press, 1980); and S. Van Kirk, "Many Tender Ties": Women in Fur Trade Society, 1670–1870 (Winnipeg: Watson & Dwyer, 1980).

4. Cree women's narratives of trapping are becoming available. These texts unfold in a genre similar to those of the Carrier: with quiet warmth, humor, and modesty rather than bravado and heroism. R. Flannery, *Ellen Smallboy: Glimpses of a Cree Woman's Life* (Montreal: McGill-Queen's University Press, 1995).

5. Archaeological studies and historical ethnography have yet to offer detailed descriptions of the Southern Carrier economy prior to the nineteenth century, hence we make no reference to a more distant past.

6. Archeo Tech Associates Consulting Anthropologists, *An Aboriginal Sustenance Impact Assessment of the Quesnel River Gold Development Project, Near Quesnel, B.C.* (Victoria, B.C.: Ministry of Energy, Mines and Petroleum Resources, 1993), 12–14.

7. Historian Arthur Ray commented on the significance of feasting with beaver: "The Western Carrier [those of Babine Lake and the Bulkley Valley] were very fond of beaver meat, which was an important item on feast menus, particularly at very important funeral feasts." Ray, "Men of Property and the Exercise of Title," 302.

8. In 1994 Caroline Mufford collected Julie George's memories of her life.

9. In 1951 the Alcan Corporation flooded a huge tract of land to generate electricity for an aluminum smelter to be located on the Pacific Coast. Many Carrier lost their traditional resource territories, for which they received no compensation at the time. The Cheslatta Nation was forcibly removed from their home village and other Southern Carrier relocated to trap and hunt after their traplines were flooded. Ootsa Lake was formed by this damming of one arm of the Nechako River, and in the process the Peters family lost their traplines.

10. Catherine Peters shared her life story with Caroline Mufford in 1994.

11. The Carrier hold more than one view on who is most vulnerable to the power of the otter. For example, some say it is anyone under twenty.

12. We employ "seminomadic" to indicate the seasonal movements through the traditional lands, all of which were governed by complex laws of land tenure and resource management.

13. V. Kobrinksy, "Ethnohistory and Ceremonial Representation of Carrier Social Structure" (Ph.D. diss., University of British Columbia, Vancouver, 1973); A. G. Morice, "Are the Carrier Sociology and Mythology Indigenous or Exotic?" *Proceedings and Transactions of the Royal Society of Canada*, ser. 1, sect. 2 (1892): 109–26.

14. J. Cruikshank, *Life Lived Like a Story* (Lincoln: University of Nebraska Press, 1990); R. Ridington, *Swan People: A Study of the Dunne-za Prophet Dance* (Ottawa: Canadian Ethnology Service, Mercury Series No. 38, National Museums of Canada, 1978); J. Fiske, "Gender and Politics in a Carrier Indian Community" (Ph.D. diss., University of British Columbia, Vancouver, 1989).

15. Carol Naziel and Rhonda Naziel, *Stories of the Moricetown Carrier Indians of Northwestern B.C.* (Moricetown, B. C.: Moricetown Indian Band Council, 1978), 16.

16. Bridget Moran with Mary John, *Stoney Creek Woman (Sai'k'uz Ts'eke): The Story of Mary John* (Vancouver: Tillacum Press 1988), 32.

17. Ibid.

18. J. Hackler, "The Carrier Indians of Babine Lake: The Effects of the Fur Trade and the Catholic Church on their Social Organization" (Unpublished manuscript, 1958).

19. Two copper mines have been closed on Lake Babine, in the heart of the nation's traditional territory. A plan for environmental management of the effects of these mines anticipates a century of careful monitoring of the wastes left behind. Lake Babine Nation leaders are now negotiating their role in these plans. They are also working toward negotiating protection measures with the Ministry of Forestry and the forestry corporations with tree licenses in the Babine territories.

20. First Nations of British Columbia (with rare exception) have never ceded land in treaties, nor have they been compensated by the Canadian state for the appropriation of their lands and resources. The treaty negotiations now in process with forty-three First Nations and the federal and provincial governments comprise a trilateral negotiation of land and resource rights, compensation for losses, and the establishment of the First Nation's legal jurisdiction over community governance, justice, land, and resource management, and so on. The British Columbia Treaty Commission arose from a 1990 trilateral agreement that established the terms of the process for each of the three governments involved. The federal and provincial governments have entered into the process in the hopes of establishing greater economic certainty vis-à-vis resource rights and of eradicating more direct and radical strategies on the part of First Nations struggling for their rights.

21. Moran and John, *Stoney Creek Woman*, 74.

22. J. McLean, *John McLean's Notes of a Twenty-five Years' Service in the Hudson's Bay Company*, ed. W. S. Wallace (Toronto: Champlain Society, 1932); D. Harmon, *A Journal of Voyages and Travels in the Interior of North America* (New York: Barnes and Co., 1903); A. G. Morice, "The Western Denes: Their Manners and Customs," *Proceedings of the Royal Canadian Institute*, 3d ser., vol. 6, no. 7 (1889): 109–74; Hudson, *Traplines and Timber*.

23. Estimating women's caloric production is not easy and is open to debate. However, from observations made by Fiske in 1984, it is clear that Carrier women undertake almost all responsibility for processing food, for netting freshwater fish, and for netting salmon in those regions where salmon is a primary food source (with the exception of the Babine, where more men are observed participating in all aspects of procurement and processing of fish). Men may kill and butcher large game much more frequently than women, but women process it, a more time-consuming task. Gathering is predominantly a female activity, and berries remain significant in the diet. Hudson's 1983 data also indicate the larger contributions of labor on the part of women. Of course, as Susan Walter points out, women also serve as the only source of nourishment for the very young, through nursing infants. Other societies in which women produce more than 50 percent of the diet include horticultural societies such as the Houdenosaunee. Walter's survey of food storing foraging societies exposes the biases in earlier studies in which food acquisition alone is equated with subsistence production, described in the studies available to her as primarily male labor. Thus low estimates of women's contribution routinely fail to include preservation as a subsistence contribution. Susan Walter, "Food Storage, Contributions to Subsistence and the Relative Status of Men and Women in Foraging Societies" (Unpublished Manuscript, 1984).

24. Hudson, *Traplines and Timber*, 135.

25. Brody, *Maps and Dreams*, 196.

26. Ibid.

27. Edwin W. Ardener, "Belief and The Problem of Women," in *Perceiving Women*, ed. S. Ardener (New York: Wiley Books, 1975), 1–28.

28. J. Fentress and C. Wickham, *Social Memory* (Oxford: Blackwell Press, 1992), 138.

29. Ibid., 139.

30. Gender differences in Carrier narration have been noted by Fiske in relation to historical political economy. Women, more so than men, historically position their memories in relation to family events (a common motif is to date an event in relation to the birth of a child or death of a parent), but they also identify different "external" or "public" turning points in their social history. For example, women and men may identify different economic moments as "good" or "bad" times depending on their individual capacity to secure jobs. Jo-Anne Fiske, *Gender and Politics in a Carrier Indian Community* (Unpublished dissertation, University of British Columbia, 1989), chap. 3.

Carolyn Podruchny Festivities, Fortitude, and
Fraternalism: Fur Trade Masculinity
and the Beaver Club, 1785-1827

IN 1785, wealthy fur trade merchants in Montreal founded the Beaver Club, an elite dining club restricted to men who had wintered in the North American interior, often referred to as "Indian Country." Although the Beaver Club existed alongside other dining and entertainment clubs in Montreal, it was unique in its membership, raison d'être, and rituals. The club was initiated to provide a forum for retired merchants in which to reminisce about the risky and adventurous days of fur trading, and a forum for young fur traders to enter Montreal's bourgeois society.[1] The initial membership of nineteen expanded to a peak of fifty-five, as the club met regularly until 1804. Following a three-year suspension, dinners were then resumed. It probably began to decline after the merger between the North West Company and Hudson's Bay Company in 1821, when the business center of the fur trade moved from Montreal to Hudson Bay. Evidence shows that members continued to meet until 1824, when the club ended. Efforts to resurrect the club in 1827 were unsuccessful.

The Beaver Club is a well-known institution of the Montreal fur trade. Many scholars have glorified the exclusive fraternity and the extravagant style of the dinners, and idealized the strength of the men who wintered in "Indian Country." Although mention of the Beaver Club is widespread, details are few, and its treatment is uncritical, romantic, celebratory, and lacking in historical context.[2] This chapter explores the social meaning of the Beaver Club for its members and for wider Montreal society. The club should be seen as a variant of men's club typical of the North Atlantic world in the late eighteenth and early nineteenth century.

Fraternal association provided a forum for men to establish business connections, share ideas, and construct and cement a common culture of shared values and social ideals. One of the most important of these ideals was the respectable man. Club rules and rituals defined the substance and boundaries of respectable behavior. The Beaver Club was distinct from many fraternal associations because it embodied a fascination with the "wild" and "savage." Men who had braved the unknown, encountering what they thought were strange, exotic, and potentially menacing natives, and surviving the rigors and dangers of travel by canoe, came together in Montreal to remember and honor their rugged adventures in the North American interior. In some ways fur trade merchants appropriated the "rugged" and "wild." Although they did not actually share the physical experiences of their laborers or the natives with whom they traded, they pretended to have done so in their reminiscences. At the same time members forged a bourgeois civility, which excluded women and the working class. In the privacy of the club, the fur traders could enjoy acting in a rough manner while upholding their respectable reputations to the outside world. In some ways the divergent ideals of respectability and rowdiness reflected a transition from an earlier fur trade society dominated by rough and ready traders whose claims to status and power came solely from their success in the trade, to a later society dominated by a professional, mostly English and Anglican, elite, who brought urban middle class ideals to their management of the fur trade.

I. Bourgeois Men's Clubs

Montreal was a mercantile city that relied on the fur trade and international import-exports for its economic survival until 1821. It served as the financial heart for a large part of the fur trade in North America. After 1770 its local economy became more vigorous, with a growing population and diversification of economic interests.[3] Although Montreal and Quebec City constituted the major urban centers of the Canadian colonies, their populations in the mid-eighteenth century reached only five thousand, less than half the size of New York, Philadelphia, and Boston, the largest cities in the Thirteen Colonies.[4] Montreal's middle class, which included businessmen, liberal professionals, and colonial officials, were the beneficiaries of the post-Conquest economic growth. Within this group the merchant bourgeoisie increased in number, diversity, and power. Fur trade merchants' prestige and influence were especially strong. This group of more than one hundred men made fast fortunes in the fur trade, bought property, gained political power, and became a part of the governing class of the colony. Partners in Montreal fur trade firms were commonly referred to as bourgeois. The dozen or so large companies began to pool resources in the early 1770s and eventually merged into the North West Company in 1784.[5]

As Montreal flourished, clubs became important institutions for urban sociability. Increasing affluence and leisure time among merchants led to the growth and popularity of clubs that provided organized forums for social entertainment, fellowship, and business networking. Similar patterns existed in eighteenth-century England, where voluntary organizations fostered a new sense of social order in towns, promoted urban advancement, were committed to intellectual innovation and social improvement, transmitted new ideas, and contributed to public vitality. Clubs played significant social and cultural roles in the transition from a preindustrial order to a modernizing industrial society by promoting social division based on class and wealth rather than rank and status, and by stressing harmony and order within the middle class.[6] In eighteenth-century America, fraternities, such as the Freemasons, accompanied the growth of market relations and towns. Clubs forged patronage relationships, which formed the primary means of survival and advancement in the eighteenth-century business world. Merchants relied heavily upon the reputation and ties of trust provided by clubs.[7] In Montreal, sodalities, such as the Beaver Club, helped to cement the bonds between members of the bourgeois class, provided vehicles for business and social bonding, and instilled values that helped shape their attitudes and behavior.

The Beaver Club dinners were part of a large continuum of vigorous socializing among fur traders and Montreal's bourgeoisie. Men and women entertained regularly, and one of the most popular activities was dining. In December 1797, Colonel George Landmann had not been in Montreal for more than twenty-four hours before receiving invitations to dine for the next ten days from army officers, government officials, and merchants. His descriptions of feasting and hard drinking extended to parties held by fur traders before spring fur brigades set out.[8] Montreal businessman and fur trader Joseph Frobisher's dining diary from 1806 to 1810 illustrates his participation in the broad circuit of dining and parties among Montreal's social elite. Even though Frobisher was not in the best health, he frequently dined out or entertained in his home every night of the week.[9] Although men and women frequently dined together, fraternization among men was formalized in clubs and associations, such as the Beaver Club. Other men's dining clubs that formed part of the pattern of socializing among Montreal's bourgeoisie included the Brothers in Law Club, which, like the Beaver Club, allowed members of the same occupation to meet in a convivial setting. This exclusive group of Montreal lawyers met several times a year to dine, between 1827 and 1833.[10] Others included the Bachelor's Club, the Montreal Hunt Club, and the exclusive Montreal Fire Club, to which many Beaver Club members belonged.[11]

Several Beaver Club members and many of their guests became members of the Masonic order, one of the most prestigious and well connected fraternal associations in the North Atlantic world. Although it drew men from many backgrounds, its character was bourgeois, and like the Beaver Club, it helped its membership forge a bourgeois identity. Sir John Johnson, an Indian department official and member of the legislative council of Lower Canada, was a regular guest at Beaver Club dinners. He was appointed the Masonic Provincial Grand Master for Canada in 1788. His father, Sir William Johnson, a prominent merchant and superintendent of Indian affairs for northern British North America, founded one of the first Masonic lodges in New York in 1766. Beaver Club member William McGillivray became Provincial Grand Master of the District of Montreal. His younger brother, Simon McGillivray, also a Beaver Club member, became a Freemason in 1807 and was appointed provincial grandmaster of Upper Canada in 1822.[12] Many lodges were founded at fur trade and military posts in the late eighteenth century, such as Michilimackinac, Niagara, Cataraqui, and Mackinaw. As well, colonial military regiments, whose officers regularly attended Beaver Club dinners, were closely tied to early masonic lodges.[13] The last meeting of the Beaver Club was held at the Masonic Hall Hotel.[14] These ties with Freemasonry aided the fur traders in business and politics. Fur trade scholar Heather Devine has found that the rapid success of Scottish Nor'Westers as merchants was due to their entry into Sir William Johnson's political, social, and economic networks. Through patronage, Johnson established close ties with some Scottish émigrés, particularly Simon McTavish.[15] These ties seemed to persist into the nineteenth century in Montreal, as Sir John Johnson was a regular guest at the Beaver Club.

The club was comprised mainly of men who either worked for or were sympathetic to the North West Company. Members included the most powerful men in the fur trade business, such as Charles-Jean-Baptiste Chaboillez, Maurice Blondeau, Benjamin Frobisher, Joseph Frobisher, Thomas Frobisher, James McGill, John McGill, William McGillivray, Duncan McGillivray, and Roderick McKenzie, as well as some of the most famous explorers of the North American interior, such as Alexander Henry the younger, Alexander MacKenzie, and Simon Fraser.[16] Some members were less socially prominent, and a few had dubious backgrounds, such as interpreter and trader Joseph-Louis Ainsse, who was accused of plundering at Michilimackinac, who betrayed a commandant, and who embezzled from the Indian Department. American trader Peter Pond, described as violent and unprincipled, was suspected of being involved in the murders of at least three

fur traders.[17] However, in the context of the Beaver Club, these social differences were often flattened, and suspect backgrounds were ignored in the
interests of maintaining a respectable appearance. Fur traders who worked in
rival companies, such as the XY Company, were not welcome, even if they
had been members previously. For example, Alexander McKenzie was elected to the Club in 1795, disappeared from its records while he was a partner
of the XY Company, but was reelected in 1808, four years after the XY
Company's dissolution. At the same meeting former XY partner A. N.
McLeod was also elected. Another XY Company partner, John Gregory, was
initially elected in 1791, but does not reappear in the club minutes until
1809.[18] Some well-known fur traders, such as David Thompson and Daniel
Williams Harmon, never became members, probably because they spent most
of their lives in the northwest.[19]

Beaver Club folklore extolled the political and economic power of its
members. Member James Hughes recalled the club as the "acme of social
attainment and the pinnacle of commercial success in Lower Canada,"
proudly reported distinguished visitors to the club, and hinted that the fur
traders controlled affairs of state.[20] Guests included militia officers, government officials, businessmen, and professionals, such as judges, lawyers, and
doctors, as well as distinguished visitors to Montreal, including John Jacob
Astor, Washington Irving, and Thomas Moore. The political and economic
networks formed between fur trade businessmen, colonial officials, Indian
Department administrators, and military officers were encouraged by their
regular socializing. Members and guests were often connected through family as well as through business. For example, the frequent guest Alexander
Auldjo was a leader among Montreal businessmen, supporter of the English
Party, and member of the Scotch Presbyterian Church. David David, a fur
trader, businessman and militia officer who became a Beaver Club member in
1817, was appointed director of the Bank of Montreal in 1818. Another frequent visitor was John Forsyth, a successful merchant actively involved in
improving Montreal's financial infrastructure, a militia officer, and a member
of the legislative council.[21]

Meetings were held in the off-season of the trade once a fortnight from the
first week in December until the second week in April. Beginning at four in
the afternoon, dinners often lasted until four in the morning.[22] Dinners were
held in various Montreal hotels and taverns, such as City Tavern, Richard
Dillion's Montreal Hotel, Palmer's Hummums, and Tesseyman's, as was
common for private parties, business and political meetings, and gatherings of
male friends in the eighteenth century.[23] The passing around of a calumet, or

peace pipe, marked the beginning of the Club's formal rituals, continuing with a speech, or "harangue," made by the evening's president, and formal toasts.[24] Dinner fare included country food, such as braised venison, bread sauce, "Chevreuil des Guides" (stew), venison sausages, wild rice, quail, and partridge "du Vieux Trappeur," served in crested glass and silverware.[25] After dinner, the club became more informal, as men began to drink more heavily, sing voyageur songs, and reminisce about the good old fur trading days. Festivities continued until the early morning, with men dancing on the tables, reenacting canoeing adventures, and breaking numerous bottles and glasses. The approbation of rough and rowdy behavior, at odds with the urbane civility of other Montreal dining clubs, especially those where women were included, allowed fur traders a private space in which to embrace rugged masculine ideals.

II. Gender, Class, and Fraternalism

The Beaver Club was instrumental in developing the gender and class identities of its members. It brought bourgeois men together in an insulated setting and promoted representations of idealized masculinity. Gender formation and class formation were closely associated in the late eighteenth- and early nineteenth-century North Atlantic world. Some scholars, such as British middle class historians Leonore Davidoff and Catherine Hall, argue that class and gender always operate together, and that class always takes a gendered form.[26] As bourgeois men came together in business and fraternal orders, they began to limit the boundaries of their collective identity. The increasing marginalization of women from the world of public commerce after the Conquest extended to their exclusion from fraternal associations, which were often seen as extensions of men's business interests. Bourgeois men also sought to distinguish themselves from other classes. They generally considered the lower orders as their social and economic inferiors and, despite their aspirations to gentry, they often called the higher orders their moral inferiors.[27] Through fraternal associations, the bourgeois were able to consolidate their class and forge bourgeois harmony.

Women were excluded from most fraternal associations for various reasons. One of the key components to middle-class constructions of femininity and masculinity was the division between the public sphere, the realm of rational activity, market forces, and production, and the private sphere, the realm of morality, emotion, and reproduction. Although men and women moved in both these spheres, men appropriated the former, while women dominated the latter.[28] The subsequent marginalization of women in the public sphere contributed to the exclusion of women from club meetings, as fraternal associations were frequently associated with men's trade and business. Like many other men's clubs, Beaver Club meetings were held in taverns, where few middle-class women ventured. Hall argues that taverns were increasingly defined as inappropriate settings for women who wished to maintain their gentility, as temperance movements became an important component of the evangelical project to raise the moral tone of society.[29] Other scholars suggest that the absence of women was important to the process of forging masculinity. Mark Carnes's study of fraternal associations in Victorian America argues that their rituals provided solace and psychological guidance, away from women, for a young man's passage from the maternal affection of childhood to manhood.[30] In the all-male atmosphere men could practice distinctive social behaviors, such as smoking, swearing, gambling, and drinking, with little interruption. In her work on American mariners, Margaret Creighton asserts that these masculine activities were not meant to make the men more appealing to women; rather, they made them more acceptable to other men.[31] Men were subject to gender expectations generated by both sexes. Away from women, men could focus on themselves, cultivate their own desires and identities, and escape the pressures of women's expectations. In the Beaver Club, fur traders were able to revere their lives in the North American interior, where, away from their Euro-American wives and mothers, they pursued their aspirations for rugged adventure.

Fur trade laborers, such as voyageurs, interpreters, and guides, were almost never included in Beaver Club festivities. The social organization of the Montreal fur trade firmly divided partners from low-ranked workers.[32] In the mid-eighteenth century, some men were able to rise from the rank of worker to manager, but by the time of the emergence of the North West Company in the 1780s, the hierarchy was firmly in place. Older fur traders counseled young clerks to be obedient and polite to superiors, to be self-important when out in the field, and to hold themselves apart from their laborers to command respect and submission.[33] However, bourgeois attitudes to lower orders could be complex and contradictory, especially for fur traders who had lived and worked alongside their labor force in an isolated and dangerous setting. Many fur trade bourgeois admired voyageurs for their strength and skill, and established relationships with them built on trust and interdependence. At the same time most fur trade bourgeois considered voyageurs to be thoughtless, irrational, and rude.[34] Club rituals imitating voyageurs helped the bourgeois to distance themselves from their workers. The romanticization of voyageurs' activities cast them as exotic curiosities. At the same time, bourgeois men appropriated voyageurs' experiences in the fur trade. They reminisced about paddling canoes and running through rapids, even though this was the work of the voyageurs. The bourgeois did not risk their lives in rapids and portages, carry back-breaking packs, paddle at outrageous speeds, nor survive on minimal food, as did the voyageurs. Rather, they directed crews, managed accounts, distributed food, and had better rations than their voyageurs. Both the distancing from and the imitation of voyageurs reflected a code of ethics that applauded rugged behavior of the bourgeois in the right settings.

Most eighteenth- and nineteenth-century bourgeois admired upper orders, and cherished noble values such as courage, loyalty, prowess in combat, and gallantry in love.[35] This admiration was not unproblematic, as the bourgeois found aristocratic behavior often at odds with many of their notions of respectability and honor. Nonetheless, members of higher social orders were not excluded from the Beaver Club. The desire to achieve the status of a gentleman inspired in the fur trade bourgeois a fascination for nobility and aristocracy. Although many Anglophone merchants were hostile to the old seigneurial order, they were nonetheless influenced by it. Military service, purchasing noble titles, and acquiring property were common ways that the bourgeoisie could associate themselves with nobility and aspire to gentry.[36] Fur trade bourgeois usually procured their own crest and motto, which were important signifiers of membership in the gentry.

Aristocratic association was a common theme in club folklore. Members honored nobility, such as the Duke of Kent, Lord Selkirk, and Lord Dalhousie, the governor-general of Canada, by inviting them to club dinners.[37] For example, at an 1894 auction Brian Hughes was delighted to buy his grandfather's snuffbox bearing the inscription: "The Earl of Dalhousie to James Hughes, Esq., in remembrance of the Beaver Club, May 24, 1824."[38] Club members also tried to imitate nobles through lavish spending and material accoutrements. Hughes relates his grandfather's memories of members richly adorned with their medals, ruffles, gold lace, gold-clasped garters, and silver-buckled shoes. Members often displayed their wealth through hospitality to their peers and to visitors.[39] When traveling through Montreal in the early nineteenth century, John Lambert describes how the "Nor'Westers'" lavish displays of hospitality inspired both jealous resentment and "interested deference" in nonmembers.[40]

Status anxiety may have been behind the merchants' desire to cultivate a strong noble demeanor. One British visitor in 1820, Edward Talbot, cautioned his readers about the vanity and lack of refinement of the newly rich merchants in Montreal, originally servants or mechanics "of low origin and scanty acquirements" who made fortunes in the fur trade. Talbot was appalled by the aristocratic pretensions of this group, but grudgingly admitted that some members of the North West Company belonged to the highest class in Montreal society.[41]

Despite their affinity for the aristocracy, bourgeois values also reflected the struggles of a vigorous urban elite to establish independent claims to power and status. Davidoff and Hall assert that the British middle-class challenge to aristocratic hegemony was based on their claim to moral superiority.[42] Robert Nye has found that the French bourgeois were preoccupied with moral discipline, inner values, and control of reproduction and sex to carefully regulate inheritance strategies.[43] Many similarities can be found with the fur trade bourgeois, who earned their position through hard work, careful planning, and merit. One of the club's medals was inscribed with the motto "Industry and Perseverance," which emphasized the efforts of men rather than their birthright.[44] Loyalty and commitment were also important ideals to club fraternity, as members were expected to attend the meetings if in town, and were forbidden from hosting parties or accepting other invitations on club days.[45] Like other bourgeois, the fur traders were encouraged to marry within their social group. For example, John Forsyth married the daughter of prominent Quebec merchant Charles Grant; Joseph Frobisher married the daughter of Jean-Baptiste Jobert and niece of Charles-Jean-Baptiste Chaboillez, founding members of the Beaver Club; Simon McTavish married the daughter of Chaboillez; and William McGillivray married the daughter of Beaver Club member Sir John McDonald of Garth.[46] However, many of the Northwest Company bourgeois married Native or mixed-blood women, especially after spending many years in the interior. These marriages were often strategies for building trading alliances and surviving in the bush.[47] Some, such as McGillivray, abandoned their country wives when they left the interior to become merchants in Montreal.[48]

In the Beaver Club gender and class divisions came into sharp relief, as membership was explicitly restricted to bourgeois men. However, the club was less selective of ethnicity and religion. Of the nineteen initial Beaver Club members, eight were French Canadian, six were Scottish, three were English, and two were American.[49] Although Scots came to dominate the Montreal fur trade and the Beaver Club, a French Canadian presence persisted.[50] The inclusion of a variety of ethnicities and religious affiliations reflected the composition of people involved in the Montreal business and fur trade world. The fraternal rituals of the club helped to smooth over tension arising from ethnic and religious difference. Hall suggests that clubs and voluntary associations in late eighteenth- and early nineteenth-century Britain gave their members a sense of collective identity, which helped unite men of different religious backgrounds, trades, and classes.[51] The same was probably true of the Beaver Club, which helped smooth ethnic and religious differences between its members.

The club was characterized by an odd tension between its efforts to promote harmony and a collective bourgeois identity, and its hierarchical nature. The ideal of egalitarianism was manifested in the club's organizational structure. Each member had an equal vote in electing new members, deciding on fines for those who had broken club rules, and in other club affairs. Also, members took turns rotating as president, vice president, and cork of the club, enforcing general equality without challenging the structure of hierarchy.[52] The privacy of the club probably contributed to the spirit of egalitarianism. Members felt the privilege of belonging, being set apart from the rest of society, and sharing in secrets from the outside world.[53]

Exclusivity expressed in numerical limits helped to maintain social hierarchy. Initially the Beaver Club began with nineteen men, but was expanded to forty with eight honorary members by 1807, to fifty and ten honorary members in 1815, and by 1816 the limit was fifty-five members and ten honorary members.[54] Only men who received a unanimous vote and met the club requirements could join. Bourgeois respectability required wealth and leisure, as the men were expected to dedicate time and money to club. Members had to purchase a gold medal recording the date of their first winter spent in the interior. They were fined for breaking club rules, such as failing to attend a dinner if they were in Montreal, not wearing their medals to the dinners, and forgetting to notify the secretary of guests they intended to bring to dinner.[55] Members were required to pay for their dinners even if they did not attend club meetings, and were only excused from the fee if they were ill.[56] Social pressure to drink large amounts of alcohol at the meetings was high, and men had to pay for their drinks.[57]

The club also served to distinguish fur traders from other bourgeoisie. The condition that men had to winter in the interior to join the club verified the candidate's strength and fortitude. Members were differentiated from guests by their medals, which served as a common marker to identify the members as a group. Private dinners that excluded guests were held at the beginning of every year to plan the year's events.[58] Only members had voting privileges, and each was provided with a printed book of the club's mandate, the rules and regulations, and membership list.[59]

The club's five formal toasts reflected the tension between the ideals of an emerging urban bourgeoisie, and those of an older rough and ready fur trade society. The first toast, "the mother of all the saints," paid respect to the church, while toasts to the king and the fur trade honored the state and commerce. The rules and regulations did not indicate allegiance to any specific church, and members ranged from Roman Catholics to Presbyterians to Anglicans. The toast to "the mother of all the saints," probably the Virgin Mary, may have been a convenient way to acknowledge the importance of religion without restricting devotion to a single church. At the same time, the toast may have paid homage to an earlier fur trade world dominated by Roman Catholicism. In the toast to "voyageurs, wives, and children," the fur traders venerated themselves and the institution of the family. It is unclear whether the toast to "voyageurs, wives, and children" referred to the fur traders themselves and their families, or to those the fur traders considered their dependents, that is, their workers, wives, and children. Finally, the last toast, to absent members, could be seen as a tribute to fraternity and brotherly love. By acknowledging these values through ritual toasts, fur traders reinforced bourgeois standards of virtue among themselves and taught them to young clerks, as the club served to initiate young fur traders and bring those who had spent years in the North American interior back into respectable society.[60] Formal toasting was a way to draw the group together to participate in a unified activity, sharing similar sentiments about religion, occupation, and masculinity that were different from that of the larger society. Perhaps the jovial and convivial atmosphere allowed these men to reassert older values while recognizing their contradiction within a changing world.

Two Beaver Club members, Simon Fraser and John McDonald of Garth, wrote a memorandum in 1859, near the end of their lives, which captured the spirit of fur traders' masculine ideals:

> We are the last of the old N[orth]. W[est]. Partners. We have known one another for many years. Which of the two survives the other we know not. We are both aged, we have lived in mutual esteem and fellowship, we have done our duty in the stations allotted us without fear, or reproach. We have braved many dangers, we have run many risks. We cannot accuse one another of any thing mean & dirty through life, nor done any disagreeable actions, nor wrong to others. We have been feared, loved & respected by natives. We have kept our men under subordination. We have thus lived long lives. We have both crossed this continent, we have explored many new points, we have met many new Tribes, we have run our Race, & as this is probably the last time we meet on earth, we part as we have lived in sincere friendship & mutual good will.[61]

III. The Gentleman and the Wild Man

The fur trade bourgeois differed from other North Atlantic bourgeoisie in their masculine ideals and in their struggles to attain respectable status. As merchants, the fur traders often worked independently of social hierarchies and were open to a wide variety of cultures.[62] Merchants have been described as adventurers, gamblers who took risks for which they expected a high return.[63] The fur trade brought them into the midst of the wild, where they experienced first hand the wonders of exotic people and places. Fur traders struggled to manage their fascination with the wild and savage while operating within an urban context of respectability. They cultivated respectability and patriotism in order to secure business contacts, and also were subject to the exigencies of their class. Yet, the rough skills learned by the fur traders in their perilous adventures were a source of pride, and they helped to create a distinction between "refined" women and "rough" men in an urban context.

The traders thus constructed their own particular type of masculinity, combining bourgeois ideals of respectability with their rugged and wondrous fur trade experiences. These two impulses were not dichotomous nor necessarily in conflict, as strength was important to respectability and honor. The Beaver Club became a safe and private forum for honoring coarse and rude behavior, such as excessive drinking and carousing, not acceptable for bourgeois men in public settings. At the same time, gentility was represented in the club's stately settings, formal rituals, and illustrious assembly. Visitors, such as Landmann, commented on the wild feasting and hard drinking that went on during club dinners, and yet gratefully recalled the "greatest civilities" received from club members.[64] While the club helped fur traders to reconcile their desires to be both rough and gentle, however, it also served to emphasize boundaries between civilized bourgeois society on the one hand, and on the other the rough bush society of voyageurs, country wives, and Natives.

Some of the most interesting aspects of the Beaver Club were the formal and informal ceremonies of the meetings. The solemn rituals instilled meaning in the club's ideals, while the revelry provided a place and time in which to cement fraternal bonds. Rituals and ceremonial occasions can be seen as sites of struggles between competing representations, serving as markers for collective identity.[65] The dominant impulse in the rituals was a romanticization of the fur trade, which emphasized its importance in the men's lives, but also eased anxiety about the lack of fit between fur trade life and urban bourgeois society.

The tension between the fur traders' desire to be refined and to be rash found expression in the structure of club meetings. The dinners began formally, following specified rituals, but then developed into wild and reckless parties. The fixed scheduling of club dinners contributed to the formal atmosphere. Formality was also expressed in codes of dress. At club functions members were obliged to wear their medals on blue ribbons or on black ribbons to honor a member's death.[66] The dinner itself reflected a tension between the savage and the civil. Country food, such as wild rice and venison, was served in crested glass and silverware in stately settings.[67] After the formal rituals of club dinners, informal socializing and frolicking could begin. A defined social space was an important part of the fraternal process because it was a time to solidify bonds and express brotherly love and harmony. Conversations must have often turned to business, with deals discussed and strategies developed.[68] However, the time for play at the dinners was also a time to turn tables, reverse meanings, and poke at the social order expressed in the rituals and rules of the club. Frequent amusements were the singing of voyageur songs, such as *La claire Fontaine* and *En roulant ma boule.*[69] James Hughes's stories include an account of the men arranging themselves on the floor, then imitating the vigorous paddling of a canoe and mounting wine kegs to "shoot the rapids" from the table to the floor.[70] Rules ensured that every member could drink as he pleased after the toasts had gone around, firmly dividing the formal ritual from informal play.[71] In winter 1797 Landmann described in detail a wild club party: initially all men consumed a bottle of wine during the dinner, but after the married men retired, leaving the bachelors to "drink to their health," the party really began in "right earnest and true highland style," which involved war whoops, singing, heavy drinking, breaking plates and glasses, and dancing on the tables. Landmann estimated that 120 bottles of wine had been consumed at the dinner by about twenty men.[72]

In the eighteenth century, consumption of alcohol was considered a gratifying and convivial activity and accompanied almost every social occasion. In the Beaver Club it contributed to the building of trust and friendships.[73] Lambert felt that the wild abandon of the fur traders' spending and celebrating was well deserved considering the rigors and risks of fur trading.[74] Perhaps many of the members considered the wild revelry a necessary release from the tension and discomfort of their experiences in the bush. Hughes also recounted that retired fur traders tried to recreate the "untrammeled license" that they enjoyed in the wilderness.[75] Club dinners provided a safe social space for licensed wildness and drinking closely associated with release. Holding one's liquor was a source of pride. At one party Landmann admired Alexander Mackenzie and William McGillivray for being the only two men remaining in their seats when everyone else had passed out.[76] Excessive drinking could have been a demonstration of wealth. Lambert hints that the North West Company bourgeois aroused the jealousy and resentment of Montreal society for their lavish spending and incredible hospitality, which was meant to display wealth.[77]

However, disapproval of excessive drunkenness in public, and especially alcoholism, led the bourgeois to confine heavy drinking and wild abandon to an appropriate context. In a letter to John Askin, Alexander Henry inquired if he enjoyed his visit to the Beaver Club, where he no doubt joined in the merriment of drink, and a few paragraphs later criticized a late colleague for excessive drinking.[78] In the late eighteenth century public drunkenness and swearing were increasingly condemned.[79] Serious drinking was recognized as a social ill, and associated with poverty, misery, disease, and death.[80] Beaver Club members may have been especially cautious to define a framed time and place for their wild abandon.

Some rituals especially captured the tension in fur traders' attitudes toward their bush experiences. Passing the calumet,[81] common to many Native cultures, often marked the beginning of conferences or treaties, and paid tribute to spirits.[82] Although the fur traders probably appreciated the solemn and sacred nature of the calumet, a greater appeal must have lain in the exotic aspects of adopting Native traditions. Traveler John Palmer noted that Indian manners, customs, and language, especially war whoops, were closely imitated at club dinners.[83] The attitude of the fur traders toward Natives was complex and often contradictory. Fur traders lived with Natives, often married them, depended on them for survival, and traded with them. Respect and common understanding existed in the relationship. Yet, to the fur traders, Natives were a savage people, both appealing and dangerous. The tradition of bourgeois traders marrying Native women created a particular anxiety for the bourgeois to distance themselves from Native influences in a respectable urban environment. Fur traders were fascinated with the savage, and the safe and constricted atmosphere of the club allowed them a place and time to explore and revel in savagery, while maintaining a respectable distance. Ritualizing Native customs may have provided a way for the bourgeois to both dissociate from and honor them. Also, exotic rituals instilled romance in fraternal orders, and spoke to the desire for spiritualism. Passing the peace pipe around must have underscored the values of brotherly love and fraternity, as Club rules refer to the calumet as the "usual emblem of Peace."[84]

A significant aspect of fraternal bonding was reminiscing about fur trade experiences, an activity that was so highly valued it was part of the mandate published in the members' club rules.[85] In retelling his own adventures, each member asserted claims to valor and strength, while also renewing links of friendship and camaraderie.[86] Reminiscing allowed members to recast their fur trade memories by highlighting acceptable aspects of that life, such as the manly honor of completing difficult journeys, while silencing other memories, such as abandoned country wives and families. Yet at the same time, retelling their experiences may have allowed many to mourn their country families and friends, and their lost youth. Reminiscing was an essential method in teaching and revering the masculine values of strength, courage, fortitude, and perseverance gained in fur trade experience. A poem presented to the club by John Johnston on 19 November 1814 described the pleasure of meeting together with the wanderers of Canada's wide domain, "to recount the toils and perils past." While urging members to participate in the War of 1812 to protect the fur trade, the poem complimented traders for their force, skill, and "manly heart," and lauded their brave suffering in difficult situations.[87] Military service was valued because it provided evidence of a man's courage and honor. Fur traders reminded each other to protect their honor, to avoid imposition, and to always defend themselves when attacked. Not only was strength in action highly valued, but also strength in rhetoric. One clerk congratulated another for his force and elegance with words and manly roughness with his argument in his letters.[88] The motto of the Club, "fortitude in distress," clearly indicated the primacy of the masculine ideals of ruggedness, might, and courage. The mandate of the Club proudly asserted that all initial members had been fur traders from an early age, referring to them as "voyageurs."[89] Members even considered changing the name to the "Voyageur Club."[90]

There was no clear definition of the term *voyageur*. It was used for all hardy travelers, and yet often the term referred only to French Canadian fur trade laborers. Regardless of the bourgeois' use of language, their attitudes toward fur trade workers were no less ambiguous than their attitudes toward Natives. The Beaver Club toast to "voyageurs, wives and children" may have been another example of the bourgeois trying to mimic their workers by calling themselves voyageurs. By singing voyageurs' songs, and by reenacting canoeing, fur traders could identify with voyageur toughness and rugged risk-taking masculinity, while they distanced themselves from their men in the everyday world. At the same time, the bourgeois appropriated the voyageurs' experiences and culture, as they revered the activities and adventures of their workers, in which the bourgeois did not participate.

IV. Conclusions

Fur traders were different from other elite men in Montreal. Their experience in the fur trade was foreign to respectable urban society but was not easily forgotten by its participants. Their rough ways formed in bush society were both a source of anxiety and a source of pride. The Beaver Club provided them with a forum in which to make sense of their past experiences, cast them in a positive light, and assert their particular brand of the ideal man. At the same time, the Beaver Club was primarily a respectable men's dining club, where Montreal's bourgeois society met to forge business alliances, exchange information, share ideas, and cement social ties. Although the club allowed members to indulge in idealization of the savage and an older rough and ready fur trade world, the respectable man remained the dominant ideal.

At club meetings, secluded from women, the lower orders, and Native people, Montreal's bourgeois men could focus on themselves, cultivate their own desires and identities, and affirm their values. Men could honor strength, courage, and perseverance, all acceptable aspects of bourgeois masculinity, but they could also venerate risk taking, the spirit of adventure, and a taste for the exotic, qualities that boarded on the rough and uncouth. The privacy of the Club allowed the traders to indulge in rough behavior, while protecting their respectable reputations. These masculine ideals also brought the distinction between rough men and refined women into greater relief. The secluded fraternal setting, where men shared their memories and emotions, could not be confused with the domestic sphere, which was the domain of women.

Notes

1. I use the term *bourgeois* in this chapter sometimes to refer to the emerging middle class. However, in the Montreal fur trade merchants and managers were referred to as "bourgeois." Although most of the fur trade bourgeois were part of Montreal's bourgeoisie, the terms have distinct meanings.

2. For examples see Lynn Hetherington, "Canada's First Social Club," *The University Magazine* 9 (April 1910): 296–305, esp. 297, and Robert Watson, "The First Beaver Club," *The Beaver* Outfit 262, no. 3 (December 1931): 334–37, esp. 335. Many works on fur trade and Montreal history cite frequently George Bryce, *The Remarkable History of the Hudson's Bay Company including that of the French Traders of the North-West, XY, and Astor Fur Companies* (Toronto: William Briggs, 1900) and *Mackenzie, Selkirk, Simpson: The Makers of Canada* (Toronto: Morang & Co., Ltd., 1910); Clifford P. Wilson, "The Beaver Club," *The Beaver* Outfit 266, no. 4 (March 1936): 19–24, 64; Donald Creighton, *The Empire of the St. Lawrence* (Toronto:

MacMillan Co., 1956), 27; Marjorie Wilkins Campbell, *The North West Company* (New York: St. Martin's Press, 1957) and *McGillivray: Lord of the Northwest* (Toronto and Vancouver: Clarke, Irwin & Co. Ltd., 1962). An exception is provided by Lawrence J. Burpee, who does not cite his evidence, but discusses primary and secondary sources within the text. Lawrence J. Burpee, "The Beaver Club," *Canadian Historical Association Annual Report* (1924): 73–91. Another exception is Jennifer Brown, whose brief mention of the Beaver Club describes its role of easing the transition of fur traders back into community life after long absences in the interior. Jennifer S. H. Brown, *Strangers in Blood: Fur Trade Company Families in Indian Country* (Vancouver: University of British Columbia Press, 1980), 44.

3. Louise Dechêne, "La Croissance de Montréal au XVIIIe Siècle," *Revue d'histoire de l'Amérique française* 27, no. 2 (septembre 1973): 163–79, esp.167; Jean-Paul Bernard, Paul-André Linteau, and Jean-Claude Robert, "La Structure professionnelle de Montréal en 1825," *Revue d'histoire de l'Amérique française* 30, no. 3, (decembre 1976): 383–415, esp. 390–91. Fernand Ouellet argues that the Montreal fur trade began to decline as early as 1803, but admits that "even in decline, the famous fur trade would continue to exert a considerable influence on certain elements of society." Fernand Ouellet, *Economic and Social History of Quebec, 1760–1850* (Ottawa: Institute of Canadian Studies, Carleton University, 1980), 181–82, 186.

4. David T. Ruddel, *Québec City, 1765–1832* (Ottawa: Canadian Museum of Civilization, 1987), 23.

5. Fernand Ouellet, *Lower Canada 1791–1840, Social Change and Nationalism*, trans. Patricia Claxton (Toronto: McClelland and Stewart, 1980), 38–39, 63, and *Economy, Class, & Nation in Quebec: Interpretive Essays*, ed. and trans. Jacques A. Barbier (Toronto: Copp, Clark, Pitman, 1991), 79–80; and Brown, *Strangers in Blood*, 35–36. See also Creighton, who describes the political program of the Montreal merchants in *Empire of the St. Lawrence*, 23, 35–55.

6. Peter Clark, "Sociability and Urbanity: Clubs and Societies in the Eighteenth Century City," The Eighth H. J. Dyos Memorial Lecture (Leicester: University of Leicester, Victoria Studies Centre, 1986), 17–19, 23.

7. Steven Conrad Bullock, "The Ancient and Honorable Society: Freemasonry in America, 1730–1830," (Ph.D. diss., Brown University, 1986), 5, 78, 84.

8. George Landmann, *Adventures and Recollections of Colonel Landmann, Late of the Corps of Royal Engineers* (London: Colburn and Co., 1852), 232–33, 295–96. Ottawa, National Archives of Canada, Masson Collection, Miscellaneous Papers, MG19 C1, vol. 44, microfilm reel #C-15639, "Notes By Roderick McKenzie on books read by him . . . ," Part One, n.d. pages 11–19; Charles Bert Reed also describes the parties at Fort William in *Masters of the Wilderness* (Chicago: University of Chicago Press, 1914), 70–71. Reed's article on the Beaver Club is almost entirely a quotation of Brian Hughes describing the stories he was told by his grandfather, James Hughes, who was a Beaver Club member. Burpee is skeptical about much of the information provided by Hughes because many of the particulars are inconsistent with other historical sources. Burpee, "The Beaver Club," 89–90.

9. Ottawa, National Archives of Canada, McTavish, Frobisher & Company Collection, MG19 A5, vol. 4, Journal of Joseph Frobisher, 1806–10.

10. Montreal, McCord Museum of Canadian History Archives, M21413, Brothers in Law Society of Montreal Minute Book, 1827–33.

11. The Bachelor's Club was listed frequently in the Journal of Joseph Frobisher and mentioned in a letter from James Caldwell, Montreal, to Simon McTavish, New York Coffee House in London, 5 December 1792. Montreal, McGill Rare Books, MS 431/1, Simon McTavish Correspondence, 1792–1800. The Montreal Hunt Club was formed in 1826, with Beaver Club member John Forsyth as its first president. Marcel Caya, ed., *Guide to Archival Resources at McGill University* (Montreal: McGill University Archives, 1985), 3:294. Many Beaver Club members belonged to the Montreal Fire Club, which operated between 1786 and 1814, with a membership limit of fourteen. It was formed to provide mutual assistance in case of fire, as well as convivial association. Montreal, McGill Rare Books, MS 437, Montreal Fire Club Minute Book, 1786–1814. Some of the clubs seemed to be class based, and not exclusive to men. In the late 1790s, Isaac Weld describes a club of Montreal's "principal inhabitants," both men and women, which met once a week or fortnight to dine. Isaac Weld, Jr., *Travels Through the States of North America, and the Provinces of Upper and Lower Canada, During the Years 1795, 1796, and 1797*, 4th ed., 2 vols. (London: John Stockdale, 1807), 1:315.

12. A. J. B. Milborne, *Freemasonry in the Province of Quebec, 1759–1959* (Knowlton, QC: P.D.D.G.M. G.L.Q., 1960), 40, 67–68; J. Lawrence Runnalls, "Simon McGillivray 1783–1840," *The Papers of the Canadian Masonic Research Association* (Hamilton: 44th Meeting of the Association of The Heritage Lodge, No. 73, A.F. & A.M., G.R.C., 1966), 3:1487–89.

13. John E. Taylor, "Freemasonry in Old Canada and the War of 1812–15," *The Papers of the Canadian Masonic Research Association* (Toronto: 23d Meeting of the Association, A.F. & A.M., G.R.C., 1958), 2:783, 787; A. J. B. Milborne, "The Murals in the Memorial Hall, Montreal Masonic Memorial Temple," *The Papers of the Canadian Masonic Research Association* (Montreal: 8th Meeting of the Association, A.F. & A.M., G.R.C., 1953), 1:255–57.

14. Montreal, McCord Museum of Canadian History Archives, M14449, Beaver Club Minute Book, 1807–27, Original, 3 February 1827, 120. Photostats and typescripts can also be obtained at McGill Rare Books and the National Archives of Canada.

15. Heather Devine, "Roots in the Mohawk Valley: Sir William Johnson's Legacy in the North West Company," in *The Fur Trade Revisited: Selected Papers of the Sixth North American Fur Trade Conference, Mackinac Island, Michigan, 1991*, ed. Jennifer S. H. Brown, W. J. Eccles, and Donald P. Heldman (East Lansing: Michigan State University Press, 1994), 217–42, esp. 228–30. Also see Brown, *Strangers in Blood*, 36–38.

16. It is difficult to determine whether Simon McTavish, general director of the North West Company, was a member of the Beaver Club. His name does not appear in the Minute Book, but he is listed as a member since 1792 in the 1819 issue of the

Rules and Regulations of the Beaver Club: Instituted in 1785 (Montreal: W. Gray, 1819), McCord Museum of Canadian History Archives, M144450, 10 (the name "De Rocheblave" is written on the front cover). Some scholars assert that fur traders disliked McTavish so much that they never invited him to join, or that "the Marquis" himself refused to meet his colleagues on an equal footing in the Club. Burpee, "The Beaver Club," 74–75.

17. David A. Armour, "Ainsse (Ainse, Hains, Hins), Joseph-Louis (Louis-Joseph)," in *Dictionary of Canadian Biography* (hereafter *DCB*) (Toronto: University of Toronto Press, 1983), 5:7–9; Barry M. Gough, "Pond, Peter," in *DCB*, 5:681–86.

18. Beaver Club Minute Book, 4, 26, 47.

19. This is suggested by Burpee, "The Beaver Club," 75.

20. Reed, *Masters of the Wilderness*, 75, 77, 79, 80.

21. Gerald J. J. Tulchinsky, "Auldjo, Alexander," in *DCB*, 6:18–20; Elinor Kyte Senior, "David, David," in *DCB*, 6:179–81; Gerald J. J. Tulchinsky, "Forsyth, John," *DCB*, 7:309–11; Bruce G. Wilson, *The Enterprises of Robert Hamilton: A Study of Wealth and Influence in Early Upper Canada, 1776–1812* (Ottawa: Carleton University Press, 1983), 12–13.

22. Reed, *Masters of the Wilderness*, 69.

23. Thomas Brennan, *Public Drinking and Popular Culture in Eighteenth-Century Paris* (Princeton, N. J.: Princeton University Press, 1988), 8; Kym Rice, *Early American Taverns: For the Entertainment of Friends and Strangers* (Chicago: Regnery Gateway, 1983), 88.

24. *Rules and Regulations*, 3; Beaver Club Minute Book, 2.

25. For an example of a Beaver Club menu, see Jehane Benoît, "Wintering Dishes," *Canadian Collector* vol. 20, no. 3 (May/June 1985): 25–27. For mention of Beaver Club glass and silverware, see Watson, "The First Beaver Club," 337.

26. Leonore Davidoff and Catherine Hall, *Family Fortunes: Men and Women of the English Middle Class, 1780–1850* (Chicago: University of Chicago Press, 1987), 13, 30.

27. Ibid., 18–23. Also see Robert A. Nye, *Masculinity and Male Codes of Honor in Modern France* (New York: Oxford University Press, 1993), 8, 31–33.

28. Davidoff and Hall, *Family Fortunes*, 13, 25, 29.

29. Catherine Hall, *White, Male and Middle Class: Explorations in Feminism and History* (New York: Routledge, 1992), 158.

30. Mark C. Carnes, *Secret Ritual and Manhood in Victorian America* (New Haven, Conn. and London: Yale University Press, 1989), 14.

31. Margaret S. Creighton, "American Mariners and the Rites of Manhood, 1830–1870," in *Jack Tar in History: Essays in the History of Maritime Life and Labour*, ed. Colin Howell and Richard J. Twomey (Fredericton, N. B.: Acadiensis Press, 1991), 132–63, esp. 147.

32. Brown, *Strangers in Blood*, 35, 47–48.

33. Toronto, Archives of Ontario, George Gordon Papers, MU 1146, G. Moffatt, Fort William to George Gordon, Monontagué, 25 July 1809.

34. For example, see W. Kaye Lamb, ed., *Sixteen Years in Indian Country: The Journal of Daniel Williams Harmon, 1800–1816*, (Toronto: MacMillam Company of Canada Ltd., 1957), 197–98.

35. Davidoff and Hall, *Family Fortunes*, 18; Nye, *Masculinity and Male Codes of Honor*, 32.

36. Ouellet, *Economy, Class, & Nation*, 62, 80, 94–95, 109.

37. Campbell, *The Northwest Company*, 130, 140; "Incidents, Deaths, &c." *Canadian Magazine* 2, no. 11 (14 May 1824): 473.

38. Reed, *Masters of the Wilderness*, 57–58.

39. Ibid., 68, 75.

40. John Lambert, *Travels Through Canada, and the United States of North America, in the years 1806, 1807, & 1808. To Which are Added, Biographical Notices and Anecdotes of Some of the Leading Characters in the United States,* 2 vols. 2d ed. (1813; London: C. Cradock and W. Joy, 1814), 295–96, 524.

41. Edward Allen Talbot, *Five Years' Residence in the Canadas: Including a Tour through Part of the United States of America in the Year 1823*, 2 vols. (London: Longman, Hurst, Rees, Orme, Brown and Green, 1824), 2:282–84. John Duncan also criticizes the Montreal bourgeoisie for their deficiency in enterprise and public spirit. John M. Duncan, *Travels Through Part of the United States and Canada in 1818 and 1819*, 2 vols. (Glasgow: Wardlaw and Cunninghame, 1823), 2:156–57.

42. Davidoff and Hall, *Family Fortunes*, 18–20, 30.

43. Nye, *Masculinity and Male Codes of Honor*, 32–34.

44. Hetherington, "Canada's First Social Club," 298.

45. Beaver Club Minute Book, 2; *Rules and Regulations*, 5.

46. Tulchinsky, "Forsyth," 311; Fernand Ouellet, "Frobisher, Joseph," in *DCB*, 5:331–34, esp. 333 and "McTavish, Simon," in *DCB*, 5:560–67, esp. 566; Campbell, *McGillivray*, 111.

47. Brown, *Strangers in Blood*, 81–110; Van Kirk, *"Many Tender Ties": Women in Fur Trade Society in Western Canada, 1670–1870* (Winnipeg, Manitoba: Watson and Dwyer Publishing, Ltd., 1980), 28–52

48. Campbell, *McGillivray*, 68; Brown, *Strangers in Blood*, 90; Van Kirk, *Many Tender Ties*, 50.

49. Beaver Club Minute Book, 3.

50. For example, F. A. Larocque and J. M. Lamothe were elected in 1815 and Dominique Ducharme attended the last meeting in 1827. Beaver Club Minute Book, 94, 112, 121.

51. Hall, *White, Male and Middle Class*, 157.

52. Beaver Club Minute Book, 1–2; *Rules and Regulations*, 5–6.

53. Bullock found the same with the Freemasons. Although the organization kept its work and rituals secret, they participated visibly in public life and believed they were working toward a public, rather than a private, good, and they demanded public honor. Bullock, "The Ancient and Honorable Society," 4–5.

54. Beaver Club Minute Book, 1, 90, 113; *Rules and Regulations*, 5.

55. *Rules and Regulations*, 3–6. Hetherington discusses three surviving medals at the Chateau de Ramezay in Montreal and at the Library of the Parliament Buildings in Ottawa, as well as some privately owned plates and snuff boxes. Hetherington, "Canada's First Social Club," 298. Watson mentions that cups and silver plates bearing the mark of the Beaver Club were put up at auctions throughout the country. Watson, "The First Beaver Club," 337. Also, a picture of a gold brooch of a beaver, said to be worn by wives of Beaver Club members, appears in "The HBC Packet," *The Beaver*, Outfit 264, no. 3 (December 1933): 5–6.

56. For an example of a member charged for a dinner he did not attend, see Beaver Club Minute Book, 21 January 1809, 32. For an example of a member excused from dinner fees because of illness, see Beaver Club Minute Book, 53, 82.

57. See the accounts listed at the end of every dinner in the Minute Book.

58. For example, see the first meeting of the years 1815–16 and 1816–17, Beaver Club Minute Book, 97–98, 113.

59. *Rules and Regulations*, 4.

60. Ibid., 3.

61. Montreal, McCord Museum of Canadian History Archives, M18638, Memorandum recording the meeting of Simon Fraser and John McDonald of Garth, the last two surviving partners of the North West Company, 1 August 1859, Original. Published in W. Kaye Lamb, ed., *The Letters and Journals of Simon Fraser, 1806–1808* (Toronto: MacMillan Company of Canada, 1960), 271.

62. Brown, *Strangers in Blood*, 2–3.

63. Wilson, *The Enterprises of Robert Hamilton*, 12, 20–21.

64. Landmann, *Adventures and Recollections*, 233–34.

65. Nye, *Masculinity and Male Codes of Honor*, 10–11.

66. Beaver Club Minute Book, 1–2; *Rules and Regulations*, 5.

67. Benoît, "Wintering Dishes," 25–27; Watson, "The First Beaver Club," 337.

68. Reed, *Masters of the Wilderness*, 68.

69. *Rules and Regulations*, 3; Reed, Masters of the Wilderness, 68.

70. Reed, *Masters of the Wilderness*, 68.

71. Beaver Club Minute Book, 1; *Rules and Regulations*, 6.

72. Landmann, *Adventures and Recollections*, 234, 238.

73. Rice, *Early American Taverns*, 98. Bullock found that for Masons convivial drink-

ing and conversation were very important for specific expressions of brotherly love and fraternity (Bullock, "The Ancient and Honorable Society," 62).

74. Lambert, *Travels Through Canada*, 295.

75. Reed, *Masters of the Wilderness*, 65.

76. Landmann, *Adventures and Recollections*, 296; Rice, *Early American Taverns*, 98.

77. Lambert, *Travels Through Canada*, 295–96; 524. Clark found that in eighteenth-century English clubs conspicuous consumption and excess were an essential ingredient of club sociability, Clark, "Sociability and Urbanity," 20.

78. Alexander Henry, Montreal, to John Askin, Strathbane, 9 May 1815, *The John Askin Papers, Vol. 2, 1796–1820*, ed. Milo M. Quaife (Detroit: Detroit Library Commission, 1928–31), 781–83.

79. Clark, "Sociability and Urbanity," 21.

80. Rice, *Early American Taverns*, 101.

81. *Rules and Regulations*, 3.

82. Basil Johnston, *Ojibwa Ceremonies* (Toronto: McClelland and Stewart, 1982), 33, 160.

83. John Palmer, *Journal of Travels in the United States of America and in Lower Canada, Performed in the Year 1817; Containing Particulars Relating to the Prices of Land and Provisions, Remarks on the Country and the People, Interesting Anecdotes, and an Account of the Commerce, Trade, and Present State of Washington, New York, Philadelphia, Boston, Baltimore, Albany, Cincinnati, Pittsburg, Lexington, Quebec, Montreal, &c.* (London: Sherwood, Neely, and Jones, 1818), 216–17.

84. Other bourgeois fraternities also imitated Native culture, the most obvious being the Improved Order of the Red Men, established in the United States in 1834. Carnes describes in detail the order's rituals and language, inspired by Native culture, such as sachems invoking the "Great Spirit of the Universe" and pale-face warriors fearlessly facing death. Unfortunately Carnes's only explanation for why Native culture was chosen as a model for the fraternity is that the men who were transforming America into an urban, industrial society desired to recreate a primitive past. Mark C. Carnes, "Middle-Class Men and the Solace of Fraternal Ritual," in *Meanings for Manhood: Constructions of Masculinity in Victorian America, ed. Mark C. Carnes and Clyde Griffen* (Chicago: University of Chicago Press, 1990), 37–52, esp. 39–45.

85. *Rules and Regulations*, 3.

86. Reed, *Masters of the Wilderness*, 69.

87. Beaver Club Minute Book, 83.

88. Frederick Goedike, Aguiwang, to George Gordon, Michipicoten, 29 October 1811, George Gordon Papers.

89. *Rules and Regulations*, 1.

90. Beaver Club Minute Book, 28 September 1807, 6–7.

Susan Sleeper-Smith[1] Furs and Female Kin Networks:
The World of Marie Madeleine
Réaume L'archevêque Chevalier

WOMEN RARELY appear in fur trade literature. The best known are the Native and Métis wives of British fur traders whose lives are the focus of Sylvia Van Kirk's *Many Tender Ties* and Jennifer Brown's *Strangers in Blood*.[2] Few historians, however, have pursued the issues of gender raised by these two books almost twenty years ago.

American historians have not produced a seminal work comparable to that of either Van Kirk or Brown.[3] Instead, the fur trade resonates with more popular notions about a masculine frontier. Here men escaped social constraints, braved the rigors of an untamed landscape, tested the limits of physical endurance, and when sufficiently resourceful, achieved success. These traders married Native women, some in the "custom of the country,"[4] but others in more formal arrangements that endured until the death of a spouse. Their wives appear, however, as inconsequential, the silent partners of rugged adventurers.

French fur traders were eager to marry Native women, particularly socially prominent women with extensive kin networks. Fictive and affine kin networks ensured Euro-American men access to furs. The exchange of trade goods for peltry occurred on a face-to-face basis along a kinship continuum. Seventeenth- and eighteenth-century French fur traders were assimilated into a world structured by Native American custom and tradition. Traders who married indigenous women were routinely transformed into fathers and brothers, since women, from an indigenous perspective, did not marry out.[5]

The intermarriage of traders and Native women resulted in increasingly complex kin networks.[6] Although these networks remain largely unidentifiable, there is one group whose identity is known and that can be studied. These are the French fur traders and their Native wives whose kin network was structured by the umbrella of frontier Catholicism.[7] The few remaining baptismal registers reveal a great deal about the nature of fur trade society.

They depict a complex social system where one was less an individual and more a member of a larger kinship group. Lives were intricately woven into densely constructed webs of kinship.[8]

Native women appear repeatedly in baptismal registers, their identity often disguised by Christian names. Identifying the names of female converts unscrambles the otherwise meaningless jumble of names that crowd the pages of these documents. For instance, at Michilimackinac, the Langlade, Bourassa, and Chaboyer women were frequent godmothers to each other's children and grandchildren. Their names span the eighteenth century and their godmothering roles were subsequently assumed by their daughters and granddaughters. They played an integral role incorporating diverse people into Catholic fur trade society. These women were the godmothers to converts who lived near Michilimackinac, to Native and African American slaves and their children, to the offspring of transient traders, and to the children of unconverted Native American women, such as "a female Savage called Catherine, of the Sauteux nation, daughter of the pagan savage called mouus. . . who brought her son to be baptized."[9]

The deliberate construction of female kin networks illustrates the centrality of Native women in fur trade society. Men denied inclusion in these networks were often part of an anonymous herd, transient traders who appeared one season only to disappear the next. Traders who married well remained resident in specific areas.

How women constructed familial and fictive kin networks is best understood by examining the lives of Native women who converted to Catholicism, married French traders, and who then repeatedly reappeared in the baptismal registers as mothers and godmothers. Marie Madeleine Réaume, an eighteenth-century Iliniwik woman, exemplified that process[10]. Although she could sign her name, she left no personal record. What we know about her life is drawn from other sources: baptismal and marriage registers, reimbursement records kept by fort commandants, letters and petitions written by her husband, and references made about her and her children in the letters of French and British officials.

Madeleine spent most of her life at Fort St. Joseph, an inconsequential military installation but important fur trade community on Lake Michigan's southeastern shore. Her marriages to two traders and those of her five daughters to fur traders were indicative of this eighteenth-century society. Madeleine's life spanned seventy years of the century and its longevity facilitated her deliberate construction of a kin network that eventually stretched north to Michilimackinac, northwest to Green Bay, northeast to Montreal, and south to Cahokia and to St. Louis.

Fort St. Joseph was established by Robert LaSalle in 1679.[11] A decade later the first permanent mission was established by Father Allouez, a seasoned veteran of the Green Bay area assigned to the Illinois country.[12] Several Potawatomi clans migrated south from Green Bay. By 1692, the French estimated that over two hundred warriors could be recruited from among the southwest Michigan Potawatomi. This equated with twelve hundred Potawatomi living near or at the post. Several hundred Miami also lived in an adjacent village.[13]

Figure 1. **French Posts and Settlements in the Seventeenth and Eighteenth Centuries.**

St. Joseph was part of a riverine network of forts designed to establish French control of western trade routes and to thwart British encroachment. Located on the St. Joseph River, this fort was a short canoe trip from Lake Michigan to Illinois Country. In the spring, when the winter snow melted, and in the fall, when the seasonal rains arrived, the St. Joseph River valley flooded. The once-dry land became a lake, and Native people paddled up the St. Joseph to the Kankakee, along the Illinois River, and then, to the Mississippi.

Like other western outposts, Fort St. Joseph was closed shortly after the 1696 royal ban on the western fur trade.[14] Many illegal traders remained in the upper country despite the injunction against trade and the threat of confinement to French galleys if apprehended. The removal of French troops left illicit traders increasingly dependent on their indigenous kin. Intermarriage guaranteed survival.[15] During this tumultuous time, Madeleine was born in Illinois Country. Her father, Jean Baptiste Réaume, an illicit trader, became the Fort St. Joseph interpreter when it was reestablished in 1717.[16] Later, he moved to Green Bay, where Madeleine's sister was raised.

At the age of twenty-four, Madeleine married Augustin L'archevêque,[17] an Illinois Country fur trader. The next day she gave birth to a daughter. With this first child, Madeleine established a baptismal behavioral pattern that followed each subsequent birth. She chose Iliniwik women or her own daughters, rather than French women, to serve as godmothers. Each godfather, however, was French: the fort commandant, his sons, an interpreter. Over the next fifteen years, gave birth to at least four daughters. Only with the birth of the last child, a son, did Madeleine deviate from this pattern when she chose a godfather with a Native mother. All four daughters took the first name of their mother, Marie, also a common baptismal name. Each was distinguished by her second name. The daughters lived to maturity, but the son probably did not reach adulthood.[18]

We know little else about the first four decades of Madeleine L'archevêque's life, other than the names of her children and their godparents. She first appears in the official fort records after her husband's death, when she provisioned France's indigenous allies gathered at St. Joseph to help fight the Chickasaw.[19] The Widow L'archevêque was paid for "one fat pig, a heifer, an ox, four pairs of snowshoes, a bark canoe, and another fat pig." Other invoices indicate that the widow, in addition, supplied sacks of wheat, oats, and corn.[20]

Madeleine's household also supplied grains and vegetables to French traders who wintered in the southern Great Lakes. Fur trade permits allowed each trader to take two canoes into the upper country, and limited cargo space was devoted almost entirely to trade goods. Fur traders depended on an indigenous food supply. Native women controlled productive resources, and Madeleine, her daughters and slaves, produced an agricultural surplus that was central to the success of the St. Joseph fur trade.

Madeleine's fur trade interests became more apparent when she established kinship ties to the Michilimackinac fur trade. In the summer of 1748, this thirty-nine-year-old widow took three of her children on the long journey north. Here, her young son was baptized and two of her daughters were married. Members of two prominent Michilimackinac fur trade families, the Langlades and the Bourassas, signed as godparents at the baptism [21] and witnesses at the weddings.[22] Seventeen-year-old Marie Catherine L'archevêque became the wife of a Trois Revières trader.[23] Fifteen-year-old Marie Joseph Esther L'archevêque's bridegroom appears to have been related to the Montreal merchant with whom Madeleine's father had traded.[24] Joseph Esther was the only daughter baptized at Michilimackinac, and her young marital age suggests her mother arranged this match. Eventually Joseph Esther was widowed and then remarried. Of all her siblings, Esther repeatedly reappeared in later written documents.[25] The newlyweds returned to Madeleine's St. Joseph household. These marriages ensured a larger share of the St. Joseph trade, however, Madeleine's family remained one of many in this trading community.

Madeleine used another more transparent marital strategy to garner a larger share of the St. Joseph fur trade. At the age of forty-one Madeleine gave birth to a son whose father was Louis Therèse Chevalier, a well-known Michilimackinac trader[26] Madeleine and Louis were later married at the St. Joseph mission, six months after young Louis' birth. She was forty-two; her husband thirty-nine.[27]

Marriage to Louis Chevalier established familial kinship ties to the Michilimackinac fur trade and guaranteed Madeleine's kin a stable supply of trade goods. Louis and his sixteen siblings were raised at Michilimackinac; each married among other fur trade families.

Madeleine, despite her age, was an attractive marital prospect. Louis apparently severed the less constrictive ties of his country marriage to an Odawa woman.[28] Marriage to Madeleine offered access to a new and valuable source of furs. Prior to Louis' marriage the Chevalier family were infrequent participants in the St. Joseph trade. Although Louis' father purchased a trade permit in 1718 he subsequently returned to Michilimackinac. He reappeared once in 1730, probably hired as a guide by two Montreal merchants.[29]

Louis' older sister Charlotte had lived at Ft. St. Joseph for over twenty years and was married to the blacksmith, Antoine Deshêtres. The reimbursement records from the post commandant to Deshêtres were for his work as a blacksmith. There is no direct evidence of his involvement in the St. Joseph trade.[30]

The marriage of each of Madeleine's daughters solidified kinship ties to the Chevalier family and to the even larger fur trade community in Montreal. Louis's younger brother Louis Pascal Chevalier married a L'archevêque daughter.[31] Another sister married her stepfather's Montreal trading partner, Charles Lhullic dit Chevalier. The groom was a forty-five-year-old widower. The bride, Angelique L'archevêque, was twenty-one.[32] Madeleine's youngest daughter, seventeen-year-old Anne, also married a fur trader. Like her sisters, she too remained part of the St. Joseph community.[33]

The kinship ties that linked people also joined communities. Probably contemporaneous with Madeleine's marriage to Louis, her two eldest daughters, their husbands, and their children moved to Fort Pimiteoui, now Peoria, and eventually to Cahokia.[34] Their movement strengthened the family's involvement in the Illinois trade. Madeleine's fourth daughter, Marie Amable, and her husband also eventually left Fort St. Joseph and joined their L'archevêque kin at Cahokia.

Kin linkages established by marriage were then reinforced by the godparenting roles that siblings played to each others' children. Madeleine's daughters were frequent godparents to their nieces and nephews.[35] Godparents lived in the community, but they also came from nearby, as well as from distant posts. Louis Chevalier's siblings became godparents to L'archevêque grandchildren, and Madeleine's daughters were godmothers of Chevalier grandchildren.

By the 1750s, the St. Joseph community changed dramatically. The French population decreased when many fur trade families moved to Detroit. There was, however, a dramatic increase in the number of furs gathered at Fort St. Joseph. During this decade more engagements or contracts for hiring canoemen were issued than in any previous period.[36]

Previous to Pontiac's Rebellion, the St. Joseph River Valley became a predominantly indigenous universe. Simultaneously, the number of Catholic converts increased dramatically even though the mission no longer had a resident priest.[37]

Catholicism had evolved as a socially integrative tool, a frontier Catholicism with Madeleine as its most important lay participant.[38] The St. Joseph mission incorporated indigenous people as well as *Panis*, or Native slaves. Madeleine was the godmother to Marie Jeanne, a thirteen-year old slave as well as to Therese, a forty-year-old Potawatomi woman.[39] One Miami couple, Pierre Mekabika8nga [40] and his wife, had their "indian style marriage" sacramentally sanctioned by the priest.[41] The baptisms of their four adult daughters revealed their link to the L'archevêque-Chevalier family. One daughter selected Louis Chevalier as her godfather; two other daughters chose Madeleine as their godmother.[42]

Before the outbreak of the American Revolution, the rhythm of daily life had changed dramatically in the St. Joseph River Valley. Agriculture evolved as increasingly important. Madeleine and her Native kin shared abundant harvests, and both produced sufficient surplus to feed the residential and transient populations. This market for agricultural produce as well as for furs lent stability to the region. Late eighteenth-century traders became brokers of foodstuffs as well as of furs. They shipped boatloads of corn, barrels and *mokocks* or baskets of sugar, as well as furs to Michilimackinac and Detroit.[43]

The St. Joseph Potawatomi drew distinctions about the quality of the grains they raised. They classified the less fully matured as more fit for animal than human consumption. In 1778, Louis Chevalier arranged a meeting between the Potawatomi and the British Lieutenant Governor of Detroit, Henry Hamilton. Hamilton failed to bring the presents and liquor necessary to seal the bonds of friendship, and one of the river valley's more prominent Native Americans, Gros Loup, honored him with an appropriate gift. In his journal Hamilton recorded that Gros Loup gave him "3 large baskets of young corn, dried pumpkin and kidney beans, saying that such coarse fare might serve my cattle if I could not eat it myself."[44]

Most historians have assumed that crops like wheat, because they required extensive milling, were not grown by Native Americans, but in the fertile midwestern river valleys wheat was harvested in the eighteenth century.[45] Mills were constructed by both Native Americans and Jesuits. In Father Marest's Illinois village, not only did the Jesuits have their own mill, but the Iliniwik owned two mills.[46]

> In addition to raising a large supply of Maize, the Indians thereabouts produce also considerable Wheat. There are three grist-mills; one of these is a wind, another a horse mill; the third, a guern. They have oxen, cows, horses, fowls. . . .[47]

In the St. Joseph River valley, farms, with their framed houses, cultivated fields, and fruit orchards, marked the St. Joseph landscape.[48] Madeleine's property in the St. Joseph River Valley included "ten houses, good lands, orchards, gardens, cattle, [and] furniture. . . ."[49] A master carpenter had lived in the community and had built a house for a medal chief. There was also a stone jail built by the community's blacksmith.[50]

Although farms and framed houses distinguished St. Joseph as having agricultural dimensions, this farmscape was different from New England and New France. Here the French were a distinct minority within a larger indigenous society. Gendered divisions of labor reflected those of Native American society, not those of Euro-America. In Native society agriculture was women's work. Madeleine's daughters and their children remained part of their mother's matrifocal household, an ever-expanding labor force over which Madeleine exercised control. The daughters did not establish separate households until they left the St. Joseph community.[51]

Fort St. Joseph was never heavily garrisoned. New France officials relied on fur traders to maintain Native American loyalty. The last effective commandant, Francois Marie Picote, Sieur de Bellestre, was appointed to the St. Joseph post in 1747. He was rarely present, as his role as a peace negotiator required frequent and extended appearances in Detroit and Montreal. In 1757, the stepson of the governor general of New France, Marquis de Vaudreuill, was the last commandant, but Louis de Varier stayed less than two years and left by 1759.[52]

After France's defeat in the French and Indian War, British soldiers replaced an almost nonexistent French garrison at Fort St. Joseph. Their presence was short-lived. When Pontiac's supporters attacked the fort in 1763 there were only fourteen soldiers. Ten died in the attack, and the other four were exchanged for Indian prisoners at Detroit.[53]

The fort was never again staffed with a military garrison. Ten years of peace ensued. The British became increasingly dependent on Louis Chevalier to secure Native American allegiance. Louis claimed loyalty to a new foreign master but simultaneously frustrated British efforts to control the fur trade. In 1773, four English traders were murdered near St. Joseph. The British suspected Chevalier, but they were in no position to remove him.[54]

The British decision to rely on Chevalier became increasingly problematic with the outbreak of the American Revolution. St. Joseph was in a strategic location. It was a convenient staging area from which the British could attack St. Louis. In addition, because the post was ungarrisoned, it could easily be captured by either the Spaniards or the American rebels. From here an attack could be launched on British posts, particularly Detroit or Michilimackinac.[55]

Britain did not have sufficient military forces to secure the post. Unable to triumph through force, Britain sought Native allies. Allegiance was kin-based. Madeleine and Louis Chevalier were kin allies while the British remained outsiders.

The lieutenant governor of Michilimackinac, Patrick Sinclair, openly disliked Chevalier and was determined to thwart Chevalier's influence.[56] Governor Haldimand ordered the removal of traders, whose loyalty was questionable, from living among the Indians. Sinclair used this pretense to forcibly remove fifteen families from St. Joseph.[57] Ironically, Louis Ainssé, Louis Chevalier's nephew, was placed in charge of the expedition. He arrived from Michilimackinac with seven canoes. While people packed what they could into the canoes, Ainssé completed a census of the evicted inhabitants. At the time of removal Madeleine was seventy-one and Louis was sixty-nine.

English traders soon arrived at St. Joseph, but they never secured control over the community. Madeleine's kin network thwarted British intentions. Her daughters and their fur trade husbands, who lived in Illinois Country, had no intention of allowing rivals to achieve ascendancy. Shortly after the French removal, the British traders were attacked by an invading force from Cahokia. Members of Madeleine's Illinois kin network, Tom Brady and Jean Baptiste Hamelin, led the raid.[58] Brady had recently married Madeleine's widowed daughter, Marie Joseph, and Hamelin kin were frequent godparents for St. Joseph children.[59]

The invaders arrived in early December of 1780. They overpowered the British traders, loaded their trade goods on packhorses, burnt what they could not carry, and set fire to British storehouses and buildings. They headed toward Chicago. Lieutenant Dequindre, now the British Indian agent for St. Joseph, arrived shortly after their departure. He set out in pursuit. Somewhere in the vicinity of present-day Michigan City, Indiana, he overtook them and killed four, wounded two, and captured seven Cahokians.[60]

Two months later, the L'archevêque-Chevalier kin were part of a second attack, larger in scope and launched from Illinois Country under the Spanish flag. Madeleine's son, thirty-year-old Louis Chevalier, was the guide and interpreter. The invasion force was large. The Potawatomi reckoned the number to be "one hundred white people and eighty Indians led by Sequinack and Nakewine."[61] Historians' estimates are lower, perhaps sixty-five men, some from St. Louis and others from Cahokia, and a large Indian contingent. On 12 February 1781, St. Joseph was plundered anew. The young Louis Chevalier negotiated with the Potawatomi to allow the invaders to surprise the British traders. Following the successful attack Chevalier divided the British trade goods among his Native friends and relatives.[62] A large supply of corn, set aside by the British for their planned assault on St. Louis, was burned. The attack was devastatingly effective, and the invaders were gone when Lieutenant de Quindre arrived the next day. DeQuindre failed to convince the Potawatomi to join him in pursuit of the raiders. Without their support, retaliation was futile.[63]

The 1781 attack, viewed as an insignificant skirmish of the Revolutionary War, allowed the L'archevêque-Chevalier kin network to prevent the British from controlling the St. Joseph fur trade. At the conclusion of the war the same kin network, albeit with new faces, returned to the river valley. Like their predecessors, those who intermarried with their Native American trading partners were the most successful. Kinship remained the central determinant of success in the St. Joseph fur trade.[64]

Boundaries between Native American and French society were at best ill-defined. Communities like St. Joseph were neither extensions of French nor of Native societies. Nor were the residents of eighteenth-century St. Joseph a distinct Métis people.[65] Identity was embedded in kin networks. People defined themselves by their relatives, while outsiders identified them as either French or Indian. Although the British identified Louis Chevalier as French, they referred to his son, Louison, by Madeleine as Indian. Louison's allegiance resided with the Potawatomi, and along with them he probably received gifts from the Spanish at St. Louis.[66] Another of Chevalier's sons, Amable, by his first Odawa wife, was identified by the British at Michilimackinac as a chief of his people. He served as a lieutenant in the British Indian Department. Amable's brother, probably lived at St. Joseph, and during the French removal was identified as absent and "at war." His wife and child resided at St. Joseph, to be cared for by Madeleine's kin network.[67]

Madeleine, like her husband Louis, resided in a world where one's identity had neither ethnic nor national connotations. Kin networks transcend and confuse the questions posed by historical analysis. While we may ask where loyalties resided, with the French, British, or Native American, the malleable boundaries of fur trade society identified loyalty by kin networks. In the indigenous universe of the eighteenth-century Great Lakes, kin networks were complex, rarely recorded, and highly malleable. These networks, with their diversity and multiplicity of names, contributed to anonymity while simultaneously, as in Madeleine's case, contributing to her importance.

Madeleine lived in St. Joseph for seventy years. Like the community, Madeleine's life underwent many changes, but those changes were always defined by the kin networks that also defined the fur trade. She was the daughter of a fur trader, married to two fur traders, and her five daughters married fur traders. Two of her daughters lived in the community for thirty-five years, until the British forcibly removed them. Twelve of her godchildren were baptized at St. Joseph. Because of marriage and baptism, Madeleine's kin network stretched throughout the western Great Lakes. Marriage was a planned extension of that network. Ties were further complicated and expanded through the fictive kin of godparents. The network was permeable, malleable, and complex, but it was also highly discriminatory. Many fur traders passed through the St. Joseph River Valley; those incorporated into female kin networks often remained permanent inhabitants.

Native women of the Illinois Country socially reproduced the matrifocal households of their indigenous culture, which found fertile soil in the St. Joseph River Valley. Fur trade husbands joined their wife's household. Their presence brought women, who already controlled the household's productive resources, ample supplies of trade goods. Among indigenous kin, trade goods reinforced ritual gift giving and secured new sources of power for women like Madeleine. Boldly apparent in the eighteenth-century landscape was the increasing power of these matrifocal households. Those who ignored Madeleine's kin networks were denied a share of the St. Joseph fur trade.

Neither the threat of war nor a military presence ensured control of the St. Joseph community. Warfare did not always disrupt communities. Instead, warfare at St. Joseph was the means by which related kin networks kept control of the fur trade. The British understood the ties that so clearly bound the French to the Native Americans of the Great Lakes. Major Arent Schuyler DePeyster, the Michilimackinac commandant, remarked, "The Canadians I fear are of great disservice to Government but the Indians are perfect Free Masons when intrusted with a secret by a Canadian most of them being much connected by marriage."[68] Unfortunately, DePeyster understood only part of the story. The ritual of baptism had escaped his notice.

Ever-expanding female kin networks facilitated the evolution of colonial fur trade society in the western Great Lakes. These women incorporated, under the umbrella of Catholicism, the kinship behaviors of indigenous society. In doing so they appropriated honor, prestige, and authority and exercised a more invisible mode of domination. Madeleine's life demonstrates that the fur trade was far from a masculine universe.

Notes

1. I would like to thank Keith Widder and Anne Meyering for commenting on early versions of this paper. JoAnne Fiske, coeditor of this volume, offered invaluable criticism during the revision process.

2. Sylvia Van Kirk, *Many Tender Ties: Women in Fur Trade Society*, 1670–1870 (Winnipeg: Watson and Dwyer, 1980; Norman: University of Oklahoma Press, 1980); Jennifer S. H. Brown, *Strangers in Blood: Fur Trade Families in Indian Country* (Vancouver: University of British Columbia Press, 1980; Norman: University of Oklahoma Press, 1996).

3. The most recent work to focus on the Great Lakes during the colonial period is Richard White's *The Middle Ground: Indians, Empires, and Republics in the Great Lakes Region, 1650–1815* (New York: Cambridge University Press, 1991).

4. "Marriage 'after the custom of the country' was an indigenous marriage rite which evolved to meet the needs of fur trade society. . . . Although denounced by the Jesuit priests as being immoral, the traders had taken their Indian wives according to traditional native marriage rites and distinct family units had developed." Van Kirk, *Many Tender Ties*, 28. See also Brown, *Strangers in Blood*, 81–110.

5. Sylvia Van Kirk, "Toward a Feminist Perspective in Native History," in *Papers of the Eighteenth Algonquian Conference*, ed. William Cowan (Ottawa: Carleton University Press, 1987), 386.

6. Intermarriage between traders and Native American women is discussed in Brown, *Strangers in Blood*; Kirk, *Many Tender Ties*; Jacqueline Peterson and Jennifer S. H. Brown, eds., *The New Peoples: Being and Becoming Métis in North America* (Manitoba: University of Manitoba Press, 1985), especially Jacqueline Peterson's "Many Roads to Red River: Métis Genesis in the Great Lakes Region, 1680–1815," 37–73; Lewis H. Thomas, ed., *Essays on Western History* (Edmonton: University of Alberta Press, 1976), especially Sylvia Van Kirk's "The Custom of the Country: An Examination of Fur Trade Marriage Practices," 49–68, and John E. Foster's "The Origin of the Mixed Bloods in the Canadian West," 71–80; John Mack Faragher, "Americans, Mexicans, Métis: A Community Approach to Its Imperial Past," in *Under An Open Sky: Rethinking America's Western Past*, ed. William Cronon, George Miles, and Jay Gitlin (New York: W.W. Norton, 1992), 90–110; James A. Clifton, ed., *Being and Becoming Indian: Biographical Studies of North American Frontiers* (Prospect Heights, Ill.: Waveland Press, 1989), especially Gary Clayton Anderson's "Joseph Renville and the Ethos of Biculturalism," 59–81; Jacqueline Peterson, "'Wild' Chicago: The Formation of a Multi-Racial Community on the Midwestern Frontier, 1816–1837," in *The Ethnic Frontier*, ed. Melvin G. Holli and Peter d'A. Jones (Grand Rapids, Mich.: Eerdmans, 1977), 25–73; Robert E. Bieder, "Scientific Attitudes Toward Indian Mixed-Bloods in Early Nineteenth-Century America," *Journal of Ethnic Studies* 8 (summer 1980): 17–30.

7. The term *frontier Catholicism* suggests that lay Catholics were instrumental in the spread of eighteenth-century Catholicism. This was a result of the scarcity of priests. The role lay people played in the transmission of dogma is unclear.

8. Two baptismal registers and one wedding register are part of this research and include "The St. Joseph Baptismal Register," ed. Rev. George Paré and M. M. Quaife, *The Mississippi Valley Historical Review* (hereafter *MVHR*) 12 (June 1925 to March 1927): 201–39; "The Mackinac Register, 1696–1821: Register of Baptisms

of the Mission of St. Ignace de Michilimakinak," *Collections of the State Historical Society of Wisconsin* (hereafter referred to as *WHC*) (Madison, 1910), 19:1–162; "The Mackinac Register, 1725–1821: Register of Marriages in the Parish of Michilimakinac," *WHC*, 18:469–513. The original St. Joseph Register is in the archives of the Quebec Seminary.

9. "Mackinac Register," in *WHC*, 19:23.

10 Clarence Alvord states that "The Handbooks of American Indians gives the following derivation of the name: "'Illiniwek, from ilini 'man,' iw 'is' ek plural termination, changed by the French to ois.'" Clarence Alvord, *The Illinois Country, 1673–1818* (Urbana: University of Illinois Press, 1987), 31.

11. For a detailed description of Fort St. Joseph as a military post under the French see Dunning Idle, "The Post of the St. Joseph River During the French Regime, 1679–1761," (Ph.D. diss., University of Illinois, 1946). Information on the fort can also be found in Ralph Ballard, *Old Fort Saint Joseph* (Berrien Springs, Mich.: Hardscrapple Books, 1973); Gérard Malchelosse, "Genealogy and Colonial History: The St. Joseph River Post Michigan," *French Canadian and Acadian Genealogical Review* 7, nos. 3–4 (1979): 173–209; Mildred Webster and Fred Krause, *French Fort Saint Joseph: De La Poste de la Riviere St. Joseph, 1690–1780* (privately printed, 1990). Some of the genealogical information in these articles is problematic. Other secondary articles on Fort St. Joseph contain information that is even less historically accurate.

12. The Jesuits actually established a mission in 1686 but this land grant was not confirmed by the French court until almost three years later. Concessions, Versailles, 24 May 1689, *Archives Nationales, Colonies* (hereafter *ANCol*), ser. B, 15:218, 223. Margry, Pierre Découvertes et Éstablissements des Francais dans le Sud de l'Amerique Septentrionale, 1614–1698: Memiors et Documents Originaux 5, (Paris: Maisonneure, 1879–88).

13. Cadillac's estimate was done when he was commandant at Michilimackinac. James A. Clifton, *The Prairie People: Continuity and Change in Potawatomi Culture, 1665–1995* (Lawrence, Kansas: Regent's Press, 1977), 83; W. Vernon Kinietz, *The Indians of the Western Great Lakes, 1615–1760* (Ann Arbor: University of Michigan Press, 1965), 309–10.

14. Louis XIV in 1696 abolished the granting of fur trade licenses while permitting Forts St. Joseph, Michilimakinac, St. Louis des Illinois, and Fort Frontenac to remain open. The price of beaver was reduced and the traders were told to return to the colony. Contrary to the royal edict, at least two hundred coureurs de bois remained in the west. W. J. Eccles, *The Canadian Frontier, 1534–1760* (Albuquerque: University of New Mexico Press, 1974), 129–31.

15. "In spite of the prohibition against trading in the Indian country there have always been Frenchmen who have gone there, and who not daring to come back into the Colony remained among the nations: they are called coureurs de bois." Joseph L. Peyser, *Letters from New France: The Upper Country, 1686–1783* (Urbana: University of Illinois Press, 1992), 88.

16. The first official reference to Jean Baptiste Réaume was in 1720 when New France governor, Vaudreuil, sent him to the reestablished Fort St. Joseph post with two canoes loaded with gifts for the Miami. Marie Madeleine Réaume first appeared in the St. Joseph Register when she was listed as a godmother in March of 1729 and was identified as the daughter of Simphorose Ouaouagoukoue and the post's interpreter, Sieur Jean Baptiste Réaume. "St.Joseph Register," in *MVHR*, 12:212. Réaume was also spelled Rheaume.

17. Variant spellings for L'archevêque include Larchesveque and Larche. Certificate, Montreal, signed de Villiers, 18 July 1745; *ANCol*, C11A, 117:325. In 1741 Augustin L'archevêque contracted to hire canoemen to accompany him to Illinois Country. For engagements or contracts hiring canoemen at St. Joseph from 1722–45, see *Rapport de l'Archiviste de la Province de Québec* (hereafter *RAPQ*), 1929–30:233–465.

18. The first daughter, Marie Catherine, was born the day after her mother and father were married. She was baptized on January 13, 1731. Her godparents were the post commandant, Nicholas Coulon de Villiers, and Marie Catherine, of the Illinois Nation. "St. Joseph Register," in *MVHR*, 12:213. The second daughter, Marie Esther (referred to as Marie Joseph Esther), was born sometime in 1733 and baptized one year later at Michilimackinac on 1 January 1734, "Mackinac Baptisms," in *WHC*, 19:4. The third daughter, Marie Anne, was twenty-one months and eight days old at the time of her baptism at St. Joseph in April of 1740. Her godparents were Nicholas Coulon de Villiers, the post commandant, and her older sister, Marie Joseph Esther. "St. Joseph Register," in *MVHR*, 12:218. The fourth daughter, Marie Amable, was baptized at St. Joseph on 27 July 1740, by the post commandant, Nicholas Coulon de Villiers, and subsequently by Father Lamorine on 29 June 1741. The godparents were Claude Caron and Charlotte Robert, the wife of the post interpreter. "St. Joseph Register," in *MVHR*, 12:219. The fifth daughter was Angelique (Agathe), baptized in March of 1744. Her godfather was Monsieur de Lespiné de Villiers, cadet in the Troops of Marine detachment in the colony. Her godmother was her oldest sister, Marie Catherine. "St. Joseph Register," in *MVHR*, 12:221.

19. In Ste. Genevieve, Illinois Country, French widows were more active in the local economy and were more likely to file legal grievances than either single or married women. Susan C. Boyle, "Did She Generally Decide? Women in Ste. Genevieve, 1750–1805," *The William and Mary Quarterly* 44 (October 1987): 788–89.

20. Joseph Peyser, *Fort St. Joseph Manuscripts: Chronological Inventory of French-Language Manuscripts and Their Translations and Abstracts* (Niles, Mich.: Privately printed with funding provided by City of Niles; compiled by Joseph Peyser for the Four Flags Historical Study Committee, 1978), 121, 104.

21. Two-year-old Augustin's godparents were also selected from these families and would have facilitated the child's entry in the fur trade community had he lived to adulthood. The godfather was Augustin Maras Langlade, esquire, and the godmother was Mlle. Bourassa, the elder, (Marie Catherine de La Plante), "Mackinac Register," in *WHC*, 19:24-25.

22. Several signatures are illegible, but those that are legible include members of both the Langlade and Bourassa families, "Mackinac Register," in *WHC*, 18:476.

23. The groom was Jean Baptiste Jutras (Joutras); the wedding took place at St. Ignace on 7 July 1748. Witnesses included Legardeur De St. Pierre Verchere, Bourassa, Langlade, and Charles Langlade, "Mackinac Register," in *WHC*, 18:475.

24. The wedding of Marie Joseph Esther and Jacques Bariso de La Marche took place at St. Ignace on 2 August 1748, "Mackinac Register," in *WHC*, 18:476. In 1729 Jean Baptiste Réaume owed Charles Nolan LaMarque 4,000 livres (in furs). Idle, "Post of the St. Joseph," 185; *RAPQ*, 1929–30:244–408, passim.

25. Joseph Esther was twice widowed, and at the age of forty-six on 8 June 1779, she married Thomas M. Brady. He became the Indian agent at Cahokia. She had children and grandchildren living in Cahokia until well into the 1800s. Joseph Esther had four children baptized at St. Joseph. When a second son was born in 1752 she was living at Fort Pimiteoui (Peoria). In 1753 they took this child, along with his elder brother, to be baptized at St. Joseph. Esther's children included Etienne Joseph, born in 1750; Louis, born in 1752; Marie Joseph, born in 1753; and Angelique, born in 1756. Webster and Krause, *Fort Saint Joseph*, 114–15.

26. The Chevaliers were a large French family. There were seventeen children. Jean Baptiste Chevalier and his wife, Marie Françoise Alavoine, probably moved from Montreal to Michilimackinac in 1718. Baptismal registers at Michilimackinac and St. Joseph provide information about fifteen of the seventeen children born to Jean Baptiste Chevalier and Marie Françoise Alavoine. Four—possibly six—children were born in Montreal; eleven children were baptized at St. Ignace. The children born in Montreal included Charlotte (Deshêtres, Louis (1712), Marie Joseph, and Marie Anne (Chabouillez). The eleven children baptized at the St. Ignace Mission included Constance (1719), Louis Thérèse (1720), Joseph Marguerite (1723), Marie Magdaleine (1724), Anne Charlotte Veronique (1726), Charles (1727), Joseph Maurice (1728), Louis Pascal (1730), Anne Thérèse Ester (1732), Angelique (1733), and Luc (1735). Webster and Krause, *Fort Saint Joseph*, 55–56.

27. Louis Chevalier was born in October of 1751 and baptized by his uncle, Louis Pascal Chevalier. In April of 1752 he was baptized by the priest, Father DuJaunay. His godfather was his oldest stepsister's husband, Joutras, and his godmother was another stepsister, Madeleine Chevalier. "St. Joseph Register," in *MVHR*, 12:223.

28. Webster and Krause, *Fort Saint Joseph*, 113. Chevalier's son Amable was raised among the Odawa, married an Odawa woman, and their children were baptized at Michilimackinac. "Mackinac Register, " in *WHC*, 19:93, 95.

29. In 1718 Governor Vaudreuil issued six congés for the St. Joseph post. Jean Baptiste Chevalier, Louis's father, received a permit for a canoe with two crewmen in addition to himself. Congés granted in 1717 and 1718 are linked to the letter from Vaudreuil and Bégon dated 11 November 1718; *ANCol*, C11A, 38:85–88vo; also see John M. Gram's "The Chevalier Family and the Demography of the Upper Great Lakes," unpublished paper in the archives of the Mackinac Island State Park Commission, Lansing, Michigan; *RAPQ*, 1929–30: 278.

30. Charlotte Chevalier Deshêtres lived at St. Joseph with her family for over twenty
    years. Charlotte first appeared as a godmother at the St. Joseph mission in 1730,
    "St. Joseph Register," in *MVHR*, 12:213. Charlotte and Antoine Deshêtres moved
    to Detroit sometime in 1750 or 1751. Webster and Krause, *Fort Saint Joseph*,
    118–19.

31. Marie Magdelaine L'archevêque appears to have been one of Madeleine's daugh-
    ters but this cannot be confirmed by the baptismal registers. Louis Pascal was bap-
    tized at Michilimackinac on 22 July 1730. He died prior to 1 January 1779. Louis
    Pascal and his wife had four children baptized at St. Joseph between 1758 and
    1773, "St. Joseph Register," in *MVHR*, 12:223n. 38; *WHC*, 8:490; *WHC*, 19:3;
    Webster and Krause, *Fort Saint Joseph*, 120–21.

32. The Chevaliers were partners, but they were not related. Charles Lhullic
    Chevalier's trading partner now became his stepfather-in-law. Charles and
    Angelique were married at St. Joseph, and three of their children were baptized
    there. Chevalier died in 1773. He was about sixty-four. His death was the last entry
    in the St. Joseph Baptismal Register. Webster and Krause, *Fort Saint Joseph*,
    115–17; Idle, "Post of the St. Joseph," 253–54n. 104; "St. Joseph Register," in
    MVHR, 12:230.

33. The register does not mention the marriage of Anne L'archevêque and Augustin
    Gibault. When she served as godmother to the daughter of her sister Marie Joseph
    in 1756, she was identified as Anne L'archeveque. By 1758, she was identified as
    the wife of Gibault. "St. Joseph Register," in *MVHR*, 12:228, 230.

34. Marie Amable married Jean Baptiste François Lonval. Lonval's ties were to the
    fur trade community at Trois Rivières. The Lonvals settled in Cahokia where they
    appear on the 1787 Cahokia census. Webster and Krause, *Fort Saint Joseph*,
    117–18; "St. Joseph Register," in *MVHR*, 12:231, 233–34.

35. Both Joseph Esther's and Marie Amable's children were baptized at the Fort
    St.Joseph mission. Four of Esther's children were baptized there. In 1753 her sis-
    ter Catherine was the godmother to her sixteen-month-old son, Louis, and to her
    three-year-old son, Etiennne Joseph. Esther's sister Anne was the godmother to
    her three-year-old daughter, Marie Joseph. In 1756, Esther's sister Magdeleine
    was the godmother to her five-month-old daughter, Angelique. "St. Joseph
    Baptismal Register," in *MVHR*, 12:225, 225–26, 228. In 1761, Amable's two-
    month-old daughter was baptized at St. Joseph, "St. Joseph Register," in *MVHR*,
    12:233–34.

36. Idle, "Post of the Saint Joseph," 182; *RAPQ*, 1929–30:233–465.

37. The prolonged absence of priests at frontier missions led lay Catholics and even
    non-Catholics to perform baptisms. Priests were only intermittently assigned to
    the St. Joseph mission but did serve continuously from 1750 to 1761. During other
    times the post was reliant on the missionary priests assigned to Illinois Country—
    generally they resided at either Cahokia or Kaskaskia. Growth of the frontier
    Catholic church was hampered in 1762 when the French government decreed sec-
    ularization of the Jesuits. The Supreme Council of New Orleans put the decree

into effect on 3 July 1763. Father Meurin was allowed to remain in Illinois Country at Ste. Genevieve on the Spanish side of the river. Priests from other orders were at the St. Joseph mission in 1761, 1768, and 1773. A new missionary priest, Father Gibault, was assigned to Illinois Country in 1773. "St. Joseph Register," in *MVHR*, 12: 204–5; George Paré, *The Catholic Church in Detroit, 1701–1888* (Detroit: Wayne State University Press, 1951), 78–103. For an account of the banishment see Reuben Gold Thwaites, ed., *The Jesuit Relations and Allied Documents LXX* (hereafter *JR*) (New York: Pageant Book Co., 1959).

38. The term *baptized conditionally* appears frequently in baptismal registers and indicates that a child had previously received lay baptism when a priest was unavailable. For an explanation of the term *baptized conditionally*, see "The Mackinac Register," *WHC* 19:7n. 25.

39. "St. Joseph Register," in *MVHR*, 12:218, 238.

40. The numeral 8 appears throughout the St. Joseph Baptismal Register and indicates the phonetic equivalent for parts of Native American languages that were not spelled in French. S was a digraph or shorthand for ou.

41. His godfather was Mr. Marin de la Perriere and his godmother was Madeleine de Villiers, his wife. Her godfather was Louis Metivier, a master carpenter, and the godmother, Marie Fafard, his wife. Five years later Marie, Pierre's wife, died. "St. Joseph Register," in *MVHR*, 12:221–23.

42. On 22 April 1752, one of Pierre's daughters, 8abak8ik8e, was baptized. She was about thirty-five years old and took the name Marie as her Christian name. Louis Chevalier signed as the godfather. On 1 May 1752, three more of Pierre's children, all women were baptized, one was twenty-six or -seven, the second was twenty-five, and the third was fifteen or sixteen. The eldest, a widow and identified as Temagas8kia, took the name of Marguerite. Her godmother was Marguerite of the Saki nation. Both other daughters elected Marie Madeleine Réaume Chevalier as their godmother. The middle daughter, age twenty-five, was identified as being married to Pi8assin, who was listed as still unconverted. The third daughter took the name Suzanne. "St. Joseph Register," in *MVHR*, 12:222–23.

43. In Illinois Country fur traders had also learned to diversify their economic pursuits. For a description of an agricultural community along the banks of these fertile river valleys, see Winstanley Briggs, "Le Pays des Illinois," *The William and Mary Quarterly* 47 (January 1990): 30–56; Richard White also discusses the issue of economic diversification: "On the Great Lakes the French had created a market not only for beaver and menues pelleteries but also for venison, canoes, fish, corn, and bear oil." White, *Middle Ground*, 211.

44. John D. Barnhart, *Henry Hamilton and George Rogers Clark in the American Revolution with the Unpublished Journal of Lieutenant Governor Henry Hamilton* (Crawfordsville, Ind.: R.E. Banta, 1951), 115–16.

45. There was an average of 140 frost-free days in the lands that rimmed the southern Great Lakes, known as the Prairie Peninsula. Although corn remained the most

economically important grain, other grains were also harvested. James A. Brown, *Aboriginal Cultural Adaptations in the Midwestern Prairies* (New York: Garland, 1991), 57.

46. Pénicault's Relation in Margry, *Découvertes et éstablissements* 5:375–586; Father Gabriel Marest to Father Germon, JR, 66:218–95; also in Father Watrin's summary of his work among the Kaskaskia, JR, 70:218–95.

47. E. B. O'Callaghan, ed., *Documents Relative to the Colonial History of the State of New York* (Albany: Weed, Parsons and Co., 1855–87), 9:891.

48. Plum, crabapple, and cherry trees grew along the river bottoms. The Jesuits in the seventeenth century attested to the lushness of the St. Joseph River Valley and to the profusion of wild grapes that grew along riverbanks. The dune area around southern Lake Michigan also produced large quantities of huckleberries, wild currants, gooseberries, and blackberries. Brown, *Aboriginal Cultural Adaptations*, 60; *JR*, 55:195.

49. "Petition of Louis Chevallier," reprinted from the Haldimand Papers, Canadian Archives, Ottawa (Lansing, Mich.: Michigan Pioneer Historical Collection) 13:61. Hereafter referred to as *MPHC*.

50. A jail was constructed by the blacksmith Antoine Deshêtres. It was made of stone and measured eight feet by ten feet. Certificate, St. Joseph, signed Piquoteé de Belestre, 13 May 1750. *ANCol*, C11A, 96:313. The post interpreter, Pierre Deneau dit Detailly, submitted a certificate to receive 1,000 livres for building a house for a medal chief. Certificate, St. Joseph, 30 April 1760, *Archives Nationales* 7, 345:99.

51. The term *matrifocal* conveys that women in their role as mothers are the focus of relationships and that such women slowly evolved as "the centre of an economic and decision-making coalition with her children." Raymond Smith, "The Matrifocal Family," in *The Character of Kinship*, ed. Jack Goody (New York: Cambridge University Press, 1973), 125.

52. Ballard, *Old Fort Saint Joseph*, 25–26.

53. Peyser, *Letters from New France*, 215–16; Ballard, *Old Fort St. Joseph*, 44–46.

54. Malchelosse, "St. Joseph River Post," 191; *WHC*, 11:116 and 18:367.

55. In 1779 the British Ministry planned a two-pronged attack on Spanish Territory. Both the villages in the south surrounding New Orleans as well as those near St. Louis were part of the plan. Michilimackinac and Detroit were to serve as the staging areas for the St. Louis assault. Alvard, "Conquest of St. Joseph," 404.

56. Sinclair to Haldimand, in *WHC*, 11:153.

57. Keith R. Widder, "Effects of the American Revolution on Fur-Trade Society at Michilimackinac," in *The Fur Trade Revisited: Selected Papers of the Sixth North American Fur Trade Conference, Mackinac Island, Michigan, 1991*, ed. Jennifer S. H. Brown, W. J. Eccles, and Donald P. Heldman (East Lansing: Michigan State University Press, 1994), 303.

58. Joseph and Agathe Hamelin Normand had three children baptized at St. Joseph in 1765, 1766, 1767. Louis Pascal Chevalier and Louis Hamelin were godfathers.

Webster and Krause, *Fort Saint Joseph*, 122–23; "St. Joseph Register," in MVHR, 12:235–6.

59. John Francis McDermott, ed., *Old Cahokia: A Narrative and Documents Illustrating the First Century of its History* (St. Louis: St. Louis Historical Documents Foundation, 1949), 128; Webster and Krause, *Fort Saint Joseph*, 123; Idle, "Post of the St. Joseph," 182, 188.

60. McDermott, *Cahokia*, 31, Malchelosse, "St. Joseph River Post," 204–5; Paré, *Catholic Church*, 47.

61. "Indian Council: At a Council held at Detroit 11th March, 1781, with the Pottewatimies from St. Josephs, Terre Coupé and Coeur de Cerf," MPHC, 10:453–55.

62. The attack was led by Eugène Pouré dit Beausoleil. The number of men who accompanied him varies in different historical accounts. Helen Hornbeck Tanner, in *Atlas of Great Lakes Indian History*, estimates the number at "65 Spanish militia and an estimated 100 Indians" (Norman: University of Oklahoma Press), 72. At the time of the census taken by Ainssé in 1799, the Chevalier sons, Louis and Amable Chevalier, were not listed among the people forcibly removed. It is also possible that Pieniche Chevalier was another son of Louis Chevalier. He was listed as a member of the French community but was not removed to Michilimackinac. He was listed as "in war."

63. Descriptions of the attack on and destruction of Fort St. Joseph include Peyser, *Letters from New France*, 219–21; A. P. Nasatir, "The Anglo-Spanish Frontier in the Illinois Country during the American Revolution, 1779–1783," *Illinois State Historical Society Journal* 21 (October 1928): 291–358; Ballard, *Old Fort St. Joseph*, 46–48; Malchelosse, "St. Joseph River Post," 204–6; Rufus Blanchard, *The Discovery and Conquest of the Northwest* (Chicago: Cushing, Thomas, and Co., 1880), 165–66; B. A. Hinsdale, *The Old Northwest* (New York: Townsend, 1888), 173–74; Charles Moore, *Northwest under Three Flags* (New York: Harper & Bros., 1900), 257–60; McDermott, *Cahokia*, 31–32, 200. A less reliable version of the attack is contained in Clarence W. Alvard's "The Conquest of St. Joseph Michigan, By the Spaniards in 1781," *Michigan History* 14 (1930): 398–414.

64. Recent fur trade studies that have reexamined the impact of the fur trade on Native American society contend that Native Americans were active agents and not mere consumers whose loyalty could be purchased with cheaper goods. Bruce Alden Cox, "Natives and the Development of Mercantile Capitalism: A New Look at 'Opposition' in the Eighteenth Century Fur Trade," in *The Political Economy of North American Indians*, ed. John N. Moore (Norman: University of Oklahoma Press, 1993), 87–93.

65. Peterson, "Many Roads to Red River," 41.

66. "Report of the Various Indian Tribes Receiving Presents in the District of Ylonia or Illinois, 1769," "Report of Don Pedro Piernas to Gov. O'Reilly, Describing the Spanish Illinois Country, Dated October 31, 1769," and "Report of the Indian Tribes who Received Presents at St. Louis, Dated November 15,

1777," in Louis Houck, ed., *The Spanish Regime in Missouri: A Collection of Papers and Documents Relating to Upper Louisiana*, 2 vols. (Chicago: R. R. Donnelley & Sons Co., 1909), 1:44–45, 66–75, 141–49.

67. MPHC, 16:115–16; 10:407.

68. "DePeyster to Haldimand," June 1779, in *WHC*, 11:131–32.

SECTION 2

New Visions

Peter Cook[1] # Symbolic and Material Exchange in Intercultural Diplomacy: The French and the Hodenosaunee in the Early Eighteenth Century

INTERPRETING INTERACTIONS between North American Native peoples and Europeans in the sixteenth, seventeenth, and eighteenth centuries requires an adequate account of the patterns of exchange between indigenous and colonial societies. "The fur trade" is often used as a kind of shorthand to describe economic exchanges over much of the continent—although the term tends to obscure the great variety of goods and services exchanged between First Nations and colonials in this period.[2] Indeed, from an indigenous perspective, one might well speak of "the cloth trade" or "the kettle trade." More fundamentally, the commonsense meaning of trade does not easily accommodate exchanges occurring in contexts that cannot be imagined as a kind of market. For example, when the Anishinaubaek or Hodenosaunee met the French in council—in an obvious "diplomatic" or "political" context—furs, beads, European manufactured goods, and other items were passed back and forth according to established protocols. Was this trade?

In seeking to understand such council exchanges, I have found it necessary to address the habit of constituting economics and politics as relatively autonomous domains. Habit is perhaps too mild a word for it: these received categories of analysis have retained their basic distinctiveness in both scholarly and everyday usage, despite the numerous attempts that have been made in the scholarly domain to demonstrate a fundamental interrelatedness. This is perhaps because the meaningfulness of these terms depends upon their situation in a larger system of oppositions rooted in the basic taxonomies of Western thought. Council diplomacy appears to "naturally" fit under the rubric of the political; conversely, the seventeenth- and early eighteenth-century annual fur fairs at Montreal seem an equally clear example of economic activity. This naturalistic partitioning was evident in the explicit economism of early and mid-twentieth-century scholars like Harold A. Innis and George

T. Hunt, for whom the transhistorical imperatives of market forces and technological improvement determined the political behavior of Native groups in the period of European colonization.[3] The practice of diplomacy was of little importance save to elucidate the effect of these forces upon Native decision making. The later formulation of Abraham Rotstein, working under the influence of theoretical developments in economic anthropology, reversed the tables by insisting that within North American Native societies, as within precapitalist societies generally, "trade functioned within the context of political relations . . . and was subordinated to the over-riding requirements of security."[4] Although Rotstein spent little time studying Native political practices for their own sake, his approach accorded them prominent explanatory weight, since "primitive" economies were alleged to be embedded within properly sociopolitical institutions. What was formerly understood as economic behavior was now deemed to be essentially political.[5]

Scholarly debates over the interpretation of intersocietal exchange have evolved considerably since these early formulations. Nevertheless, the subtle effect of oppositional categories has continued to make itself felt—no longer with respect to the validity of economic models, but rather to the broader question of practice.[6] When Bruce Trigger summed up the debate between formalists and substantivists in 1985, and reviewed the evidence relating to the fur trade in the St. Lawrence lowlands in the first half of the seventeenth century, he concluded that Native trading practices were embedded in political and social institutions, but nevertheless exhibited important elements of economic rationalism, insofar as the Hurons, Montagnais, and Algonkins "sought to profit by exchanging goods with other tribes for more than they had paid for them, by playing off foreign trading partners to lower the price of goods, and by asking for more than the standardized rate of exchange as evidence of friendship and goodwill." If other Native behaviors suggested the absence of an economic consciousness—such as the observed inelasticity of Native demand for goods—Trigger explained this by reference to subsistence patterns, which among hunter-gatherers discouraged the accumulation of surplus goods, or to internal social obligation, which among the Hurons meant that chiefs and traders were expected to redistribute profits as presents in various ceremonial contexts, and were rewarded for doing so.[7]

In thus ascribing Native trading practices, and hence the diplomacy associated with them, to an overarching rationalism exercised within the constraints of traditional subsistence patterns and social customs, Trigger was quite deliberately reacting to interpretations that portray Native people as exotic Others, and their lifeways as incommensurable with those of

Europeans—such views usually entailing claims that Natives were totally impervious to European influences, were not dependent on trade goods, and were impressed by the symbolic rather than the utilitarian value of European trade goods. Trigger labeled these views "romantic," in contrast to his avowed intent of showing that Native peoples were as rational as the Europeans they encountered in seventeenth-century North America.[8] Trigger's elaboration of this distinction gives rise to a series of oppositions, whereby the terms "rational," "universal," "utilitarian," and "literal" find their antitheses in the "cultural," the "idiosyncratic," the "nonutilitarian," and the "metaphorical." Universally rational calculations are associated with problem solving, strategy, adaptation, experience, and observation, while culture is viewed as exerting a constraining effect upon actors.[9] At the center of this framework, then, is a set of more or less homologous oppositions that one is tempted to view as precipitates of a deeply rooted tension in the theoretical underpinnings of modern social science.

The negotiation of such basic dichotomies has been a preoccupation of Pierre Bourdieu since the 1970s, and his ideas go some way toward permitting a critical and reflexive approach to the system of oppositions sustaining the antimony between "reason" and "culture" as explanatory concepts. In general, Bourdieu has sought to explain practices in a manner that recognizes, on the one hand, the rationality, or interestedness, of actors while emphasizing, on the other hand, the socially constructed sources of meaning and of rationality itself. The second half of this chapter seeks to apply these ideas to the symbolic and material exchanges involved in early eighteenth-century council diplomacy on New France's western frontier. In the first half, I explore the implications of Trigger's contrast between rationalistic and romantic interpretations and evaluate some recent historical writing in this context.[10]

According to Trigger, "rationalist explanations seek to account for human behavior in terms of calculations that are cross-culturally comprehensible." Strategies and calculations are the products of this rationality operating within individual minds, and are especially evident "with respect to those matters that relate most directly to . . . material well-being." Economic behaviors are consequently more susceptible to rational reevaluation and change than religious beliefs and customs, which are inherently conservative. This position is grounded in a materialist view of culture inspired by Karl Marx's thesis that modes of production determine the general characteristics of social life.[11] An explicit corollary is that economic practices and technology, or more generally the nature of a society's relations to the natural world, are the driving forces of social change.[12]

In a distinguished lecture in archaeology published in 1991, Trigger advocated the marriage of this Marxian principle with the rationalist philosophy of Jean-Paul Sartre. For Trigger this meant that social scientists should

> view human behavior as the product of an interaction between the ability of individual human beings to foresee at least some of the consequences of what they do and the sort of constraints on human behavior, both physical and imagined, that such calculations must take into account.

These constraints, which include external forces as well as cultural constructions, operate "through the individual consciousness and ability to calculate, not in some automatic way."[13] Trigger writes that "practical reason has the ability to transcend culture,"[14] and argues that over the long term, the basic human cognitive ability to reason pragmatically allows people to "adjust cultural perceptions so that they accord sufficiently with the real world."[15] I infer from these arguments that, for Trigger, "practical reason" is precultural, transhistorical, and universal in human beings. It follows that different cultures are "historical precipitates"[16] of a pragmatically determined mode of production that is itself a consequence of the encounter between practical reason and certain external, objective realities.

Although few other students of Native-European relations in the northeast have been as explicit about their theoretical assumptions as Trigger, several recent works underline the powerful attraction of "romantic" views. Christopher Miller and George Hamell, reacting to the occultation of the ideological aspects of intercultural trade relations in the literature, argue that the emphasis on Native rationality in the fur trade fails to take into account the archaeological and historical evidence indicating that trade in nonutilitarian European goods—the baubles and trinkets of an older historiography—was significant during the early contact period. As Miller and Hamell point out, Trigger himself noted that "trading in exotic goods has often played a role that was out of all proportion to its utilitarian significance"—in this case, European trade goods reaching the Huron country in the immediate precontact period (ca. 1580–1610) seemed to have had little technological impact, but far-reaching political consequences, as the Hurons concentrated their settlements and sought to expand trade contacts with Algonkians.[17] Surveying archaeological sites pertaining to protohistoric Woodland Algonkian, Siouan, and Iroquoian groups, Miller and Hamell observed European copper and glass alongside "spiritually charged native items in ceremonial contexts," (e.g., ossuaries and grave-sites), and deduced that, in some cases, Natives accepted manufactured European goods as substitutes for symbolically loaded native objects, such as native copper, exotic stones, and marine shells.

The authors' reconstruction of the mythic world of Native peoples in the northeast underlines the significance of this process. These objects represented "wealth," that is, ensured physical, spiritual, and social well-being to their owner, not least because of their extraordinary provenance—for Natives believed objects like crystal, native copper, catlinite, and shell (implicated by their respective colors with basic symbolic schemes and thus accorded ideational and aesthetic value) to be obtained through reciprocal exchanges with powerful other-than-human beings. Miller and Hamell infer from indigenous accounts of first contact that European goods and their bearers were initially assimilated into these mythic categories, although the authors distinguish between this initial phase—during which Natives perceived themselves to be involved in reciprocal exchanges with supernatural beings for supernatural goods—and a subsequent phase of "disenchantment [which] was predominantly the result of the fur trade" and of European diplomacy. The former "increasingly pushed intercultural exchange out of the symbolic ceremonial realm and into the realm of the white marketplace," while the latter involved the extensive presentation of gifts in contexts of war and antisocial activities (e.g., exclusive alliances). This in turn laid the ground for a potential "nativistic" reaction and a shift in attitude toward "trinkets," leading to a transition, in the minds of Natives, from ceremonial exchange to economic exchange—a transformation that occurred under the effects of a conjuncture that saw the articulation of "Indian resources, land and labor into the market," and the combined effects of European population pressure, climatic change, disease, alcohol, and warfare.[18]

Trigger has displayed a guarded acceptance of this interpretation, apparently considering its archaeological and ethnographic analyses to be the most convincing elements. Trigger's own thesis that Natives initially reacted to Europeans on the basis of "traditional religious beliefs," but subsequently experienced a "'cognitive reorganization' in which the rational component inherent in the mental processes of every human being began to play the dominant role," resembles the disenchantment theory advanced by Miller and Hamell.[19] Neither theory of transition, however, has been the subject of sustained investigation, and both function to some extent as mere devices for the reconciliation of otherwise opposing perspectives.

The work of Marshall Sahlins exerts an important influence upon that of Miller and Hamell, and the former's theoretical positions illustrate the variance between Trigger's position and theirs. Marshall Sahlins begins, like Trigger, with a note from Karl Marx: namely, that "production [is] the appropriation of nature within and through a determinate form of society. It follows that a mode of production itself will specify no cultural order unless and until its own order as production is culturally specified." A particular social formation is thus the "cultural assumption of external conditions," producing a "definite symbolic scheme which is never the only one possible." While Sahlins and Trigger might agree that culture must conform to material constraints in order for a society to be viable, Sahlins departs from this consensus by rejecting the possibility of a practical reason, or a sense of self-interest, that is somehow prior to culture. Rather, "it is culture which constitutes utility."[20] Sahlins's interpretation of late eighteenth- and early nineteenth-century Hawaiian history depends heavily on the concept of cultural logics that determine the positions taken by actors in various situations. If for Trigger the dynamic force in history is in the long-term the encounter between practical reason and an external reality taking place in spite of cultural constraints, for Sahlins it is in the dialectic between culturally constituted categories and the social effects of putting those categories to work in changing circumstances.[21]

Trigger and Sahlins by no means represent wholly opposite viewpoints. Both reject rigid notions of social evolution, ecological determinism, and historical materialism. Both emphasize the ability of actors to determine their own history through meaningful action, and in their empirical work both scholars have sought to produce sympathetic historical accounts of indigenous peoples in the context of European expansionism. Yet they are opposed along the lines of a basic antimony that, at the risk of gross simplification, might be referred to as the question of whether people are all the same or whether they are all different.[22]

Two recent works further illustrate the sense of exotic difference, as well as Sahlins's impact on North American historiography. Richard White's *The Middle Ground* (1991) and Matthew Dennis's *Cultivating a Landscape of Peace* (1993) share the goal of elucidating Native decision making relating to war, alliance, and trade with Europeans. Dennis's study of Hodenosaunee-Dutch and Hodenosaunee-French relations emphasizes the vastly different cultural worlds to which each of these groups belonged, and seeks to show how the first two-thirds of the seventeenth century bore the imprint of different cultural projects. While Dutch traders sought profits in the fur trade, and French Jesuits and governors sought to dominate the Hodenosaunee religiously and politically, the Five Nations themselves were constantly motivated by the desire to achieve peaceful relations with the intruders by means of the logic of the Great League of Peace. As embodied in the Deganawidah Epic, the Hodenosaunee concept of peace was founded upon the ideal of domestic harmony, and was thus predicated upon consanguinity and shared values. The metaphor of the longhouse sheltering the Mohawk, Oneida, Onondaga, Cayuga, and Seneca under one roof could be extended to encompass new peoples—in particular, the European invaders. The Deganawidah Epic, for Dennis, is the functional equivalent of the Hawaiian myths used by Sahlins to interpret early contacts between Hawaiians and Europeans.[23]

Dennis proceeds to reinterpret the political history of the northeast before 1664 in the light of these respective projects. The Hodenosaunee endeavor to incorporate the French into the longhouse seemed most promising when Jesuits came among them, but soured when these men refused assimilation and intermarriage. For, according to Dennis, the Hodenosaunee sought to establish kinship and domesticity in purely literal terms, as evidenced by their reluctance to release French captives. Naturally this emphasis on a culturally driven quest for peace makes it difficult to explain Hodenosaunee warfare generally, and events such as the dispersal of the Huron in 1648 and 1649 particularly. Dennis's solution is to explain Hodenosaunee attacks as a response to the "rebuffs" they received from the French and the latter's Native trading partners:

> Satisfied with their autonomous way of life and their separate prosperity, and hard-pressed by New France to reject peace with the Iroquois, [the Hurons] snubbed the Five Nations in favor of New France's affections. Consequently, the Huron-Iroquois conflict continued, amid numerous attempts by the Five Nations to effect a peaceful amalgamation, until the Hurons were eventually devastated by poor harvests, famine and disease, French-induced factionalism, and, by 1649, Iroquois assaults.[24]

The period closes with the Hodenosaunee weakened by European diseases, politically isolated, subject to aggressive Jesuit proselytization, and understandably frustrated by their lack of success in assimilating the French into the longhouse. In an epilogue, Dennis affirms that the multiple crises of the 1660s and 1670s compelled the Five Nations to recognize

> that a mechanical application of traditional formulas would not allow them to construct the peace they sought. Holding firmly to the essence of Deganawidah's dream, and forging new mechanisms to make it manifest in their world, the Iroquois began to develop a new foreign policy [which involved] accepting fictive, or symbolic, over literal kinship, and social separation rather than amalgamation.[25]

The Hodenosaunee appear here as a monolithic society of "cultural dopes," alternating between optimistic overtures of peace and violent fits of peevishness.[26] In sympathetically seeking to overturn the historiographical myth of Hodenosaunee bellicosity—a task already accomplished by an earlier group of historians—and to emphasize the sophistication of

Hodenosaunee political culture, Dennis has imposed upon historical actors a straitjacket-like conception of culture that reduces practice to stubborn attempts to achieve a literally defined cultural project, and rationality to a dim awareness of its success or failure. Nor is the notion of ideological transformation any more sophisticated: Dennis's thesis that the Hodenosaunee finally ceased trying to "mechanically" apply the formula of literal domesticity and kinship may simply be a product of his own mechanistic conceptualization of culture.

Richard White's broad synthesis of Native-European relations in the Great Lakes region before 1815 parallels Sahlins's project of demonstrating that the articulation of indigenous economies with a global European market (e.g., the fur trade in North America, or the sandalwood trade in the Hawaiian islands) was frequently mediated by the impact of local cultural schemes. In the Great Lakes region, this meant that Europeans were obliged to accommodate Native models of exchange and alliance in order to fulfill their own mercantile and imperial aims. But where Sahlins addresses the possibility of structural transformations in Hawaiian symbolic schemes and society, White's focus is the process of mediation—a process that allegedly had a structure unto itself. This was the "middle ground": a "common conception of suitable ways of acting," "a mutually comprehensible, jointly invented world, rather than a traditional set of procedures." This "customary world" rested on a "bedrock of common life"—for thus White characterizes the coexistence of French traders and Native peoples in the Great Lakes region— and "resulted from the daily encounters of individual Indians and Frenchmen with problems and controversies that needed immediate solutions." Formal elements of the middle ground were "cultural fictions," because they emerged from the often crude attempts of two groups to manipulate each other's cultural forms. These transformed forms were nevertheless authenticated through negotiation and practice. Consequently, the middle ground had a logic of its own, which was neither fully Algonkian nor fully European.[27]

White's model aims to transcend the "pervasive dichotomy" of acculturation or resistance that marks accounts of Native-European interaction, and in so doing avoids explanations that hinge either on "rational" Native responses to the fur trade, or on cultural persistence for its own sake. It does so by positing the creation of a new symbolic and institutional order that mediated between Native and European societies. In formulating the concept of "the middle ground," White is obviously sensitive to current theoretical concerns about describing cultural systems in processual rather than static terms.[28] Yet the focus on the "middle ground" as a buffer between the world economy and

Native lifeways obviates any need to investigate ideological transformations in Native societies. Native rationality—understood as the exercise of culturally determined preferences—apparently retained its precontact contours, just as Natives in the Great Lakes region allegedly remained technologically independent vis-à-vis European traders, at least during the French regime.[29] As an interpretive device, the "middle ground" merely delays the inevitable narratives of acculturation and resistance evoked in the book's epilogue.

My point in this brief exposition is not to discount interpretations that are considerably more complex than I have allowed here, but to flesh out the current dichotomization of ethnohistorical approaches. Insofar as analyses of the fur trade incorporate the perspectives and methods of ethnohistory, they are likewise bound to display the influence of oppositional categories. But various strands of recent social theory, of which Pierre Bourdieu's is one, would seem to support a theoretical middle ground between notions of universal rationalism and cultural relativism.[30]

Social reproduction rather than cultural contact has provided the context for Pierre Bourdieu's efforts toward developing an adequate theory of practice and of the subject. Nevertheless, his critique of existing theories is germane to Trigger's contrast between rationalistic and romantic interpretations of Native-European relations. Bourdieu addresses the antimony that opposes the objectivist viewpoint (in the structuralist tradition of Lévi-Strauss) to the subjectivist viewpoint (in the tradition of Sartre). In discerning the continuity, regularity, and patterned nature of social practices, the objectivist defines the homologies and oppositions that seem to govern them, frequently resorting to the language of laws, codes, and rules. Yet, argues Bourdieu, it is clear that the actors themselves are not consciously obeying laws or rules, except in those limited areas of social practice where rules are actually made explicit and enforced. So what, then, motivates an agent to produce practices that nevertheless seem to harmonize with the actions of others? The rational actor theory of the subjectivists would locate the principle of action in the constant exercise of logic or reason by individuals who somehow all share the same preferences. Presumably, this is the principle of practice implicit in Trigger's rationalism. But Bourdieu balks at the notion of a "subject 'without inertia,'"[31] that is, without durable dispositions, or ingrained habits of doing or thinking a certain way. What looks rational to the observer may in fact be a matter of unthinking habit for the actor, while the "rational" calculations of an actor may seem absurd to the outsider. One cannot simply assume the universality of any subset of possible human preferences.

Bourdieu has developed methods of accounting for social practices that avoid, on the one hand, constant reference to the concept of culture as being itself a motivating principle, and, on the other hand, the dualism of Trigger's rationalist formulation, which relies upon the distinction between reason and cultural beliefs.[32] There are two aspects of Bourdieu's thought that I have found useful in getting around this opposition. First is the concept of habitus, or ways of being that are inculcated in each actor as he or she grows within a community. These are not rules that we follow consciously; instead, they are classificatory schemes that are transmitted, internalized, and put into practice every day without attaining the level of discourse: they are implicit in the social organization of space, time, and of the body itself.[33] The ongoing application of these schemes produces the regularity or patterned nature of society that the outsider may observe, but that the actor experiences as the flux and uncertainty of everyday life. What distances this even further from the principle of the rule, or custom, or tradition, is that the calculation of interest enters into the determination of practices. There is no predetermined fit between schemes and types of situations, especially new situations: actors are constantly engaged in correcting the results of practice by developing new strategies.[34] Strategy, or interest, is not understood by Bourdieu in terms of universal tendencies toward maximizing productivity or economic well-being. Yet Bourdieu does employ an economic analogy in viewing strategies as calculated efforts to manipulate various forms of capital. He is a materialist in the sense that he views social hierarchies and the structure of the symbolic order as being ultimately grounded in the distribution and control of material capital, but he sees actors as principally concerned with struggles over what he terms symbolic capital. It is this second concept that is most relevant to understanding interaction between Europeans and Native peoples in the early period of colonization in the northeast.

The notion of symbolic capital subsumes what people subjectively feel as honor, prestige, respectability, authority, and so on. Part of what makes symbolic capital valuable is that it may be converted into economic capital, or "invested" in order to produce material effects. In an example drawn from his early fieldwork in Algeria, Bourdieu shows how symbolic capital in the form of prestige and renown attached to a family name help the family maintain networks of relationships with kin and clientele that come in handy during peak labor periods: rather than maintain a large workforce all year round, the family merely "cashes in" on its symbolic capital and draws in clients when time comes for the harvest. The disposition of eighteenth-century Anishinaubaek hunters to share game with kin obeyed a similar logic: "In giving food Ojibway people made an investment in long-term goodwill and helped to assure their own future well-being."[35]

Still, the amassing of symbolic capital clearly involves considerable effort and important symbolic and material investments, in the form of courtesies and gifts. Paradoxically, the "means eat up the ends: the action necessary to ensure the continuation of power and prestige themselves help to weaken it."[36] In order to maintain honor, prestige, or simply to achieve recognition for acting in an officially approved manner, one must constantly renew symbolic and material investments. Bourdieu refers to this as a gentle mode of domination, or as a form of symbolic violence, which the actors themselves speak of in terms of credit, confidence, obligation, personal loyalty, or a code of honor.[37] It is from this perspective that we must consider European descriptions of Native leadership in the northeast. The following statement, by the intendant Antoine-Denis Raudot, is typical:

> [One becomes war chief] by the great deeds he has done, and by the support of young men which he attracts by means of gifts, for usually these chiefs are the worst clad of the whole nation as they give everything in order to be esteemed.[38]

To speak of gift giving in terms of domination and violence may seem strange and even disrespectful when applied to practices that are described in terms of generosity; it is not meant to be. Rather it outlines the modes of political action and leadership that may obtain in "societies without a State."[39]

In the context of early eighteenth-century council diplomacy, Bourdieu's approach allows an account of gift giving that does not imply a stark contrast between rational and mythical motivations. Rather, it asks us to see how a variety of actors manipulate and transform various forms of capital, and to examine the effects of these transactions and the reactions of actors to them. A French-Onondaga council of 1707 may serve as an example of this process. It was in many ways an unremarkable council, by comparison with the other councils that took place at Montreal and Quebec in the early eighteenth century.[40] The frequent participation of Onondagas and Senecas in councils at Montreal in this period reflected their position in contemporary trade and alliance networks. Removed from the direct influence of the English at Albany, and exposed to the attacks of French allies from the upper great Lakes, these two nations had every reason to maintain good relations with the French. Alliance with the English did not guarantee protection and military assistance in case of conflict with the French and their allies; moreover, trade with the French was an alternative to overdependence on Albany. Finally, having adopted several influential Frenchmen, they were inclined to perform ceremonies of condolence upon the deaths of these men, their spouses, or their close relatives.[41]

In mid-August 1707, a delegation of Onondagas arrived at Montreal for a council with the governor of New France, Philippe de Rigaud de Vaudreuil. It was a crucial political juncture. Three years before, Odawas from Michilimakinac had captured several Hodenosaunee near Fort Frontenac. Both the Senecas and the Onondagas had asked the French governor to approach the Odawas on their behalf, on the basis of the agreements reached at Montreal in 1701. Thus, in 1704, the Onondaga orator Ohonsiowanne (La Grande Terre) requested the mediation of the French governor:

> We remind you however, Father, of what was said at the general peace; namely, that you would hold all your children within your embrace, and should any be attacked, he would not avenge himself with his own hands, but instead would appeal to you. That is what we have done by this belt.[42]

The Odawas accepted Vaudreuil's mediation during a series of councils at Montreal in 1705, and by 1707 had returned the captive Hodenosaunee and all but one of the slaves they had promised to give as compensation for their coup.[43] While the French were relieved to have helped prevent further hostilities between their allies and the Five Nations, this diplomatic reconciliation made it possible once again for western Natives to travel to Albany through the land of the Hodenosaunee.[44] Accordingly, in 1707 the Onondagas were interested in renewing their ties to the French, and ensuring that good relations would prevail—despite the ongoing imperial conflict (the War of the Spanish Succession) between the French and the English. The recent death of Jacques Le Ber provided the occasion for a Condolence Council that would achieve these ends.[45]

The unnamed Onondaga orator opened the council by evoking the purpose of the condolence ceremony they were about to conduct, saying, "My father, our custom is to weep when we experience a great loss; do not be surprised therefore to see us weep as we do, it is the custom of our land which your predecessors have always practiced as well as our elders."[46] He then proceeded to offer seven gifts of wampum in succession: the first to "cover" Le Ber; the second, to mourn the land of the French and all those who had died upon it; the third, to kindle a fire to talk of peaceful matters; the fourth and fifth, to banish sorrow and melancholy with strong medicine; and the sixth, to attach a sun in the sky to warm the minds of humans. Lastly, he asked that the French smiths repair their arms.[47]

Vaudreuil's reply the following day approved the conduct of the Onondagas. Reiterating their proposals, the governor gave gifts of wampum to accompany his responses. He mourned the land of the Onondagas, exhorted them to peace at the fire they had kindled, offered a metaphorical emetic to expel all bad thoughts, and stayed the sun in its course so that its light would illuminate the land forever. Vaudreuil's first response to the Onondagas made explicit the Native origin of the protocols of intercultural diplomacy:

> You have said, my children, that your custom was to weep when you experienced a great loss, and that I was not to be surprised to see you weep as you did because it was a custom of your land, that my predecessors had formerly recognized, in order to maintain, by means of this way of weeping for the dead, unity between nations, in that each took part in the losses of the other. I am pleased to see you so inclined towards peace and the good relations I wish to have with you. I thank you for covering the body of Monsieur Le Ber.[48]

Vaudreuil pointed to an important difference between the Hodenosaunee and the French—the pattern of ritualized mourning ("weeping for the dead") that characterized intergroup relations among the Hodenosaunee was "a custom of your land" (but not of his)—yet nonetheless agreed that these exotic practices provided the structures that made intercultural diplomacy possible, for he acknowledged the precedent of his predecessors' participation in councils patterned after the condolence ceremony of the People of the Longhouse.[49]

In council, Native discourse explicitly linked gifts to functions like covering the dead or clearing minds. One could account for the rationality of such overtures of peace on the grounds of a universal human preference—but this would reduce the Onondaga's words and actions to simple metaphor, a deliberately obtuse way of saying something that could be said just as well literally. One could argue that the Onondaga acted thus because custom so dictated, or because he felt instructed to do so by some mythical text, such as the Deganawidah Epic. Indeed, had an outsider demanded explanation, some such text might well be invoked as a means of legitimating his action. Bourdieu's method asks us to view the Onondaga's behavior as a practical effort to mobilize the symbolic schemes of the Hodenosaunee habitus toward the achievement of concrete aims. The performance of the Condolence Council implied that the Onondaga were to the French as one moiety was to another among the Onondaga, or, at another level, among the five Peoples of the Longhouse collectively. As William Fenton writes,

> The typical Iroquois community and tribe had two such moieties, or ways of grouping and serving one another in crises. Moiety functions are mainly ceremonial: they act reciprocally to condole and bury each other's dead; they perform games like lacrosse, which drain internal tensions; and many ritual acts are conceived and acted as one side supporting the other.

This dualistic relationship was homologous with many others in Hodenosaunee society and polity, including the basic division between men and women, between the father's and mother's line of the bilateral nuclear family, and between the forest and the village. The aim of ritual practices was to reconcile the tensions between oppositional categories, to reconstitute society in a harmonious fashion.[50] Although close attention to form may well be a feature of ritual, leading outsiders to deduce the existence of rules governing behavior, it is because actors constantly mobilize the same basic schemes to resolve new problems that practices take on the aura of custom. The process of "invention within limits" creates possibilities for improvisation, and requires the constant monitoring of the reactions of others to one's own actions.[51] In the context of intercultural diplomacy, it meant observing the French reaction to the Condolence Council, and to the gifts of wampum passed across the council fire.

In council, the French carefully reciprocated the gifts of the Onondaga, as they did in every French-Hodenosaunee council of the period without fail. The dispatches of the French governor, however, revealed the different context in which he understood these exchanges. Required to defend himself against charges of corruption, Vaudreuil explained to his superiors in France that the value of wampum, furs, hides, and other things that he received personally in councils with Natives was far less than the cost of bread, wine, tobacco, and other presents that he was obliged to give in return. The cost of diplomatic gifts was perceived as onerous by French officials; in particular, the condolence ceremonies conducted by large Iroquois delegations were deemed burdensome but necessary concessions to diplomacy. The French attitude can only be understood with reference to their practice of calculating the monetary value of these exchanges.[52] In addition to gifts of wampum, the French provided Native diplomats with various services and goods. Although we lack direct evidence in this particular case, we may assume that the Onondagas had their arms repaired by a gunsmith at the expense of the French, who paid qualified smiths a fixed rate for such work.[53] On occasion the canoes of diplomats were also repaired by the French. Moreover, the Onondagas were no doubt boarded at the Montreal residence of the baron Charles Le Moyne de Longueuil, their adopted son, although when Natives of other nations came to Montreal the governor himself was responsible for the keep of the sizable delegations.[54] Finally, Native diplomatic conventions also required hosts to provide parting gifts to traveling ambassadors: in the early eighteenth century, parting gifts given by the French usually mirrored the inventory of trade goods that Natives preferred. From time to time, these goods were itemized in the colonial administration's accounts, where the focus lay on the monetary value of objects, rather than on the recipient or instrumental value of the gift.[55]

There is good evidence that Native peoples also carefully calculated the value of gifts in diplomatic contexts. When a speaker of the Odawa related to Vaudreuil the diplomatic events at Detroit in 1706, he gave detailed accounts of the type and quantity of gifts that were exchanged as the Odawa, Huron, and Miami nations sought to end a conflict that divided them. Another such detailed account was given by a Potawatomi speaker in 1712. In 1717, during a council at Detroit, Odawa and Potawatomi delegates lavished trade goods and wampum upon a group of Miamis, whereas the Huron envoys gave only one white blanket to show that they were unhappy with the settlement.[56] In these accounts, Natives did not calculate value in monetary terms—and yet they acted as though the number and nature of gifts mattered.

According to Bourdieu, "symbolic capital is always *credit*, in the widest sense of the word, i.e. a sort of advance which the group alone can grant those who give it the best material and symbolic *guarantees*."[57] The recognized modes of transforming economic capital into symbolic capital differ, however, from society to society. In societies where exchange is consciously expressed as gift giving, everything takes place as if the significance of a gift resided principally in the manner, timing, and intent with which it is given. By virtue of being similarly disposed to (mis)recognize the exchange of gifts as so many ways of clearing minds, wiping tears from eyes, clearing throats, flattening the land, and so forth, Iroquoians and Algonkians were able to offer each other reasonably good symbolic and material guarantees on any investment of capital. That is, the recipient of a gift was disposed to acknowledge the giver's credit, or future claim. The economic and social consequences of redistribution, which are masked by Native discourse, are nevertheless taken into account in the calculation of credit, since both the giver and recipient are aware of the practical activity, or labor (both spiritual and physical), entailed in the production of different kinds of gifts.

Early eighteenth-century Frenchmen were another matter. The French were no strangers to the symbolic exchanges and credit that served to build clienteles and instill loyalty. It was thus possible for them to perceive the effect of gift giving as a kind of patronage.[58] In many ways, then, intercultural council diplomacy worked smoothly, for both French and Native diplomats were attentive to the reciprocity of investments of symbolic and material capital. But the French were equally disposed to refuse the conversion of economic capital into symbolic capital, or credit. They did this when they spoke, as

Vaudreuil did, of the monetary value of gifts, thus stripping exchange of its social meaning.

The following observation of the Jesuit Joseph-François Lafitau can be explained in terms of a clash over the conventions of converting capital:

> The [Natives] think that no matter of business can be concluded without [wampum] belts of this sort. . . . The Europeans, knowing or caring little about their practices, have upset them somewhat in this respect, by keeping their belts without responding with similar ones. To avoid the inconveniences arising from this, they have adopted the fashion of no longer giving any more than a very small number of the belts, excusing themselves on the grounds that their wampum supply is exhausted. They make up the rest by bundles of buck and deerskin in exchange for which they are given merchandise of little value so that negotiations between the Europeans and them have become a trade.[59]

The Natives to which Lafitau referred were probably the people of Kahnawake, where he lived from 1712 to 1717, for the records of diplomacy involving the French and the Five Nations for that period reveal even exchanges of belts between parties. But this passage is suggestive of the practical difficulties of making symbolic investments when one's partner in the exchange is inclined to perform different calculations in the process of conversion.

The respective habitus of the Hodenosaunee and the French provided each group with schemes that could be strategically mobilized in order to resolve conflicts. The Onondagas' pursuit of symbolic exchanges with the French and their observation of kinship obligations with respect to individual Frenchmen were beneficial to them in obtaining French support in the settlement of conflict with the Odawas of Michilimakinac and the subsequent resumption of peaceful trade through their land. Such a policy was rational to the extent that the French reaction bore some resemblance to the reciprocal bond implied by the Condolence Council. The French policy of selectively adopting the forms of Hodenosaunee diplomatic practice and of engaging in reciprocal gift giving was rational insofar as it accorded with European notions of ceremony and patronage and advanced French imperial aims; yet it was occasionally deemed irrational—at least fiscally so—because of the perceived cost to the Marine treasury. If dissimilar dispositions inevitably muddied the conventional congruences that provided the basis for intercultural business, however, this had not, by the early eighteenth century, provoked an abandonment of these forms.

It is perhaps fitting that a Condolence Council should be the focus of an attempt to negotiate the antimony between rationalistic and romantic

Table 1.

PARTICIPATION OF NATIVE NATIONS IN FIFTY-SIX COUNCILS AT
MONTREAL AND QUEBEC, 1703-25
Number of Councils Attended

Nation	1703–5	1706–10	1711–15	1716–25	Total
Hodenosaunee	1	1	3	2	7
Mohawk	1	1	-	-	2
Oneida	1	-	-	-	1
Onondaga	4	5	1	1	11
Cayuga	2	-	-	-	2
Seneca	4	2	3	1	10
Huron	2	-	2	-	4
Illinois	-	-	1	-	1
Kickapoo	-	-	1	1	2
Menominee	-	2	1	-	3
Miami	2	-	1	1	4
Odawa of Detroit	2	1	1	-	4
Odawa of Michilimackinac	2	4	3	1	10
Potawatomi	1	1	5	2	9
Sauk/Fox	-	1/-	2/1	1/2	4/3
Saulteur (Ojibwa)	-	1	1	1	3

Sources: Archives des colonies (Paris), C11A, Correspondance générale, Canada, vols. 21 to 47, National Archives of Canada, MG 1, microfilm, reels F-21 to F-47; Francis Jennings, William N. Fenton, Mary A. Druke, and David R. Miller, eds., *Iroquois Indians: A Documentary History of the Diplomacy of the Six Nations and Their League* [microform collection] (Woodbridge, Conn.: Research Publications, 1984), reels 6 to 9.

Note: The data for the Hodenosaunee include instances where all five nations were indeed present, as well as councils where the participants were identified only as "Iroquois" (the French term for the Peoples of the Longhouse).

interpretations of Native-European interaction in the northeast. In exploring the theoretical opposition outlined by Bruce Trigger and implied by other scholars, and in arguing for the practical utility of symbols and the mediation of practices by what amounts to a symbolic order, the habitus, I do not intend a call to revisionism. Rather, following a strand of social theory developed by Bourdieu, my aim is to critically address the classifications by which scholars interpret behavior in the hope of building methods for conceptualizing cultural contact, and more specifically, the entanglement of European and Native North American societies in the early modern period. Examining French-Onondaga council diplomacy in the light of Bourdieu's theory of symbolic capital and its conversion, it is possible to see how diplomatic practices of the early eighteenth century entailed symbolic and material exchanges that were rationally motivated, and yet, for all that, rooted in specific cultural schemes.

It has been suggested that in Bourdieu's theory of practice, actors "seem doomed to reproduce their world mindlessly, without its contradictions leaving any mark on their awareness," until a crisis, such as contact with a previously unknown culture, arises.[60] This judgment is perhaps too harsh. Certainly, in *Outline of a Theory of Practice*, the focus is on social reproduction, rather than on cultural transformation. Yet it is precisely for this reason that the model is well suited to diachronic analyses spanning one or several generations—that is, the chronological framework of most historical studies. The evolutionary perspectives of cultural materialists may well suggest that over the long term, societies make "rational" adjustments to ecological and economic circumstances; but this does not mean the principle behind practice can be nothing other than a universal rationality. Instead, such adjustments may be interpreted as the result of complex interactions between external circumstances, practices motivated by the habitus, and the consequences, both intended and unintended, of individual and collective actions.[61] Bourdieu's method offers the possibility of an empirical investigation of sociocultural change, based on a series of studies of the structures of the habitus at different points in time. The persistence of specific symbolic schemes might then be clarified, and reductionist models of ideological transformation considerably nuanced.[62] Finally, Bourdieu's approach suggests criteria for the selective adoption of elements drawn from both "rationalistic" and "romantic" interpretations. The respective insights of materialist social science and interpretive emics are simply too compelling to be abandoned to opposite sides of an increasingly polemical debate. To borrow a phrase from the Requickening Address of the Hodenosaunee, it may be time "to gather the scattered firebrands and rekindle the fire."[63]

Notes

1. I am grateful to Louise Dechêne, Catherine M. Desbarats, Frans Koks, D. Peter MacLeod, and Colin Scott for commenting on earlier versions of this work. I also wish to thank Bruce Trigger for responding to my questions back in May 1994, at a time when I was beginning to work out some of the ideas contained in this paper. Bruce White and the editors of this volume offered invaluable criticism during the period of its revision, which was undertaken with the support of a Social Sciences and Humanities Research Council of Canada Doctoral Fellowship. All translations from the French are my own.

2. Francis Jennings has noted that "the fur trade" is in this sense a misnomer (*The Ambiguous Iroquois Empire* [New York: W. W. Norton, 1984], 61). Bruce White has explored Anishinaubaek and Dakota perspectives on the objects of exchange in "Encounters with Spirits: Ojibwa and Dakota Theories about the French and Their Merchandise," *Ethnohistory* 41, no. 3 (1994): 369–405.

3. George T. Hunt, *The Wars of the Iroquois: A Study in Intertribal Trade Relations* (Madison: University of Wisconsin Press, 1940); Harold A. Innis, *The Fur Trade in Canada: An Introduction to Canadian Economic History*, rev. ed. (Toronto: University of Toronto Press, 1956).

4. Abraham Rotstein, "Trade and Politics: An Institutional Approach," *Western Canadian Journal of Anthropology* 3, no. 1 (1972): 1.

5. The formalist—substantivist debate of the 1960s and 1970s was considerably more complex than this, but was to some extent determined by uncritical definitions of the "economic" and the "political." A contemporary attempt to address the problem of defining "economics" was Robbins Burling, "Maximization Theories and the Study of Economic Anthropology," *American Anthropologist* 64, no. 4 (1962): 802–21. My thanks to Bruce White for providing this article. For a reflection on the theoretical and ideological context of the debate, see Barry L. Isaac, "Retrospective on the Formalist-Substantivist Debate," *Research in Economic Anthropology* 14 (1993): 213–33.

6. Over a decade ago Sherry Ortner suggested that "a new key symbol of theoretical orientation is emerging, which may be labeled 'practice' (or 'action' or 'praxis')." The central concern of this broad trend was to understand how everyday human behavior related to the reproduction of social systems, and to develop an adequate theory of human motivation. "Theory in Anthropology since the Sixties," *Comparative Studies in Society and History* 26, no. 1 (1984): 126–66, esp. 144–60; 127 (quotation).

7. Bruce G. Trigger, *Natives and Newcomers: Canada's "Heroic Age" Reconsidered* (Kingston and Montreal: McGill-Queen's University Press, 1985), 183–94; 193 (quotation).

8. Bruce G. Trigger, *The Children of Aataentsic: A History of the Huron People to 1660*, rev. ed. (Kingston and Montreal: McGill-Queen's University Press, 1987), xix–xx, xxvi–xxvii. See also Bruce G. Trigger, "Early Native North American Responses

to European Contact: Romantic versus Rationalistic Interpretations," *Journal of American History* 77, no. 4 (March 1991): 1195–1215.

9. Trigger, *The Children of Aataentsic*, xx–xxi; Trigger, "Early Native North American Responses," 1196–1200.

10. Other writers have recently challenged the use of rigid oppositional categories in ethnohistory. See especially B. White, "Encounters with Spirits," 370–71, 393–96. A more tentative approach is taken by David Murray, "Through Native Eyes? Indian History/American History," in *Visions of America since 1492*, ed. Deborah L. Madsen (New York: St. Martin's Press, 1994), 57–72.

11. Trigger, *The Children of Aataentsic*, xxi (quotation), xxii.

12. "Although it is impossible for a society to distinguish clearly between its own technological knowledge and other forms of belief, it is the former that has transformed humanity's relations with the natural world, and by doing so, the nature of human society and values." Bruce G. Trigger, "Hyper-relativism, Responsibility, and the Social Sciences," *Canadian Review of Sociology and Anthropology* 26 (1989): 787.

13. Bruce G. Trigger, "Constraint and Freedom—A New Synthesis for Archaeological Explanation," *American Anthropologist* 93, no. 3 (1991): 555–56.

14. To which he adds, "some societies are more consciously oriented toward such a privileging of reason than are others." Trigger, "Early Native North American Responses," 1196.

15. Trigger, "Constraint and Freedom," 555.

16. Ibid., 559.

17. Christopher Miller and George R. Hamell, "A New Perspective on Indian-White Contact: Cultural Symbols and Colonial Trade," *Journal of American History* 73, no. 2 (1986): 312–15; Trigger, *The Children of Aataentsic*, 243–45.

18. Miller and Hamell, "A New Perspective," 316–17, 320–21, 326–27. Hamell has pursued this line of argument further in another paper in which he presumes the existence of a shared precontact Northeastern Woodland Indian cosmology— which he describes—and elaborates a set of speculative propositions that can be summarized as follows: initial Amerindian responses to European trade goods reflected the assimilation of certain goods into a traditional mythical reality; the subsequent influx of symbolically charged trade goods led, however, to a reification of this mythical reality and ultimately to its restructuration (or even its replacement, e.g., by Christianity—described as a kind of cargo cult) so that it might better "fit the present reality of the contact experience." "Strawberries, Floating Islands, and Rabbit Captains: Mythical Realities and European Contact in the Northeast During the Sixteenth and Seventeenth Centuries," *Journal of Canadian Studies* 21, no. 4 (1986–87): 72–94.

19. Trigger, *The Children of Aataentsic*, xxxii–xxiv; Trigger "Early Native North American Responses," 1204–6, 1210 (quotation).

20. Marshall Sahlins, "Cosmologies of Capitalism: The Trans-Pacific Sector of 'The World System,'" in *Culture/Power/History: A Reader in Contemporary Social Theory*, ed. Nicholas B. Dirks, Geoff Eley, and Sherry B. Ortner (Princeton: Princeton University Press, 1994), 413; Marshall Sahlins, *Culture and Practical Reason* (Chicago: University of Chicago Press, 1976), viii.

21. See Marshall Sahlins, *Historical Metaphors and Mythical Realities: Structure in the Early History of the Sandwich Islands Kingdom* (Ann Arbor: University of Michigan Press, 1981). An important aspect of Sahlins's project is the integration of structure and historical process: while structuralist analyses elucidate cultures, historical analyses demonstrate how actors put structures into practice and, in the process, transform them. Some of the issues raised by this and similar projects are obviously connected to questions of practice and to the reason/culture dichotomy I have outlined here: see Nicholas Thomas, *Out of Time: History and Evolution in Anthropological Discourse* (Cambridge: Cambridge University Press, 1989).

22. "The dual messages of anthropology . . . have in part to do with the efforts on the one hand to show that 'primitive' people are rational, despite the manifest conflicts between their beliefs and what we 'know' to be true, and on the other hand to maintain the otherness of the people studied, either out of respect for their concrete way of life or as a mirror for our own." Craig Calhoun, "Habitus, Field, and Capital: The Question of Historical Specificity," in *Bourdieu: Critical Perspectives*, ed. Craig Calhoun, Edward LiPuma, and Moishe Postone (Chicago: University of Chicago Press, 1993), 61–88; 65 (quotation).

23. "The work of Marshall Sahlins has influenced my ideas on these matters." Matthew Dennis, *Cultivating a Landscape of Peace: Iroquois-European Relations in Seventeenth-Century America* (Ithaca and London: Cornell University Press, 1993), 85n. 20.

24. Ibid., 224, 227 (quotation).

25. Ibid., 268. Marshall Sahlins is again on hand to consecrate this alleged ideological transformation (269).

26. "'Cultural dope' is a term used by [Anthony] Giddens to refer to the image of the actor as a robot in the work of the sociologist Talcott Parsons." Stanley R. Barrett, *The Rebirth of Anthropological Theory* (Toronto: University of Toronto Press, 1984), 12n. 1.

27. Richard White, *The Middle Ground: Indians, Empires, and Republics in the Great Lakes Region, 1650–1815* (Cambridge: Cambridge University Press, 1991), 50, 56 (quotation), 80–82, 87, 90, 93, 323 (quotation). White also likens the customary world of the middle ground to the notion of an "invented tradition" (323n. 16).

28. For reference to this dichotomy, see ibid., ix. For theoretical orientations, see 52n. 4.

29. For the argument against material dependence, see ibid., 128–41. The "subversive" nature of European goods adopted by Natives is mentioned (103–4), but does not become a central part of the analysis.

30. For a bibliography of Bourdieu's works and discussion of his methods, see Richard Harker, Cheleen Mahar, and Chris Wilkes, eds., *An Introduction to the Work of Pierre Bourdieu: The Practice of Theory* (New York: St. Martin's Press, 1990), and Calhoun, LiPuma, and Postone, eds., *Bourdieu*.

31. Pierre Bourdieu, *The Logic of Practice*, trans. R. Nice (Cambridge: Polity Press, 1990), 56. See also Charles Taylor, "To Follow a Rule . . . ," in Calhoun, LiPuma, and Postone, eds. *Bourdieu*, 45–60.

32. Having made this analytical distinction between reason and culture, Trigger notes that it is not always possible to distinguish the effects of one from the other: over time, recurrent rational decisions may become culturally encoded, while "irrational" conventions may actually serve utilitarian ends (Trigger, *The Children of Aataentsic*, xxi). Clearly, the exercise of reason, or the attuning of actions with objective possibilities, is bound up with the many manifestations of culture, such as myths, proverbs, legends, scientific theories, and so on.

33. Pierre Bourdieu, *Outline of a Theory of Practice*, trans. R. Nice (Cambridge: Cambridge University Press, 1977), 80–94. Gender is deeply implicated in the elaboration of many such schemes, as indicated in Bourdieu's interpretation of the Kabyle house (*The Logic of Practice*, 271–83). See also Françoise Héritier, *Masculin/féminin: la pensée de la différence* (Paris: Odile Jacob, 1996).

34. Bourdieu, *Outline*, 76–78, 123–24. Thus Bourdieu's model of practice is situated between the possibility of "unpredictable novelty," which is implicit in rationalist models, and on the other hand the model of near-mechanical cultural reproduction. It is "invention within limits." Bourdieu, *Outline*, 95–96.

35. Ibid., 180; Bruce M. White, "'A Skilled Game of Exchange': Ojibway Fur Trade Protocol," *Minnesota History* 50 (1987): 230.

36. Bourdieu, *Outline*, 184.

37. Ibid., 183–94. Here Bourdieu echoes the classic statement of reciprocal gift giving as a feature of societies everywhere: Marcel Mauss, *The Gift: The Form and Reason for Exchange in Archaic Societies,* foreword by Mary Douglas, trans. W. D. Halls (London: Routledge, 1990).

38. "Parmy ces anciens sont les chefs de guerre, ils le deviennent par les belles actions qu'ils font, par l'amitié de la jeunesse qu'ils s'attirent par les présents qu'ils leurs font; car ordinairement ces chefs sont les plus mal vêtus de la nation donnant tout pour se faire aimer." Camille de Rochemonteix, ed. *Relation par lettres de l'Amérique septentrionale (années 1709 et 1710)* (Paris: Letouzey et Ané, 1904), 82. For a similar description of Native leadership that stresses the virtue of liberality, see "Abrégé de la vie et coustumes des sauvages du Canada," [1723], Archives des Colonies (France) [hereafter AC], C11A, 45, f° 172v.

39. Cf. Robin Ridington, "The Medicine Fight: An Instrument of Political Process among the Beaver Indians," *American Anthropologist* 70, no. 6 (1968): 1152–60; reprinted in *Little Bit Know Something: Stories in a Language of Anthropology* (Iowa City: University of Iowa Press, 1990). See Pierre Clastres, *Archeology of Violence*, trans. Jeanine Herman (New York: Semiotext(e), 1994), chap. 8, esp. 112–18 for

a reflection on power and debt in "societies without a State." Mary Druke has used historical sources to describe Hodenosaunee expectations of leaders in the colonial period: "Structure and Meaning of Leadership among the Mohawk and Oneida during the Mid-Eighteenth Century," (Ph.D. diss., University of Chicago, 1982), 132–41.

40. See table 1 for French-Native councils in this period. For descriptions of council diplomacy, see Michael K. Foster, "On Who Spoke First at Iroquois-European Councils: An Exercise in the Method of Upstreaming," in *Extending the Rafters: Interdisciplinary Approaches to Iroquoian Studies*, ed. Michael K. Foster, J. Campisi, and M. Mithun (Albany: State University of New York Press, 1984), 183–207; Michael K. Foster, "Another Look at the Function of Wampum in Iroquois-White Councils," in *The History and Culture of Iroquois Diplomacy*, eds. F. Jennings, William N. Fenton, Mary A. Druke, and David R. Miller. (Syracuse: Syracuse University Press, 1985), 99–114; and Daniel Richter, *The Ordeal of the Longhouse: The Peoples of the Iroquois League in the Era of European Colonization* (Chapel Hill: University of North Carolina Press, 1992), 39–49.

41. Hodenosaunee delegations came to Montreal to mourn governor Louis-Hector de Callière in 1704, Paul Le Moyne de Maricourt in 1704, Jacques Le Ber in 1707, the Jesuit Jacques de Lamberville in 1710, female family members of Louis-Thomas Chabert de Joncaire and Louis Maray de La Chauvignerie in 1712, Louis XIV in 1717, Claude de Ramezay in 1725, and governor Vaudreuil in 1727.

42. "Nous nous resouvenons cependant notre père de ce qui a esté dit à la paix générale, que vous teniez tous vos enfans sous vos esselles, et que le premier qui se trouveroit offencé, ne se vangeroit pas par ses mains, mais qu'il viendroit s'en plaindre à vous, c'est ce que nous sommes venus faire par ce collier." Parolles de la grande terre . . . du 18e octobre 1704, AC, C11A, 22, f° 52.

43. After separate councils with Vaudreuil, the Hodenosaunee and Odawas met together to arrange the reparations. Parolles des outaouais aux Iroquois du 23e aoust 1705 [et] Reponces des Iroquois, AC, C11A, 22, f° 255–255v.Vaudreuil had served as the go-between, presenting a parcel of beaver pelts, a belt of wampum, and a red calumet to the Hodenosaunee on behalf of the Odawa as a means of opening a channel of communication between the two groups. Parolles des out-auois de michilimakina . . . du 22e aoust 1705, AC, C11A, 22, f° 261.

44. Richter, *Ordeal of the Longhouse*, 223.

45. Jacques Le Ber (ca. 1633–1706) arrived in Canada in 1657 and married the sister of Charles Le Moyne de Longueuil the following year. He became a prominent Montreal merchant and was a lessee of Fort Frontenac after 1682. Yves F. Zoltvany, "Jacques Le Ber," *Dictionary of Canadian Biography*, 14 vols. to date (Toronto: University of Toronto Press, 1966–1994), 2:389–91. Le Ber's nephew, the Baron de Longueuil, was adopted by the Onondagas in the late seventeenth century.

46. "Mon père, nostre coustume est de pleurer quand nous faisons une perte consid-érable, ne soyés pas surpris si vous nous voyez pleurer comme nous faisons, c'est

la coustume de nostre pays que vos prédécesseurs ont toujours pratiqués aussy bien que nos anciens." Parolles des sauvages Onnontagués à Monsieur le gouverneur général le 16e aoust 1707, AC, C11A, 26, f° 86.

47. The term wampum refers to tubular beads made of marine shells. These beads could be strung together to form something resembling a rosary ("une branche de porcelaine") or woven to form belts (referred to by the French as "colliers de porcelaine"). Although similar European glass beads were available, the descriptions of eighteenth-century observers like Bacqueville de La Potherie and Pierre François-Xavier de Charlevoix indicate that the Hodenosaunee continued to use marine shells from the Atlantic coastline to manufacture wampum belts for use in councils. Claude-Charles Le Roy [Bacqueville de La Potherie], *Histoire de l'Amérique septentrionale*, 4 vols., (Paris: Nion, Didot, 1722; facsimile ed., Ann Arbor: University Microfilms, 1969), 3:34–35; Pierre F.-X. de Charlevoix, *Histoire et description générale de la Nouvelle-France avec le journal historique d'un voyage fait par ordre du roi dans l'Amérique septentrionale*, 6 vols. (Paris: Nyon, P.-F. Giffard, 1744; reprint, 3 vols., Ottawa: Éditions Élysée, 1976), 3:209–10.

48. "Vous m'avés dit bien mes enfans que vostre coutume estoit de plûrer quand vous faisiés quelque perte considérable, et que je ne devois pas estre surpris de vous voir plurer comme vous faisiez parce que c'estoit une coutume de vostre pays, que mes prédécesseurs avoient mesme authorisée autrefois, afin d'entretenir par cette façon de pleurer les morts, l'union parmy les nations en prenant part aux pertes que l'on fait les uns, et les autres, je suis bien aise de vous voir dans les sentiments si conformes au bien de la paix, et à la bonne intelligence que je veux tousjours entretenir avec vous, je vous remercie d'avoir couvert le corps de Mr Lebert." Reponce de Monsieur le gouverneur général aux sauvages Onnontagués du 17e aoust 1707, AC, C11A, 26, f° 87v.

49. For the Condolence Council as a paradigm for diplomatic councils, see William N. Fenton, "Structure, Continuity and Change in the Process of Iroquois Treaty Making," in *The History and Culture of Iroquois Diplomacy*, ed. Francis Jennings, William N. Fenton, Mary A. Druke, and David R. Miller, 3–36, esp. 18–19. Such councils between the People of the Longhouse and the French had occurred since the mid-seventeenth century.

50. Fenton, "Structure, Continuity, and Change," 9–14; 10 (quotation). See also Richter, *Ordeal of the Longhouse*, 18–23; and Dean R. Snow, *The Iroquois* (Cambridge, Mass.: Blackwell, 1994), 5. For a cogent historical analysis of ritual as a means of reconciling the "dynamic tensions" or contradictions inherent in any sociocultural order, see Jean Comaroff, *Body of Power, Spirit of Resistance: The Culture and History of a South African People* (Chicago and London: University of Chicago Press, 1985).

The French colonial archives contain a document dated to 1666 that outlines the nine "families" of the "Iroquois nation"; it is in fact a description of the clans ("familles") and moieties ("bandes") of the Seneca, and includes copies of Seneca pictographs illustrating the meeting of clans in council and the use of wampum. AC, C11A, 2, f° 263–69. The pictographs are reproduced in William N. Fenton,

"Northern Iroquoian Culture Patterns," in *Handbook of North American Indians*, vol. 15: *Northeast*, ed. Bruce G. Trigger (Washington, D.C.: Smithsonian Institution, 1978), 299.

51. Fenton, "Structure, Continuity, and Change," 28; Bourdieu, *Outline*, 16–17.

52. Vaudreuil to Pontchartrain, 14 November 1709, *Rapport de l'Archiviste de la Province de Québec* (1942–43): 438–39; Louvigny's complaint about Iroquois condolence councils following the deaths of Ramezay, Longueuil's own wife, and Vaudreuil is in his dispatch to the council, 31 October 1725, AC, C11A, 47, f° 133–133v. See also Catherine M. Desbarats, "The Cost of Early Canada's Native Alliances: Reality and Scarcity's Rhetoric," *William and Mary Quarterly*, 3d ser., 52, no. 4 (1995): 609–30.

53. See Begon to Council of Marine, 13 November 1717, AC, C11A, 37, f° 64, for a reference to the smith Pierre Gauvereau, "le seul bon armurier qui soit à Québec," who was retained by the Crown to repair Native weapons according to a fixed tariff that was considerably lower than the colonial market value for his services. At Detroit, the commandant was required to maintain a smith at his own expense, along with an intepreter. Both were crucial in intercultural diplomacy. Vaudreuil and Begon to council of Marine, 26 October 1719, AC, C11A, 40, f° 58v–59.

54. Like other French agents among the People of the Longhouse, Longueuil requested and received special allowances (gratifications) from the king to cover the expense of maintaining visiting diplomats.

55. See, for example, "Estat de la depense qui a esté faitte pour accomoder l'affaire des Outa8as du Saguinan qui avoient tuez des Miamis," Detroit, 15 September 1717, AC, C11A, 39, f° 30–31. During the 1730s and 1740s, the intendant Gilles Hocquart kept fastidious accounts of gifts and services provided to Native diplomats and warriors. Desbarats, "The Cost of Early Canada's Native Alliances," 618–27.

56. Parolles de Miscouaky . . . le 26 Septembre 1706, AC, C11A, 24, f° 246–49; Parolles de Makisabé chef P8t8atamis du 17 aoust 1712, AC, C11A, 33, f° 86v–88v; Vaudreuil to the Council of Marine, 30 October 1718, AC, C11A, 39, f° 152v–153v.

57. Bourdieu, *Outline*, 181. *Crédit* is also the word used to describe the prestige that French diplomats acquired with Native groups.

58. Cornelius J. Jaenen has indicated that "French culture attached great importance to etiquette, precedence, and protocol, so that there was an immediate receptivity and appreciation of North American formalities and practices in this domain. There seems to have been a genuine enjoyment on the part of certain pompous governors of the protracted ceremonies," which included gift giving. "The Role of Presents in French-Amerindian Trade," in *Explorations in Canadian Economic History*, ed., Duncan Cameron (Ottawa: University of Ottawa Press, 1985), 232. See also Sharon Kettering, "Gift-giving and Patronage in Early Modern France," *French History* 2, no. 2 (1988): 131–51.

59. Joseph-Francois Lafitau, *Customs of the American Indians Compared with the Customs of Primitive Times* [1724], 2 vols., ed. & trans. W. N. Fenton and E. C. Moore, (Toronto: Champlain Society, 1974–77), 1:311.

60. Comaroff, *Body of Power*, 5–6.

61. This is how I construe Bourdieu's call for "a complete description . . . of the relations between the habitus, as a socially constituted system of cognitive and motivating structures, and the socially structured situation in which the agents' interests are defined, and with them the objective functions and subjective motivations of their practices." *Bourdieu*, 76.

62. The history of Native-European encounters in northeastern North America may in fact prove to be too restricted an arena in which to implement the kind of project required by Bourdieu's method. In particular, it is by no means clear that the data regarding Native societies of the seventeenth and eighteenth centuries will bear the weight of interpretations that, like Bourdieu's, rely on detailed ethnographic fieldwork.

63. The eleventh matter of the Requickening Address of the Six Nations (Brantford), quoted in Elisabeth Tooker, "The League of the Iroquois: Its History, Politics, and Ritual," in *Handbook of North American Indians*, vol. 15: *Northeast*, 438.

Laura Peers[1] Fur Trade History, Native History, ⫯ Public History: Communication and Miscommunication

AS MICHAEL PAYNE noted at the Sixth Fur Trade Conference, fur trade history has always been closely connected to public history sites.[2] One of the most important recent developments in both fur trade historiography and public history has been a new focus on First Nations/Native American[3] cultures and histories. Since 1994, I have been analyzing the messages communicated about Native people at a number of reconstructed "living history" sites that use costumed staff to interpret period buildings. Historically, these were places of interaction between Native peoples and Europeans. They are still such places, but today they are tourist destinations, places where history is enacted for education and entertainment. Adding Native interpretation to public history sites has resulted in complex interactions between fur trade history, Native history, and public history.

The sites I have been working at are scattered across the Great Lakes in Canada and the United States, range temporally across two centuries, and, historically, involved several different Native peoples. Colonial Michilimackinac, now tucked under the bridge that spans the Straits of Mackinac in Michigan, was an eighteenth-century nexus for the Great Lakes fur trade, where diplomacy and corn to fuel the canoe brigades were as much a part of the fur trade as furs. Hundreds of Odawa, Ojibwa, Métis, and other Great Lakes peoples came to this site every year to trade, visit, and negotiate political agreements. The North West Company Fur Post, located between modern Minneapolis and Duluth in Minnesota, was the tiny wintering quarters of John Sayer, his Ojibwa wife, and a few staff in 1804–5, while they traded with local Ojibwa people. Old Fort William in present-day Thunder Bay, Ontario, was the North West Company's western depot, a thriving little community of Europeans, mixed-blood people, and Ojibwa whose numbers swelled with the annual rendezvous of the canoe brigades each summer. It has been reconstructed to depict aspects of life as it is thought to have been

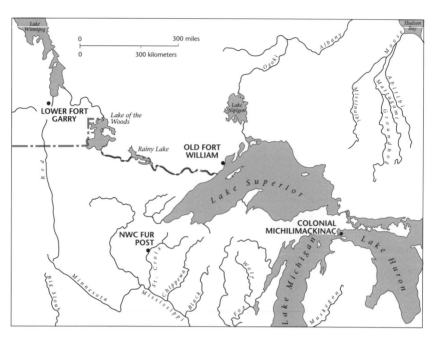

***Figure 1.* Locations of Reconstructed Fur Trade Sites.**

like in and around the post in the summer of 1815. Lower Fort Garry is just north of Winnipeg, Manitoba; it was a Hudson's Bay Company depot and provisioning post for the western trade, and now interprets the 1850s and the local Ojibwa and northern Cree peoples who lived nearby. My analysis of these sites has relied on data gathered through participant observation, archival and secondary source research, and interviews with administrators, interpreters, support staff, scholars, and visitors.

These four reconstructions were chosen for this study to examine whether, despite being in different countries and operated by diverse heritage agencies, they focused on similar messages about the fur trade and the roles of Native people in it. They are representative of several dozen historic sites across the continent that have added Native interpretation programs since the mid-1980s. The sites are operated by federal (Lower Fort Garry), provincial, and state (the three others) heritage agencies, are of different sizes (the North West Company post has just one palisaded rowhouse, while Old Fort William has 42 buildings) and have visitor numbers ranging from 15,000 at the North West Company Fur Post to 120,000 at Colonial Michilimackinac. Despite such disparities, these four sites have gone through similar processes of development in adding Native interpretation, and they communicate similar information about Native peoples and Native-White relations in the past.

Historic reconstructions offer a compelling medium to explore past lives, to experience the physical details of everyday life in the past, and to engage visitors in direct, face-to-face communication about history. These are exciting places, where academic research on the fur trade can be disseminated to a wider audience. Since the early 1980s, fur trade studies have emphasized the experiences and agency of Native peoples in the trade and the nature of their interactions with Europeans. The knowledge gained from this research has not only enhanced our understanding of the past, but has the potential to teach and affect the approximately 350,000 people who visit these four places each year. As my interviews with visitors revealed, the vast majority of them have never before had the opportunity to speak to a Native person, and derive what little they know of Native cultures from popular media and stereotypes. The basic messages that fur trade sites can communicate about Native peoples—that Native people adapted creatively to the trade, that some Natives and Whites were able to bridge cultural differences, that Native people were astute traders, and that Native people had sophisticated cultures of their own—are often new ideas to visitors. This is information that can help to change the continuing negative assumptions about Native peoples that still sour Native-White relations and maintain inequalities in North American society.

Today, the four reconstructions examined here use Native interpreters and dwellings to interpret the historic presence and roles of Native people. This is a recent development that has taken place since the mid-1980s at most sites, although Old Fort William's Native encampment was begun in the mid-1970s. Such change reflects the shift within historiography since the 1960s and 1970s toward the inclusion of minority peoples and their historic experiences, as well as efforts by Native peoples since the 1970s to gain control over public and scholarly representation of their cultures and pasts. Part of a worldwide trend within the global context of decolonization, Native peoples across North America have critically explored and problematized the relationship between the dominant elements of nation-states and their academic and public representations of minority groups.[4]

This has been an especially contentious issue for museums and historic reconstructions, as Native people have challenged the traditional authority of curators, the messages communicated by exhibits, and the very function of museums.[5] Native people now demand to be consulted and included in planning and implementing exhibitions and interpretive programs at historic sites and museums. As well as seeking to change the relationship between heritage institutions and themselves, Native people seek to change the narratives told by these places, to voice their own perspectives on history and the complex relationship between past and present.[6] Lower Fort Garry, Old Fort William, Colonial Michilimackinac, and the North West Company Fur Post have all found themselves in the middle of these demands and changes.

The recently added Native encampments and staff at these reconstructions have, however, been grafted onto sites that were originally intended to tell episodes in the history of the dominant society and its conquest of North America. For many decades, the fur trade was portrayed in both history texts and historic sites as the introduction of European commerce and culture into the heart of the continent as a prelude to settlement, a "link between savage wilderness and civilization."[7] In this older narrative, the fur trade became a vehicle by which Europeans penetrated the wilderness, brought North America into a global market, and came to possess the continent. Alternatively, fur trade posts were interpreted as the beginning of European civilization in the wilderness, as rough-hewn pioneer villages with beaver skins.[8] Lower Fort Garry, for instance, was interpreted for some time as "a little Scottish village on the Red River."[9]

This portrayal of the fur trade as a foundation of national history emphasized the deeds of European men and downplayed the roles of Native people. This is typical of national history as a genre, which reinforces the identity of members of the dominant class and legitimates the existence of the nation and its control over its territory and the peoples within its boundaries.[10] National histories thus tend to efface and deny the very different perspectives on the past that colonized groups acquire. As Randall McGuire notes, "just because two peoples share a common history does not mean that they shared a common experience."[11] The history of the fur trade has traditionally not been told—either in texts or in the form of "living history"—from the perspectives of Native people. On the contrary, historic sites have tended to be funded by various levels of government: they have been *state* or *national* historic sites, voices of the dominant society, and they have traditionally advertised themselves with claims of authenticity, stating that they portray history "as it really was."

The four reconstructed fur trade posts considered here were rebuilt in the 1960s and 1970s to commemorate themes in national history, and with their palisades, their large buildings, their cannons and muskets, they present a perspective grounded in the dominant society, and do indeed tell part of the story of the European conquest of North America. Given this context, the addition of a Native presence to these sites, and the particular messages they communicate about Native people in the fur trade, becomes a subject of great interest. Initially, the non-Native administrators of several of these sites intended to include Native people, but only as examples of friends or foes of European expansion. In early displays, administrators did not expect Native people to tell their very different historical experiences.[12]

In theory, the addition of Native interpreters and encampments to historic reconstructions is intended to allow Native people to voice their perspectives on the past. But how well is this process working? What messages are actually communicated about the fur trade and Native people? What intrigues me most about this study is that despite having different vantages on the fur trade, and despite their unique contemporary situations, all of these sites deliver similar messages about Native people in the fur trade. In the portrayal of Native life and Native-White relations, they show patterned, consistent differences between the roles that Native people are known to have fulfilled in the past, and those portrayed at the reconstructions, as well as between the nature of Native-White relations in the past and those shown in the present.

Like other "living history" sites, all of these places use reconstructed living and work areas of fur trade posts, furnished with reproduction possessions and trade goods, and staffed by people in period clothes representing persons who would have lived and worked there, to interpret the fur trade to modern visitors. Artifacts and activities related to the fur trade and Native people are quite standard, even generic. There are trade goods, of which the most consistently seen are beads, cloth, blankets, powder and shot, trade silver, traps, knives, and axes; fur traders, voyageurs, and their personal possessions; and one or more Native house structures to show the material culture of the people who would have traded there. Costumed interpreters display typical Native daily activities and technology of the place and era, usually including cooking, tanning hides, packing furs, making bark containers, and sewing moccasins.

While the physical details of the fur trade that are depicted are well researched and evocative, they seem too uniform. True, the material culture of the trade was relatively standard, at least in terms of the types of goods involved and the types of activities performed at certain posts. Still, it seems simplistic and misleading to represent the complexity of the fur trade by an insistently repetitive set of artifacts consisting of a blanket, a beaver hide on a stretcher, some beads, and a musket. I suspect that this portrayal of a generic fur trade material culture exists partly because of the commonalities in fur post inventories, but partly also because such goods have iconic meanings that resonate with the public's (and, until the last few decades, with scholars') expectations of the fur trade. Blankets, beads, axes, guns, and shot represent to visitors tokens of the civilization offered by fur traders to the savages in the wilderness; they connote the still-popular assumption that Native people became dependent on European trade goods; and they thus affirm the underlying assumption that European cultures have always been superior to those of "Others."

Furthermore, the intensely detailed and evocative portrayal of life and material culture that these reconstructions excel at redirects the visitor's gaze away from the actual human and intercultural relationships involved in the fur trade, and the way in which such relationships created the historical situation that is recreated.[13] When visitors watch dramatic cannon firings by men in elaborate uniforms, they seldom ask what the relationship between the military and Native people was at the site historically; when they see women working in painstakingly reconstructed period kitchens, they seldom ask who these women are (were they Native? Métis? European?) and how they came to live and work inside the fort. Reconstructed buildings and interiors should be a backdrop for the interpretation of the Native-White relations involved in the establishment and maintenance of trading posts. Trading goods and shops should be the basis for showing the act of trading itself; not just the simple exchange, but the personal relationships and local politics involved.

Historic sites also show a patterned minimization of the numbers of Native people and the size of local Native encampments. Despite the fact that all of these forts were, in their historic incarnations, small islands of Europeans surrounded and visited by large Native populations, the Native areas at these sites today are all very small compared with the reconstructed European areas. While the European areas tend to be recreated in meticulous detail, matching the building sizes to archaeological foundation marks, the Native camps tend to be much more representative: examples of kinds of lodges or seasonal ways of life rather than replicas of specific camps or populations at specific historical moments. This disparity is partly due to the fact that the European parts of the sites were reconstructed first, during the 1960s and 1970s, which one Parks Canada historian refers to as "the era of the big budget,"[14] while the Native encampments have been added more recently, during an era of severe budget cuts. Old Fort William, for instance, has increased the size and quality of the Ojibwa camp recently, but budgets are simply not what they once were: the camp still has just four conical bark-covered lodges and two work areas in its camp, while the area inside the palisade includes forty-two large, imposing buildings. Unfortunately, such disparity conveys the impression that there were very few Native people around fur posts, and that they were relatively unimportant and powerless.

All four reconstructions also show Native people as playing limited roles in the fur trade. Native people brought in furs to these sites, we are told, and furs we see—despite the fact that at Lower Fort Garry, Old Fort William, and Colonial Michilimackinac, the food and other country produce they brought was at least as important as furs (and, in fact, the areas around the forts had long been trapped out by the eras that their reconstructions now depict). Even when interpreters say this, their actions deny it. At Old Fort William, for instance, one of the daily dramas is a fur trading session that originates in the Ojibwa camp, although everyone in the encampment will tell you there was not much to be trapped around there in 1815. Food items and goods such as hides, bark, or pitch are seldom represented in quantities that suggest these goods were traded. By downplaying the role of Native people in supplying food to traders, these sites undermine their claims that Native peoples and Europeans were interdependent in the fur trade. Given that the trade in European goods is depicted but the trade in country food is not, visitors are quite likely to conclude from what they see that Europeans were independent of Native peoples, but that Native people were dependent on Europeans for trade goods. Not only has the simplicity of this assumption been challenged in recent scholarly literature, but it suggests, again, the more basic and problematic notion that European peoples and cultures were superior to Native peoples and their cultures.

These themes are reinforced by the tendency of historic sites to focus on Native domesticity in their interpretation even when much of the Native presence at fur posts was for political negotiation, visiting kin, or performing labor. Each of these four reconstructions has added an Ojibwa or Odawa living area, complete with dwellings and typical furnishings, but none makes clear the fact that Ojibwa and Odawa people came there for many different reasons. Again, the emphasis on material culture obscures the reasons for the Native presence there. Nor do the sites examine the importance of social and political ties between Native and non-Native people for the continued operation of the fur trade, or the ways in which Native people were and were not part of life at the site in general.

That sites steer away from interpreting such aspects of history is confirmed by the fact that Natives and non-Natives are virtually always shown on opposite sides of the palisade. Not only are the encampments placed well outside the palisade (at Old Fort William, for instance, the Ojibwa encampment and its bark lodges is literally in the forest, while the fort, with its squared-log and frame buildings and farm area, is in a clearing), but interaction between Native people and Europeans or Métis is seldom shown. The North West Company Fur Post is the only site to depict Native people inside the palisades on a regular basis, and European characters in any of the Native encampments are an even rarer sight. I have only ever seen one instance of meaningful interaction depicted between a Native person and a fur trader at any of these sites, even at those, such as Colonial Michilimackinac, that interpret the Métis (which must lead visitors to wonder how the Métis came to exist).

Interpretation at all reconstructions currently depicts a social and racial gulf between Europeans and Native peoples that denies the extraordinarily cross-cultural nature of the trade. Such separations reinforce the old dichotomy between the related concepts of European-civilization-history and Native-savagery-wilderness that is at the root of so much North American historical writing. They also make less believable the themes, popular in planning documents and visitor guidebooks, that the Native people shown were allies of the Europeans, and that Natives and Europeans were interdependent in the trade.

It would be far more accurate to portray some of the many different kinds of interactions between peoples in the fur trade and the cultural borrowings, syntheses, and adaptations these sparked, than to suggest that Native people and Europeans only ever came face to face over the trading counter. Furthermore, if Natives are to be depicted as allies, it is necessary to show the workings of such alliances: let us see Native decision making, intercultural friendships, Native provision of essential foodstuffs to Europeans, and the complexities of cross-cultural relationships (a fur trader dealing with an Ojibwa father-in-law, for instance). It would also be instructive to depict the darker side of these relations: suspicions, hostility, and attempts to control the trade and its politics by both sides. Right now, despite the contributions of fur trade social history to our understanding of the trade, and despite the willingness of administrators and staff to try to interpret a Native presence, I fear that what we have are still essentialized, if not stereotyped, cardboard cutouts: trader, Indian, voyageur, squaw.

The danger of communicating fur trade social history with such a simplistic perspective is that it meshes so well with the expectations of visitors. Those expectations, unfortunately, are often composed of an equal blend of ignorance and stereotypes. Visitors readily expressed their preconceptions about Native people and the fur trade in interviews, as well as directly to interpreters, both Native and non-Native.[15] To most visitors, these sites certainly do exemplify the old narrative of the fur trade as a stage in the conquest of North America: they have only to point to the palisades or walls around all of the reconstructions to raise their preconceived, American-frontier notion of Native-white relations. The function of palisades is probably the most frequently asked question by visitors, and of all the painstaking historical research by scholars that goes into a site, palisades are certainly the most evocative features for visitors. At Lower Fort Garry, where the outer stone wall is quite close to the trading shop, visitors often glance at the musket hanging over the counter and then back outside at the wall, and ask the "clerk," "I guess everyone around here had one of those to keep the Indians out, eh?"

In this still-widespread perception, the fur trade, "Indians," palisades, and muskets feature in a standard Hollywood Western plot line about the frontier. The frontier is popularly thought of as a place deep in the wilderness, to which European settlers brought the light of civilization, of Christianity, of Western technology, and of agriculture. As Richard White has noted, we have imbued such things as covered wagons and log cabins with "latent narratives" about "migration, primitive beginnings, and ultimate progress."[16] For centuries, the frontier has been thought of in the popular imagination as "the engine of progress and the domain of real men who dominated other men and nature. . . ."[17] The "real men," of course, were European; those dominated were Native. The frontier has come to be thought of as a sort of crucible for North American society: a place and process heated by conflict with Native peoples over access to land and resources. Our image of the frontier contains within it a set of power structures: it was a place of violent race relations, of the necessary conquest of wilderness and savages to establish European civilization.

These living history sites are visited largely by Euro-Americans and Euro-Canadians: the four considered here receive about 350,000 visitors annually, of which well over 90 percent are Caucasian. As is typical of visitor profiles at other historic reconstructions, about half of the visitors have some post-secondary education and an average household income of $50,000 or more, figures well above the average for the North American population.[18] In short, the majority of visitors to these reconstructions are members of the dominant society.

Very few of these visitors have ever met a Native person or have any detailed knowledge about Native cultures, either past or present. They derive what information they have from popular media—movies, novels, the news—and from stereotypes about Native people that are woven into the fabric of North American culture. As result, at historic sites one hears—repeatedly and constantly—visitors war-whooping, greeting costumed Native staff by saying, "How!," making comments about braves and squaws and scalping, and asking questions about the efficacy of Native technology ("how do you stay warm in winter?"). As visitors move from the Native to the non-Native areas, they also comment on what they see as the contrast between the "primitive" way of life in the encampment and the more "civilized" way of life inside the palisades. This discourse assumes the social and technological inferiority of Native cultures, and that peoples of European descent "naturally" and rightfully dominated (and dominate) Native peoples.

Given visitors' predilection for such responses, it is not enough to stock a carefully reconstructed post with exact replicas of items that were used there: sites need to be aware of what messages visitors actually receive from the artifacts displayed and from the different areas of a site, and act accordingly. It is too easy to assume that if one gets the physical details of a place correctly reconstructed, then one is also telling the correct story about the site, when in fact those objects are acting as commonly understood symbols that simply reinforce stereotypes.[19]

At Colonial Michilimackinac, for example, where the Native encampment is rather sketchily representative of the historic Native presence at the site, administrators included a war post when they built the camp in 1991–92. While the war post is there, certain other aspects of Native life at Michilimackinac are not represented in the camp: there are no councils shown, no visits with Métis or European kin inside the palisade, no quantities of corn being traded. By itself, without evidence of other aspects of Native life, the war post suggests savagery and the worst stereotypes about Native peoples. This is the exact opposite of the historic theme that it is intended to suggest, which is alliance with the British and "Native contributions to British military efforts from Michilimackinac during the American Revolution."[20] For the majority of visitors with whom I spoke, however, the war post suggests Native attacks on Europeans rather than Native military support of Europeans.

The miscommunication surrounding the war post reminds us of the need to focus on the actual processes of communication between these places, their furnishings, interpreters, and visitors. At historic reconstructions, which privilege physical artifacts and sensations, interaction between visitors and interpreters almost always begins with a question about an artifact or a building ("What is that?" "Isn't it cold in here in winter?"). The best interpreters use these questions to link what the visitor sees to the historic forces that produced the era interpreted at the site. Site staff need to think carefully not just about documentary research on material culture, but on which items of material culture can be used to communicate desired themes and information—and how to deal with documented items that send the wrong messages.

There is, then, a set of common images and artifacts used to represent Native peoples in the fur trade, a standard way of spatially organizing the sites, and a set of messages that is repeated at each reconstructed fur post. These commonalities transcend the histories and contemporary politics and situations of individual sites. European participation in the fur trade is over-represented; Native participation is underrepresented. European reliance on Native labor, on political and social relations with Native people, and on the crucial food and country goods supplied by Native people is likewise under-represented. Interpreters' verbal messages attempt to compensate for the physical distortions of the past that visitors see at these places, but are under-mined by the physical evidence and the popular narratives about the past that reconstructions conjure up for visitors. Like the artifacts that are chosen to furnish reproduction dwellings, historic sites are in many ways superficially authentic, highly selective in their representation of the past, and communi-cate problematic (and often inaccurate) messages. While the addition of Native encampments is intended to add perspectives that have traditionally been omitted from the writing and enactment of history, actually doing this and communicating a more balanced view of the fur trade or Native per-spectives on the trade is evidently more complex than site administrators had anticipated.

Similarly, while eager to add Native staff, perspectives, and interpretation, sites are not yet dealing with the dynamics and implications of placing Native people on display for a largely non-Native visitorship. The public display of Native peoples and cultures has a long history, and has generally been con-trolled by Europeans and emphasized stereotyped and exoticised images of Native peoples. Such displays began shortly after contact with the kidnapping of Native people to be kept as living curiosities in the courts of Europe. Later, groups of Native people were brought to Europe to perform public entertain-ments, and displayed at World's Fairs as a "primitive" note to play up the wonders of civilization displayed elsewhere at the fairs. These displays cul-minated, if you will, with the participation of Native people in Buffalo Bill's show, where they played roles in performances that were continued in the plots of Hollywood westerns.[21] In many instances, the "ethnic" or "cultural" tourism that has developed around the world in recent years comes danger-ously close to perpetuating such colonialistic ideology and dynamics.

What saves these four reconstructions from participating in this tradition is the agency and agendas of their Native interpreters. There is a second tra-dition of Native cultural performance, which was developed out of colonial forms by Native people to serve their own needs. These performances were and are intended to educate non-Native audiences about Native cultures and to persuade the wider society of the value, sophistication, and humanity of these cultures; they have included dance, song, recitations, theater, lectures, and costumed craft demonstrations.[22] Native interpreters who work at historic sites today draw on a long tradition of demonstrating and performing elements of their cultures for tourists, of understanding tourist expectations of "Indians," and responding to these, and of challenging prejudice and stereotypes through their performances.

Native interpreters are perfectly aware of the implications of being gawked at by non-Native visitors for eight hours a day, and work hard to find ways of responding creatively and positively to the often racist, almost always stereotyped way in which visitors view them. To be a Native woman trying to communicate pride that one's ancestors had a rich culture and were integral to the fur trade, and to hear fifty times a day the line, "Go stand with the squaw and I'll take your picture," has the potential to turn historical interpretation into a demeaning travesty. Native interpreters at these sites respond to this discourse: their self-perceived mission is to challenge and replace it by educating non-Native audiences about the worth and dignity of Native cultures. Freda McDonald, an Ojibwa elder who works at Old Fort William, said that she is able to forgive a great deal of what tourists say and do by reminding herself that they have been raised in ignorance, on the wrong version of history. She takes great satisfaction in teaching those people. Marie Brunel, who headed the Native staff at Sainte-Marie for years, similarly said that "If we can just reach one person, teach one person that we are real human beings, then it's all worth it."

Note that these interpreters are using the messages they communicate about their cultures in the past to challenge prejudice in the present. Such approaches to interpretation remind scholars that for minority and formerly colonized peoples, what is said about the past very much affects the present. Jonathan Hill has expressed this most forcefully:

> To successfully resist ongoing systems of domination, racial or ethnic stereotyping, and cultural hegemony, the first necessity of disempowered peoples, or of marginalized subcultural groups within a national society, is that of poetically constructing a shared understanding of the historical past that enables them to understand their present conditions as the result of their own ways of making history.[23]

The stakes in such struggles are crucial: being able to voice one's own perspective on the past and to control one's heritage, David Lowenthal reminds us, is "essential to autonomy and identity."[24] First Nations people would add that it is essential to cultural survival and self-determination. Native interpreters are using their personal, family, and community histories to challenge too-simple, exclusive national histories; they are struggling to replace popular, "master narratives of cultural disappearance and salvage . . . [with] stories of revival, remembrance, and struggle."[25]

Both academic and public historians have been slow to acknowledge and deal with this: since both traditions are rooted firmly in the dominant society, the role of history and its representations in reinforcing the status quo has been taken for granted. It has taken the addition of minority perspectives on the past to make scholars think about whose history is represented, and how the past is related to the present. The challenges of decolonization and multiculturalism are beginning to lead us past initial attempts to add the perspectives of cultural "Others" to existing historiographical frameworks and to rethink the purposes and audiences for historical writing and reconstructions.

Such revision is in its infancy, however, and at present Native history, fur trade history, and public history sites still coexist rather uneasily at times. One such uncomfortable conjuncture occurs at Colonial Michilimackinac, where Odawa interpreters portray Great Lakes Native life and the role of Native people in the fur trade; they especially try to communicate that Native people were crucial allies of the traders at Michilimackinac. Some of that site's static displays are waiting to be updated, however, and one of the older ones is a diorama illustrating the capture of the fort by Ojibwa warriors in 1763. This graphic model and its text focuses on the brutality of Native people involved in the attack (the figures in the diorama include warriors scalping fallen British officers and pools of gore), but does not explore Ojibwa motivations for the attack with equal force. When one Odawa interpreter was in public school, her class came to the fort, and saw the diorama. As she explains it, she was one of a few Native students in the class. After her class had viewed the display, one of the non-Native students looked at her and said, "So you're an Indian!"—with all the negative connotations that term could bear. The display is still there, and as a staff member in 1994, she was still dealing with its reinforcement of negative stereotypes about Native people.

Colonial Michilimackinac's administrators certainly never intended to reinforce negative stereotypes with that display, nor did they intend to put their Native interpreters on the spot with its effects on visitors. What they, like many public historians, failed to consider was the conjuncture of perspectives that the diorama and the Native encampment would be bringing together and the pain—not just interpretive dilemmas, but real emotions—that such a conjuncture might cause for Native interpreters. That display is due to be replaced soon, but I include this incident here because it suggests many of the challenges involved in revising historical messages at reconstructions, how much the past entwines with the present in the lives of the Native peoples whose histories we now seek to add to these places, and why Native interpreters see themselves as giving oppositional, "Other Half" perspectives and information.

As part of the process of revising the way they represent the past, historic sites are increasingly expected to consult and collaborate with local Native groups and even to make their sites forums for discourse between cultures.[26] Administrators and staff at all four of these reconstructions have begun the process of forging lasting and serious relationships with the descendants of the Native people involved at the fur trade at their sites. As yet, this work is seldom noticeable to the casual visitor, but it is certainly gaining momentum and promises exciting developments ahead.

This outreach work is taking several forms. As part of the process of forging ties with local Native communities, sites are sponsoring events that encourage Native people to visit. At Old Fort William, "Ojibwa Keeshigan" is a festival lasting several days in which the culture and heritage of local Ojibwa people is celebrated. Similarly, in 1995, Lower Fort Garry sponsored a regional First Nations art festival to take place on the grounds. While these activities may be tangential to what usually takes place there, they function to communicate to a Native audience that the site is trying to update its messages, that it is open to comments from a Native audience, and that it wants a Native audience—a far cry from the past.

Sites are also formally seeking advice and perspectives from Native people on the history they portray. Ojibwa and Odawa scholars, local elders, and cultural resource people have contributed to the review and planning process for Native interpretation at Old Fort William, Pine City, Colonial Michilimackinac, and Lower Fort Garry since 1990.[27] It will be a few more years yet before this advice is fully implemented, but sites reflect a willingness not only to broaden the range of their Native interpretation, but to portray oppositional history, to add notes of contention to a genre of historical representation that has been remarkably harmonious.[28]

In an even more remarkable development, Old Fort William and another reconstruction, Fort Langley National Historic Site near Vancouver, have begun to develop a perception of themselves as places for Native peoples to explore their histories. At Old Fort William, recently retired manager Armin Webber told me of his strong feeling that "50 percent of the Native encampment is to serve the needs of the Native community, and 50 percent is to serve the [site's] needs." Webber emphasized that many aspects of early-nineteenth-century Ojibwa culture interpreted at the fort could not be seen at powwows, craft classes, or other contemporary venues within the local Native community. At Fort Langley, the Sto:lo First Nation sees the fort as an opportunity to teach its members about their history and about culture at a specific point in time, before the overlay of twentieth-century pan-Indianism.[29] These are drastic shifts in intent and concept for public history, and signal continued evolution and learning on the part of historic sites.

Conclusion

In their contemporary operational struggles, these sites remind us that the fur trade is a nexus of contested histories that continue to affect the identities of and relationships between Native peoples and members of the dominant society. The struggle to add Native interpretation and perspectives to public history sites has been a difficult one. Initial development of Native encampments has produced well-documented but still skewed representations of Native cultures and Native-White relations, and sites need to analyze the messages that visitors actually receive to improve their communication of desired messages about Native peoples and their pasts. Still, these four reconstructions should be commended for having made a determined effort to add Native people to the histories they depict and for working toward presentations of more balanced views of the past. Furthermore, such efforts are in most cases still in their first decade of experimentation and have occurred despite the serious budget cuts and staff reductions that have plagued public heritage agencies during this time.

Now that they have faced these initial challenges, historic sites are beginning to consider the implications of bringing together very different views of the past. Native people have made it clear that they are unwilling to be represented in only minor roles in the history of the dominant society of North America, which these sites have traditionally reiterated. While scholars have done much to promote the idea of Native agency within the fur trade, producing revisionist studies focusing on cultural florescence and adaptive strategies that occurred among Native groups in response to the early trade, there is a strong voice coming from within contemporary Native communities that insists the fur trade played a very negative role in their pasts, as a force of cultural disruption and an early form of colonial relations between Europeans and Native peoples. Creating partnerships with Native groups, and strengthening Native interpretation programs, will increasingly require confronting uncomfortable conjunctures of fur trade history, Native history, and public history.[30] To paraphrase both Edward Said[31] and James Clifford,[32] whose histories are being represented at these places? By whom, and in whose voices? And for whom, and for what purposes?

"Living history" and historic reconstruction is a very unwieldy, complex, and difficult medium. It is also a very powerful one. Historic sites have large audiences and, by the compelling physical and face-to-face nature of communication they use, have the potential to educate, to explore the human realities of the past and their legacy in the present, and to challenge the stereotypes about the past that continue to affect Native communities in the present. For most of the visitors I interviewed at historic sites, these were sites of first contact: they had never before had the opportunity to speak to a Native person, to explore ideas and stereotypes face-to-face with a person about whom they thought such things. In many cases, these were powerful encounters, that engaged visitors of all ages and backgrounds, and sowed the seeds for further learning in a way that no other media could. Attempts by historic sites to develop relationships with Native communities and to acknowledge Native perspectives on the fur trade are fascinating developments that exist at the intersections between fur trade history, Native history, and public history. While these junctions are often contentious, and sometimes contradictory and painful, they are also vital to explore, to portray, and to communicate to both scholarly and public audiences.

Notes

1. I would like to thank the administrators and interpreters at these sites for generously permitting me to conduct research on their sites and for assisting my work in so many ways. Research for my Ph.D. dissertation, on which this chapter is based was carried out in 1994 and 1995 and was funded by the Social Sciences and Humanities Research Council of Canada and McMaster University. This article is dedicated to the memory of Lily McAuley, the engaging Cree "half-breed" woman who was speaker at the banquet of the Sixth North American Fur Trade Conference and who died in 1994 of breast cancer. Lily worked for many seasons at York Factory and Churchill. She inspired many of us to continue to try to understand, explore, and cherish the human side of the fur trade, and to try to represent these complexities at public history sites.

2. Michael Payne, "Fur Trade Social History and the Public Historian: Some Other Recent Trends," in *The Fur Trade Revisited: Selected Papers of the Sixth North American Fur Trade Conference*, ed. Jennifer S. H. Brown, W. J. Eccles, and Donald P. Heldman (East Lansing: Michigan State University Press, 1994), 484.

3. I will refer to First Nations and Native American populations throughout the article as "Native."

4. As a sampling of the scholarly literature considering these relationships and their implications, see James Clifford, *The Predicament of Culture: Twentieth-Century Ethnography, Literature, and Art* (Cambridge: Harvard University Press, 1988); Edward Said, "Representing the Colonized: Anthropology's Interlocutors," *Critical Inquiry* 15 (1989): 205–25; Edward Said, Orientalism (London: Routledge, 1978); and Bruce Trigger, "The Past as Power: Anthropology and the North American Indian," in *Who Owns the Past?*, ed. Isabel McBryde (Oxford: Oxford University Press, 1985).

5. Anna Laura Jones, "Exploding Canons: the Anthropology of Museums," *Annual Reviews in Anthropology* 22 (1993): 201–20; Ivan Karp and Steven D. Lavine, eds., *Exhibiting Cultures: The Poetics and Politics of Museum Display* (Washington, D.C.: Smithsonian Institution Press, 1991); Task Force on Museums and First Peoples, *Turning the Page: Forging New Partnerships Between Museums and First Peoples* (Ottawa: Assembly of First Nations and Canadian Museums Association, 1992).

6. Michael Ames, Julia Harrison, and Trudy Nicks, "Proposed Museum Policies for Ethnological Collections and the Peoples They Represent," Muse 6, no. 3 (1988): 47–52, Michael Ames, "Biculturalism in Museums," *Museum Anthropology* 15, no. 2 (1991): 7–15 Ivan Karp, Christine Mullen Kreamer, and Steven Lavine, eds., *Museums and Communities: the Politics of Public Culture* (Smithsonian Institution Press, 1992); Karp and Lavine, eds., *Exhibiting Cultures*.

7. Robert Coutts, *Lower Fort Garry: An Operational History, 1911-1992* (Ottawa: Parks Canada Microfiche Report Series 495, 1993), 1; see also Michael Payne and C. J. Taylor, "Animated Adventures in the Skin Trade: Interpreting the Fur Trade at Historic Sites," paper presented to the Rupert's Land Research Centre Colloquium, Winnipeg, 1992; and A. J. B. Johnston, "Toward a New Past: Reflections on the Interpretation of Native History Within Parks Canada," unpublished ms., 1994.

8. Payne and Taylor, "Animated Adventures in the Skin Trade," 8, 12; Payne, "Fur Trade Social History and the Public Historian," 489-91.

9. Robert Coutts, personal communication, 1994.

10. David Lowenthal, *The Past is a Foreign Country* (New York: Cambridge University Press, 1985), 44; Ana Maria Alonso, "The Effects of Truth: Re-presentations of the Past and the Imagining of Community," *Journal of Historical Sociology* 1 (1988):33; Ellen Badone, "Ethnography, Fiction, and the Meanings of the Past in Brittany," *American Ethnologist* 18 (1991): 539; Martha K. Norkunas, *The Politics of Public Memory* (Albany: SUNY Press, 1993).

11. Randall H. McGuire, "Archaeology and the First Americans," *American Anthropologist* 94, no. 4 (1992): 816. See also Jonathan D. Hill, "Contested Pasts and the Practice of Anthropology," *American Anthropologist* 94, no. 4 (1992): 809–15; Jonathan Friedman, "The Past in the Future: History and the Politics of Identity," *American Anthropologist* 94, no. 4 (1992): 837–59.

12. Patricia Jasen, "Imagining Old Fort William: Romanticism, Tourism, and the Old Fort, 1821 to 1971," *Papers and Records*, vol. 18, Thunder Bay Historical Museum

Society, 1990; Barbara A. Johnstone, "Lower Fort Garry Complete Conversion to National Historic Site Plan # 1" (Hudson's Bay Company Archives [Provincial Archives of Manitoba], HBCA E.97/53, 1960); Barbara A. Johnstone, "A Broad Outline of Exhibit Stories for Lower Fort Garry National Historic Park" (Hudson's Bay Company Archives [Provincial Archives of Manitoba], HBCA E.97/53, 1962).

13. See Catherine A. Lutz, and Jane L. Collins, *Reading National Geographic* (Chicago: University of Chicago Press, 1993), 280.

14. C. J. Taylor, *Negotiating the Past: the Making of Canada's National Historic Parks and Sites* (Montreal: McGill-Queen's, 1990), 169-90.

15. See Laura Peers, "'Playing Ourselves': Native Histories, Native Interpreters, and Living History Sites," (Ph.D. diss., Department of Anthropology, McMaster University, 1996) for a more complete description of this topic.

16. Richard White, "Frederick Jackson Turner and Buffalo Bill," in James Grossman, ed. *The Frontier in American Culture* (Berkeley: University of California Press, 1994), 12–13.

17. White, "Frederick Jackson Turner and Buffalo Bill," 49.

18. This information is taken from Randi Korn and Associates, "Enemies to Allies: Cultural Accommodations in the Western Great Lakes, 1760–1783. A Front-End Evaluation: Part II," unpublished consultant's report for Colonial Michilimackinac, 1995, with comparative data from: Eric Gable, Richard Handler, and Anna Lawson, "On the Uses of Relativism: Fact, Conjecture, and Black and White Histories at Colonial Williamsburg," *American Ethnologist* 19, no. 4 (1992): 792, 803 for Williamsburg; Richard Prentice, *Tourism and Heritage Attractions* (London/New York: Routledge, 1993), 4, 54–58 for British heritage tourism. Informal conversations with site directors also support these trends.

19. McGuire, "Archaeology and the First Americans," 817; Lutz and Collins, *Reading National Geographic*, 220.

20. Phil Porter, "Encampment at Pe-quod-e-nonge: Native American Interpretation at Colonial Michilimackinac," unpublished site training document, 1992, 44.

21. There is an extensive literature on Native cultural performances in colonial contexts. See Olive Dickason, *The Myth of the Savage* (Edmonton: University of Alberta Press, 1984), 205–12; J.C.H. King, "A Century of Indian Shows: Canadian and United States Exhibitions in London 1825–1925," *European Review of Native American Studies* 5, no. 1 (1991): 35–42; Susan Labry Meyn, "Who's Who: The 1896 Sicangu Sioux Visit to the Cincinnati Zoological Gardens," *Museum Anthropology* 16, no 2 (1992): 21–26; Neil Harris, *Cultural Excursions: Marketing Appetites and Cultural Tastes in Modern America* (Chicago: University of Chicago Press, 1990); Richard Slotkin, "The 'Wild West,'" in *Buffalo Bill and the Wild West* (Exhibition catalogue: no ed. given; The Brooklyn Museum and Buffalo Bill Historical Center, 1981); Sarah J. Blackstone, *Buckskin, Bullets, and Business: a History of Buffalo Bill's Wild West* (New York: Greenwood Press, 1986).

22. For discussions of some of these performances and their meanings to Native performers, see James M. McClurken, *Gah-Baeh-Jhagway-Buk: A Visual Culture History of the Little Traverse Bay Bands of Odawa* (East Lansing: Michigan State University Museum, 1991); David Blanchard, "For Your Entertainment Pleasure—Princess White Deer and Chief Running Deer—Last 'Hereditary' Chief of the Mohawk: Northern Mohawk Rodeos and Showmanship," *Journal of Canadian Studies* 1, no. 2 (1984): 99–116; Peers, "'Playing Ourselves.'"

23. Hill, "Contested Pasts and the Practice of Anthropology," 811.

24. David Lowenthal, "Conclusion: Archaeologists and Others," in *The Politics of the Past*, ed. Peter Gathercole and David Lowenthal (London: Unwin, 1990), 302.

25. James Clifford, "Four Northwest Coast Museums: Travel Reflections," *Exhibiting Cultures: the Poetics and Politics of Museum Display*, ed. Ivan Karp and Steven D. Lavine (Washington, D.C.: Smithsonian Institution Press, 1991), 214.

26. Ames, "Biculturalism in Museums," 14.

27. See, for instance: Wesley L. Andrews, "Appropriate Representation, Cultural Interpretation and Exhibit Policy: A Perspective for Consulting with Native American Indian Communities in Northern Michigan," consultant's report prepared for the Mackinac Island State Park Commission, 1995; Sandra L. Goodsky (O-zhaa-wazsh-ko-ge-zhi-go-quay), *Angwaamass—It's About Time: A Research Report on the Ojibwa-European Fur Trade Relations From an Ojibwa Perspective*, report prepared for the Minnesota Historical Society's North West Company Fur Post, 1993.

28. Thomas Schlereth, *Cultural History and Material Culture: Everyday Life, Landscapes, Museums* (Ann Arbor, Mich.: UMI Research Press, 1990), 347–75.

29. Keith Thor Carlson and Albert "Sonny" McHalsie, "The Sto:lo Nation and the Fort Langley National Historic Site: Overcoming Pan-Indianism and Defining Sto:lo Culture and Tradition" paper presented to the Second Columbia Department Fur Trade Conference, Vancouver, Wash., 1995.

30. See also Payne and Taylor, "Animated Adventures in the Skin Trade," 15, on another related dilemma in public history, the realization that Native people are only interpreted in the context of the fur trade or perhaps of missionization, as if they had no lives, no histories, apart from that which their involvement with Europeans gave them. There are two exceptions to this, that I know of: the Wanuskewin site in Saskatchewan, and the new Waswagoning site at Lac du Flambeau. Both of those sites are operated by Native people.

31. Edward Said, "Representing the Colonized."

32. Clifford, *The Predicament of Culture*.

Bruce Alden Cox Whitemen Servants of Greed: Foreigners, Indians, and Canada's Northwest Game Act of 1917

We need to anthropologize the West: show how exotic its constitution of reality has been. . .

Paul Rabinow, "Representations . . ." in *Writing Culture*

LET US begin with a thought experiment. Consider the phrase, "conservation in northern Canada." What comes to mind? Is it muskox, wood buffalo, or caribou? And what of the conservation measures themselves? Perhaps closed hunting seasons, or resrictions on trading in animal parts? Now suppose we learn that similar concerns came before public gatherings in the early part of this century? Has nothing changed? Let us admit at once that it is no easy task to follow Paul Rabinow's advice. How can we anthropologize someone who talks just like we do? Nevertheless, Rabinow's project is a worthy one. Let us then look for the exotic in an otherwise unremarkable setting, the Canadian Commission of Conservation, which held annual conferences around the time of the Great War. These conferences gathered together federal and provincial politicians and civil servants, along with experts and advocates from Canada and the United States. Prominent there was Gordon Hewitt, author of *Conservation of the Wild Life of Canada*. Dr. Hewitt used the 1917 conference to raise his concerns over the plight of northern wildlife. Who was responsible for that plight? Hewitt felt that it was American market hunters along with Native hunters. But here he meant "nontraditional" Native hunters, though he did not say who they were. Hewitt felt that the foreign and Native exploiters were two sides of the same coin, and thus subject to the same remedy. The remedy, Dr. Hewitt urged, lay in new legislation, directed mainly against the Americans. These were foreign trappers and traders whose sole desire was to "enrich themselves . . . in the quickest manner possible."[1] This article attempts to reconstruct the climate of opinion that led to the passage of that law, the precedent-setting 1917 act.

That act was first mooted, as we have seen, at an annual conference of the Conservation Commision. After Hewitt, and the politicos, one of the most prominent members of the commission was Duncan Campbell Scott. Scott, a self-published poet, was deputy superintendent general of indian affairs. This was the highest civil service position in Canada's Indian Department. Scott's views on foreign hunters were much what we have just seen from Dr. Hewitt. Nevertheless, Duncan Scott held these views on non-Natives long before 1917. For Scott, such non-Native trappers were "Whitemen servants of greed." This was a phrase from Scott's 1905 poem, *On the Way to the Mission.*[2] In this poem, two whitemen stalk an Indian dragging a toboggan loaded with what they suppose is his winter's catch of fine furs. The two kill the Indian, only to discover that the heavy toboggan holds a young woman's body, on its way to be buried at the Mission. Such "servants of greed," Scott later made clear, were not found among the major trading establishments. Scott castigated only the "foreigner," without a permanent establishlment and "only cash in hand."[3] Throughout Scott's prolific popular writings on Indians, there were recurring images of fires "waning," "dying away in ashes."[4]

The race has waned and left but tales of ghosts,

That hover in the world like fading smoke . . .

Now their vaunted prowess is all gone,

Like a moose-track in the April snow.[5]

In the northern forests, Scott held, "the Aboriginal hunter is supreme no longer, ..." "Gone is the fiction that he is superior in these pursuits. The White man equals him as a trapper, and holds his own on the trail and in the canoe."[6] Scott was consistent. If Indian life was "a fire that was waning," Indians should be no threat to northern wildlife, unlike the "foreign trapper and free trader."

Fires waning, footprints fading, embers fading away—these are seductive images. Did they seduce the writer as well as his readers? Or did Scott scatter such phrases through his writings more for their calculated effect than through settled conviction? Furthermore, did Scott truly believe that Indians held no threat to northern wildlife, and that foreigners and white interlopers did? These questions admit of no easy answer. Nevertheless, it is clear that Scott had reason to hope that he was right about the Indian hunters. The 1919 conference of the Conservation Commission did much to show the quandary in which Scott had to operate as superintendent of the Indian Department. Scott spoke that year to an audience ready to believe the worst of Indian hunters, and of the Indian Department for mollycoddling them. This was an audience who thought they had a good idea "of the destruction that it was possible for a single Indian to execute." That remark came from F. Bradshaw, provincial game guardian for Saskatchewan, although he attributed it to an anonymous correspondent. Bradshaw understood all too well the dilemma under which Scott and his department operated: "The more moose meat the Indian secures the less beef the agent will have to provide."

> I venture to say that the average Indian agent encourages, rather than dis-courages, the illegal killing of big game. He feels it incumbent upon himself to keep expenses down to a minimum that he may present a report that is favorable to the Administration in regard to its avowed policy of making the Indian self-sustaining, so far as it is possible to do so.[7]

Scott temporized:

> We wish to preserve the game; at the same time, we wish to have our Indians well fed, but we do not wish the hunters to feed themselves entirely on the game of the country.[8]

In his prepared remarks, Scott claimed that Indian hunters were often made the scapegoats for overhunting actually done by white sports hunters. No one there would accept that claim, however. This was a crowd that wanted some-one else to blame! It was left to W. F. Tye, of Montreal, to came up with a for-mula that the crowd would buy. Recall, Tye argued, that whites taught the Indians their bad habits; Indians overhunted "in imitation of the white man." That was just the ticket. No one objected to blame being apportioned in this left-handed, roundabout manner. They were also willing to hear Tye's reme-dy, which he outlined for delegates at the conservation conference.

> If you are going to preserve the game the first thing to do is to make the white man obey the law. The white man makes the laws, Indian does not; the white man is used to obeying laws, the Indian is not. First make the white man obey the laws, and the Indian will, in the course of time, follow.[9]

That is exactly the tack taken by the Northwest Game Act of 1917. In the early summer of that year, Scott, Hewitt, and others from the Conservation Commission drafted a revised N. W.T. Game Act. Just as Tye proposed, they directed the new act against those likely to teach Indians bad habits. The new law, for example, imposed a license system directed at foreign trappers and traders. What did the government have against "peddler traders from the south?" That question was asked in the House debate on the bill by Frank Oliver, who had been indian affairs minister in Sir Wilfred Laurier's previous

Liberal government. Oliver, publisher of the *Edmonton Bulletin*, also wondered whether the "estimable theorists" from the Commission of Conservation were familiar with the actual condition in the North?[10] Exactly! Nevertheless, Oliver's point was lost on the Canadian House of Commons, which passed the Northwest Game Act in July 1917.

Although the new act was supposed to be directed mainly against foreign hunters, much of its force was directed against all hunters, white and Aboriginal. The act's provisions included an absolute ban on hunting wood buffalo, musk-oxen, elk, and white pelicans, with a ten-year ban on hunting wild swans, and a shorter ban on hunting eider ducks.[11] The House, as Frank Oliver complained, had acted without knowing the North, taking on itself "a right of life or death" over all the people of that northern country. Nevertheless, the act was sold to the public as a measure against foreign inter-lopers in the North. Thus, some evidence of interlopers was needed to get the ball rolling. This article attempts to track down those rumored "peddler traders from the south" whose "invasion" was needed to spur the House to action.[12]

The trail takes us back to the late winter of 1914. Arctic explorer Vilhalmur Steffansson wrote to the Conservation Commission from Fort Macpherson, which he visited on one of the three Canadian Arctic expeditions he led between 1906 and 1918. Steffansson may have been the first Canadian voice in this period to view wildlife resources with alarm: "caribou were killed for their hides, for their tongues, for 'sport,' [by] Eskimos and even White men." Steffansson also made passing reference to the American schooner *Teddy Bear* trading into the Coronation Gulf. Teddy bears perhaps brought to mind another Teddy, Theodore "Teddy" Roosevelt, the twenty-sixth president of the United States! In any case, Steffansson's brief mention sufficed.[13] The letter's passing mention of Yankee trading schooners with provocative names evidently set alarm bells ringing in Ottawa. The Royal Northwest Mounted Police also commissioned their own report on interlopers in the North. The Mounties' report complained of "Beach Combers" and "Squaw Men" in the Arctic, "in every way detrimental to the Natives."[14] Steffansson's letter went from the Conservation Commission to the office of the prime minister, Sir Robert Borden. Sir Robert, who now graces the Canadian $100 bill, sent it back to Scott's Department of Indian Affairs.[15]

Superintendent Scott decided that he needed his own report from the North. He found the man to do it in Henry Bury, who had the summer before served as a junior clerk to the government party "paying treaty" to the Indians of Great Slave Lake.[16] Treaty 8 called for an annual payment of five dollars to each family head; every summer officials of the Indian Department traveled north to "pay treaty." Scott found a way to send Bury to survey northern wildlife while conserving the department's funds. In 1915, Scott once again sent Bury as junior clerk to the Treaty 8 party, with his traveling expenses and modest salary of $100 per month included in the Treaty Commission's budget.[17] Thus it was that in May 1915, Bury once again set out for the Great Slave Lake region of the Northwest Territories. There, as "acting clerk," he was charged with keeping track of treaty annuities paid to the Crees, Chipewyans, Dogribs, and other Indians of the region. Bury was also expected to write a report on the wildlife of that vast area, "equivalent in size to the whole of European Russia," Bury reckoned. The party traveled quickly over that great area. They reached Fort Chipewyan on Lake Athabasca on 7 June, and were back in Edmonton before the end of August.[18]

Bury was not the only one writing a report, of course. Bury's superior, Treaty Inspector Henry Conroy, also reported, in passing, about wildlife and Indian hunters. Conroy's remarks, which came from an experienced northern observer, leave a very different impression from Bury's. The treaty inspector found that "Caribou had been plentiful" at Lake Athabasca during that winter's hunt.[19] One man's plenty may be another's slaughter, of course. Bury had been sent north to find slaughter, and he had found it. He claimed, for example, that Indian hunters on Lake Athabasca were carried away by their blood lust. Once the hunt began, Bury believed, those hunters were seized by "primordial instinct" to the point where they "continue slaughtering right and left."[20] That is a striking image, but not one that Bury took in at first hand. Recall that he was a visitor during springtime who commented on the winter caribou hunt! In fact, his report makes clear that he was never a witness to scenes of "wholesale slaughter." Bury wound up his 1915 report by admitting that more information was needed.[21] Evidently the Indian Affairs Department thought so as well. In 1916, Superintendent Scott once again sent Bury to the Great Slave Lake region, this time with the princely expense allowance of $3,999.14.[22]

Bury's 1916 report caused more of a stir in Ottawa than his first one had. For example, it made the "drastic" suggestion that private companies should not be given a free hand with northern resources, which "should be developed for the welfare of the country. In that case why are private corporations permitted to exploit these national resources for their own particular benefit?"[23]

Bury had posed what was undoubtedly a sensible question, but it was not what they wanted to hear in Ottawa. Private corporations, provided they were "the established traders [who] took a paternal interest in the hunters," were viewed in a favorable light by Scott and his Conservative Party masters.[24] No one in Ottawa paid Bury's suggestions on that point any mind. Nevertheless, Bury's second report contained a warning that they were bound to heed in Ottawa. Recall that Steffansson had mentioned the American trading schooner *Teddy Bear* in his letter to the Conservation Commission that had started the ball rolling in 1914.[25] Thus, when Henry Bury also made the "American connection," he was assured of an attentive audience back in Ottawa. Bury by then had a permanent appointment in Scott's department, so that his time in the N. W. T. was limited. "The exigencies of my own Departmental duties," Bury noted in the letter covering his report, prevented, for example, his "spending some time in the bison habitat."[26] In fact, he evidently sailed directly north to the Mackenzie River Delta. Nevertheless, somewhere en route across the Great Slave Lake and down the Mackenzie River he discovered the American menace. "I have indisputable evidence," Bury warned, that American fur traders mean to bring in "White and Colored trappers from Alaska." Such "evidence," however, all came from the mouth of Mr. C. W. Dawson, a fellow traveler on the Mackenzie River steamship. Dawson claimed to represent a firm of Seattle fur traders.

> C. W. Dawson, who travelled from Edmonton to the mouth of the Mackenzie, informed me that his firm was bringing last summer as many as 200 trappers from Alaska to exploit the fur resources of northern Canada. They propose to open a chain of posts and trap the country in much the same way that they did at one time in Alaska.[27]

Were these travelers' tales, meant to while away long evenings on deck under the midnight sun? Perhaps they were. Nevertheless, back in Ottawa, they believed it all. Gordon Hewitt commented on the 1916 report in a letter to the deputy head of the Commission of Conservation. In it, Hewitt complained that "conditions as previously reported were mild compared with the serious state of affairs existing at present." Hewitt went on to complain that American traders had dared to offer "somewhat higher prices" for furs, including white fox skins. With this sort of "extermination," Hewitt expostulated, "the white fox would soon become a rare animal."[28] Extermination, however, Dr. Hewitt believed, was something that was done only by interlopers. Never mind that the Hudson's Bay Company also extracted "vast quantities of valuable furs," including five thousand white fox pelts per year, according to Bury's first [1915] report, which Hewitt must have seen.[29] Nevertheless Hewitt's mind was filled with images of extermination. "Every possible step" should be taken, Dr. Hewitt urged in his reply to the deputy head of the Commission of Conservation.[30] Sir Clifford Sifton, another former Liberal cabinet minister, now chairman of the Conservation Commission, agreed with Hewitt. Correspondence in this case followed much the same paper trail as for Vilhalmur Steffansson's letter two years before. Sifton wrote the prime minister, Sir Robert Borden, with a copy to W. J. Roche, minister of indian affairs. Dr. Roche promised to give his "immediate and attentive attention" to the new legislation that Hewitt had demanded.[31]

By July of 1917, Hewitt, along with Scott and a few others, had drafted the new Northwest Game Act. In debate over that bill in the House of Commons, the government side kept very much to the Hewitt's line. Thus, on 21 July, Dr. Roche claimed that this was legislation "designed to hit those who are coming in for exploiting purposes."[32] That assertion begs two questions. First, was this truly the main thrust of the legislation? Second, were there Americans in the North in any numbers during this period? Let us deal at once with the second question. Recall that the new act was directed against a problem that was thought to be already in existence. Thus, the fairest test of the claims made by Hewitt and the Conservation Commission lies in counting the Americans who turned up in the Northwest Territories shortly after World War I. Consider, then, the early years after the revised act was put in place, ending, let us say, on the tenth anniversary of Bury's first report, in 1925.

We can get a good idea of the presence of foreigners in the N.W.T. by looking at the reports that the new act set in motion. The act charged J. B. Harkin, commissioner of dominion parks, with its administration and with reports on its enforcement. The act came just in the nick of time, Harkin felt, to stave off the "alien interests" who had "contemplated introducing large numbers of [foreign] hunters into the North."[33] Such was Harkin's position in 1917, on the eve of the new law's passage. Soon, however, Harkin was in a position to keep track of such interlopers, since they now required a license. The first complete figures come from 1919–20; in the year ending in March 1920, 171 men bought hunting licenses. Over three-fourths (131) were residents, while just over a tenth, 18, were "non-resident British." That is, only 10 percent of the hunters were from southern Canada. Furthermore, only 22 hunters bought "non-British, non-resident," or American licenses. Regarding trading, Americans bought only 9 of the 166 trading licenses sold.[34]

Was this the promised invasion of "foreign trapper-traders?" Hardly. On New Year's Day of 1922 the administration of the Northwest Game Act passed from the Dominion Parks Branch to the newly created Northwest Territories Branch of the Department of the Interior. In that same year (1921–22), only one American bought a trading license.[35] In 1923, the year in which Duncan Campbell Scott warned American readers about "foreigners" among the North's petty traders, the director of the Northwest Territories administration reported that only eight Americans bought nonresident trading licences.[36] The year following, 1924–25, only one "foreigner" bought a trading license.[37] The winter that ended the decade, 1929–30, told a different story. On 24 October 1929, the American stock market suffered its Black Thursday; a worldwide depression was looming. In 1929–30, over 550 white trappers came to the Territories, 50 of them Americans. Nevertheless, only six trading licenses were sold to Americans during the winter of 1929–30.[38]

Table 1.

AVERAGE NUMBER OF HUNTING LICENSES SOLD IN THE NWT, 1919–25

	Number	Percentage
Residents	142	69
Nonresident Canadians	44	21
"Foreigners"	19	9
Total	205	99

Source: Author's computations, based on Interior Department figures for 1919–25; from Canadian government Sessional Papers nos. 25 (1919), 12 (1923,1924, and 1925). See notes 33–37 for detailed citations.

Table 2.

AVERAGE NUMBER OF TRADING LICENSES SOLD IN THE NWT, 1919–25.

	Number	Percent
Residents	168	94
Nonresident Canadians	6	3
"Foreigners"	5	3
Total	179	100

Source: Author's computations, based on the same Canadian government sources as in table 1. See notes 33–37.

The Honorable Dr. W. J. Roche warned the Canadian House of Commons in 1917 about the impending invasion of the northern forests by Americans. Where were these interlopers? Tables 1 and 2 show that, during the first half decade of the new game act, most white men who hunted or trapped in the Territories were resident there. (Aboriginal residents do not appear in these tallies, as they needed no licenses.) In fact, section 20(2) of the act puts the "onus of proof as to his bona fide residence" on the trapper himself. Further, even among the nonresident trappers, most were Canadians, not Americans, by a ratio of more than two to one. Regarding traders, residents outnumbered nonresidents by a ratio of nearly twenty to one, and American traders were rare indeed. It is clear that only a few Americans were in the Territories when the Mounties began to sell trading licenses during the winter of 1917–18, and even at the end of the 1920s, there were still only a handful of American traders in the Northwest Territories.

We have seen that very few Americans set up as traders in the Northwest Territories. Nevertheless, perhaps the handful of Americans who did come caused problems out of proportion to their numbers? There is little evidence of that. RNWMP Commissioner A. B. Perry reported in November 1918 that "The general condition as to law and order" in the NWT during the year just passed was "very satisfactory." The Mounties were then in a position to know well the "general condition as to law and order," with detachments at Fort Fitzgerald, Fort Simpson, Fort Resolution, Fort Macpherson, and Herschel Island and, in 1919, at the mouth of the Coppermine River on the Arctic Coast. Furthermore, "our patrols in the Northwest Territories are very extended," Commissioner Perry reported, "covering as they do all ordinary routes of travel and visiting the different settlements and Indian reserves."[39] Furthermore, Section 6 of the act made all members of the RNWMP game officers. They were thus well placed to apprehend "Yankee pedlars . . . invading the field," as Scott had put it.[40] They rarely found them; the Mounties found, however, that more traders were coming to the North in the post-war years. Did "the competition of rival traders" cause "the lot of the Indian [to] become harder," as Scott had warned?[41]

RNWMP Commissioner Perry had a different view:

> More traders are visiting the Arctic and the competition in purchasing furs is more keen, a decided benefit to the natives. The fur catch of 1918 [1918–19] was disappointing but the high prices paid compensated for this. . . . (my emphasis)[42]

Things would have looked very different in the North, as compared to their interpretation in Ottawa. Northerners would have seen no American "invasion," for example, and who knows what they would have made of Henry Bury's brush with a supposed "primordial" lust for slaughtering wild game? Section 4(4) of the act imposed an absolute ban on hunting the wood buffalo. Were they indeed at risk? Were the caribou then at risk? In spite of Henry Bury's two fact-finding missions, no one knew for sure. In fact, reliable figures concerning wildlife populations in the Northwest Territories were simply unavailable in this period, as Dr. Hewitt himself admitted to the National Conference on Conservation in 1919.[43] The boom in fur prices after the Great War brought more small traders into the Northwest Territories. Nevertheless, they were never a source of difficulty for the Indians and Inuit, despite what Superintendent Scott had predicted. In fact, the new traders provided a benefit to the native fur producers.

Frank Oliver had warned the House against "theorists," who had little "practical knowledge of the facts or the conditions in the country affected," but nevertheless held an "absolute right of life or death over the people of that country."[44] Frank Oliver was both right and wrong in the advice he gave to the House of Commons when the new game act was being debated. That is, nobody knew for sure which animals were in trouble in the North. He had that right. On the other hand, Oliver, a newspaper publisher and former Liberal cabinet minister, may have misread the members on the government side. Did he believe that the government and the Conservation Commission operated in a permanent state of absence of mind? If that is what he believed, that estimate would have been wide of the mark. The House did not aim at American market hunters but hit the northern natives by mistake. As we see from their discussions, the white conservation lobbyists always had both targets in their sights. "First make the white man obey the laws," W. F. Tye advised the Conservation Commission; that done, aboriginal hunters would soon follow suit. That was exactly the tack taken by the 1917 Game Act.

Only the white hunters were required to buy licenses, and to be sure, Native hunters were granted partial exemptions from some provisions of the law. Nevertheless, let us look closely at the language of those exemptions. To be sure, Section 4(3) exempted "Indians or Eskimos" who were inhabitants of the Northwest Territories from closed seasons on moose, deer, caribou, and so on. Generous? Hardly, when this section extended the same exemption to any "bona fide inhabitants" of the Northwest Territories. The general intent of Section 4(3) can be deduced from its last line, which exempts "explorers or surveyors" from the various closed seasons, when they are in need of such game "to prevent starvation." Furthermore, no one, Native or white, could kill wild swans during a ten-year closed season, and no one, as we have seen, could legally kill wood buffalo, musk-ox, elk, or white pelicans.[45] The act was color-blind; it might grant exemptions to anyone in need, but made no concessions to aboriginal rights. In fact, the act seemed to see the northern aboriginal peoples as individuals who occasionally might need to hunt out of season, if only to "prevent starvation." The 1917 act made no concessions to treaty rights, nor to any sort of collective rights. In fact, the authors seemed unwilling to distinguish between Indian and white hunters, thus ignoring the collective nature of much Native hunting.

> Native hunting was a communal activity more than an individual one. All adult members of a hunting band played important roles in insuring a successful hunt and all members benefitted from the spoils. Many traditional culture-affirming rituals centred on hunting as well.

On the other hand:

> As understood by wildlife conservation policy-makers, however, hunting was an individualistic excercise of self-development and self-affirmation. They refused to recognize the communal context in which the native hunted, treating Indian and white hunters alike as possessive individualists. . . .[46]

"We must anthropologize the West," Paul Rabinow advises in the opening epigram. That may not be so difficult here; the construction of reality that underlay the Northwest Game Act seemed exotic enough. Exotic elements extend to poet-lawmakers, travelers' tales retold, hunters carried away by "primordial instinct," rapacious Yankee market hunters, and so on. All the elements of melodrama—or perhaps farce—are present. Nevertheless, something is lost if these events are seen only as melodrama. Nor does that reading exhaust the implications of Paul Rabinow's epigram for this study of the Canadian wildlife conservation movement around the time of the Great War. There is clearly more to be said about conservationists' constructions of reality during this period. In fact, their constructions were exotic, not only in the sense just considered, but in another sense as well.

Consider the Commission of Conservation's construction of threats to wildlife. For these wildlife advocates, such threats never came from the home team. Can you remember the telling epigram that cartoonist Walt Kelly put in the mouth of the title character of that comic strip from my college days? Kelly's Pogo Possum gave a new twist to an American military maxim: "We have met the enemy, and he is us." Exactly. Nevertheless, Kelly's wry saying would gain no support at the annual conferences of the Commission of Conservation. There, the enemy of wildlife was always the exotic other: Indians carried away by blood lust, or rapacious American market hunters. For the members of the comission, as noted earlier, wildlife exploitation was something done by interlopers. Frank Oliver asked the lawmakers what they had against peddlers from the south.

What indeed? Yet few spoke up against the new law, either in the Commission or in the House of Commons, when the Northwest Game Act was debated. In the same vein, a brave few scolded the conservation conferences about always blaming otherwise unattributed wildlife depredations on Native hunters. Yet these were always lone voices. Most delegates probably left the conservation conferences convinced of the destruction of wildlife that Indians might execute. They pondered the mischief supposed to come from "Charley Grey-Eyes," "Johnny Rain-in-the-Face" and the "Big Chief Company,"[47] and although they probably wanted stronger fare, they were willing to go along with the Northwest Game Act. And why not? Didn't it strike at the American market hunters? After all, weren't they the ones teaching the Indians "bad habits"?

The conservationists believed, most of them, that Indians were the principal threat to northern wildlife. Section 4(1) of the act closed spring and summer hunting, to northern Natives and everyone else. Although the new law was touted as a measure against white interlopers, as we have seen there were never many of them around. In fact, the whole number of whites hunting in the Northwest Territories in this period was never more than a few hundred. The numbers of Native hunters were easily greater by a factor of ten. When Henry Conroy gave the lie to Bury's 1915 report of caribou slaughter, he also reported "paying treaty" to 730 adult Indians around the Great Slave Lake, in the southern part of the N. W. T. In 1921, Commissioner Conroy brought another 1,900 adult N. W. T. Indians into treaty, and these figures leave out Inuit, Métis, and other nontreaty aboriginal peoples. Finally, in 1922, Bury's successor brought another 150 adults at Fort Liard into treaty.[48] Who, then, was the Northwest Game Act directed against? That boils down to the question: Who was there? The preponderance of N.W.T hunters were Natives, then and now.[49] "Directed against" is the operative term here, of course. There is no evidence that provisions of the act were enforced against Natives in this period. Perhaps nobody expected the new bill to be enforced. Such nonenforcement would only confirm what the sports hunters who frequented the conservationists' conferences believed all along. Nevertheless, they wanted a stick to beat the "Big Chief Company" with, even if nobody would use it for the present. The conservation lobbyists got just that in the Northwest Game Act of 1917. Since the policy makers were ignorant of whether northern Indians were overhunting or whether northern wildlife was at risk, these measures were, on their face, unfair to northern Natives. They placed, in principle, wide restrictions on what northern Natives could hunt, and when they could hunt it. Frank Oliver was right: these were matters of life and death, restrictions put in place by men who had little practical knowledge of conditions in the country affected, and less of the people of that country.

Notes

1. C. G. Hewitt, "Conservation of the Fur Resources of Northern Canada," in *Report of the Eighth Annual Meeting, Commission of Conservation* (Montreal: Federated Press, 1917), 120–21; *The Conservation of the Wild Life of Canada* (New York: Scribner's, 1921); also see F. Tough, "Conservation and the Indian: Clifford Sifton's Commission of Conservation, 1910–1919," *Native Studies Review* 8, no. 1 (1992): 61–74.

2. D. C. Scott, "On the Way to the Mission," in *Selected Poems of Duncan Campbell Scott*, ed. E. K. Brown (1905; reprint, Toronto: Ryerson, 1951), 40. For a biography of Scott, see E. B. Titley, *A Narrow Vision: Duncan Campbell Scott and the Administration of Indian Affairs in Canada* (Vancouver: University of British Columbia Press, 1986).

3. D. C. Scott, "The Aboriginal Races," *American Academy of Political and Social Sciences, Annals* 107 (1923): 65.

4. D. C. Scott, *John Graves Simcoe* (Toronto: Oxford University Press, 1927), 76.

5. D. C. Scott, "Indian Place Names," in *Selected Poems of Duncan Campbell Scott*, ed. E. K. Brown (1905; reprint, Toronto: Ryerson, 1951): 37.

6. Canada, House of Commons, Sessional Paper no. 27, *Annual Report of the Dept. of Indian Affairs*: D. C. Scott, "Report of the Deputy Superintendent General," 7. (Hereafter Sessional Papers.)

7. D. C. Scott, "The Relation of Indians to Wildlife Conservation," *National Conference on Conservation of Game, Fur-Bearing Animals and Other Wild Life, Commission of Conservation, February 18 and 19, 1919* (Ottawa: King's Printer, 1919), 19–21; "Discussion," 26–27 and 38–39. For another perspective on federal-provincial relations, see T. Morantz, "Provincial Game Laws at the Turn of the Century: Protective or Punitive Measures for the Native Peoples of Quebec?" *Papers of the Twenty-Sixth Algonquian Conference* (Winnipeg: University of Manitoba, 1995), 275–90.

8. Scott, "The Relation of Indians," 21.

9. "Discussion," 38–39.

10. Canada, *Debates of the House of Commons*, speech by F. Oliver, 21 July 1917, 3667.

11. Canada, *Northwest Game Act*, S. C. 1917, 7–8 Geo. 5, 36, section 4.

12. Canada, *Debates of the House of Commons*, 21 July 1917, 7–8 Geo. 5 1917, 3674.

13. Public Archives of Canada (hereafter PAC), MG 26 H: V. Steffansson, letter to Sir Clifford Sifton, 8 February 1914, *Robert Borden Papers*, 185:101562 and 101566–67. Teddy bears were named after Theodore Roosevelt, who served as the U.S. president from 1901–9.

14. PAC, MG 26H, G. L. Jennings, "Report to the Commissioner, R.N.W.M.P.," 11 April 1914, *Borden Papers*, 185:101533.

15. PAC, MG 26H, W. J. Roche, letter to Sir Robert Borden, 30 March 1914, *Borden Papers*, 185:101527.

16. Canada Sessional Paper no. 1, Part H, 1916, "Auditor General's Report, 1914–1915," 4.

17. Canada Sessional Paper no. 1, Part H, 1917, "Auditor General's Report, 1915–1916," 4.

18. PAC, RG 85, H. J. Bury, "Report on the Game and Fisheries of Northern Alberta and the Northwest Territories," 6 November 1915, vol. 664, file 3910, and vol. 2:1; Canada Sessional Paper no. 27, 1917, "Report of Henry A. Conroy, Inspector for Treaty No. 8," 79, 81.

19. Canada Sessional Paper no. 27, "Report of Henry Conroy, 'Treaty No. 8,'" 80. In fact, Conroy chided Indians for not killing more caribou and salting them away against future need.

20. PAC, RG 85, Bury, "Game and Fisheries," 5, 6.

21. Ibid., 17–18

22. Canada Sessional Paper no. 1, Part H, 1918, "Auditor General's Report, 1916–1917," 5.

23. PAC, RG 85, H. J. Bury, "Report Concerning the Game, Fur and Fishery Resources of the Northwest Territories, Supplementary to Report Submitted November 6th, 1915," 4 October 1916, Ottawa, vol. 666, file 3915, pp. 7, 8.

24. Scott, "The Aboriginal Races," 65.

25. PAC, MG 26H, Steffansson, letter to Clifford Sifton, 185:101563.

26. PAC, RG 85, H. J. Bury, letter to J. B. Harkin, 4 October 1916, vol. 666, file 3915.

27. PAC, RG 85, Bury, "Report," 4 October 1916, 8.

28. PAC, MG 26H, G. Hewitt, letter to James White, Commission of Conservation, 14 November 1916, 187:102816, 102817.

29. PAC, RG 85, Bury, "Game and Fisheries," 14.

30. PAC, MG 26H, G. Hewitt, letter to James White, 187:102818.

31. MG 26H, C. Sifton, letter to Sir Robert Borden, 11 December 1916; W.J. Roche. letter to Sir Clifford Sifton, 27 November 1916, *Borden Papers,* 187:102819-20.

32. *Debates*, 21 July 1917, 3674.

33. Canada Sessional Paper no. 26, 1917, J. B. Harkin, "Report of the Commissioner of Dominion Parks," 12.

34. Canada Sessional Paper no. 25, 1920, p. 3. These figures apply only to non-natives; only they were required to buy licenses.

35. Canada Sessional Paper no. 12, 1923, p. 110.

36. Canada Sessional Paper no. 12, 1924, "Report of the Director, Northwest Territories and Yukon Branch," O. S. Finnie, 154.

37. Canada Sessional Paper no. 12, 1925, p. 135.

38. Canada, *Department of Interior, Annual Report*, (1929–30), 150.

39. Canada Sessional Paper no. 28, 1919, pp. 11, 8; Sessional Paper no. 28, 1920, p. 15.

40. Scott, "The Aboriginal Races," 65.

41. Ibid.

42. Sessional Paper no. 28, 1920, A. B. Perry, "Commissioner's Report," 15.

43. C. G. Hewitt, "The Need of Nation-wide Effort," *Conference on Conservation* (Ottawa: King's Printer, 1919), 12–13.

44. Debates, 21 July 1917, 3667.

45. *Northwest Game Act*, Sections 4(3) and 4(1).

46. D. Gottesman, "Native Hunting and the Migratory Birds Convention Act: Historical, Political and Ideological Perspectives," *Journal of Canadian Studies* 18 (fall 1983): 85.

47. D. C. Scott, "The Relation of Indians," 19–21; "Discussion," 24, 26.

48. Sessional Papers no. 27, 1917, H. A. Conroy, "Report," 79–80 (author's computations); Canada, Dept. of Indian Affairs, *Treaty No. 11 and Adhesion, With Reports, Etc.* (1926; reprint, Ottawa: Queen's Printer, 1967), 5, 11.

49. B. A. Cox, "Prospects for the Northern Canadian Native Economy," *Polar Record* 22, no. 139 (1985): 393–400.

SECTION 3

New Versions of Old Tales

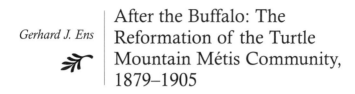

Gerhard J. Ens

After the Buffalo: The
Reformation of the Turtle
Mountain Métis Community,
1879–1905

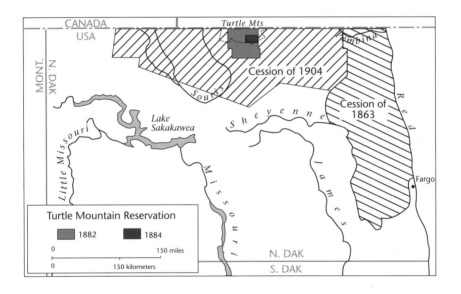

Figure 1. **Turtle Mountain Métis Community.**

HISTORIANS WRITING about the Turtle Mountain Chippewa (Ojibwa) and Métis have focused almost exclusively on the Indian policy of the American government and have emphasized the tragic nature of their story. Gregory Camp, commenting on the period from 1870 to 1920, has written, "During this era of Indian policy reform, this northern Plains tribe experienced a familiar pattern of land loss, poverty, and despair."[1] My intention is not to dispute or revise this historiography, but to provide a different perspective. I am not going to retell the tragedy of land loss and poverty, although these surely occurred, but rather explain how the Métis of Turtle Mountain

139

were able to reestablish a community after the buffalo, the mainstay of their economy for most of the nineteenth century, had disappeared in the 1870s.

This chapter will examine the origins of this community in the period 1870 to 1905 and examine the strategies, both political and economic, that the Métis used to reformulate an identity and community. In particular, the chapter focuses on a specific group of Red River Métis from St. François Xavier (in Manitoba), and from Pembina and St. Joseph in the United States. These Métis followed the receding herds to southern Saskatchewan and Montana in the 1860s and 1870s, and returned to the Turtle Mountain region of Manitoba and North Dakota after the buffalo disappeared, in an attempt to start a new life. They adapted to a different kind of fur trading, combined with small-scale agriculture, and were involved in the tribal (treaty) and reservation politics of the Turtle Mountain Chippewa. These strategies of community and alliance building were successful in creating a viable Métis community in the twentieth century.

The Métis community in question is located in north central North Dakota along the Manitoba border. The Turtle Mountains, or more accurately hills, occupy several hundred square miles in both North Dakota and Manitoba. They stand out as an oasis of forests and lakes on what was once a vast tree-less prairie. Hundreds of lakes, and even more sloughs, in the area made this a land of plenty. Buffalo, deer, elk, wildfowl, berries, fish, and other fur-bearing animals were plentiful in the early nineteenth century, when the Chippewa and Métis began congregating in this area.

The Turtle Mountain Chippewa were a branch of the Great Lakes Chippewa. In the late eighteenth and early nineteenth century they moved onto the plains, initially as fur trappers for the various trading concerns. They then adopted an equestrian buffalo-hunting tradition as trapping opportunities declined after the first decade of the nineteenth century. By 1805, a group of Chippewa had formed a permanent band at Pembina around the trading post of Alexander Henry the Younger. A splinter group of this Pembina band also became established at Turtle Mountain, where food resources were more abundant.[2] It was at these locations that they came into contact with French and Scottish fur traders who married extensively into the band. By 1819, there was an extensive Métis and Chippewa population around Pembina, some of whom moved to the fledgling Red River Settlement at St. François Xavier in the 1820s.

The ties between the Chippewa and Métis were more than simply familial or kin based. Since both groups relied heavily on large buffalo hunts that took them south and west deep into Sioux territory, they formed a close alliance for protection. The Métis who organized buffalo hunts out of Red River and Pembina often had large numbers of Chippewa accompanying them on their month-long hunts. Likewise, the Métis would attend the Chippewa hunts while maintaining their distinct band organization. In 1858, a Grand Council of the Chippewa, Sioux, and Métis met to establish a peace treaty, the relative boundaries of the various groups, and their buffalo-hunting privileges. At this time the Métis were recognized as a distinct group allied to the Chippewa. The grand chief of the Métis was Jean-Baptiste Wilkie of St. Joseph, who was recognized as an equal to the Chippewa chiefs.[3]

In the 1850s and 1860s, as the buffalo began retreating westward and the market for winter buffalo robes expanded, those Métis involved in this trade moved further west where they could still find buffalo in the early winter. It was during this period that wintering villages were established at places such as St. Joseph in the Pembina Hills, the Turtle Mountain region, and in the Souris River Basin. These wintering villages provided both the population level needed for social existence and the requisite numbers for protection from raiding Sioux bands. Large numbers of the Red River Métis and the Pembina Métis now centered their economic life in these wintering villages, which provided an excellent base from which to organize summer buffalo hunts, practice small-scale horticulture, and receive religious and educational services from Roman Catholic priests, and provided a residence near enough to the buffalo herds to get the prime winter buffalo robes, which were bringing high prices by the 1850s.

These communities experienced a crisis in the early 1870s when the buffalo all but disappeared from the region. To continue in the buffalo robe trade the Métis of Red River, St. Joseph, Turtle Mountain, and the Souris area relocated again. Large buffalo herds still existed but they were now found further west, in Montana, Saskatchewan, and Alberta, in areas such as the Judith Basin, Wood Mountain, Cypress Hills, Milk River, and Battle River. Oral histories compiled from surviving Turtle Mountain Métis in the 1930s repeatedly stress how they and their families loaded up their life's belongings and made the trek to Montana to follow the buffalo.[4] By the early 1870s villages like St. Joseph were deserted.

The buffalo-hunting life of these Métis continued in Montana until about 1881–83 when the last of the large herds disappeared. With their way of life coming to an end the Plains Métis were faced with a limited number of options. Some stayed in Montana, working as hired labor on ranches. Others moved north into Canada to enroll in the Indian treaties being signed in the 1870s or to take scrip. After 1885 scrip allotment was the method the

Canadian government used to extinguish Métis claims in the Northwest.[5] Still others returned to the communities they had originally left further east in the 1870s. A large number of the Métis formerly from St. François Xavier, St. Joseph, and the Turtle Mountain regions who had some Chippewa ancestry moved back to Turtle Mountain in the period 1879–83. Their decision was prompted not only by their familiarity with the region and the knowledge that other game still existed there, but also because other opportunities had recently opened up.

By the early 1880s negotiations between the U.S. government and the Turtle Mountain Chippewa raised the possibility of a treaty that might provide a land allotment for the Métis of the area when a reservation was created. The Métis saw this as an opportunity not only because of their Chippewa ancestry, but also because of the history of Chippewa/U.S. treaty negotiations. During the 1863 negotiations that led to the Red Lake and Pembina Chippewa Cession of land west of Red River to Devil's Lake, the Métis had played a large role in the negotiations. The Chippewa chiefs had insisted on land provisions for their Métis relatives. Of the approximately one thousand Natives who gathered at the treaty negotiation site, present-day Crookston, Minnesota, 653 were Métis. This treaty, which was signed in 1863, did not make the Métis a party to the treaty, but article VIII did stipulate that each male Métis related to the Red Lake or Pembina Chippewa who was a citizen of the United States would receive a homestead of 160 acres to be selected at his option in the limits of the tract ceded to the United States.[6] In 1864 this was changed to a grant of scrip redeemable for 160 acres of land located on any of the lands ceded by said treaty in lieu of all future claims for annuities.[7] The treaty, ceding some 11 million acres of land to the federal government, provided for the annual payment of $20,000 to be distributed among the Chippewa in per capita payments for a period of twenty years. Reservations were created at Red Lake and White Earth, Minnesota.[8]

While the chief of the Turtle Mountain Band, Little Shell, participated in the negotiations and signed the treaty, he and his band were not given a reservation. They were expected to remove to the White Earth Reservation. Little Shell, however, refused to reside on this reservation and maintained that his band retained claims to the unceded lands around Turtle Mountain. Thus, when the U.S. government finally got around to negotiating the cession of the 10 million acres of land around Turtle Mountain in the early 1880s those Métis of Chippewa descent who had not taken scrip in 1863–64 felt there was an excellent opportunity to reestablish themselves at Turtle Mountain. The refusal of American officials to recognize the Métis claims in 1863 on an equal basis with the full-bloods, however, meant that if the Métis wanted recognition in the Turtle Mountain area, they would have to claim tribal status. The Chippewa accepted this strategy, as Métis numbers would bolster their claims for a larger reservation.

The arrival of white settlers to the Turtle Mountain region in the late 1870s and the resulting land disputes finally pushed the United States to begin negotiations with the Turtle Mountain Chippewa to cede the approximately 10 million acres in the region. To allay the fears of the Turtle Mountain Chippewa and Métis about the encroaching white settlement, President Chester Arthur signed an executive order in 1882 creating a twenty-two township reservation along the Canadian border in Dakota Territory. This was followed a year later by a Congressional appropriation of $10,000 to aid in the relocation of the Turtle Mountain Chippewa to the new reservation.[9] It was this news, along with earlier rumors, that induced many of the Plains Métis who had ties to the Turtle Mountain Chippewa to return from their wintering quarters in Montana.

With the expectation of receiving treaty land, these buffalo-hunting Métis began trickling back in 1879–80. For example, in 1879, Antoine Brien and Charles Gladu, members of a wintering band of 150 Métis families in the Milk River area, decided that better opportunities existed by returning to the Turtle Mountains.[10] Francois Morin and his family, having followed the buffalo on the plains from 1870 to 1883, decided in 1883 to give up their river lot in St. François Xavier, Manitoba, and resettle at Turtle Mountain.[11] These kinds of decisions were made by literally hundreds of Métis families as the buffalo hunting economy disappeared between 1879 and 1883. By 1884, the Indian commissioner for the area reported that thirty-one full-blood Chippewa families and 1,200 Métis individuals were living in the Turtle Mountain area.[12] By 1892 the attorney for the Turtle Mountain Chippewa Band, John Bottineau, a Métis himself, estimated that the members of the band now living on or near the reservation numbered more than 2,100, and all but a few hundred were Métis (see table 1).[13]

While waiting for land grants, these Métis squatted on reservation land or in the surrounding area. They built houses, planted gardens, and in summer worked as hired labor on area farms or the railway.[14] They collected buffalo bones, for which they received $15–20 a ton, thereby raising enough cash to buy supplies for the winter. During the winter they hunted elk and deer for food. They trapped muskrat and weasel for the pelts that they sold to fur dealers in Wakopa, St. John, and Dunseith. There was also a market for chopped firewood, which they hauled to the nearby towns of St. John, Rolla, Belcourt, and Dunseith.[15]

Table 1.
ENUMERATIONS OF THE TURTLE MOUNTAIN CHIPPEWA AND MÉTIS,
1888-1904.

	Full Blood Chippewa	Métis	**Total**
I.O. report of 1884	31[a]	1,200	
I.O. report of 1885	192	1,206	1,398
I.O. report of 1886 [b]	282	963	1,245
I.O. report of 1887 [b]	309	817	1,126
I.O. report of 1891			2,144
McCumber roll of 1892 [b]	283	1,476	1,759
Davis roll of 1904	201	1,893	2,094

Sources: "Turtle Mountain Band of Chippewa Indians," U. S. Congress, vol. 36, no. 3878, 56th Cong., 1st sess., 1900, S. Doc. 444, 5, 142–3; *St. Ann's Centennial: 100 Years of Faith* (Rolla, North Dakota: Star Printing, 1985), 93.

[a] Number of families

[b] Enumerated only those living on the reservation

As these Métis returned to Turtle Mountain in ever increasing numbers, the Catholic Church sent Rev. John F. Malo to the area in 1882. He quickly built St. Claude Church on the eastern slopes of the mountain, where many of the first Métis had settled. By 1884 the chapel had become too small, and it was decided to move the mission to the nearby town of St. John, where a larger church was built.[16] In the same year the Sisters of Mercy from Yankton, South Dakota, established an Indian Industrial school and convent at Belcourt about twelve kilometers south of St. John. When Belcourt became the major population center in the Turtle Mountain area in the late 1880s,[17] Father Malo moved to Belcourt and constructed a new church there. In 1887 another church, St. Michael's (later St. Anthony's), was built on the western fringe of the reservation and a day school was run out of the church.[18] By the 1880s the Catholic Church provided much of the institutional basis for Métis community life in the area. This was in contrast to full-bloods in the area, who followed a more traditional Indian way of life and were less sedentary.[19] James H. Howard, an ethnographer who did fieldwork in the area, noticed distinct cultural differences as late as the 1950s. The full-bloods, on the one hand, spoke Ojibwa, continued to practice their own native ceremonies such as the sun and grass dances, and avoided the Church. The Métis, on the other hand, spoke English, French, or the Michif jargon, were almost 100 percent

Roman Catholic, and avoided Indian ceremonies.[20] These differences would play a role in dividing the community as it negotiated with the government for a land base.

The wait for land was a long and frustrating one. It was caused by the U.S. government's reneging on their original grant of a large reserve, disputes over which Métis would be allowed onto band rolls, and an internal dispute within the Turtle Mountain band on how to divide the land they would receive. In 1882, in response to desperate pleas of the Turtle Mountain Chippewa for a reservation with distinct boundaries in the face of incoming white settlement, President Chester Arthur set aside a reservation comprised of a twenty-four by thirty-two mile tract in Rolette County, along the U.S./Canadian border. The government, however, soon changed its position. In 1883, Congress appropriated funds to move the entire band to the White Earth Reservation in Minnesota. When the Chippewa resisted all attempts at removal, a special agent was sent to the reservation to report on the situation and make recommendations.

Agent Cyrus Beede reported that the tribal population had been grossly overestimated. He argued that all the Métis on the reservation were Canadian in origin, despite their protestations to the contrary. The result was the reduction of the reservation from twenty-two townships to two. The remainder of the reservation was returned to the public domain.[21] With the arrival of more white settlers, and with the Chippewa and Métis refusing to move, conflicts inevitably arose in the 1880s. Problems occurred when white settlers claimed land outside the boundaries of the small reservation on which a tribal member, usually a Métis, had squatted. Other conflicts arose over taxation. The Chippewa and Métis refused to pay county taxes on the understanding that they were exempt from property taxes as long as the U.S. government held their lands in trust. When county officials then began taxing cattle and tried to confiscate the cattle in lieu of taxes the threat of violence became very real.[22]

In an attempt to finally clear up these problems, the House of Representatives Committee on Indian Affairs sent out a three-member commission to settle the ten-million-acre claim. They again tried to convince the Chippewa to move to the White Earth Reservation. The Turtle Mountain Chippewa and Métis again refused to move. Instead they demanded the Turtle Mountain Reservation be restored to its 1882 boundaries. The commission had to return to Washington without any agreement. Congress then created a second commission in 1892 headed by Senator P. J. McCumber to reach an accord that did not call for the removal of the Chippewa. New problems, however, emerged, principally with who was to be included on tribal rolls, and the size of the reservation. These issues were further complicated by a split in the ranks of the Chippewa and Métis at Turtle Mountain.

The full-bloods did not want to take their land in severalty. The Métis, many of whom were already doing well, were in favor of individual allotments. The full-bloods, led by Chief Little Shell, were also adamant that the size of the reservation be increased. The reservation had been reduced in size in 1884 because Beede had not counted the Métis as tribal members, claiming they were all Canadian-born. Chief Little Shell and his faction argued that all Métis with kin ties to the Turtle Mountain Chippewa be included on tribal rolls. Many of the American-born Métis at Turtle Mountain, on the other hand, having waited more than ten years for land grants, were willing to exclude some Canadian-born Métis from tribal rolls. They were willing to accept a small reservation as long as they were able to locate their allotments on the public domain around Turtle Mountain.[23]

Exploiting this split, the McCumber Commission ignored Chief Little Shell and his council and arranged for the election of a new thirty-two member council composed of sixteen Métis and sixteen full-bloods. The document that was eventually agreed upon bore the signatures of this council of thirty-two and some 258 male heads of family, most of whom were Métis. It allowed for $1 million compensation for the ten-million-acre Turtle Mountain claim.[24] The commission also drew up a tribal roll including 1,476 Métis and 283 full-bloods.[25] A total of at least 177 Métis were rejected as being Canadian-born.[26] The agreement further stated that all members of the band unable to secure land on the reservation would be allowed to take Indian homesteads without charge on the public domain, and still be entitled to a share of all tribal funds, annuities, and property.[27]

In the following year Little Shell and his council regained control over the Turtle Mountain Band. They repudiated the agreement made in 1892,[28] and lobbied Congress not to ratify the McCumber Agreement, to reinstate the Métis dropped from the tribal rolls, and to increase the size of the reservation. This campaign was successful in that Congress did not ratify the agreement, but a new treaty was not forthcoming for another twelve years.

When an agreement was finally reached in 1904, however, it represented a victory for those Métis who had promoted the 1892 agreement, and the defeat of Little Shell's faction. In the intervening period, Little Shell, disheartened with the lack of progress, had left for Montana with a significant number of his full-blood members. In 1900 he died, weakening the opposition to the 1892 agreement. Many of the Canadian-born Métis, who had been left off the tribal roll in 1892, returned to Canada after 1901 when the Canadian government made a new offer of scrip to those Métis who had not received it in 1885–86. As such the Métis and remaining full-bloods at Turtle Mountain were ready to accept the 1892 terms by 1904. This bill passed both the House and the Senate in 1904.[29] It was ratified by a majority of the adult males of the Turtle Mountain Band in a general council convened for that purpose in 1905. This agreement was largely the 1892 agreement, with minor modifications.

The agreement of 1904 provided for no expansion of the reservation, nor were any Métis dropped from tribal rolls in 1892 reinstated.[30] The agreement also entailed the implementation of the allotment of land in severalty.[31] At this time a new tribal roll was compiled by Charles Davis, the Indian superintendent for the reservation. This roll included 201 full-blood Chippewa and 1,893 Métis (see table 1). By 1904, the Turtle Mountain Band was largely a Métis band. The allotment of land to band members, however, was complicated because the size of the reservation was so small. Since every enrolled member of the band (including women and children) was granted a 160-acre allotment only 326 members received allotments on the reservation. The majority of the band received their allotments from the public domain. Many received allotments close to the reservation, but many others found their claims located in western North Dakota in the Trenton-Williston area, others in eastern Montana, and still others in South Dakota.

To interpret this process only in a tragic light—the allotment policy as a wholesale dispersal of the band and the rapid sale of many of these allotments as an unprecedented land loss[32]—is to ignore the way in which many of the Métis of Turtle Mountain viewed these grants. Many of those who had been given land in western North Dakota or eastern Montana moved there in the early twentieth century. They spent some years making improvements, sold the land, and used the proceeds to reestablish themselves in the Turtle Mountain area. For example, Freeman Belgarde, who was allotted 40 acres on the western edge of the Turtle Mountains and 120 acres in Montana briefly relocated to Montana to sell his land there. He then moved back to Turtle Mountain where he rented extra land adjacent to his small farm.[33] Ambroise Lafontaine moved to his allotment at Froid Lake, Montana, in 1905. He farmed there for six years, sold it, and then moved back to Turtle Mountain.[34] William Davis, who did receive land at Turtle Mountain, still moved to Montana in 1906 since many family members (his wife, sons, and grandsons) received allotments there. Again, these Montana lands were sold and the extended family moved back to Turtle Mountain to live on Davis's original allotment, later buying additional land.[35] Many of those returning to Turtle Mountain without land to settle on moved into Belcourt or onto land owned by a family member. This was possible because a family did not need much land to survive in Turtle Mountain. As Pete Delorme noted in an interview in 1993, "there weren't a lot of real farms around the reservation." People did not go into large-scale farming because they did not have the equipment. Most kept a few cows for butter and cream, and maintained a garden. Well into the twentieth century the Métis of Turtle Mountain still trapped and hunted in winter, chopped firewood for sale in area towns, and worked on threshing gangs and railway gangs in summer.[36] It was a way of life they had followed since moving back to Turtle Mountain in the early 1880s.

If the Turtle Mountain Métis adopted a Chippewa tribal affiliation to gain a land base and organize a coherent community, however, they did not assimilate to a Chippewa tribal culture. Interviews conducted with Métis elders in the 1990s (most of whom had been born in the early years of the twentieth century) show that they saw themselves as different and distinct from the small number of full-blood Chippewa on the reservation. As children they had been afraid of these Indians. They lived in different parts of the reservation and followed different religious and economic pursuits. Mostly Catholic, the Métis looked askance at the yearly sun dance held by the full-blood Chippewa.[37] It has only been in the last thirty years, after the last vestiges of Chippewa tribalism disappeared, that the Métis of Turtle Mountain have begun to revive Chippewa cultural practices and incorporate them into their identity.

Today the "Turtle Mountain Chippewa" are the largest Native community in North Dakota. With tribal enrollments in the area well over 18,000, this community is, as well, largely a Métis community. Today the Tribal Council is made up completely of Métis members, and the Métis heritage and history is celebrated every year on the reservation.[38] The significance of their story in the last two decades of the nineteenth century is not of dispersal and dispossession, but rather of the successful reformulation of a community and identity. While it is certainly true that the Turtle Mountain Métis were poor in relative terms for most of the first half of the twentieth century, it is also true that they built and maintained a unique community and identity through the politics of tribal affiliation, economic adaptation to a unique environment, and the maintenance of their cultural traditions.

Notes

1. Gregory S. Camp, "Working Out Their Own Salvation: The Allotment of Land in Severalty and the Turtle Mountain Chippewa Band, 1870–1920," *American Indian Culture and Research Journal* 14, no. 2 (1990): 19. See also Gregory S. Camp, "The Turtle Mountain Plains-Chippewa and Métis, 1797–1935," Ph.D. diss., University of New Mexico, 1987; Stanley N. Murray, "The Turtle Mountain Chippewa, 1882–1905," *North Dakota History* 51, no. 1 (winter 1984): 14–37.

2. Gregory S. Camp, "The Chippewa Fur Trade in the Red River Valley of the North, 1790–1830," in *The Fur Trade in North Dakota*, ed. Virginia L. Heidenreich (Bismarck: State Historic Society of North Dakota, 1990), 35–43. See also Jacqueline Peterson, "Gathering at the River: The Métis Peopling of the Northern Plains," in *The Fur Trade in North Dakota*, 50–53.

3. Affidavits of Michael Gladue and Louis La Fromboise locating the dividing line between the Sioux Indians and the Turtle Mountain Chippewa Country, as settled between them, 9 February 1892. Reprinted in "Turtle Mountain Band of Chippewa Indians," U.S. Congress, vol. 36, 56th Cong., 1st sess., 1900, S. Doc. 444, 1900, 151–52.

4. These interviews were conducted under the New Deal's WPA projects in the 1930s and are found on microfilm in the Historical Society of North Dakota Archives (Bismarck, N.D.), Historical Data Project, Rolette County.

5. During the 1870s the Canadian government negotiated a series of seven Indian treaties in western Canada. Those Métis who had kinship ties to the various bands were allowed to enter treaty. Following the Métis rebellion of 1885 in what today is Saskatchewan the Canadian government established a commission to extinguish the claims of the Métis residing in the Northwest on 15 July 1870 in areas that had already been ceded by treaty. Allotments were to be in money scrip worth $160 for Métis heads of family and $240 for children of Métis heads of family. A few weeks later another Order-in-Council allowed Métis children to take land scrip for 240 acres if they so desired. A later Order-in-Council (16 July 1899) extended scrip to all Métis born in the Northwest Territories between 15 July 1870 and 16 July 1885. Other rulings also provided for scrip to be granted to those Métis who had taken treaty but wished to withdraw in order to receive scrip. In response to these various scrip offerings many Métis who had moved to the United States returned to Canada to take advantage of these opportunities.

6. "Report of R. V. Belt on the Turtle Mountain Chippewa, November 13, 1888," reprinted in "Turtle Mountain Band of Chippewa Indians," U.S. Congress, vol. 36, no. 3878, 56th Cong., 1st sess., 1900, S. Doc. 444, 140–43. See "Treaty with the Chippewa-Red Lake and Pembina Bands, 1863," in *Laws and Treaties*, ed. Felix Kappler, 5 vols. (Washington, D. C.: Government Printing Office, 1912), 2:853–55.

7. Kappler, *Laws and Treaties*, 2:861–62.

8. Ibid. The treaty also stipulated that the trading debts of the Red Lake and Pembina Chippewa would be settled and a proviso was included, that allowed the president of the United States to reserve up to $5,000 from the annual payment for agricultural or educational improvements.

9. Gregory S. Camp, "The Turtle Mountain Plains-Chippewas and the Métis, 1797–1935," 117–18.

10. Historical Society of North Dakota Archives, Interview with Gregoire Brien (1930s), WPA Historical Data Project, Rolette County.

11. Winnipeg, Provincial Archives of Manitoba [hereafter PAM], RG 17, Parish Files, Lot 47, St. François Xavier.

12. Excerpts of the Indian Commissioner Reports, reprinted in "Turtle Mountain Band of Chippewa Indians," U.S. Congress, vol. 36, no. 3878, 56th Cong., 1st sess., 1900, S. Doc. 444, 142.

13. Ibid., "Statement of the case by John B. Bottineau, attorney for the Turtle Mountain Indians, Senator P. J. McCumber, a member of the said committee, being present with the Committee," (1892), 4–5.

14. In 1885 Rolette County, which encompassed that portion of the Turtle Mountain in United States territory, had a population of 2,232, and 414 farms, with 5,124 acres of improved land. By 1887 the county produced 13,200 bushels of wheat, 210 bushels of corn, 22,940 bushels of oats, and 3,110 bushels of barley. *Resources of Dakota* (1887)

15. Historical Society of North Dakota Archives, Interviews with Louis Allary, Freeman Belgarde, Gregoire Brien, Louis Desjarlais, Ambroise Lafontaine, Albert Wilkie, Albert Laviolette, Joseph Lagemodier, William Davis, and Michael Davis (1930s), WPA Data Project, Rolette County. *St. John: City at the End of the Rainbow* (1982), 36.

16. *St. John: City at the End of the Rainbow*, 32.

17. Belcourt was located within the reservation (unlike St. John) and quickly became the administrative center for the band.

18. *St. Ann's Centennial: 100 Years of Faith, 1885–1985* (Rolla: Star Printing, n.d.), 30–78.

19. Ibid., 91, 98.

20. James H. Howard, *The Plains-Ojibwa or Bungi: Hunters and Warriors of the Northern Prairies with Special Reference to the Turtle Mountain Band. Reprints in Anthropology* 7 (1977): 8.

21. Camp, "Working Out Their Own Salvation," 21–24.

22. Camp, "The Turtle Mountain Plains-Chippewa and the Métis, 1797–1935," 127–28.

23. These positions emerge fairly clearly in the documents published in "Turtle Mountain Band of Chippewa Indians," U.S. Congress, vol. 36, no. 3878, 56th Cong., 1st sess., 1900, S. Doc. 444, 1–173.

24. "Articles of agreement and stipulations made and concluded at Belcourt, in the County of Rolette and the State of North Dakota, by and Between Porter J. McCumber . . .," reprinted in ibid., 15–19.

25. "Statement of the case by John B. Bottineau, attorney for the Turtle Mountain Indians, Senator P. J. McCumber, a member of the said committee, being present with the Committee," (1892), reprinted in ibid., 4–5.

26. "Turtle Mountain Band of Chippewa Indians," 35.

27. "Articles of agreement and stipulations made and concluded at Belcourt, in the County of Rolette and the State of North Dakota, by and Between Porter J. McCumber . . .," 16.

28. "Minutes of the Council Proceedings of December 6 and 8, 1893," reprinted in "Turtle Mountain Band of Chippewa Indians," 125–26.

29. Senate Bill 196 and House Bill no.12,689.

30. There was no increase in the $1 million compensation to the band for lands ceded; however, in 1946, with the establishment of the Indian Claims Commission, the Turtle Mountain Band filed a claim for just payment of lands ceded in 1904 and this was settled in 1980 for a large cash settlement, the disbursement of which was still under negotiation in the early 1990s.

31. Camp, "Working Out Their Own Salvation," 28–29.

32. Ibid., 29–36.

33. Historical Society of North Dakota Archives, Interview of Freeman Belgarde (1930s), WPA Data Project, Rolette County.

34. Historical Society of North Dakota Archives, Interview of Ambroise Lafontaine (1930s), WPA Data Project, Rolette County.

35. Historical Society of North Dakota Archives, Interview of William and Michael Davis (1930s), WPA Data Project, Rolette County.

36. Interview of Peter Delorme, *Turtle Mountain Times,* 17 November 1993. Howard, *The Plains-Ojibwa or Bungi Hunters and Warriors of the Northern Prairies with Special Reference to the Turtle Mountain Band,* 28–30.

37. See interviews in *Turtle Mountain Times* in the early 1993–94; Howard, *The Plains-Ojibwa or Bungi: Hunters and Warriors of the Northern Prairies with Special Reference to the Turtle Mountain Band,* 7–8.

38. See Murray, "The Turtle Mountain Chippewa," 14; *St. Ann's Centennial: 100 Years of Faith,* 89–104; *Turtle Mountain Times,* various issues throughout 1994.

Janet E. Chute Ojibwa Leadership during the Fur
ᛉ Trade Era at Sault Ste. Marie

Introducing the "Cranes"

No other Ojibwa group during the mid to late fur trade era attracted as much attention from traders and colonial administrators as the "Crane" band of Sault Ste. Marie. The Cranes were descendants of an individual, or perhaps a select number of individuals, who possessed the Crane totem mark, or *dodem*, as an identifier. Their high profile stemmed from their ability to argue persuasively, and occasionally defiantly, on behalf of their group's long-term interests. At the turn of the eighteenth century the British at Michilimackinac feared that the Cranes might obstruct safe passage of goods and freight between Lakes Huron and Superior.[1] Yet sufficient written and oral data exist regarding this group for one to surmise that Crane leaders rarely acted rashly in their economic or political transactions with outsiders. At least as early as 1760 they were committed to maintaining a milieu conducive to the preservation of Native cultural values, and during the first three decades of the British colonial regime, their warlike penchant and strategic location made them a formidable entity to be reckoned with by both Native and non-Native brigades seeking entrance to Lake Superior by way of Sault Ste. Marie.

New Light on an Old Controversy

What was the organizational character of the Crane group? Was it patrilineal? did its composition and structure change as a result of the fur trade? The nature of the impact of the fur trade on Ojibwa leadership in the Upper Great Lakes area has been the subject of controversy for many years. Harold Hickerson claimed that Ojibwa groups prior to the arrival of Europeans to the Sault area resided in patrilineal village clans, with leadership decisions made by the group as a whole.[2] Powerful chiefs, he suggested, only emerged during the fur trade era when a rise of individualistic values carried over into the

153

sphere of intergroup relations and radically modified group structure and composition. James G. E. Smith and Edward S. Rogers similarly regarded high-profile leadership as an epiphenomenon of the fur trade milieu. They argued, however, that protohistoric bands were not patrilineal, but rather that new forms of leadership came to be engrafted upon an earlier, flexible bilateral band society without major modification to the groups themselves.[3] By contrast, Charles Bishop contended that the Ojibwa's central role in a vital prehistoric trade in copper, chert, ocher and perishable items would have fostered aggressive leaders who at all times could negotiate effectively in the trading forum.[4] To Bishop, organizational characteristics exhibited by the late seventeenth century constituted elaborations of earlier prototypes, with trade and war alliances among group leaders continuing to determine internal structuring of the units involved, as they had in the past.

In this chapter, these positions are reviewed in the light of historic and ethnographic evidence pertaining to the Cranes. For 150 years, leaders at the Sault bore the Crane totem, or *dodem*, an animal symbol inherited in the male line and used as both a personal and a group identifier. Internal composition, development cycle, nature and transmission of leadership, and the strategic

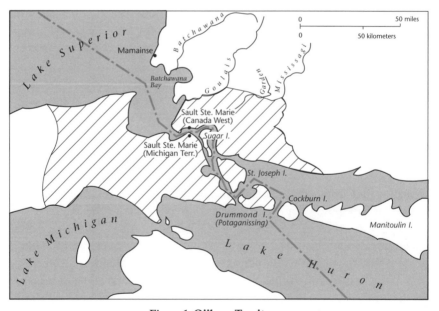

Figure 1. Ojibwa Territory.

position of the Cranes vis-à-vis other groups are examined from the perspective of values upheld by this group. This stance echoes Hickerson's viewpoint that values play an important role in the nature of group organization and maintenance, but questions the assumption that values are always necessarily altered radically by economic circumstances.

The traditional Native worldview also undoubtedly colored Crane perceptions on leadership in the past. Worldview has governed and, to a certain extent, still does govern group consensus on how leaders ought to act. According to Mary Black-Rogers, who conducted her studies of leadership among Native respondants during the 1970s and 1980s, ordinary Ojibwa individuals within the negotiating forum often demonstrated "power-control" by compelling the other side to decide on the definition of a situation.[5] Yet leaders arose with acknowledged capabilities that were not so ambiguous. While Black-Rogers admits that Ojibwa leaders provided exceptions to the usual powerless stance, she embedded the concept of Native leadership deeply within the operation of the power-belief system to reveal subtle rationales lying behind such exceptional modes of behavior. Each individual was expected to be self-sufficient, but those with great powers were charged with a special responsibility to use their gifts to aid others, less fortunate. This sharing relationship did not always develop; gifts might be misused for selfish ends, but it was the socially sanctioned behavior to which leaders must conform if they wished to maintain their status within their group. While a leader's gifts—seen as blessings bestowed by spiritual agencies—remained covertly expressed except in certain ritualized settings, demonstration of their working to the benefit of the group in the economic and political spheres assured others of the consistency with which their headmen used such powers to further the welfare of their own people. In so doing a leader attracted followers to his group and retained them over time. From this perspective lineal characteristics could be overridden by ideological considerations, which raised the necessity for competent leadership behaviour above and beyond any need to replicate the lineal social structure. Crane leadership, for its continuance, depended as much on its ability to exercise power in conformity with prevailing cultural norms and values, as on its possession of the "right" *dodemic* mark.

Holders of the Crane *dodem* referred to themselves as belonging to the *Bo.wating.inini.wug*, or "people of the rapids," which comprised an Ojibwa group entity recorded at Sault Ste. Marie as early as 1640.[6] From this is derived the term Batchewana, used to designate one of the two local Ojibwa bands presently residing near Sault Ste. Marie. It has also been posited that

Outchibous, denoting a group encountered by French missionaries in the early seventeenth century, may bear relation to the Ojibwa term *Otchitchak*, or "Crane."[7] According to oral tradition, the Crane band at Sault Ste. Marie split about 1670, with a prominent chief of the Crane *dodem* migrating to Chequamegon, near Lapointe, Wisconsin.[8]

The fact that the chief who represented Sault Ste. Marie at peace negotiations in Montreal in 1701 drew a crane symbol as his or his village's identifying mark on the French document [9] suggests that chiefly succession *may* have followed a lineal pattern by this time, although conclusive evidence for lineality is lacking. Yet the presence of a chief known as Kecheokanajeed, or "Great Crane," living around 1750, from whom all Cranes at the Sault in 1800 were descended, also indicates that leadership succession and group membership may not necessarily have followed the same rules. There are problems with Bishop's contention that Ojibwa leaders, such as those of the Cranes, exhibited competitive traits characteristic of Melanesian "big-men" that induced their groups to attach themselves firmly to their headmen through their exercise of solely lineal principles. Although thought provoking, this argument is weakened on the one hand by the fact that during the height of the Maritime fur trade, Micmac and Malecite chiefs also acted as "big-men," but with no concomitant development of lineality within their bands' social organization.[10] On the other hand, historical and genealogical evidence relating specifically to the composition of the Crane group tends to uphold Smith and Rogers's contention that Ojibwa bands themselves have always remained primarily bilateral, with group membership determined by linkages through consanguineal and affinal ties to a prominent nodal core group—usually a leader and his wives. In 1736, for instance, warriors of the Sault nation were reported as both "Cranes" and "Catfish," so the group was composite at this date even if the chiefly hierarchy were solely "Cranes."[11] During the fur trade era *leadership succession* may have developed lineal traits, while admittance to group membership may have remained primarily bilateral—and exercised through both male and female kinship linkages.

Another important aspect of the Ojibwa belief system overlooked by Bishop's argument involves the *dodem*. While often regarded solely as a group identifier, the *dodem* also retained a spiritual and moral component. During the early 1980s the author had opportunities to speak on the subject with several prominent members of the Pine family at Garden River, near Sault Ste. Marie, who, although they did not possess the Crane dodem themselves, knew many of the traditions surrounding the *dodemic* naming system and could trace Crane ancestry either through their grandfather's or their great grandfather's maternal line.[12] One of these individuals, Mr. Daniel Erskine Pine Sr., stressed that Ojibwa leaders acted in conformity with group norms concerning headship, since every person had a purpose for which one's dodem acted as a spiritual guide.[13] Actions not in keeping with the Ojibwa moral system would cause one's *dodem* to flee, leaving the soul to wander aimlessly, especially after death. A chief would employ his *dodem* as an identifier in the negotiating forum so as prevent his personal name—particularly a name associated with his source of power or blessings—from being bandied about promiscuously by others. Since a Sault leader thus would assume his *dodemic* identity with outsiders, the bilateral group he represented would come to be known as "Cranes," not only because he held that mark, but also because its members were seen to be under the express protection of the person bearing the Crane *dodem*. The band would be called *the Cranes*, because they were under a Crane's care.

Opportunities for ambitious men at the Sault lacking the Crane mark to exercise such protective aegis would have been limited, however. As head chiefs were usually polygynous, with large numbers of children, numerous individuals of a chief's *dodemic* designation were always potential candidates in the event of a leadership vacancy. Generations of leaders with the same *dodem* became an entrenched phenomenon in the Upper Great Lakes Native community. Moreover, by allocating gifts and honors to individuals identifiable by a mark they recognized, traders and colonial authorities aided in sustaining the preeminence over time of a group characterized by a specific *dodem*. In this way, the *dodemic* unit with its lineal traits assumed functional prominence during the colonial and fur trade era as a structural entity engrafted upon the Ojibwa kinship universe.

A final problem with Bishop's hypothesis resides in his suggestion that chiefly roles were restricted solely to those of "civil chief" and "war chief." To Bishop, reciprocal alliances for trade and war, sustained at exchange feasts, upheld a chiefly elite. Yet on reading nineteenth-century ethnographic accounts it appears that many other leadership roles existed, with that of civil chief being only the most prominent. Such roles, almost all achieved rather than ascribed, included that of *mishinoway*, a kind of "economical aid to the chief"[14]; *oskabewis*, a messenger and minor spokesperson under the direction of the head chief[15]; *kekedowenine*, an advocate who acted whenever disputes arose within the band[16]; *tebahkoonegawenene*, a judge in such disputes; and the anikeogima, a "step-below chief" or subchief.[17] Other ranked statuses existed within the medicine societies, particularly the Grand Medicine Society, or *Midéwiwin*, a forum for expressing power-control in ways that conferred considerable prestige within the Upper Great Lakes Native community.

None of these roles was mutually exclusive. A subchief, usually the head of a winter hunting unit, often traded on behalf of his extended family group. "Trading chiefs" were men whose success in procuring furs became formally recognized by traders and fur companies. This did not preclude civil chiefs from acting as the principal trading negotiators on behalf of their entire band either, since their duties involved negotiating with outside agencies. Yet the head chief, or *ogima*, was not primarily a centralizing and distributing agent for material wealth. His principal role was to establish and sustain political linkages with other powerful agencies in order to secure a stable milieu for his group.

The Cranes retained their political aegis until the first decades of the nineteenth century. Active in the medicine societies, in warfare and negotiations, they appeared elaborately and often richly dressed at councils, the men bedecked with silver ornaments, silk turbans, regimental coats trimmed with ribbons and, occasionally, both French and British medals and other military insignia. Henry Rowe Schoolcraft, the Indian agent at the American Sault from 1822 to 1842, felt it imperative to discover the principles governing succession within the Crane band in order to weigh the respective claims of potential chiefly successors whenever a prominent Crane leader died. Schoolcraft traced the Cranes' genealogy back to a patriarch by the name of Great Crane. Great Crane had been recognized as a head chief around 1750 by the French, and had four sons, the eldest of whom, Maidsosagee, maintained four wives and had about twenty children.[18] The Crane civil chief at the time of Schoolcraft's arrival was Shingabaw'osin, an elderly man who had only one son, Kebay Nodin, but surrounded himself with sons-in-law as well.

Despite Schoolcraft's emphasis on patrilineal succession, being well placed within the Crane hierarchy was not the only criterion for leadership. War prowess, negotiating ability, strong oratorical skills, the ability to proffer wise advice in council, and the right to regulate the membership of one's group counted highly. Territorial prerogatives also formed an important constituent. Crane leaders traditionally wielded aegis over the Canadian Sault and most of Michigan's Upper Peninsula.

Their location at the Sault conferred numerous strategic advantages upon the Cranes. No trade passing north along the St. Mary's River escaped their detection. A respectful attention had to be paid to their presence, as they were known to be hostile if treated too casually by passing strangers. In the eighteenth century the Sault had remained marginal to the nearest principal seat of French colonial power at Detroit. Large assemblages of Native visitants met annually at the rapids to exploit the abundant whitefish, trade, perform ceremonies, hold festivities, and wage war with the Iroquois, Foxes, Menomonies, and Dakota. Band leaders accepted French gifts and goods but did not always conform to the wishes of French policy. The terms were rarely strictly businesslike. According to Native cultural logic, the French were kinspeople, and should act as such by graciously and responsibly supplying Native needs.[19] For their part, the French authorities highly valued the Ojibwa as allies against the British on the Albany. French geopolitics subordinated trade to an instrument of empire; by 1700 goods might even be traded at a loss in order to keep bands loyal to the French cause.[20]

Such conditions enabled leadership candidates to amass surpluses in furs, which they frequently exchanged for instruction in an esoteric form of traditional knowledge associated with the *Midéwiwin*, or Grand Medicine Society. This last point is significant, for exchange of peltry for power has until recently constituted an important yet oft-overlooked consequence of the fur trade. Entry to the ranks of recognized power-holders in the Upper Great Lakes area traditionally required four distinct achievements: a vision experience; the recording of this vision-inspired knowledge on bark scrolls known as *ke.kee.wins*; the active demonstration of the possession of power on the warpath or in the councils of one's nation; and finally, a formal recognition by other power-holders that one must be treated as a colleague and no longer as a mere aspirant.[21] Yet the specialized knowledge requisite to participate in the revitalization ceremonies of the Grand Medicine Society had to be purchased, and the required payment in peltry, even into the nineteenth century, was high. Many of the Cranes, among them Kaygayosh, the third-eldest son of Maidosagee, stood out as noted *Midéwiwin* practitioners. Kaygayosh's apprentice, Shingwaukonse, was said to have paid his mentor over forty packs of beaver skins, each pack weighing one hundred pounds at a time when beaver was worth eight to ten dollars a pound.[22] Despite the exorbitant cost, however, so many contenders desired to join the *Midéwiwin* that reforms had to be made to restrict entrance even further. Under a revised policy, introduced by Eskebugecoshe, also called Flat Mouth, a *Midéwiwin* practitioner and civil leader from Leech Lake, Wisconsin, new candidates had to have two, rather than merely one mentor, undoubtedly with a concomitant escalation in costs of instruction.[23]

Ambitious young Ojibwa men, finding few leadership opportunities in their home communities during the late eighteenth century, often entered the fur trade as Native middlemen. These individuals pressed westward to escape the hegemonical sway of established chiefs, and when they amassed sufficient furs, sought the widespread prestige conferred by *Midéwiwin* membership. In their trading ventures and wars against other Native nations, they were aided and abetted by certain French traders who remained in the Upper Great Lakes region, as well as Métis persons who, owing to the exigencies of trade, often opposed colonial policy.[24] Certain of these Ojibwa rose to become civil chiefs in their own right on lands lying west and southwest of Lake Superior.

Others with similar ambitions became long-distance brigade leaders who returned each fall to their home bands in the northeastern sector of the Upper Great Lakes. These men, with their retinues, plied Lake Superior and points west for furs in the spring, and by late fall returned to exchange their peltry at Sault Ste. Marie and Mackinac. Shingwaukonse, or "The Little Pine," Kaygayosh's protégé in the *Midéwiwin*, was one such person. Although Schoolcraft claimed that Shingwaukonse "traced his lineage from the old Crane band," The Little Pine did not possess the Crane *dodem*. Shingwaukonse was a product of the fur trade, the Métis son of an Ojibwa woman and a French trader, probably Levoine Barthe of the Barthe family at Sault Ste. Marie, which maintained close kin and trade ties with the prominent merchant John Askin Sr. at Mackinac. Culturally, however, Shingwaukonse was wholly Ojibwa, since his mother left her French consort to rejoin her people while her son was in his childhood. It would not be until his escalation to the rank of civil chief in 1836, in the wake of a weakening Crane hegemony, that Shingwaukonse would see fit to employ his own distinctive *dodemic* mark— that of the Plover, a symbol that his male descendants still claim today. Prior to this date The Little Pine employed one of his two French names, either "Levoine Bart [Barthe]" or "Augustan," as a personal identifier.[25]

Shingwaukonse would become the inheritor of the Crane legacy of power and prestige, as the following section shows. Yet, since before 1836 Shingwaukonse did not act independently of the Cranes, his actions as a leader must first be examined in the light of ethnographic and historic evidence relating to the larger Crane band. After 1836 Shingwaukonse's following would not only separate from, but also draw into itself, elements of the original Crane group.

Patterns of Interaction, Defiance, and Reconciliation

The Cranes, which had ably weathered the vagaries of French and British colonial policy in the late seventeenth and eighteenth centuries, found themselves confronted by a new threat from the south following the American Revolution. As groups of land speculators and colonists crossed the

Alleghenies into the Upper Ohio Valley, repercussions from disconcerting events involving the Ohio Native populations spread northward to the Upper Great Lakes area. In 1793 the Ojibwa, all of whom were designated as "Cranes" within a roster of twelve participating nations listed on British documents of the time, joined in intertribal councils at the Miamis Rapids sponsored by the British Indian Department. This ephemeral confederacy mutually pledged to defend the Upper Ohio territory as a neutral buffer zone between competing British and American continental interests.[26]

Within two years all the Native delegates who had pinned their nascent hopes on Britain's defense of a neutral tract had their hopes dashed when in 1795 Britain relinquished all responsibility for the Ohio area under the Treaty of Greenville. That Britain acquiesced to American demands without first seeking Native input of any kind enraged the Cranes, who immediately used their strategic position to harass British trade. A French trader warned the British at Mackinac that Maidosagee's people had attacked several traders of British extraction. Even John Tanner, a Britisher then living among the Ottawa, found it expedient to move westward with his adoptive Native parents, since he heard Maidosagee was "going against the whites," and he felt his position at Mackinac unsafe.[27]

Although the French and Métis traders proved less vulnerable than the British to Crane hostility, at least one, Jean Baptiste Nolin, who had purchased the old Barthe establishment at the rapids, found it suddenly expedient to offer the Cranes compensation for his use of their land.[28] On the other hand, when the Cranes burned John Sayers's premises to the ground while he was away west on a trading expedition, he could redeem so little property of any value that he had to engage in the service of the North West Company.[29] By 1798, however, willingness shown by Maidosagee's band to cede St. Joseph's Island to the British for a garrison post, as well as a tract on the north shore of St. Mary's Straits to the North West Company, demonstrated that by this date some grounds for accommodation had been reached.[30]

The Cranes' firm attachment to Britain in 1807 and 1808, despite earlier reversals in British policy antithetical to Native interests, stemmed from this group's associations with British traders for whom they had deep respect and occasionally kinship ties. John Askin at Mackinac publicly vowed to uphold Native territorial claims and engendered the belief among the Ojibwa that Britain would also uphold these rights.[31] Traders like Askin were able to retain the Sault band's confidence in the British cause at a time when many chiefs further west, after hearkening to the ephemeral appeals of Tenskwatawa, the "Shawnee prophet," brother to Tecumseh, to drive all whites into the sea, simply assumed a state of passive defiance.

John Askin Sr., before his death in 1808, specifically addressed his attention to the Cranes through Shingwaukonse, who became keeper of a wampum belt symbolizing the Crane band's allegiance to Britain.[32] In response, Shingwaukonse fought alongside four of Maidosagee's sons, Shingabaw'osin, Waubechechauk, Sessaba, and Mucketdaywucket, in numerous encounters with the Americans during the War of 1812, and led the last of the war parties from the Sault against the Americans in 1814.[33] Until 1820 Shingwaukonse remained in contact with the elder Askin's son, John Askin Jr., who became Indian agent at Amherstburg. For his loyalty to Britain, Askin promised him a reserve for his people on the north shore of the Sault rapids, although Shingwaukonse did not exercise territorial prerogatives over the area for many years.[34]

After 1816 the political world as the Cranes had known it changed radically. The British sent a clear message that strong Ojibwa leaders would prove an embarrassment. In 1819 Indian Department officials recognized Nebenagoching, the eight-year-old son of a Crane leader named Waubechechauk, or White Crane—who had fallen in action during the War of 1812—as the Sault head chief;[35] undoubtedly a concession to American fears concerning British influence among the Ojibwa along the international boundary. While the British agency on Drummond Island, located westward of Manitoulin Island in Lake Huron, continued distributing annual presents to the western tribes as they had done during the war, none of their Native allies had been included in the peacemaking proceedings. As Lieutenant Colonel Robert McDouall, Commander at Drummond Island, commented, peace with the United States favored expedience and discretion. "Through me," he lamented, "the Western Indians were taught to cherish brighter hopes. . . . How have such prospects been realized?—they are abandoned at their utmost need, and [are] about to be immolated on the altar of American vengeance."[36]

Captain Thomas G. Anderson, the British Indian agent resident on Drummond Island, had another suggestion. His answer lay in weaning the bands away from the fur trade and placing them in agricultural settlements away from the international border, divorced from the traders who originally had generated their attachment to the British Crown.[37] The reticulate kinship linkages that characterized many Ojibwa-trader relationships were to be completely ignored. Henceforth the Native peoples would be dealt with apart from any considerations of their former trading partners.

The Cranes, it seemed, would either have to vacate the American Sault or stand their ground when the Americans laid claim to their lands at the rapids.

They initially responded to this new challenge with the characteristic defiance they had shown in the past. In 1816, two American military expeditions narrowly escaped being fired on by Ojibwa canoeists in the St. Mary's Straits.[38] Then, when an official party from Washington under General Cass arrived in 1820 to gain a surrender of land at the Sault for a fort, one of Maidosagee's younger sons, Sessaba, sought to avenge Waubechechauk's death at the hands of the British during the War of 1812 by hauling down the American flag and kicking over the tobacco proffered by the Americans.[39] The Crane hierarchy acted with candor by appointing Shingwaukonse as a disinterested mediator in the dispute. Shingwaukonse was a good speaker, and since he was not Waubechechauk's blood relative, his oratorical powers might readily be called upon to mollify the vengeful Sessaba and permit the surrender to proceed peacefully[40] The Ojibwa received no annuities or other compensation under the 1820 treaty other than the promise of unmolested access to the rapids fishery. Shingwaukonse's efforts as a *kekedowenini* succeeded and, in consequence, the Cranes settled down to an uneasy accommodation with an American fort in their midst and their rapids tract divided by an international boundary.

Radical Changes in the Fur Trade after 1816

The new international boundary did more than simply divide the waters at the Sault. It heralded the implementation of new trade restrictions. In 1816 American legislation banned British traders from American soil and granted monopoly rights to American trade enterprises operating at fixed stations.[41] It was a long remove from the earlier French era that saw goods traded at a loss to keep Ojibwa loyal to the French Crown. Certain traders, such as Charles Ermatinger at the British Sault, continued to trade south of the border for a while through their Ojibwa kin. Married to a daughter of Chief Katawabedai at Fond du Lac, Ermatinger received furs from southwest of Superior until retiring to Montreal in 1828. Shingwaukonse also regularly travelled into interior Minnesota and Wisconsin during the 1820s and 1830s to acquire peltry destined for British posts.

Certain traders pressed northward to compensate for the loss of the southwestern trade. Xavier Biron and Augustan Nolin invited Ojibwa from Fon du Lac to join them when they entered into an agreement with the Hudson's Bay Company to provide stiff competition for the North West Company near Michipicoten, on the north shore of Lake Superior.[42] Others not so fortunate were left foundering for a livelihood. With the unification of the Hudson's Bay Company and the North West Company in 1821, many former company personnel found themselves unemployed. Some of these individuals, mostly Métis, joined with independent traders retiring from Drummond Island and Penetanguishene and settled in the environs of the British Sault.

As a result, over thirty Métis homesteads suddenly materialized along the shoreline on the British side of the rapids. Most of the men were engaged in the Sault fishery, although some worked as boat builders, guides, canoe men, carpenters, and translators for the Hudson's Bay Company. Illicitly, they participated in the whiskey trade. Many were married to Native women; those who were not tended to take wives from the Sault band. No longer were opportunities available for these Métis to enter the northern or western trade, and even on the immediate home front, horizons were limited. Furbearers had declined dramatically in numbers by 1830. According to Factor George Keith at the Hudson's Bay post at Michipicoten, "Black and Brown bears, lynx, fisher, martin, mink, cross, red + silver foxes, beaver + otter, Wolves and Wolverines are almost exterminated, as are the moose and red deer."[43] In 1831, owing to scarcity of furs, Governor George Simpson of the Hudson's Bay Company relegated the Sault to a mere supply depot.[44] Two years later the powerful American Fur Company lobby pressured the Hudson's Bay Company to restrict all operations, including those of the Ojibwa associated with them, solely to the British side of the international boundary.

Despite these restrictions, fur brigades under Shingwaukonse's headship still plied each year to the Hudson's Bay post operating at La Cloche on the north shore of Lake Huron, enjoyed a feast provided by the company, and traded some of their furs before proceeding on to part with the rest of their peltry at the British distribution of presents at Penetanguishene. During these years Shingwaukonse launched a major campaign calling for the American Ojibwa, with whom he had regular contact on his trading expeditions, to remain loyal to the British interest. His appeals rarely fell on deaf ears. Head chiefs west of Lake Superior railed against the high prices set by the American trading monopolies.[45] New racist policies, moreover, undermined the rights of chiefs to determine their bands' membership. When a Crane chief from Chequamegon, Wisconsin, requested government assistance to prevent Métis not associated with his band by kinship or friendship from using resources in his territory, the American subagent found he had to follow government directives that excluded all Métis from Ojibwa lands, not merely those whom the chief regarded as poachers.[46]

The Sault Cranes, by contrast, still felt they had organizations other than government agencies that they could approach to assist them in protecting their territorial and resource rights. When Kaygayosh, who assumed the

Crane leadership following Shingabaw'osin's death in 1828, and Shingwaukonse, acting as Kaygayosh's mishinway, found the American Indian agent reluctant to assist them in preventing non-Natives from poaching at the rapids tract reserved under the treaty of 1820 and at other fishery locations used extensively by the Ojibwa,[47] they turned for help to the Hudson's Bay Company on the Canadian side. The company, in response, welcomed the opportunity to restrict non-Native access to fisheries upon which it itself relied, and for several years actively supported this Native cause.[48]

Further problems arose, however, when, under the joint sponsorship of the British Indian Department and Lieutenant Governor Sir John Colborne, an Anglican missionary, William McMurray, arrived to establish a farming community at the rapids. Shingwaukonse initially favored the plan, and travelled to Toronto with McMurray to request housing materials and agricultural implements. When Shingwaukonse proposed Garden River, an old supply depot for brigades lying just east of the British Sault, as the best location, however, both the Indian agent and the missionary adamantly rejected the chief's choice, and located the mission instead on the old Ermatinger estate.[49]

A second disturbing incident for the Ojibwa concerned the intention of one prominent British Indian agent, Thomas G. Anderson, to move all the Métis at the British Sault to St. Joseph's Island on the pretext that Métis traders were poor neighbors for incipient Native farmers. Since 1819 Anderson had remained true to his goal of establishing government-controlled Native farming communities on the western frontier. His definition of "Métis" nevertheless included some prominent members of the old Crane band. Waubechechauk's son, Nebenagoching, fell into this category since his mother had been a daughter of a Sault trader, Jean Baptiste Perrault. Even Shingwaukonse's eldest son, Pierre Lavoine, was among those enumerated who would be relocated to St. Joseph's Island.[50]

For Shingwaukonse to deny these Métis individuals his support would have been tantamount to relinquishing his responsibility toward the Cranes as a whole. So when Anderson deprived Nebenagoching in 1835 of his British medal and chiefly status, allegedly owing to Nebenagoching's whiskey smuggling, and conferred these on Shingwaukonse,[51] the latter immediately rose up as the Métis' advocate. Anderson, seeing the futility of any attempt to control this new turn of events by resorting to divide-and-conquer techniques, pressured Shingwaukonse and his followers to move to Manitoulin Island. The chief adamantly refused, and relocated his family and followers to Garden River, where, with the assistance of local Métis, they began building their own log cabins and cultivating crops well beyond the scrutiny of Indian Department officialdom.[52]

The Crane Band Fissions

Throughout 1835 and 1836 Shingwaukonse's following continued to grow. Two of Maidosagee's grandsons, Kabaosa and Waubmama, wed daughters of Shingwaukonse and made Garden River their permanent home. Members of the Biron, LaRose, and Boissoneau families relinquished their Métis identities to join with the Ojibwa. Despite its rising population, however, the Garden River community still remained an integral part of the group united under Kaygayosh's headship. It was Schoolcraft's policies, rather than any action on the part of The Little Pine, that finally split the Crane band. When fitting out an Ojibwa delegation to participate in treaty making in Washington in 1836, the agent arbitrarily appointed a subchief of an intrusive group, originally from Lapointe, at the western extremity of Lake Superior, which possessed the Caribou, rather than the Crane, *dodem*, as the Sault's leading Native representative.[53] In so doing, Schoolcraft undermined the Crane leadership, although the group retained its paramount place at the Sault. Kaygayosh's death later the same year, however, resulted in the rise of Shingwaukonse, rather than one of Maidosagee's progeny, to the rank of civil chief.

Like Kaygayosh before him, The Little Pine continued to look for new economic opportunities for his people in the wake of the declining fur trade. Fish taken at the rapids, he declared, could be sold profitably to feed the expanding western settlements. With logging and mineral exploration presenting alternative possibilities, in preparation he claimed exclusive territorial prerogative over local timber and mineral resources. He even challenged the Hudson's Bay Company's right to occupy land at the Sault because it had failed to honor a promise to hold a feast for the Ojibwa each spring. The old Crane band accepted their new dynamic chief because he had shown himself to have power as a noted war chief, spokesperson, and *Midéwiwin* practitioner. He controlled the membership of his band, and exercised territorial jurisdiction over a large tract on the north shore lying between Thessalon and Batchewana Bay. His adoption after 1836 of the Plover *dodem* as an identifying mark on petitions and deeds testified to his assumption of the rights and responsibilities of civil chieftainship.[54]

Shingwaukonse still had to prove to the southwestern Ojibwa, who hearkened to his vision of the future, that he could indeed make things happen on their behalf. Not only did their territories suffer from the cutting edge of resource exploration, but dwindling numbers of fur- bearing animals threatened to destroy their economic and social fabric. Worse, they feared complete loss of their political autonomy, for in 1837 news reached these bands that they might be removed west of the Mississippi in five years.

The Ojibwa chiefs who hearkened most closely to Shingwaukonse were some of the most traditional in their worldview. Eshkebugecoshe of Leech Lake, for instance, was a high-ranking member of the *Midéwiwin* who prized his chiefly autonomy. Shingwaukonse, too, remained a proponent of the traditional cosmological order, overlaid by a thin veneer of Christianity, for his son, Ogista, claimed that his father destroyed his *Midéwiwin* paraphernalia only shortly before his death.[55] Shingwaukonse employed Ojibwa tenets of power-control to capture sources of knowledge and power in a context that blended Ojibwa, Métis, and Victorian English traditions. Combined with his determination to preserve an environment in which Ojibwa values could survive was a resilient faith, rooted deep in the traditional Ojibwa worldview, that a supreme power would reimburse the Native population for the difficulties they had suffered. The Creator, Shingwaukonse declared repeatedly, had endowed the Ojibwa with rich mineral, timber, and other resources within their former hunting tracts to sustain them when the animals had finally disappeared.[56] As his life, his mode of retaining control remained characteristically Ojibwa, and chiefs like Eshkebugecoshe responded because they knew exactly the kind of appeal Shingwaukonse was making. It was a prophecy of the future, highly structured and reasoned according to the Ojibwa belief system, and it called upon all power-holders, Native as well as non-Native, to actualize its hidden promises.

Shingwaukonse was able also to unite the entire Crane band. Oshawano, a Crane chief on the American side, and Nebenagoching, the Crane chief at the British Sault, joined with Shingwaukonse and at least two local Métis leaders in forcibly exercising their ancient territorial rights to land and resources by going so far in 1849 as to dispossess a copper mine north of the Sault. The two Cranes and The Little Pine then entered the Robinson-Huron treaty negotiations with the British Crown the following year as a unified chiefly elite. The Indian Affairs Department had so little idea of the composition of the Sault bands that it is doubtful they ever realized they had included an American Crane chief in their negotiations. It was to take nine years before this "mistake" was discovered and rectified by the deletion of Oshawano's synonymous name, Cassaquadung, from the Robinson treaty lists in 1859.

The year 1850 was the swan song of the Crane group. It never acted as a unified political entity again. The British Sault band under Nebenagoching, the American Sault band under Oshawano, and the Garden River band under Shingwaukonse separated geographically and politically into three distinct identities. Yet news of this outcome did not reach the southwestern chiefs until several years later. Still believing Shingwaukonse to have obtained some of his goals over land and resources on the British side of the rapids, head chiefs including Eshkebugecoshe petitioned in 1853 for permission to settle at Garden River and elsewhere along the northern shore of Lake Superior.[57] Their plight aroused little sympathy in British government circles, however. Soon afterward the American government rescinded their threat to remove the Ojibwa westward—Eshkebugkecoshe and his fellow chiefs would stay where they were.

Conclusion

Charles Bishop has presented an intriguing hypothesis by asserting that trade structured the internal nature of Ojibwa bands. Certainly the decline of the fur trade, with its concomitant reduction in high-profile trading alliances among the Ojibwa trading elite, had consequences in the Upper Great Lakes area that were nothing short of catastrophic. Yet the nature of Shingwaukonse's campaign in the twilight of the trading era, rooted as it was deep in the traditional Ojibwa worldview regarding power and power's proper recognition, demonstrated that to point to structured systems of trade relations as primary social determinants might be engaging in some measure of misplaced causality. To reduce such a vital element of the Ojibwa belief system as the *dodem* to something akin to a modern company's logos, may emphasize the fact that it functioned as a group designator—in addition to being an individual identifier in ways that governed marriage patterns and the extension of kin obligations to nonkin—but it ignores its role in the Ojibwa's ideological responses to the vicissitudes of economic and political change. Shingwaukonse only employed his own *dodem*, the Plover, apart from the Crane mark of his maternal kin, when he saw himself as assuming a role that granted him an opportunity to act independently to preserve a cherished cultural milieu. To this chief, as to his followers, mineral deposits, timber, and fish were as much gifts as the animals had been; to be taken, treated with respect, and subjected to exchanges endowed with meanings that, for the Ojibwa, transcended the commercial. To emphasize the importance that the value system espoused by the Garden River chief still holds for Ojibwa today, one of Shingwaukonse's great grandsons recounted the following story regarding the beliefs held by his great grandfather, and stressed the legacy for future generations that it contained:

> Manido are all valuable. Everything was put in for a purpose. That's what he said. If you run into any trouble you're the cause of it. You can bring disturbance. Only you can make a good thing or bad thing of yourself. He was really smart, just like a minister. He told others, you be proud of these gifts. Don't make fun of anything. Don't waste anything. It not for sale. If you throw it away, I'll live naked.[58]

Notes

1. National Archives of Canada (hereafter referred to as NAC), "Thomas Duggan, Storekeeper at Mackinac, to Indian Affairs, 1796," MG 19, Claus Papers, 7: 128. Reel C–1479. In the early decades of the nineteenth century the Ojibwa twice threatened American military parties passing through the St. Mary's Straits into Lake Superior. Henry R. Schoolcraft, *Personal Memoirs of a Residence of Thirty Years with the Indian Tribes on the American Frontier, A.D. 1812 to A.D. 1842* (Philadelphia: Lippincott, Grambo and Co., 1851; reprint, New York: Arno Press, 1975), 632.

2. Harold Hickerson, *The Southwestern Chippewa: An Ethnnohistorical Study. American Anthropological Association Memoir No. 92* (Menasha, Wis: American Anthropological Association, 1962), 82–84.

3. Edward S. Rogers and James G. E. Smith, "Cultural Ecology in the Canadian Shield Sub-arctic," paper presented at the IXth International Congress of Anthropological and Ethnological Sciences, Chicago, 1973.

4. Charles Bishop, "The Question of Ojibwa Clans," in *Actes du vingtième congrès des Algonquinistes,* ed. William Cowan (Ottawa: Department of Linguistics, Carleton University, 1989), 43–61.

5. Mary Black-Rogers, "Ojibwa Power Belief System," in *The Anthropology of Power,* ed. R. D. Fogelson and R. N. Adams (New York: Academic Press, 1977), 141–51.

6. Reuban Gold Thwaites, ed., *Jesuit Relations and Allied Documents, Travel and Explorations of the Jesuit Missions in New France,* 1673–1791, vol. 18 (Cleveland, Ohio: Burrows Brothers, 1896), 229–31. Hereafter referred to as JR.

7. Theresa Schenck, "Identifying the Ojibwa," in *Actes du vingt-cinquième congrès des Algonquinistes,* ed. William Cowan (Ottawa: Department of Linguistics, Carleton University, 1994), 395–405.

8. William W. Warren, *History of the Ojibway Nation* (Minneapolis, Minn.: Ross and Haines Inc., 1970), 316–17.

9. Archives nationales, Archives des colonies, Correspondance générale, Canada (C11A), F–19: 43r, "Marks of the various Indian villages. Ratification of the Peace, August 4, 1701," NAC, MG 1.

10. Tom McFeat, "The Big Men of the Northeast," in *Actes du Vingtième Congrès des Algonquinistes,* ed. William Cowan (Ottawa: Department of Linguistics, Carleton University, 1989), 232–48.

11. "Census drawn up by explorer de Chauvignerie in 1736," in E. B. O'Callaghan, ed. *Documents Relative to the Colonial History of the State of New York,* vol. 9(Albany, N. Y.: Weed, Parsons and Company, 1856), 1053–54.

12. Shingwaukonse, or Little Pine, the patriarch of the Pine family, possessed the Plover *dodem,* although his mother, was reputed to have hailed from the Crane band at Sault Ste. Marie.

13. Interviews with Ex-Councillor Daniel Erskine Pine Sr. of Garden River, Ontario, during August 1983.

14. Thomas L. McKenney, *Sketches of a Tour to the Lakes, of the Character and Customs of the Chipeway Indians and of incidents connected with the Treaty of Fond du Lac* (Baltimore: Fielding Lucas, Jr., 1827; reprint, Minneapolis, Minn.: Ross and Haines, 1972), 235.

15. J. G. Kohl, *Kitchi-Gami: Wanderings Around Lake Superior* (London: Chapman and Hall, 1860), 161–62.

16. Frederick Frost, *Sketches of Indian Life* (Toronto: William Briggs, 1904), 142.

17. Interview with Ex-Councillor Frederick E. Pine Sr. in August 1983.

18. Schoolcraft, *Personal Memoirs,* 570.

19. Richard White, *The Middle Ground: Indians, Empires, and Republics in the Great Lakes Region, 1650–1815* (Cambridge: Cambridge University Press, 1991), 129.

20. W. J. Eccles, "A Belated Review of Harold Adams Innis," *Canadian Historical Review* 90, no. 4 (1979): 419–41.

21. Henry R. Schoolcraft, *Historical and Statistical Information Respecting the History, Condition and Prospects of the Indian Tribes of the United States,* vol. 1 (Philadelphia: Lippincott, Grambo and Co., 1851), 114.

22. Kohl, *Kitchi-Gami,* 382.

23. Schoolcraft, *Historical and Statistical Information,* 5:426–27.

24. N. H. Winchell, *The Aborigines of Minnesota* (St. Paul: Minnesota Historical Society, 1911), 532.

25. Janet E. Chute, "A Century of Native Leadership: Shingwaukonse and His Heirs" (Ph.D. diss., McMaster University, Hamilton, Ontario, 1986).

26. "To the Commissioner of the United States," Petition of ten Algonquian groups signed at the Miamis Rapids, 27 July 1793, NAC, RG 10 (Indian Affairs), 8: 8525.

27. John Tanner, *A Narrative of the Captivity and Adventures of John Tanner,* ed. Edwin Jones (Minneapolis: Ross and Haines, 1956), 20.

28. J. B. Nolin, "Articles of agreement between Jean Baptiste Nolin and Quesgoitacameguiscame, sic Tamesa Mestosaguis and Bouniche." J.B. Nolin Papers (1794). Burton Historical Collection, Detroit Public Library, Detroit.

29. U.S. Congress, "Claims at the Saulte de Ste. Marie within the County of Michilimackinac." H. Rept., 20th Cong., 1st sess. Committee on Public Lands, 2 January 1828, 451–87.

30. "Report of Commissioners A. Vidal and T. G. Anderson on Visit to the Indians on the North Shore of Lakes Huron and Superior for the Purpose of investigating their claims to territory bordering on those Lakes, Appendix E," NAC, RG 10, vol. 20; "Captain Lamothe to Superintendent of Indian Affairs," n.d. (1798?), NAC, MG 19–F1 (Claus Papers), vol. 7: 262–63; "Treaty signed at St. Joseph's Island, June 20, 1787," NAC, RG 10, vol. 1841.

31. Milo Quaife, ed., *John Askin Papers*, vol. 1 (Detroit: Detroit Public Library, Burton Historical Collection Papers, 1928), 1:550.

32. F. Barlow Cumberland, *Catalogue and Notes of the Oronhyatekha Historical Collection* (Toronto: Published by authority of The Supreme Court and the Independent Order of Foresters, n. d., ca. 1910), 26.

33. Henry R. Schoolcraft, *Summary Narrative of an Exploratory Expedition to the Sources of the Mississippi River, in 1820*, Mentor L. Williams, ed. (Philadelphia: Lippincott, Grambo and Co.,1855; reprint, New York: Kraus, 1973), 79.

34. "Petition of William Shingwaukonse, 20 August, 1846," NAC, RG 10, 416: 5942.

35. "Nebenagoching. Obituary," *Sault Star*, Sault Ste. Marie, Ontario, 10 June 1899.

36. "Colonel Robert McDouall regarding Captian Payne's survey of Drummond Island, October 1815," NAC, RG 8 (British War Office Records), C–258, 399.

37. Statement of Thomas Gummersall Anderson, 9 June 1822, Archives of Ontario, Toronto (hereafter referred to as AO), MS 23 (Thomas G. Anderson Papers), microfilm reel 1.

38. Schoolcraft, *Personal Memoirs*, 632.

39. Schoolcraft, *Summary Narrative*, 76–79.

40. "Reminiscences of Events of 1820" of George Johnston, *Michigan Pioneer and Historical Collections*, 12:605–8.

41. Schoolcraft, *Historical and Statistical Information*, 1:141

42. "Post Journals, Michipocoten, 17 August and 22 August 1818," NAC, MG 20 (Hudson's Bay Company Records. Hereafter referred to as HBCA. Original records in the Hudson's Bay Company Archives in Winnipeg), B/129/a/9/1818–19.

43. "Michipicoten District, 1834. Reports on Districts," NAC, MG 20 (HBCA), B/129/e/1833–34.

44. "Sir George Simpson to Angus Bethune, 5 January 1831, Correspondence Book, Sault Ste. Marie," NAC, MG 20 (HBCA), B/194/a/6/1831.

45. Schoolcraft, *Personal Memoirs*, 293.

46. "George Johnston to Henry R. Schoolcraft, 6 January 1828," George Johnston Papers, Bayliss Library, Sault Ste. Marie, Michigan.

47. "Francis Audrain to Henry Rowe Schoolcraft, 13 June 1833," National Archives, Washington, D. C., RG 75, MI (Henry Rowe Schoolcraft Papers), Roll 71, 48.

48. "William Nourse to Angus Bethune, 12 April 1836, Correspondence Book, Sault Ste. Marie," NAC, MG 20 (HBCA), B/194/b/10/1835–36.

49. "Anderson's Journal, 1835," typescript, Thomas Gummersall Anderson Papers, Baldwin Room, Toronto Metropolitan Library.

50. "To His Excellency, Sir John Colborne K.B., Lieutenant Governor of the Province of Upper Canada, 1835," Catholic Archdiocesan Archives, Toronto, AC 2402. The Métis community, including Pierre Lavoine, the eldest of Shingwaukonse's sons, petitioned the Roman Catholic bishop for a priest to reside permanently on the Canadian side of the rapids.

51. Thomas G. Anderson to Captain G. Phillpots, 18 July 1835. AO, MG 35, Strachan Papers.

52. For an idea of the sentiments expressed by Shingwaukonse's band at this time see "Extract from the Reverend G. A. Anderson's Report of the Sault Ste. Marie and Garden River Mission, January 1849," typescript, The Reverend Canon Colloton Papers, Anglican Heritage Collection, Bishophurst, Sault Ste. Marie, Ontario.

53. Schoolcraft, *Personal Memoirs*, 524.

54. Chute, "A Century of Native Leadership," 51–52.

55. Kohl, *Kitchi-Gami*, 384.

56. *Montreal Gazette*, 7 July 1849.

57. "Petition, 1853," NAC, RG 10, vol. 198, pt. 1, 116289.

58. Interview with Frederick E. Pine Sr., 10 August 1983.

SECTION 4

Enduring Issues, New Perspectives

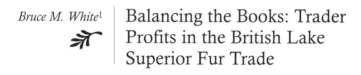

Bruce M. White[1]   Balancing the Books: Trader
Profits in the British Lake
Superior Fur Trade

HOW MUCH profit did fur traders make in their dealings with Indian people? Since the earliest days of the trade there have been widely varying estimates. The Baron Lahontan, in 1685, wrote that in the fur trade of that era, an investment in two canoeloads of merchandise worth one thousand crowns brought a return of 700 percent.[2] In contrast, Thomas Douglas, Fifth Earl of Selkirk, learned, during a fact-finding visit with various Montreal businessmen in February 1804, that:

> The Detached [Michilimackinac] traders do not in general make money which is said to be in part owing to their ambition to be chiefs & leading men in the nations they trade to, to gratify which they are extravagant in presents—There are a number of articles taken expressly for presents among which are Coats ornamented with brilliant tinsel—Hats similar—silver ornaments etc.—these are distinctive ornaments for great men—but the distribution of them is critical & often makes more enemies than friends—Rum & tobacco are presents however not subject to this difficulty.[3]

These contrasting statements represent the full range of opinion about trader profits. Both contain a grain of truth, but both require considerable interpretation. Historian Louise Dechêne examined Lahontan's estimate in her study of the Montreal-based fur trade in the seventeenth century. Dechêne noted that this was gross, not net, profit. Lahontan did not take into account trade expenses or the way in which profits were divided among various individuals. Demonstrating the way fur trade profits were shared, Dechêne analyzed the markup on five pounds of shot and the one-pound beaver skin for which it was traded in the Indian country. Five pounds of shot

175

worth 15 sols in France was shipped to Canada where it was bought by a mer-
chant trader for 30 sols. Eventually, it was traded for a fur worht 67 sols in
Montreal. The exporter of the fur sold it to a hatmaker in Paris for 168 sols.
In absolute numbers only 46.5 sols of the entire markup went for net profit.
The rest paid for transportation, storage, and the costs of operating a fur post.
For their part, the importer earned 15 percent on his investment, the supplier
earned 18 percent, the trader earned 12 percent and the exporter earned 25
percent.[4]

In light of Dechêne's detailed work with fur trade business records,
Selkirk's belief in the lack of profit in the British Great Lakes fur trade around
1800 bears similar examination. Such research is not a simple matter. In the
late eighteenth century, control of the trade in the region was fragmented,
divided among a variety of competing companies. Trading beyond Lake
Superior, because of the great distances involved, encouraged the growth of
large-scale enterprises, such as the North West and Hudson's Bay Companies.
In contrast, trade from Montreal to Michilimackinac, Green Bay, and Lake
Superior, as historian Harold A. Innis wrote, "could be financed with relatively small quantities of capital and was consequently competitive." Despite
repeated efforts, no large-scale consolidation persisted.[5] Throughout the late
eighteenth century, many operations consisted of merchant-traders who
obtained goods, usually on credit from suppliers in Montreal, and either traded them themselves or hired a variety of traders to operate small trading
posts. Furs were shipped to the supplier, who sold them in Montreal or
London and credited the trader's account.

To estimate the actual profits obtained by the many small traders and companies that operated in the western Great Lakes during the early British fur
trade, it is necessary to make use of a variety of account books, documenting
all aspects of the trade. Journals, ledgers, invoices, and canoe manifests contain figures for the goods shipped to and from Montreal, while trading journals and so-called Indian-credit books record the actual transactions involving Native customers and fur suppliers. Unlike the massive Hudson's Bay
Company Archives, the surviving records of British Great Lakes fur trade are
few and select. The complexity of the analysis carried out by Arthur Ray and
Donald Freeman in producing their classic economic study of the Hudson's
Bay Company is, thus far, out of reach for scholars of the Great Lakes fur
trade.[6] For the Great Lakes it is seldom possible to obtain complete docu-
mentation on any particular business operation. To get a clearer picture of the
trade, records from a variety of businesses must be pieced together.

The business records of Sault Ste. Marie trader Jean-Baptiste Cadot are particularly useful for answering a number of questions about the operations of small trading companies in the western Great Lakes. An influential trader and sometime government agent among the Lake Superior Ojibwa, Cadot traded with local and visiting groups. Cadot also sent traders, including his sons Jean Baptiste Jr. and Michel, to posts south and west of Lake Superior.[7] His shipments of merchandise from Montreal and of furs received are recorded in the account book of his supplier, Maurice Blondeau.[8] Information on the goods shipped to his subsidiary trading posts is recorded in a scattering of invoices.[9] The financial aspects of the actual trading process through which Cadot or the men working for him exchanged goods with Ojibwa people are not recorded in any surviving account books. Such missing information must be supplied by the business records and narratives of other traders. For example, Jean-Baptiste Perrault, writing in the 1820s, described trading methods used in the region in the 1780s, as well as some typical rates of exchange of merchandise for furs, food, and other items of trade.[10] Together this information provides a composite portrait of the business operations of western Great Lakes traders in the late eighteenth century.

There are a several approaches for estimating the fur traders' profits. One method is to compare the cost of the goods brought by traders and the value received in Montreal for furs and other items. Another method involves compiling all of the data in Cadot's accounts to determine the net profits earned by the trader. Both methods are useful, and the contrasting picture they give of trader profits is helpful for understanding the workings of the trade.

Cost Accounting

Calculating Cadot's profits in specific exchanges of furs for goods requires data on the cost of the goods in Montreal, shipping costs and other expenses, the rates of exchange current at the trading post, and the sale price of furs in Montreal. Samples of calculations based on the accounts of Jean-Baptiste Cadot, for the year 1785–86 trading are given in table 1.

The initial figures for the Montreal cost of the goods given in table 1 were obtained in an earlier study based on the Blondeau account book.[11] Blondeau assembled Cadot's merchandise in Montreal beginning in March 1785 and shipped it west in two separate canoes later in the spring and summer. In the fall of 1786 he sold the furs obtained for this merchandise. Shipping costs for the trade goods shown in table 1 were obtained indirectly from the data in this account book. In 1785, Blondeau's costs for shipping Cadot's goods to him

Table 1.

RATE OF RETURN ON MERCHANDISE TRADED IN DIRECT EXCHANGES:
ACCOUNTS OF JEAN-BAPTISTE CADOT, SAULT STE. MARIE, 1785–86
(AMOUNTS IN LIVRES)

Trade Item	Montreal Cost	Shipping Cost (%)	Shipping Cost (Amt.)	S. S. Marie Cost
2 1/2 pt. Blanket	7.2	24%	1.73	8.93
Beaver Trap	12	72%	8.64	20.64
Gun	36.9	30%	11.07	47.97
Ball and Shot (10 lbs.)	3.5	457%	16.00	19.50
Barrel of Rum	30.7	142%	43.59	74.29
Tobacco (1 carrot)	12.6	50%	6.3	18.9

cont.

Trade Item	Post Expenses (34% advance)	Total Cost	Type of Fur Traded	Qty.	Montreal Price	Rate of Return %
2 1/2 pt. Blanket	3.04	11.96	Beaver	4	54	351%
			Marten	12	58	385%
			Bear	4	96	702%
			Otter	4	96	702%
			Muskrat	60	24	101%
Beaver Trap	7.02	27.66	Beaver	4	54	95%
			Marten	12	58	110%
			Bear	4	96	247%
			Otter	4	96	247%
			Muskrat	60	24	−13%
Gun	16.31	64.28	Beaver	10	135	110%
			Marten	30	144	124%
			Bear	10	240	273%
			Otter	10	240	273%
			Muskrat	150	60	−7%
Ball and Shot (10 lbs)	6.63	26.12	Beaver	10	135	417%
			Marten	30	144	451%
			Bear	10	240	819%
			Otter	10	240	819%
			Muskrat	150	60	130%
Barrel of Rum	25.26	99.55	Beaver	15	203	104%
			Marten	45	216	117%
			Bear	15	360	262%
			Otter	15	360	262%
			Muskrat	225	90	−10%
Tobacco (1 carrot)	6.43	25.33	Beaver	4	54	113%
			Marten	12	58	129%
			Bear	4	96	279%
			Otter	4	96	279%
			Muskrat	60	24	−5%

cont.

Notes: Currency is shown in livres *ancien cours*, or Montreal currency, a money of account used in French Montreal business, and in the fur trade of the Great Lakes. In that system twelve deniers were worth one sol, and twenty sols were worth one livre. Maurice Blondeau and Jean-Baptiste Cadot both kept accounts in livres *ancien cours* (usually indicated with a # symbol in account books), although imported goods were entered into their account books in Halifax currency, the money of account used in British Montreal. A pound in Halifax currency was worth twenty-four livres *ancien cours*. In this currency twelve pence were worth one shilling, and twenty shillings were worth one pound. To simplify matters in making calculations, the smaller denominations in these two currencies have been converted to their decimal equivalents throughout this article. See Gilles Pacquet and Jean-Pierre Wallot, "Le système finacier bas-Canada au tournant du XIXe siècle," *L'Actuatlité Economique* 59 (September 1983): 473, 513. The Montreal costs of merchandise bought in 1785 and the sale price for furs sold in 1786 were obtained from the Maurice Blondeau account book, McCord Museum. The percentage of advance for shipping costs were derived from a flat £4.6 charge applied to the Montreal cost of each shipping piece listed in the David McCrae shipping invoice printed in David A. Armour and Keith R. Widder, *At the Crossroads: Michilimackinac During the American Revolution* (Mackinac Island, Mich.: Mackinac Island State Park Commission, 1978), 199–206. Because the McCrae invoice contains no record of tobacco being included in the shipment, the percentage advance was obtained by assuming a ninety-pound weight for tobacco bales and basing the value of such bales on Blondeau's 1785 tobacco purchases for Cadot. A more detailed discussion of the various shipping costs is found in B. White, "Montreal Canoes and Their Cargoes," *"Le Castor Fait Tout": Selected Papers of the Fifth North American Fur Trade Conference* (Montreal: Lake St. Louis Historical Society, 1987), 164–82. The 34 percent advance for trading post expenses was computed by dividing Cadot's total expenditures for trade goods and shipping costs in 1785 listed in the Blondeau account book into the costs listed in his 1785 invoices for the Folle Avoine and Petit Winipic trading posts listed in Jean-Baptiste Cadot Accounts, University of Notre Dame Archives. Rates of exchange of furs for merchandise were derived from Jean-Baptiste Perrault, *Jean-Baptiste Perrault marchand voyageur parti de Montréal le 28e de mai 1783* (Montreal: Boréal Express, 1978), 75; François Victoire Malhiot Accounts, McGill University Library, Rare Books and Special Collections; James Duane Doty, "Northern Wisconsin in 1820," *Collections of the State Historical Society of Wisconsin* (1876; reprint, Madison: State Historical Society of Wisconsin, 1855–1911), 7:205. In determining rates of exchange, preference was given in each case to the rate given in the earlier sources.

were an average advance or increase of 46 percent on the Montreal cost of the merchandise.[12] One way to apportion the shipping costs to each item of merchandise would be to apply a flat markup of 46 percent. However, the items of merchandise carried in Montreal canoes to the western Great Lakes varied widely in bulk, weight, and value. Cloth was expensive, light, and bulky. Iron shot and ball were cheap, heavy, and dense. To apportion shipping costs to cloth, shot, and ball by applying a percentage markup based on the average shipping cost does not adequately characterize the real costs of shipping each different kind of merchandise. What, for example, would be the cost of shipping a canoeload made up entirely of cheap, heavy, and dense shot and ball? The percentage markup necessary to pay for the costs of shipping such heavy goods would be much higher than it would be to pay for shipping a canoeload made up entirely of expensive cloth.

In fact there was never just a canoeload of shot and ball, or cloth. Fur trade suppliers filled their canoes with the full assortment of goods necessary to fill the broad range of Indian demand for European merchandise.[13] In doing so, suppliers packed the goods in such a way that they could be shipped in the most convenient form possible up the Ottawa River-French River system to reach the western Great Lakes, a thirty-day trip that included about thirty-six portages and as many *décharges*, when all or part of the goods were unloaded while the canoes themselves were floated or lined through rough water. Goods were packed into what one nineteenth-century trader referred to as a "standard portage piece," a bale, box, basket, bag, barrel, or crate designed for the convenience of the canoemen who hauled these pieces over the portage.[14] Each piece was, in a sense, interchangeable, representing a compromise among the factors of shape, size, and weight.

Given the packing process that went into shaping each portage piece, it appears that apportioning shipping expenses by assigning to each standard portage piece an equal cost is the most reasonable way to insure that each kind of merchandise bears its proper share of the expenses. In the case of Blondeau's accounts of his dealings with Cadot, no canoe manifests exist to determine exactly what was contained in each piece shipped to Sault Ste. Marie. To fill in the missing details, a combination canoe manifest and invoice for a canoeload of goods shipped to Michilimackinac by the Montreal merchants William and John Kay to the trader David McCrae in 1778 was used. This document lists both the Montreal cost of goods and the packages in which they were shipped.[15] This invoice does not include complete figures for the wages paid for the canoemen. Because of this, McCrae's shipping costs were assumed, for the purposes of these calculations, to be comparable to the 46 percent advance on the Montreal cost of goods paid by Cadot in 1785. Given that in McCrae's canoe there were 50 pieces of merchandise worth in all £500.93 Halifax currency, this averages out to a cost per piece of £4.6.[16] Taking this figure and applying it to the Montreal cost of each piece produced most of the shipping advances given in table 1, ranging from 24 percent for bales of cloth to 457 percent for ball and shot. Since the McCrae manifest did not include tobacco, the 50 percent advance in table 1 was estimated based on the assumption that tobacco was shipped in bales averaging 90 pounds. The estimated value for such bales was taken from Blondeau's account book.

Usually, cost accounting of this kind is done by present-day companies as a guide for making future business decisions, not as a method for studying the past.[17] Fur companies in the western Great Lakes made very similar calculations in determining the value of the goods shipped west. Companies needed to know what price to charge for goods they supplied to subcontractors and to employees who received goods as an advance on their wages. In contracting for three years with Jean-Baptiste Cadot Jr. in 1796, the North West Company specified the advances to be paid on the Montreal price: 40 percent for dry goods, 75 percent for tobacco, ammunition, soap, and iron tools, and 100 percent for liquor and provisions. The same advances were specified in a North West Company contract with Michel Cadot in 1803.[18]

Even more specific was the company's method for determining the value of goods at each of its posts from Lake Superior to Lake Athabasca. In an 1802 resolution ratified by the partners it was agreed that "whenever it is found from experience, that the expence of transporting Goods from Montreal to the place of Rendezvous, and from thence to the Posts in the Interior shall have encreased or diminished,—it shall be in the power of the Concern to change and alter the same according to the true expence and Cost of the Transport of such Goods." In an 1804 resolution the partners agreed that the "present Freight and advance are inadequate to form the just value of Goods at the place of Rendezvous and in the Posts of the Interior." Wholesale changes were made in the percentages for apportioning shipping costs. These percentages of markup were greater the farther west the trading post. Based on an average freight cost of £4.5 Halifax, the following advances were charged on the Kaministikwia (later Fort william) cost of goods shipped into the Fond du Lac Department, the area south and west of Lake Superior:[19]

Dry goods: Bales, Cassettes, Cases, Knives, Hats, Baskets, Kettles	26 percent
Tobacco	65 percent
Gunpowder	53 percent
Iron Works	105 percent
High Wines	130 percent
Shot and Ball	167 percent

These figures used by the North West Company in apportioning the shipping costs for dry goods, tobacco, and alcoholic beverages are not entirely comparable to those calculated using the McCrae shipping manifest. The Northwest Company added a flat 23 percent to the Montreal cost before applying these expenses. Even so, shipping costs for ammunition in table 1 were much higher than the North West Company's. There may be a variety of explanations for this. For one thing, the North West Company may have reduced costs by buying ammunition in quantity and by shipping to Michilimackinac and Grand Portage through the lower Great Lakes in lake boats. Shipping goods in this fashion reduced costs somewhat, but took longer. Only large companies could afford the investment necessary.[20]

Another important expense that needs to be taken into account in determining trader profits is the cost of getting goods to the Native communities from the Sault and the costs of maintaining trading posts. Canoes and equipment were used to ship the goods to the post, and men were needed to operate the post. The markup of 34 percent given in table 1 was computed by dividing Cadot's total expenditures for trade goods and shipping costs in 1785 into the costs listed in his 1785 invoices for the Folle Avoine and Petit Winipic trading posts. This advance was added to the value of each item of merchandise, with no attempt to apportion costs based on the type of merchandise. Rates of exchange were found from a variety of sources, chiefly the narrative of Jean-Baptiste Perrault. No additional charges were included for the shipment to Montreal of the furs, which traveled on the return trip of the canoes that brought merchandise west. As for the sale price of furs, these were obtained from Maurice Blondeau's account book, in an entry dated 6 September 1786, when the furs, obtained with merchandise sent out in 1785, were sold in Montreal.

As table 1 shows, the rate of return on investment for goods traded in direct exchange was not standard, but varied both in relation to the kinds of goods traded and the kinds of furs for which they were traded. A 2 1/2 point blanket traded for four beaver brought a rate of return of 351 percent. The same blanket traded for four otter brought 702 percent, but only 101 percent when traded for sixty muskrats. Returns were lower for a gun, which brought 110 percent when traded for beaver, 273 percent when traded for otter, and –7 percent when traded for muskrats. The shipping charges for ball and shot were 457 percent, the highest of any item in table 1, even higher than those for a barrel of rum. The beaver trap brought the lowest rate of return, varying from 247 percent for otter or bear to –13 percent for muskrat.

Based on these figures, one would be tempted to believe that the fur trade could be an extremely profitable venture in 1785, just as Lahontan had suggested it was a hundred years before. There are, however, strong reasons for suggesting that the figures in table 1 are not at all typical of the net profits traders received in their business operations. One reason is simply that the rates used in these calculations are the ones current at trading posts south and west of Lake Superior where Cadot's traders did some, but not all, of his business. Cadot also traded at Sault Ste. Marie, where rates of exchange were more favorable to Indian people. Another important reason is simply that the nominal rates of exchange between traders and Ojibwa people were not always adhered to. Actual fur-merchandise transactions varied quite a bit from the standard, probably because furs varied in size and weight, rates may have changed when goods were traded in larger quantities, and Native customers may have varied in their bargaining ability. For example, in transactions recorded between 1775 and 1778 in an account book kept by a sometime partner of Jean-Baptiste Cadot, Sault Ste. Marie trader Jean-Baptiste Barthe, a woolen blanket was worth, on the average, 2.9 beavers (or plus), though the actual rate in any particular transaction varied from 2 to 4 beavers per blanket.[21] Finally, the most important reason for not taking such rates of return as typical of a trader's entire business operation is that for traders like Cadot just a portion of their business transactions were the kind of direct, one-for-one transactions represented in table 1. Only by taking into account the full range of Cadot's transactions can we hope to obtain a clear picture of the profitability of his business.

The Balance Sheet

In the eighteenth century a trading year in an Ojibwa community near Lake Superior began with the arrival in the fall of the trader from Sault Ste.Marie or Michilimackinac, bringing a new supply of goods. Once installed in his fort or trading house he gathered members of the community and gave and received ceremonial gifts. The traders purchased food such as wild rice and sometimes made arrangements for someone in the community to hunt on a regular basis for the trading post. Goods were then given out on credit and Native people went on their fall and winter hunts, in small family groups. During the subsequent winter the trader or his men might go en drouine (a term with obscure origins), visiting families to collect the furs they produced and to trade for any surplus food they might have.[22] Similarly, community members might revisit the trading post bringing in furs or when they needed food from the trader's supply. In these cases there might be further gifts and further credit. At the end of the trading year, before the departure of the trader, certain goods were exchanged in direct exchanges and there might be concluding gifts and ceremonies.[23]

The organization of trade in this manner was something that evolved in response to the demands of both trader and Ojibwa people, their respective needs for a secure, long-term system of trade. One way or another, however, this system had to be economically viable. It had to pay for itself. If the trader gave away goods, these gifts were paid for in other ways, specifically through profit derived from direct exchanges. Similarly, if as sometimes happened because of poor hunting and trapping conditions or due to heavy competition, Native people were unable to repay the credit they were given in the fall, there had to be some offsetting income for the trader. In fact, there is some evidence that a certain amount of unpaid credit was expected, forgiven by traders who got their profit from other exchanges.[24]

Exactly what proportion of a trader's merchandise was used in gift, credit, and direct exchange is difficult to calculate. In the case of Cadot's operations there are no surviving records to provide clues. What is clear, based on work with other account books, is that there was often a correlation between particular kinds of merchandise and particular trade transactions. In the case of the trader François Victoire Malhiot at Lac du Flambeau in 1804–5, for example, cloth, clothing, and blankets made up 51 percent of the value of *drouine* transactions but only 1 percent of trades for provisions and 10 percent of gift transactions. On the other hand, tobacco and alcohol made up 26 percent of the value of *drouine* transactions, 92 percent of trades for provisions, and 68 percent of gifts.[25]

The profits traders obtained in direct trade and credit transactions offset expenditures for food purchased, gifts given, and credit not repaid. To calculate what it cost for Ojibwa people to obtain blankets, guns, rum, and tobacco, it would be necessary to take into account all the transactions in which they acquired these goods. Similarly, to do a proper apportioning of the costs of doing business to each kind of merchandise such as attempted earlier would involve taking into account all costs of doing business, including gifts, payments for food, and unpaid credit. Items actually traded for furs bore the costs of other such items given away. Unfortunately, no trading accounts have been found that are detailed enough to provide such a rigorous cost accounting. The only way to determine the effects of gift giving, food transactions, and credit on the profits of traders like Jean-Baptiste Cadot is by balancing the trader's books for an entire year or series of years, including expenses that relate to the entire business, not just to any one kind of transaction.

To balance Cadot's books, figures were used from the Blondeau account book showing merchandise purchased from Blondeau and shipped to Sault Ste. Marie and drafts or notes written by Cadot in favor of other traders or individuals and paid by Blondeau. Balancing these expenditures were the sale price of Cadot's furs in Montreal and drafts written by other traders or individuals in favor of Cadot. As seen in table 2, the resulting figures suggest a more realistic notion of the net profits obtained by traders like Cadot. Based on extremes such as a loss of 10 percent in 1783 and a return of more than 15 percent in 1784, Cadot's average rate of return on his trade investment between 1781 and 1786 was 4.46 percent.

Such figures take into account the full range of expenditures, including provisions paid with merchandise, gifts, and losses from unpaid credit. However, this data is also open to interpretation. To begin with, all the goods purchased by the trader may not have been meant for use in trade with Native people. Other goods may have been intended for personal or family use, though if Cadot's wife or others living were involved in the business, these expenses could legitimately be described as business-related. For the purposes of this analysis all goods shipped to the Sault were considered a business expense. Excluded were expenditures in Montreal for Cadot's children. As far as the supplier Blondeau was concerned, however, Cadot's business and personal life were inextricably linked, something that could be said of many family companies in a precorporate era. In addition to being a supplier and marketer of furs, Blondeau looked after Cadot's daughter and sons who lived in Montreal during this period. He purchased clothing, food, and books, and arranged for room, board, and tuition. He recorded this data indiscriminately in his account book along with the costs of trade goods, shipping preparations, and the wages of canoemen. Although all these figures for Cadot's children were left out in this attempt to balance Cadot's books, a case could be made for including at least the costs of the education of Michel and Jean-Baptiste as business expenses with some long-term value to Cadot's business, since the two sons both worked for the father beginning in the mid-1780s.

Table 2.
EXPENDITURES AND RETURNS JEAN-BAPTISTE CADOT, 1781–86
(AMOUNTS IN LIVRES).

Year	Sault Ste. Marie Merchandise	Drafts Paid	Total Expenditures	Montreal Fur Returns	Drafts Recieved	Total	Rate of Return
1781-82	15,545	3,346	18,891	18,501	593	19,094	1.07%
1782-83	32,012	1,361	33,373	30,032	0	30,032	-10.01%
1783-84	32,490	10,868	43,358	40,581	9,239	49,820	15.32%
1784-85	27,683	12,301	39,984	38,777	4,480	43,257	8.19%
1785-86	29,143	1,579	30,722	29,392	2,153	31,545	2.68%
Totals	136,873	29,455	166,328	157,283	16,465	173,748	4.46%

Notes: Amounts shown are in livres *ancien cours*. See notes to table 1 for an explanation of this currency. Calculations are based on data found in the Maurice Blondeau Account Book, McCord Museum.

The terms investment and profit are themselves subject to different interpretations given the context in which traders like Cadot operated, in which
investment opportunities, in the usual economic sense, were limited. The
small monetary returns evident in table 2 accord in some ways with the interpretation of Lord Selkirk given earlier. The costs of gift giving were, as Selkirk
stated, one reason why net trade profits did not match the elevated levels of
profit apparent in direct one-for-one exchanges. Whether or not traders like
Cadot wanted to become "chiefs," as Selkirk put it in 1804, however, is open
to question, though it is probable that Selkirk's informants would have
thought that in their improvident way traders wanted this. It was quite possible in pursuing the delicate diplomacy of trade to become enmeshed in
Ojibway leadership politics, or at least to appear to have become so. In making themselves credible in Indian eyes, traders ran a very real risk of undermining their reputations and credit ratings in Montreal. On the other hand,
looked at as a long-term business strategy, gift giving was a valuable way to
foster trust, loyalty, and status in Ojibwa terms.

For traders like Cadot, status in Native communities could even translate
into an additional source of income. Cadot was sometimes employed as a
government diplomat, and assisted in reconciling the Ojibwa people to the
British after 1760. Described as "much esteemed by Sir William Johnson,"
Cadot brought eighty canoes of Lake Superior Ojibwa to Michilimackinac in
June 1765 to meet with colonial officials. The next fall he joined Alexander
Henry the Elder to trade with the Lake Superior Ojibwa. Captain William
Howard, commandant at Michilimackinac, encouraged Cadot and Henry in
this trade because he believed that it would help insure "the Indians remain
in our Interest." Cadot was also employed directly by the British government,
receiving £80 New York currency in 1768 and £156 in 1769.[26] Much later,
Jean-Baptiste Perrault, in his reminiscences, wrote of being at Mackinac
Island in July 1787 when he observed the impressive sight of Cadot leading
many canoes of Lake Superior Ojibwa rounding one point of the island while
government diplomat Louis-Joseph Ainsse and canoes of Sioux, Sac and
Fox, Menominee and Winnebago rounded another.[27] The various nations
performed a mock naval battle in full sight of the British garrison, preparatory to signing a British-sponsored peace treaty. Ainsse and Cadot had been
sent with gifts to their respective portions of the country the year before to
announce the coming of this treaty. During this time period Cadot's sons
were involved in a short-term amalgamation of traders called the General
Society of Lake Superior and the South, though it is unclear if Cadot himself
was actually trading.[28]

Whether or not Cadot ever actually operated simultaneously as a trader and as a government diplomat, both kinds of work were intertwined, each benefiting the other. Cadot's experience as a trader meant that he was knowledgeable and influential in the Ojibwa community and could be helpful in furthering the interests of the British. His work as a government agent and distribution of gifts provided by the British bolstered his status in the community. An investment in gifts given for trade purposes was later transformed through diplomatic means into money and gifts that might have a continuing benefit for Cadot's trade business or that of his family. Cadot's business investments were subsidized with government gift giving throughout his career, making clear that in this period of the fur trade long-term relationships with Native people were complex, involving at turns the roles of patron and broker.[29]

Determining profit in the mixed context of trade and diplomacy must take into account all the various forms in which investment can take place and all the various forms of profit, both financial and social. Great Lakes fur businesses were either very profitable or close to the margin, depending on the scale of value used in the analysis. Nonetheless, assembling data on the profitability of trade in European terms is an important step for understanding the Great Lakes fur trade. This must involve making sense of existing fur trade business records and correlating a variety of case studies. If this is done, eventually a clearer picture of Great Lakes fur trade economics within eighteenth-century economics will emerge.[30]

Notes

1. This study would not have been possible without the advice and encouragement of Louise Dechêne, for which I am grateful. I would also like to thank those who offered comments, including Barton C. Barbour, Patrick Schifferdecker, William Wicken, Thomas Wien, and others who attended the conference. The assistance of Jackie Logan at the conference is also greatly appreciated. All mistakes and oversights are my own.

2. Baron de Lahontan, *New Voyages to North-America*, ed. Reuben Gold Thwaites, 2 vols. (1703; reprint, Chicago: A. C. McClurg & Co., 1905), 1:100.

3. Patrick C. T. White, ed., *Lord Selkirk's Diary, 1803–04* (Toronto: Champlain Society, 1958), 215.

4. Louise Dechêne, *Habitants et marchands de Montréal au XVIIeme siécle* (Paris: Librairie Plon, 1974), 163–70.

5. The North West Company did have operations in northern Minnesota, and for a time, in the area south of Lake Superior, but always with competition. See

Douglas A. Birk, "John Sayer and the Fond du Lac Trade: The North West Company in Minnesota and Wisconsin," in *Rendezvous: Selected Papers of the Fourth North American Fur Trade Conference, 1981*, ed. Thomas C. Buckley (St. Paul: North American Fur Trade Conference, 1984), 51–62; Harold A. Innis, *The Fur Trade in Canada: An Introduction to Canadian Economic History*, rev. ed. (Toronto: University of Toronto Press, 1970), 390; Innis book review in *Canadian Historical Review* 9 (1928): 66. The whole was discussed in more detail in B. White, "The Michilimackinac Companies: Attempts at Consolidation in the Great Lakes Fur Trade") paper presented at the Western History Conference, St. Paul, 1984.

6. Arthur J. Ray and Donald Freeman, *"Give Us Good Measure": An Economic Analysis of Relations Between the Indians and the Hudson's Bay Company Before 1763* (Toronto: University of Toronto Press, 1978).

7. For more on Cadot and his sons, the latter who usually spelled his last name "Cadotte," see Theresa Schenk, "The Cadottes: Five Generations of Fur Traders on Lake Superior," in *The Fur Trade Revisited: Selected Papers of the Sixth North American Fur Trade Conference, Mackinac Island, Michigan, 1991*, ed. Jennifer S. H. Brown, W. J. Eccles, and Donald P. Heldman (East Lansing: Michigan State University Press, 1994), 189–98.

8. The Maurice Blondeau account book is preserved in the McCord Museum, Montreal. For additional discussion of Cadot's shipments, see Bruce M. White, "Montreal Canoes and Their Cargoes," in *"Le Castor Fait Tout": Selected Papers of the Fifth North American Fur Trade Conference, 1985*, ed. Bruce G. Trigger, Toby Morantz, Louise Dechêne (Montreal: Lake St. Louis Historical Society, 1987), 164–92.

9. Jean-Baptiste Cadot Papers, University of Notre Dame Archives. The accounts contained in the microfilm of these papers in the Minnesota Historical Society are a jumble, although they were restored to their original order for the purposes of this study.

10. Jean-Baptiste Perrault, *Jean-Baptiste Perrault, marchand voyageur parti de Montréal le 28e de mai 1783* (Montreal: Boréal Express, 1978).

11. White, "Montreal Canoes."

12. The average shipping costs between 1780 and 1785 were 44.4 percent. See White, "Montreal Canoes," 188. Figures for 1785 were calculations by the author based on abstracts from the original account book.

13. A further discussion of the assortment of goods necessary to carry on the fur trade is found in B. White, "The Trade Assortment: The Meanings of Merchandise in the Ojibwa Fur Trade" (paper presented at the "Habitants et Marchands de Montreal: La Recherche sur les XVIIIe. et XVIIIe" conference in Montreal, May 1994). A published version of this paper is forthcoming.

14. White, "Montreal Canoes," 180–83. The quotation is from Paul H. Beaulieu, "The Fur Trade by Paul Beaulieu, 1880," in *Escorts to White Earth, 1868 to 1968, 100 Year Reservation* (Minneapolis: Four Winds, 1968), 77–78. The methods Beaulieu

described were from the American fur trade in the area, beginning in the 1820s, however, they were clearly derived from the earlier British and French trades.

15. The original document is in the Toronto Public Library, Quebec Papers, v. 3, 75, p. 185–89, and is found in published form in David A. Armour and Keith R. Widder, *At the Crossroads: Michilimackinac During the American Revolution* (Mackinac Island: Mackinac Island State Park Commission, 1978), 199–206. The Montreal cost of many of the goods in this invoice must be calculated by adding a 50 percent *bénéfice* or markup. See also White, "Montreal Canoes," 166.

16. See the notes to table 1 for an explanation of Halifax currency. As explained in more detail there, shillings and pence in this currency have been converted to decimal equivalents to simplify calculations made for this study.

17. R. H. Coase, "Business Organization and the Accountant," in *L. S. E. Essays on Cost*, ed. James M. Buchanan and G. F. Thirlby (New York: New York University Press, 1981), 199.

18. Michel Cadot's advance for dry goods was reduced to 33 1/3 percent in 1805. W. Stewart Wallace, *Documents Relating to the North West Company* (Toronto: Champlain Society, 1934), 92, 176.

19. Wallace, *Documents*, 195–97.

20. Innis, *Fur Trade in Canada*, 219–22.

21. These figures were computed by the author from a 1775–78 account book recording transactions with Indian people in the Jean-Baptiste Barthe Papers, Burton Historical Collection, Detroit.

22. The term was also give as *en dérouine*. See John Francis McDermott, *A Glossary of Mississippi Valley French, 1673–1850*, Washington University Studies, New Series, Language and Literature, no. 12 (St. Louis: University, 1941), 66; André Bergeron, Dictionnaire de la langue québécoise (Montreal: VLB Editeur, 1980), 179–80.

23. For a more detailed description of the process, see Bruce M. White, "A Skilled Game of Exchange: Ojibway Fur Trade Protocol," *Minnesota History* 50 (summer 1987): 229–40.

24. See Royce Kurtz, "Looking at the Ledgers: Sauk and Mesquakie Trade Debts, 1820–1840," in *Fur Trade Revisited*, ed. Brown, et al., 148; Innis, *Fur Trade in Canada*, 374.

25. These figures are compiled by the author from François Victoire Malhiot's accounts in Rare Books and Special Collections, McGill University Libraries, McGill University, Montreal.

26. On Cadot's activities early in the British Period, see *Sir William Johnson Papers*, ed. James Sullivan, 14 vols. (Albany: University of the State of New York, 1921–65), 7:50–51; 11:1804–9; Alexander Henry, *Travels and Adventures in Canada and the Indian Territories* (1809; reprint, New York: Garland Publishing, Inc., 1976), 193, 204; *Dictionary of Canadian Biography* (Toronto: Toronto University Press, 1983), 5:129; Schenk, "The Cadottes," 191. For the quotation about Cadot, see *Michigan*

Pioneer and Historical Collections, 40 vols. (Lansing, Mich.: Michigan Pioneer and Historical Society, 1874–1929), 9:530.

27. Perrault, *Jean-Baptiste Perrault*, 66. See also *Dictionary of Canadian Biography*, 5:8, for a biography of Ainsse.

28. On Cadot's activities in 1787, see *Michigan Pioneer and Historical Collections*, 11:547–50.

29. For a discussion of these terms, which have many applications to the way in which fur traders juggled a variety of roles, see Robert Paine, "A Theory of Patronage and Brokerage," in *Patrons and Brokers in the East Arctic*, ed. Robert Paine (Memorial University of Newfoundland, Institute of Social and Economic Research, Toronto: University of Toronto Press, 1971), 8–21.

30. A useful case study of this kind is found in George Fulford, "The Pictographic Account Book of an Ojibwa Fur Trader," *Papers of the Twenty-Third Algonquian Conference*, ed. William Cowan, (Ottawa: Carleton University Press, 1992), 190–233.

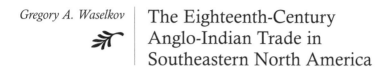

Gregory A. Waselkov

The Eighteenth-Century Anglo-Indian Trade in Southeastern North America

TRADE WITH Europeans was arguably the single greatest force for change among the Indian cultures of southeastern North America during the eighteenth century. This article focuses on two segments of this massive topic: (1) a survey of documentary and archaeological evidence on broad patterns of British and American artifact introduction and acceptance by southeastern Indians during that century; and (2) a consideration of archaeological and written evidence for the impact of this trade on the deer population of the region.

In two earlier articles I surveyed southeastern Indian trade with the Spanish and the French,[1] primarily from my vantage point as an archaeologist. This contribution complements those articles by considering British colonial and federal-period American trade during the eighteenth century. In the search for trends in British and American artifact introduction and acceptance by southeastern Native Americans, I have relied primarily on a comparison of inventories—43 lists[2] of goods that were distributed through economic exchange or as gifts to various southeastern tribes (table 1).

Even with this large number of inventories, there still remain chronological and geographical gaps in coverage. For instance, only a third of the lists date to the first half of the century, and over 50 percent relate to the Creeks or Cherokees. (It should also be noted that several of the lists dating from the 1770s and 1780s were promulgated by Spanish colonial administrations in Louisiana and Florida, but the trade goods listed therein were overwhelmingly British, not Spanish, in origin.) Despite these caveats, the sample still provides considerable information.

By using these lists, one could explore fluctuations in prices, variety, and quality of goods through time. My interest, however, has been to use these lists to interpret the archaeological assemblages recovered by excavation at early historic Indian village sites, a bias that is reflected in my discussion here.

Table 1.
SUMMARY OF ANGLO-AMERICAN TRADE GOODS AND PRESENTS
INVENTORIES RELATING TO THE SOUTHEASTERN INDIANS DURING THE
EIGHTEENTH CENTURY.

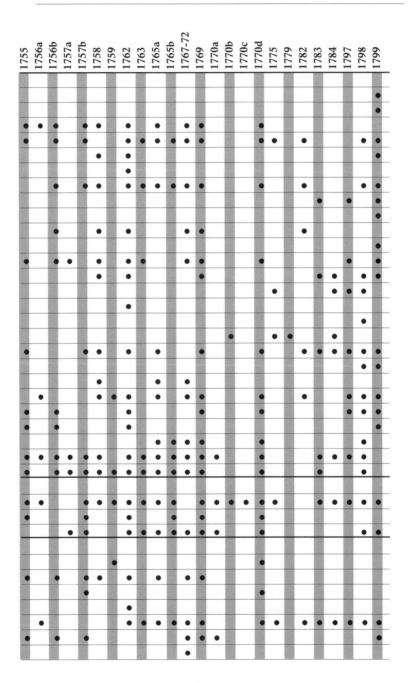

Table 1. (cont.)
SUMMARY OF ANGLO-AMERICAN TRADE GOODS AND PRESENTS INVENTORIES RELATING TO THE SOUTHEASTERN INDIANS DURING THE EIGHTEENTH CENTURY.

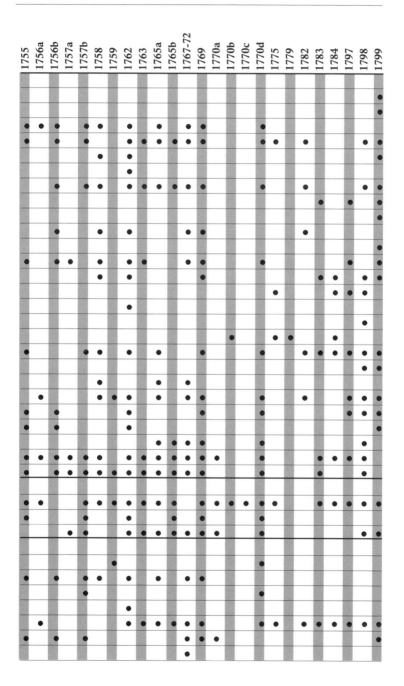

Table 1. (cont.)

	1702-15	1716a	1716b	1717	1718	1720	1724	1728	1734	1738	1739	1740	1742	1743	1748-49	1751	1752a	1752b
Shirts		•	•		•	•	•								•	•		•
Shoes (Boots)						•	•									•		
Stockings						•	•									•		
PERSONAL IMPLEMENTS																		
Animal Traps																		
Brands		•																
Burning Glasses																•		
Candlesticks																		
Combs															•	•		•
Fish Hooks																		
Hoes		•	•		•	•									•			
Jew's Harps																		
Mirrors		•			•					•	•		•	•	•	•		•
Padlocks																		
Razors											•		•	•	•			
Saddles & Tack				•			•								•	•	•	•
Strike-a-Lights		•	•													•		•
Trunks															•	•		•
Whetstones									•									
Whips							•											
PERSONAL ADORNMENTS																		
Beads		•	•	•	•	•				•	•	•			•	•		•
Bells															•			•
Buckles						•	•									•		
Buttons						•									•	•	•	•
Earrings (Brass)										•	•		•	•	•			
Paint	•				•	•			•	•	•		•	•	•	•		•
Rings								•							•			
Wire, Brass															•	•		•
[Silver]																		
Arm Bands																		
Brooches																		
Earrings															•	•		•
Gorgets																		
Medals																		
Hair Plates																		
Wrist Bands																		
IMPLEMENTS																		
[Edged Weapons]																		
Hatchets		•	•		•	•		•	•	•		•			•	•		

Table 1. (cont.)

1755	1756a	1756b	1757a	1757b	1758	1759	1762	1763	1765a	1765b	1767-72	1769	1770a	1770b	1770c	1770d	1775	1779	1782	1783	1784	1797	1798	1799
•	•		•	•		•	•	•	•	•	•	•	•	•	•	•		•	•		•	•		
								•	•			•											•	
							•	•				•												
										•														•
							•			•														
			•																					
										•														•
•			•		•	•				•	•		•	•		•						•		•
			•							•												•		•
							•		•		•	•			•		•							•
			•							•														
•			•	•	•		•	•	•	•		•	•	•	•	•				•	•			
							•			•														
•		•					•	•	•	•	•					•								
•		•		•			•	•	•	•	•				•			•	•	•	•		•	
			•				•					•	•	•								•		•
•		•					•	•		•	•											•		•
							•																	•
							•																	
	•		•	•		•	•	•	•	•	•	•	•		•	•		•		•	•		•	•
•			•		•		•	•	•	•	•		•			•							•	
									•	•														
	•			•	•		•	•	•	•			•									•	•	
•	•	•	•	•	•	•	•	•	•	•	•	•	•	•	•	•							•	
•		•	•			•			•															
•		•	•			•		•	•	•	•	•	•	•						•	•		
			•		•		•																	•
					•	•		•										•	•					
			•	•		•	•	•	•		•			•					•	•	•			•
					•		•																	
						•	•		•			•												
			•				•			•													•	
							•	•	•		•													•
•	•	•		•	•		•	•	•		•	•	•	•	•		•		•	•		•		•

Table 1. (cont.)

	1702-15	1716a	1716b	1717	1718	1720	1724	1728	1734	1738	1739	1740	1742	1743	1748-49	1751	1752a	1752b
Knives	•	•	•		•	•		•	•	•			•	•	•	•	•	•
Swords		•	•		•	•									•			
[Food-related]																		
Euro-Ceramics																		
Frying Pans																		
Kettles, Brass	•	•			•	•		•	•			•	•	•	•	•		•
Kettles, Tin															•	•		•
Spoons																		
[Sewing]																		
Needles							•			•					•	•		•
Scissors		•	•									•	•	•	•	•		•
Thread							•			•					•	•		•
[Smoking]																		
Clay Pipes						•	•			•	•				•	•		
Snuff Boxes						•												
Tobacco	•															•		
Tongs	•																	
[Firearms]																		
Gunflints	•	•	•		•	•	•		•			•	•	•	•	•	•	•
Gunpowder	•	•			•	•	•	•				•	•	•	•	•		•
Gunsmith's Tools										•	•		•	•	•			
Gun Worms																		
Holsters																		
Lead Balls	•	•	•		•	•	•	•		•		•	•	•	•	•		•
Lead Shot											•	•	•	•	•			
Muskets		•	•		•	•	•	•	•	•	•	•	•	•	•	•	•	•
Pistols		•	•		•	•											•	
[Woodworking]																		
Augers & Gimlets																		
Awls																		
Axes		•	•												•			
Chisels																		
Files																		
Hammers															•			
Nails															•	•		
Saws															•			
FOODSTUFFS																		
Rum, etc.		•		•	•													
Salt	•	•																
Spices																		
Sugar																		
Tea/Coffee																		

Table 1. (cont.)

1755	1756a	1756b	1757a	1757b	1758	1759	1762	1763	1765a	1765b	1767-72	1769	1770a	1770b	1770c	1770d	1775	1779	1782	1783	1784	1797	1798	1799
•	•	•	•	•	•	•	•		•		•	•	•	•	•	•	•	•	•		•	•	•	•
			•		•																			
						•	•				•													
						•																		
•			•	•	•	•	•	•	•	•	•	•	•				•							•
•		•			•	•		•		•	•	•	•				•							•
							•																	
	•		•			•				•	•	•	•		•									•
•		•	•		•	•	•	•	•	•	•	•		•	•	•								•
	•		•	•		•				•	•	•				•	•	•		•				
•			•	•						•	•										•	•	•
			•							•												•	•
•		•		•	•		•			•		•				•				•			•
•		•	•	•	•		•	•	•	•	•	•	•		•	•				•		•	
•		•	•	•	•	•	•	•	•	•	•	•	•	•	•	•	•	•	•	•	•	•	•
			•							•		•											•
										•		•	•										•
					•																		•
	•	•	•	•		•	•	•	•	•	•	•	•	•	•	•	•		•	•		•	•
			•								•				•							•
•		•	•	•	•	•	•	•	•	•	•	•	•	•	•	•	•	•	•		•	•	•
		•			•																	•
				•			•			•												•
			•								•	•	•	•							•
			•			•				•	•	•	•		•				•	•	•
							•			•											•
				•			•			•							•		•
				•						•									•
				•															•
				•												•	•
				•												•	•
	•			•		•		•		•						•	•	•
			•		•	•		•		•						•	•	•
								•									•
				•				•					•			•
								•						•			•

Many of the artifact categories found on the lists of trade goods were referred to by the traders in terms unfamiliar to the general public today. One goal has been to interpret the arcane jargon of the traders, so many of the terms found in table 1 are modern counterparts that, hopefully, have some significance to contemporary historians and archaeologists. A glossary at the end of the chapter offers interpretations of trader's terminology.

The single largest category comprises items of cloth that made up the bulk of the trade, items that archaeologists seldom find preserved. Most trade inventories contained strouds, duffel blankets, coats, shirts, and a variety of other cloth items. While these categories of material culture do not figure prominently in archaeological collections, we of course can often infer the existence of coats from the presence of buttons, of belts from buckles, of shoes and boots from cobbler's nails, and of uncut lengths of cloth from lead seals (the so-called bale seals.) Occasionally cloth is also preserved by proximity to copper or brass, or through some other fortuitous circumstance. While cloth and clothing may be rare from an archaeological perspective, these lists remind us of the considerable economic value such items represented in the cultural contexts of eighteenth-century Indian societies.

Some general temporal trends evident in the cloth and clothing categories include a marked increase in cloth variety after 1750, the appearance of silk in 1765, and the gradually increasing importance of cottons (particularly check, chintz, denim, gingham, and muslin) late in the century, all of which reflect rising British imports from India during that period. Larger processes were also at work, however, since variety in many trade goods categories increased with time. Items such as combs, padlocks and trunks, nested sets of tin kettles, most woodworking tools, brass wire, and, perhaps most significantly, silver ornaments are first mentioned in midcentury; animal traps, fish hooks, Jew's harps, and iron kettles appear for the first time in the late 1700s.

In a pattern that is also found on French trade lists, silver earrings appear first in the 1740s, replacing the brass earrings that had a brief period of popularity from 1738 to 1749. Silver arm bands, wrist bands, brooches, and gorgets were first itemized in the late 1750s and early 1760s, and continued in demand into the next century. This information alone should be of considerable value to archaeologists attempting to date burial assemblages. Bead researchers have been making substantial progress in determining type chronologies, and trade list data can contribute to this effort, as well. Shell wampum appears on several late eighteenth-century Cherokee trade lists, but is absent from Creek inventories until the early nineteenth century. Among glass beads, the small, wound, oval types[3] known to the traders as "barley-corns" (for their resemblance to pearls of barley) range in date from 1758 to

1784, which is probably as accurate an idea of their span of popularity in the Southeast as we will obtain. At the end of the century, the term "garnet beads" probably referred to small, wound, faceted types.[4]

Elsewhere in the summary table there are apparent gaps in the lists, artifact types of which no mention is found, even though they are known to have been obtained by native southeasterners from Europeans. For instance, brass thimbles do not appear on any of the trade lists I have seen, although they are quite common from archaeological contexts. Brass straight pins occur only twice on the lists, but are not uncommon from excavations. These lists, therefore, are not entirely reliable and should be compared critically with the archaeological record. To consider a more complex problem, brass horse bells are not listed in early eighteenth-century British accounts. We know that the interior southeastern tribes received cast brass bells from Spanish Florida until about 1704, and from the British after 1755. Between those dates, only sheet brass bells (the so-called hawksbells) were obtainable, and then almost exclusively from French trade sources.[5]

There are other apparent discrepancies between the written accounts and archaeological assemblages. Strike-a-light steels are well represented on the lists, but are, to my knowledge, rarely found archaeologically in the Southeast. Perhaps the steels have been misidentified, and they may typically remain unidentified if badly corroded. Yet the lists unequivocally indicate that they should be found and identified eventually.

Perhaps the most serious drawback to an analysis of trade lists is the tacit implication that the categories, which were assigned descriptive labels by the traders, in some way reflect the material assemblage from the viewpoint of the Indians. Ethnohistorians, of course, now recognize that Indian consumers of these goods frequently had quite different notions of function. For example, James Adair, a trader with extensive experience among the Creeks and Chickasaws, wrote in 1775 about an innovative use of belt buckles and keepers.

> The women, since the time we first traded with them, wrap a fathom of the
> half breadth of Stroud cloth round their waist, and tie it with a leathern belt,
> which is commonly covered with brass runners or buckles. . . .[6]

Straight pins were requested by some Creeks in 1753 "to streach our [deer] Skins with." Brass wire, which occurs on lists from 1748 to 1799, was described in a 1770 list of presents for the Grand Caddo as "suitable for bracelets and wormscrews."[7] There are, however, numerous indications that the Indians had other intentions for that material. Once again James Adair described an alternative function:

> Both sexes pluck all the hair off their bodies, with a kind of tweezers, made
> formerly of clam-shells, now of middle-sized wire, in the shape of a gun-
> worm; which, being twisted round a small stick, and the ends fastened there-
> in, after being properly tempered, keeps its form: holding this Indian razor
> between their fore-finger and thumb, they deplume themselves. . . .[8]

Yet another use was offered by the Creek warrior Acorn Whistler in 1752,
when he requested from Governor Glen of South Carolina, "Wire for Rings
to our Ears,"[9] by which he meant the large ear hoops Creek men created by
severing and stretching the outer ear cartilage, which was then wrapped with
copper or brass wire.

In the Southeast, throughout the eighteenth century the principal commodity traded in exchange for goods of European manufacture was deerskins. There were other types of native products, such as pelts of furbearers
(beavers, raccoons, otters, muskrats, wildcats, bears) and, late in the century,
cow hides. For a time, between about 1690 and 1716, Indian slaves captured
along the western and southern fringes of the English trading sphere dominated the trade, but slaving proved a poor basis for the stable market economy sought by colonial merchants and administrators, so deerskins eventually
regained their preeminence. Other eighteenth-century native trade goods
included beeswax, medicinal barks and roots, split cane baskets (sifters and
fanners), woven and beaded belts and garters, horse ropes or halters made of
twisted elm (wahoo) bark or silk grass, and several kinds of comestibles: dried
venison hams, hickory nut oil and bear oil (often transported in deerskin
bags), chestnuts, ground peas, and corn.[10] Still, the mainstay of the trade was
deerskins, by the thousands and hundreds of thousands per year.[11]

Admittedly imprecise modern estimates of the average number of deer
killed annually by individual Indian hunters to supply their family's domestic
consumption and trade needs range from 25 to 100, although a few historical
references mention exceptional hunters who brought in between 200 and 400
in a single year.[12] A calculation based on a midcentury Indian population of
about 55,000 for the entire region,[13] a total population:hunter ratio of 3:1,
and a middle-range annual kill estimate of 50 deer per hunter, suggests a
regional annual harvest of over 900,000 deer. Reliable figures of deerskins
actually traded to Europeans are equally suspect, but John Stuart, British
superintendent for the Southern District, in 1764 estimated that 800,000
pounds of half-dressed deerskins (at least 320,000 skins) would be obtained
that year from the entire area under British control.[14]

Despite the lack of firm figures, everyone agrees that Native American
hunters were killing large numbers of deer every year, primarily in order to

obtain the European goods they desired, including some upon which they had become dependent (such as firearms and ammunition). William Bartram wrote in 1791, "They wage eternal war against deer and bear, to procure food and clothing, and other necessaries and conveniences; which is indeed carried to an unreasonable and perhaps criminal excess, since the white people have dazzled their senses with foreign superfluities."[15] In fact, most modern writers, beginning with Verner Crane in the 1920s, have concluded that the southeastern Indians conducted "a tremendous slaughter of deer, comparable to the great wastage, by a later generation of white Americans, of the buffalo of the Great Plains. Long before 1763 the 'infinite herds' of the late seventeenth century must have been seriously diminished."[16] Modern historians and anthropologists[17] have overwhelmingly accepted this assessment. They may disagree on the timing and the rapidity of the decline in deer population, but they do not challenge the basic premise found in the title of Charles Hudson's 1981 chapter, "Why the Southeastern Indians Slaughtered Deer,"[18] that the deer population of the region was essentially extirpated by the end of the century by Indian overhunting.

Archaeological data suggest otherwise, however. Excavations at several archaeological sites of Cherokee and Creek villages occupied during the colonial and federal periods have yielded substantial quantities of deer bone in the food refuse.[19] The historical basis of this overhunting hypothesis is equally suspect.

For the interior Southeast, the region occupied by the Creek and Seminole Indians, there are two periods for which the historical records indicate a scarcity of deer. Beginning near the end of the Seven Years War, the English began to hear complaints, such as this one by a Tallasee headman in 1760: "We are a People that take great Pains in hunting having no other Way to supply our Families with Cloathing; the Game now grow very scarce and trading Goods are at an high Price. . . ."[20] At the Indian Congresses at Picolata and Pensacola in 1765, Creek headmen echoed the refrain that "deer are turning very scarce," and that hunters had to travel farther afield to find game.[21] According to the Upper Creek headman called The Mortar of Okchai,

> now many of us, are grown old & Incapable, to kill Deer enough to purchase Cloathing. We had formerly good Success in hunting but are now obliged to Cross the Cherokee River for Game, which Considerations induce me to desire, that as Deer skins are become Scarce, The Trade may be reduced in proportion, so that we may be enabled to Clothe & maintain our Families. . . .[22]

To understand the motives behind these statements, one must consider the political and economic context of the deerskin trade in the 1760s. By the time of The Mortar's speech in 1765, the French had been defeated in North America, thereby eliminating the competitive market for deerskins that Louisiana had offered the Creeks. John Stuart was under tremendous pressure from London to curtail expenses in the Southern District by decreasing the presents that had been distributed so lavishly during the war to maintain alliances against the French.[23] Those headmen who had used their access to abundant English presents to strengthen their claims of leadership by redistributing those presents to their followers were now the principal source of complaints about the scarcity of deer. Export figures for the ports of Augusta, Mobile, and Pensacola, on the other hand, show increasing quantities of deerskins leaving those ports throughout the late 1760s.[24]

If the deer population of the interior Southeast had suffered a real decline in the early 1760s, there seems little doubt that the numbers quickly rebounded. By the 1780s, Pensacola-based Panton, Leslie, & Company was shipping over 100,000 deerskins a year to England.[25] Not until the 1790s did accounts of poor hunts appear again in the historical record, such as the complaint from Zenon Trudeau (lieutenant governor of Illinois) to Governor Carondelet in 1794 that "Your Lordship will see by the report itself how small is the value of the commerce of the Missouri, which yearly decreases more and more. The introduction of merchandise increases imperceptibly, but the amount of peltries taken out by traders grow less and less."[26]

That sentiment was echoed by Benjamin Hawkins, U.S. agent to the Creek Indians, when he wrote in 1799 that "The skin trade is in decline. The hunts have been much less than they have ever been known to be in any season before."[27] During a conference held at the Creek agency in 1802, Efau Hadjo expressed an opinion evidently shared by many Creek headmen: "We are very poor, and it seems are to remain so. We could once kill game for our support, and the British or French used to pay attention to the wants of the old Chiefs. Our game is gone and we are poor, the little we get from our friends the Americans is as nothing among so many of us."[28]

Hawkins's response to reminiscences of the old days, as he explained to Secretary of War Henry Dearborn, was to recommend that the Creeks take up plow agriculture, spinning, and stock raising. In addition, "On occasions only when they stated their poverty, and contrasted the present scarcity of game and withdrawing of presents, with former times of plenty and British profusion, I recommended to them to sell some of their waste lands."[29]

Hawkins clearly had strong motivation to withhold presents from those who refused to part with their lands and adopt his civilizing program, and the consequent loss of presents would have exacerbated the economic effects caused by any real shortage of deerskins due to decline in deer population. Since there are no disinterested sources of written evidence for the disappearance of game during the federal period, additional archaeological data need to be gathered and analyzed to gain a better understanding of the transition from the deerskin trade to a plantation economy. Such a transition assuredly occurred, but the incautious acceptance of statements recorded by John Stuart and Benjamin Hawkins—the two officials principally charged with negotiating trade and land concessions from the southern Indians—is unlikely to resolve the question.

As a final thought, it might be relevant to note that the Creek Factory received 44,746 pounds of deerskins in 1801; two years later, 203,000 pounds of deerskins, mostly obtained from the Creek trade, were exported by Panton, Leslie, & Company.[30] According to the account books of these two establishments, the peltry trade declined severely in the years leading up to the Creek Civil War of 1813–14. By 1817, with only 562 deerskins received at the Creek Factory in the previous year, the deerskin trade was moribund. Yet even at that late date, the Creeks were reported to be still engaged in their annual winter hunts for deer, perhaps by then held entirely for their own consumption.[31] I think it unwise and contrary to the available evidence to conclude that the southeastern Indians extirpated deer through overhunting, without considering the political and economic context in which the deerskin trade occurred.

Glossary of Trade Terms

Cloth [Fabric]:[32]
Bombazette - A worsted wool cloth.
Broadcloth - Any cloth over a yard wide; usually a plain weave of carded wool; red (1720, 1799), black (1720), blue (1720, 1799), green (1799), and gray (1799).
Cadiz - A narrow, light woolen cloth, similar to serge; red (1718, 1748–49, 1762), body (1720, 1755).
Calico - Colored or printed cotton; furniture (1799), flowered (1718, 1782), Indian (1763, 1765, 1769), printed (1748–49, 1765, 1775), Provence (1775, 1782), Holland calico (1775).[33]
Callimancoe - Coarse mixture of wool and linen; also, a glazed linen fabric; flowered (1799).
Cambric - A thin, plain, closely woven linen, or sometimes cotton.
Check - Any fabric of plain weave with intersecting colored warp and weft stripes; common (1769, 1770), fine (1769).

Chintz - A glazed, printed cotton fabric; medallion (1799), India (1799).

Coating - A thick, heavy woolen cloth with a long nap; in crimson and gray.

Cotton - A napped fabric, usually a woolen; striped (1762, 1769).

Denim - A strong, twilled cotton cloth.

Duffel - A coarse, felted woolen cloth with a thick nap, commonly used for blankets; white (1748–49), striped (1748–49, 1799).

Flannel - A plain or twilled fabric of wool, or less often of cotton, with a brushed surface; including Baize (Bays), a coarse wool, resembling felt (1783, 1784); white (1784, 1798), yellow (1798), striped (1769), twilled (1798).

Gingham - Striped or checked cloth woven of cotton with dyed yarns.

Half Thicks - A coarse woolen cloth; purple (1762).

Kersey - A cheap, coarse, twilled wool with a heavy nap.

Limbourg (French-made counterpart to Strouds) - red (1770), blue (1770).

Linen (Garlix) - A bleached linen cloth; brown (1798), striped (1762), fine (1769, 1770), Irish (1782, 1799), French (1782), linsey (1798); also, Hollands (1762, 1799) - a plain linen.

Muslin - A fine woven cotton; plain (1799), red (1798, 1799).

Negro Cloth - A coarse, homespun cotton fabric; for powder bags (1758).

Osnaburg - A coarse, unbleached linen; for bullet or shot bags (1756, 1758).

Plains - Plain woven cotton; white (1762, 1769, 1770, 1797, 1798), red (1728), and blue (1728, 1748–49, 1755, 1762, 1797, 1798); "corded and wormed for women" (1748–49, 1755).

Serge - A light, smooth, twilled fabric of woolen weft and worsted (combed wool yarn) warp; embroidered (1755), embossed (1749, 1762), flowered (1749); also sagathy (1799) - a twilled woolen serge.

Silk - Bengal (1765, 1769, 1770), exported from India, sometimes mixed with cotton and usually striped; also sarcenet (1799) - a thin, plain-weave silk.

Stop List (Gartering, Binding) - "Lists" were selvedges cut from textiles; mazarine blue (1739, 1742, 1748–49), emerald green (1739, 1742, 1748–49), red (1739, 1742, 1748–49), silk ferret (a narrow tape; 1765, 1769, 1770), striped elastic (1797, 1798), tape (1749); red inkle (a narrow silk, wool, or linen tape or braid; 1734), gartering (1765, 1770, 1798), binding (1769, 1798).

Strouds (or Stroudwaters or Waters) - A coarse woven, dyed woolen; blue (1720, 1755, 1798), red (1720, 1755), green (1798), for flaps and matchcoats and stockings (1720), double-striped (1720), six pieces in a bale (1738), half pieces (1755, 1765); also Scarlet (1749, 1765). In 1757, Edmond Atkin specified "30 Strowds, 1/5 red, 4/5 blue—with a worm stripe & stars on each side."

Cloth [Other]:

Blankets - Most blankets (or mantles) were woolen Duffels (or Duffields), which came in white (1716, 1718, 1751), blue (1718, 1720, 1734, 1751, 1762), red (1718, 1720), striped (1718, 1720, 1734, 1739, 1742, 1743, 1755, 1762, 1770, 1783, 1784, 1798), "London striped" (1757), and shag-end or headed shag duffels (1762, 1765, 1769, 1770). These were supplied in lengths of 1 yard (1718, 1762, 1784), 1 1/2 yards (1784), or 2 yards (1718, 1762, 1784), and were shipped in bales of five blankets each (1738, 1739, 1742, 1743). Less common varieties included "black list" (1763), "Ross" or rose blankets (1798), and later 2 1/2-point (1770, 1775, 1797, 1798) and 3-point blankets (1770, 1775, 1797, 1798),[34] stroudwater (1728, 1762, 1783; see strouds, in general), limbourg blanket of 2 Castilian yards (1784).

Lace - Types included white tensy and yellow tensy (1720) and "inferior and best bed" lace (1762).

Ribbons - Red ribbons are first mentioned in 1720, by which chief's medals were to be worn. Later varieties were "tape" (1748–49, 1757), "slight" or narrow taffety (1762, 1767), "broad figured silk" (1762), figured silk and cotton (1762, 1767, 1770), Dutch prettys (1763, 1765, 1769, 1770), none-so-prettys (a linen braid with woven figures; 1757, 1765, 1767, 1772), colored safety (1765).

Clothing:

Belts - Leather belts, sometimes decorated with gilt (1748–49, 1770), may have served primarily as clothing accessories.

Coats - A wide assortment of waistcoats (1748/1749, 1755), "Ozenbrig Frocks" (1765), and "Great Coats" of stroud (1718), half thick (1716, 1718), broad cloth (1716, 1724), and duffle (1767) were available, plain or laced (1716, 1718, 1724, 1748–49).

Flaps (Girdles) - Breechclouts were made of "broad Cloth" (1724) or "stroud, blue and red" (1720), although Edmond Atkin requested "red leather girdles" in 1757.

Gloves - A pair of "Men's Yarn Gloves" is listed in the 1762 Cherokee rate schedule.

Handkerchiefs - These items came in a tremendous variety, including "Handkerchiefs of India" (1751), "Scotch Handkerchiefs" (1762), "Figured" and "printed" (1762, 1765, 1784), silk (1762, 1765, 1783, 1784, 1798), cotton (1763), "Romals" (1763, 1769, 1770, 1772, 1797, 1798), linen (1765), "Chollet handkerchiefs" (1775), and bandannas (1765, 1798); also, blue Romals of silk or cotton, imported from India, (1799). Perhaps "Kenting Necloaths" (1720) can be considered a related item of clothing.

Hats - Felted wool hats, commonly "laced" (1716, 1718, 1720, 1724) or "tinsel laced" [braided] (1748–49, 1755), were widely available. "Worsted Caps" are listed on a 1751 Cherokee rate schedule.

Petticoats - Coarse petticoats were made of calico.

Shirts - Plain and ruffled white shirts and check shirts of linen or "garlix" (1718, 1720, 1724, 1748–49, 1751, 1755), "gingham" (1762, 1765, 1770, 1775, 1783, 1784), cotton (1748–49), and unspecified materials are abundantly represented on the trade lists.

Shoes (Boots) - Leather dress shoes [with brass buckles (1720)] were presented to select individuals. A "Pair of Negro Cloth Boots" is mentioned on a 1765 Creek rate schedule.

Stockings - Hose and stockings were made of blue and red strouds (1720) or woven from woolen worsted yarn (1762).

Personal Implements:

Animal Traps - Among the varieties of traps mentioned in trade lists are "Beaver, Rat, single spring steel, & wolf traps" (1799).

Brands - Iron brands were used early in the eighteenth century to mark deerskins and slaves (1716). Horse brands appear on trade lists in 1768.

Burning Glasses - Magnifying glasses for fire starting are listed on a 1751 Cherokee rate schedule and in Edmond Atkin's 1757 instructions.

Candlesticks - Candlesticks, including some of brass and pewter (1799), appear in the second half of the eighteenth century.

Combs - Combs occurred in a variety of materials, including ivory (1748–49, 1751, 1755, 1772), horn (1748–49, 1755, 1759, 1762), bone (1762), and boxwood [from France] (1770). "Buck" or "Buckling" combs (1748–49, 1772) may have been made from antler.

Fish Hooks - Fish hooks were available by the mid-eighteenth century. Edmond Atkin rather inscrutably specified "Kirby's, flat heads for wire" (1757).

Hoes - Iron hoes at first were described as either "narrow" (1716, 1718, 1748–49) or "broad" (1716, 1718, 1720, 1748–49, 1765, 1769, 1770), including one reference to "Crawly's broad Carolina hoes" (1765). Creek factory accounts from 1801 list "weeding hoes" and "light corn hoes."

Jew's Harps - Steel versions of this instrument were listed in George Galphin's accounts ledger (1767–72). Edmond Atkin requested "smallest brass, Dutch, Jews-harps" (1757).

Mirrors - These items were uniformly termed "looking glasses" by the traders. They were produced in a variety of sizes, typically in wooden frames. A 1765 Creek rate schedule mentions painted and walnut frames. The

Cherokees were offered "Dutch Looking Glasses with Cases" in 1762.[35]

Padlocks - Small padlocks with hasps and staples were occasionally available, as well as "Large Stock Locks" and "Large Door Hinges" (1772).

Razors - Steel razors were normally listed without elaboration in the rate schedules. However, "fish skin razor cases," each with "2 London razors and 1 pair scissars," appear in lists of presents given to the Creeks in 1742 and 1743.

Saddles & Tack - Saddles and associated horse tack were important elements of the trade beginning soon after the Yamasee War, when the use of burdeners declined precipitously. Saddles were mentioned with specific references to "Women's Side Saddles" in 1751, 1762, and 1798. These were all riding saddles, as opposed to pack saddles, since virtually all were accompanied by elaborate accoutrements. Other items of tack included fringed and laced "saddle housings" [the cloth padding under a saddle—a "saddle blanket"] (1755, 1756, 1762, 1765, 1769, 1770), cruppers (1755, 1762, 1772), spurs (1762, 1765, 1797, 1798, including some plated spurs: 1798, 1799), girths (1772), and "cotton gaithers for bridlebits" (1797). Bridles came in all forms, including unspecified "bridles" (1724, 1748–49, 1755, 1756, 1762, 1763, 1765, 1783), "snaffle bridles" (1765, 1768, 1769, 1770, 1772, 1798), "curb bridles" (1772, 1798), "curb snaffle bridles" (1798), "crupper bridles" (1772), and "double bridles" (1783), "cirringles" (1798), and "half curles" (1772).

Strike-a-Lights - The "Steels" for fire starting were mentioned in lists throughout the century.

Trunks - Most of these trunks were nested sets (a nest containing up to eight trunks) made of gilt leather (1748–49, 1752, 1755, 1762, 1763, 1772).

Whetstones - Hones were described alternatively as "whet stones" (1734), "wrag stones" and "scyth stones" (1772), and "turkey oil stones" (1799).

Whips - Whips are mentioned only twice in the trade lists (1724, 1762).

Personal Adornments:

Arm and Wrist Bands - These two artifact forms, made of sheet silver, differed primarily in size. Both sometimes had "Lines about the Edge" (1758) and early nineteenth-century forms occasionally had "scalloped" edges. Silver "hair plates" (1758), "top knots" (1772), and "headbands" (1799) are also noted.

Beads - Shell wampum was provided to the Cherokees (in 1756, 1762, and 1798) by the bead or "grain." All other beads were glass, supplied by weight (by the pound) or strung (described as "necklaces," "strings," and "strands"). "Bunches" or "masses" (alternatively, spelled "mases" or "maizes") comprised multiple strands, ranging from four to a dozen depending on weight.[36] Trade list descriptions often specify only color and relative size (i.e., small or large). Exceptions include a 1738 reference to "Negro Beads" (presumably a type traded extensively to Africa); "bugles" (drawn tubular varieties listed in 1743, 1748–49, and 1757); "barley-corn" or "B.C. beads" (wound oval varieties listed in 1758, 1762, 1765, 1768, 1769, 1770, 1772, 1783, and 1784); "common," (in 1757, 1763, 1765, 1769, 1770, and 1772), which may apply to short, drawn tubular or round varieties; extremely small "seed beads" (in 1768 and 1772); "enameled" (in 1768, 1772, 1783, and 1784); "white agates" (in 1772); and "mock garnets" (1757) and "garnet beads" (1798), probably faceted wound types. Color apparently was not recorded systematically. An unusually detailed invoice dating to 1748–49 indicates "small white, purple, mongee, transparent green, transparent yellow," and "large black and yellow, white Pecado, and red Pecado" bugles.

Bells - "Hawk Bells" or "hawksbells" were small and inexpensive (appearing in 1748–49, 1752, 1755, 1757, 1759, 1763, 1765, 1769, and 1770), and certainly correspond to archaeologically recovered sheet brass, spherical types. Other terms, such as "trading bells" (1755), "horse bells" (1763, 1767), and simply "bells" (1765, 1772, 1798) could refer either to cast brass spherical or open types, though probably to the former. "Cow bells" (mentioned in 1767) were made of iron.

Brooches - Each "silver breast brooch" or "silver pin for the shirt" was valued at 2 to 3 pounds of dressed deerskins. Heart-shaped varieties were listed in 1799, but round forms predominated.

Buckles - A few scattered references to "a pair of shoes with brass buckles" (1720) and "silver[ed] brass buckles" and "9 doz. [k]nee buckles" (1772) undoubtedly underrepresent the number of buckles that must have entered the trade on shoes and belts, as well as parts of horse tack.

Buttons - "Buttons," sometimes "gilt" or "silver" but usually "brass" (1748–49, 1751, 1762, 1798, 1799), probably largely consisted of flat, one-piece, cast brass or white-metal types worn on jackets, waistcoats, or coats. Other varieties included "clopper buttons," or "bell buttons" (1720, 1756), which were two-piece metal buttons that rattled; "pea buttons" (1748–49, 1751, 1759, 1765, 1769, 1770), spherical, two-piece metal buttons, sometimes made of a white copper alloy called "Bath metal" (1748–49, 1765); and "silver sleeve buttons" (1762), which presumably were cufflinks. A 1762 Cherokee trading schedule includes the following description: "Buttons: either of Glass, or Stone: set in white Metal, or Mother of Pearl."

Earrings - The earliest varieties appear as "stone earrings" (1738, 1739, 1742, 1743, 1748–49), brass or white metal with glass or paste insets. Those without insets were known as "Bath earrings" (1748–49). "Silver earrings" or "ear bobs" or "bobs" (1748–49, 1751, 1752, 1758, 1762, 1763, 1765, 1769, 1770,

1783, 1784, 1797, 1799), made of sheet silver, quickly replaced the copper alloy varieties. Of course, all were sold or presented in pairs.

Gorgets - Crescent-shaped "Brass Gorgets, gilt, with King's Arms," and "brass lacquered gorgets" were distributed to the Creeks in 1757 and 1763, but silver types were more common, including "plain" and "chased" varieties in 1762. Round and oval forms were not available to the Creeks until 1801.

Medals - Medals, generally made of sterling silver (1765, 1770), are seldom mentioned in trade lists, but were typically presented at major conferences and congresses.

Paint - Two types of red pigment commonly traded, by weight, to the southeastern Indians were powdered "vermillion" (1705, 1715, 1718, 1720, 1734, 1738, 1742, 1743, 1748–49, 1755, 1762, 1763, 1765, 1769, 1770, 1771, 1772) and powdered "red lead" (1718, 1763, 1771, 1772). The two were frequently mixed, to extend the more expensive vermilion, and the result was referred to simply as "paint" (1751, 1758, 1759) or "vermilion mixed" (1765). Instructions to the factor at Savano Town in 1716 explained that "the Proportion of Mixture in the Paint is 2/3 red Lead and one third, Vermilion."[37] Occasionally, other pigments were offered, such as "small[t] blue, rose colour, yellow, and green" (1738, 1742, 1743, 1748–49), and Prussian blue (1757).

Rings - Finger rings were made of white metal copper alloy, "plain Bath rings" or "Bath Women's rings" (1748–49) or brass (1728, 1763, 1772), often with glass or paste insets (called "stone rings"; 1748–49, 1755, 1757, 1765).

Wire, Brass - Brass and copper wire was traded by weight (pounds) and by length (yards or spans, with a span equaling nine English inches), in various diameters (typically noted as "small and large" or "fine and coarse"). A 1770 list of presents to the Grand Caddo specified "copper wire suitable for bracelets and wormscrews."

Implements [Edged Weapons]:

Hatchets - Traders distinguished between large, heavy axes, intended principally for tree felling and log house construction, and "hatchets, (which the Indians call Tomahawks)" (1728). Although they functioned for woodworking, the hatchet's primary use was as a weapon. The trade lists mention "large and small hatchets," "oval-eyed and square-eyed hatchets" (1748–49, 1755, 1762, 1765, 1768), and "pipe hatchets" or "smoking tomahawks" (1757, 1758, 1798, 1799).

Knives - Large, straight knives with fixed handles were generally called "butcher's knives" (1716, 1738, 1748–49, 1765, 1798, 1799), "cutteau knives" (after the French term for knife; 1758, 1762, 1765, 1769, 1770, 1798, 1799), "hunter's knives" (1770), "woodcutter's knives" (1775), or sometimes "pocket

knives with sheathes" (1738, 1770). These knives had boxwood, antler, or horn handles. The other major category of knives was the "clasp" type (1716, 1738, 1752, 1755, 1762) or "buckshorn [handled] spring knives" (1739, 1742, 1743, 1748–49, 1757), also called the "common trading knife" (1765, 1769).
Swords - Small quantities of "symeters" (1720), "cutlasses" (1716, 1720), and "hangers" (1718, 1757, 1759) were available through trade and presents.

Implements [Food-related]:
Euro-ceramics - Nonaboriginal ceramics did not find a market among the Indians of the interior Southeast until the early nineteenth century. Among the exceptions appearing on trade lists were "Blue and White Juggs, Gallon and 1/2 Gallon" (1762), "4 Earthen Cups" (1763), and "1 qr. Delph Bowls," a "Milk Pott and Sugar Dish" (1772). Among Edmond Atkin's more unusual requests was one for "10 doz. Glass Tumblers" (1757).
Frying Pans - An iron "frying pan" is listed in a 1762 rate schedule for the Cherokees.
Kettles - Brass kettles, "wyer'd and bayled" (1742), were popular trade items throughout the eighteenth century. They occurred in a variety of sizes, but there is little evidence to suggest that they were sold in nested sets, as was the case in Canada. Prices were based on weight, with 1- and 5-pound sizes mentioned (1762, 1763). "Tin kettles" and "tin pots," made of tinned sheet iron, were offered in nested sets (1748–49, 1751, 1755, 1762, 1765, 1767), in sizes ranging from half pint to six gallon.[38] Cast iron pots in three gallon and six gallon sizes were presented to the Creeks in 1748–49.
Spoons - "Pewter Soup Spoons," large and small, were provided in limited quantities by a few traders.

Implements [Sewing]:
Needles - The "large needles" (1720, 1734) referred to on early eighteenth-century lists of presents for the Indians may have been needed to sew packs of deerskins. Later steel needles (including "Osnaburg needles," 1765) for sewing clothing became widely available, though "papers of pins" (1768, 1799) remained uncommon on the lists.
Scissors - "Trading scissors" were available in an assortment of sizes, including "small Steel Womens, large, and larger Scizers" (1748–49).
Thread - Early lists refer to "brown, red & Blew thread" (1720), and "blew sewing thread for Women" (1734), but later accounts mention only "white" or "whited Brown Thread" (1748–49, 1762, 1775, 1797). Other specific types include "Osnaburg, Garlix, and shoe thread" (1772), and French-made "Renne thread" (1775). Thread was sold by weight or by the skein.[39]

Implements [Smoking]:

Smoking Pipes - White clay smoking pipes, when not simply called "pipes" or "Indian pipes," were distinguished on the basis of length into two categories: "Long Pipes" (1748–49, 1755, 1765), also called "Quality Pipes" (1757); and the shorter "Hunters Pipes" or "Hunting Pipes" or "Bristol short pipes" (1738, 1739, 1748–49, 1755, 1757). In 1748–49, "Long Pipes" were packed in boxes 2 feet 3 inches long, indicating a somewhat shorter pipe length. "Pipe hatchets" or "smoking tomahawks" are mentioned in 1757, 1758, 1768, 1797, 1798, and 1799.

Tobacco - Cured tobacco was available by weight ("shag cut tobacco," 1755) or by the twist (1705, 1779).[40] Edmond Atkin specified the "best Virginia cut Tobacco, in Papers" (1757).

Tobacco Boxes - Small sheet brass or iron boxes for snuff, cut tobacco, or tinder were occasionally provided through trade.[41]

Tongs - Tongs for lighting and tamping pipe tobacco appear on one early trade ledger (1715).[42]

Implements [Firearms]:

Gunflints - English gunspalls, made of "black flint" (1755), were shipped to America in small barrels, "casks," or "rundlets," each containing four thousand to five thousand (1739, 1748–49). In 1769 and 1770, two quality grades, "common" and "fine," were specified.

Gunpowder - Traders carried gunpowder to the interior southeastern tribes in barrels (weighing one hundred pounds) or half-barrels (fifty pounds). It was then exchanged by the ounce or pound. Quality grades included "F Gun powder" (1748–49) and finer "FF Gunpowder" (1739, 1742, 1748–49, 1757).

Gunsmith's Tools - Tools provided for gun repair and maintenance include "gun plyer hammers" (1739), "claw gun hammers" (1739, 1742), "double gun hammers" (1742), and "Steel half Moon Gun Screws" (1739, 1742, 1743, 1748–49).

Gun Worms - Steel gun worms, or "wormscrews" (1770), were needed for wad extraction from rifles.

Holsters - Pistol "holsters, holster caps, and straps," which evidently were rare commodities in the southeastern trade, appear on one Cherokee rate schedule (1762).

Lead Balls & Shot - Lead was transported on packhorses in small barrels, each weighing 50 pounds or less. It was then traded in the form of bars, cast balls, cast shot, and drop shot, with prices based on count or weight. In 1748–49, twenty-six balls were produced per pound. The Grand Caddo, in 1770, obtained thirty to thirty-two calibre balls, which fit their French guns.

Shot was described as "Drop Shott" (1739), "Swan Drop Shott" (1742), "Swan Shott" (1751), "Bristol Shot" (1743), and "large Bristol Shott B" (1748–49). Swan shot was specifically prohibited from the trade in 1765.[43]

Muskets - Most firearms included on trade lists and present inventories were lightweight "Indian trading guns" (1720, 1748–49, 1759, 1765, 1767, 1769, 1772, 1783, 1784), also called by the French name, "fusils," or the English corruption, "fusees" (1770). Some of these were described more specifically as "Wilson's trading Guns" (1755, 1757) and "London Prov'd Indian Trading Guns" (1748–49). Other types of guns include "Fowling Pieces" (1755, 1765), "fine Guns with Carve'd Prov'd Barrels," and "fine Guns with Barrels inlaid with Gold" (1748–49). In at least one instance, guns were provided "in List [cloth] Cases" (1738). Gun locks were often sold separately (1751, 1762, 1769, 1770). Types included "flatt locks" and "round locks" (1748–49).

Pistols - Although pistols were infrequently included on rate schedules, reference to a pair of "Brass-Barrel Pistols" is found in a Cherokee list from 1762.

Implements [Woodworking]:

Augers & Gimlets - This category includes all sizes, from small "gimblets," some with bone handles (1762, 1772), to a "Tap Boawer" [borer] (1772), to "3/4 inch and 1 1/4 inch Augers" (1762, 1772), and "Screw Augers" (1799).

Awls - Awls appear on four 1770 lists of presents containing large numbers of French trade goods.

Axes - Trader jargon discriminated between large axes, intended primarily for tree felling and log house construction, and smaller hatchets. "Felling Axes" were specifically mentioned, as were "Broad Axes" (1748–49).

Chisels - "Heading Chisels" were rare items, mentioned in only 1772 and 1799.

Files - "Handsaw" (1762, 1772), "Cutt Saw" (1772), "Whip Saw" (1772), and "Mill Saw" files (1798) are listed exclusively on late eighteenth-century inventories.

Hammers - This category includes large and small "Carpenters Claw Hammers" (1748–49, 1762).

Nails - Hand-wrought iron nails came in 6, 8, 10, and 20 d sizes. In 1751, Governor Glen of South Carolina sent "one gross Brass Nailes" to the Creeks.

Saws - Varieties included "mill saws" (1798) and "Hand Saws Whett & Sett to work" (1748–49, 1762).

Foodstuffs:

Rum, etc. - Rum was the standard English trade liquor, "dashed" or diluted with water, and sold by the bottle or five gallon keg. Toward the end of the century, whiskey and peach brandy became available from U.S. factories (1798, 1799).

Salt - Salt was a minor trade item, sold by volume. One half bushel came in a "Bag of 3/4 Yard Osnabrigs" (1762).

Spices - Varieties included pepper and allspice.

Sugar - Sugar appeared infrequently on a few rate schedules, as "raw sugar" (1775) and "Muscavado Sugar" (1762).

Tea/Coffee - These beverages did not compete effectively with yaupon holly tea, the Black Drink, and were supplied only by independent traders George Galphin (1771, 1772) and John Fitzpatrick (1782).

Notes

1. Gregory A. Waselkov, "Seventeenth-Century Trade in the Colonial Southeast," *Southeastern Archaeology* 8, no. 2 (1989): 117–33, and "French Colonial Trade in the Upper Creek Country," in *Calumet and Fleur-de-Lys: Archaeology of Indian and French Contact in the Midcontinent*, ed. John A. Walthall and Thomas E. Emerson (Washington, D. C.: Smithsonian Institution Press, 1992), 35–53.

2. Sources of trade goods and presents inventories:

   1702–1715—[John Evans's Account Book, 1702–15], MS P/2353, South Caroliniana Library, Columbia; and [Capt. John Evans, Diary of a Journey from South Carolina to the Indian Country, 1708], Library of Congress.

   1716a—"A Schedule of the stated Prices of the Goods, as they are to be disposed of, to the Indians in Barter, viz., [at the Savano Town Factory] . . . this 9th Day of August, 1716," in *Colonial Records of South Carolina, Journals of the Commissioners of the Indian Trade, September 20, 1710–August 29, 1718*, ed. William L. McDowell Jr. (Columbia: South Carolina Archives Department, 1955), 104.

   1716b—"An Account of the Prices of Goods, settled between Col. James Moore and the Conjuror, the 30th day of April, 1716, as they are allways to be sold to his People [the Cherokees], viz.," and "Invoice of sundry Goods sent by twenty Indians, for the Charikees, to Col. Theophilus Hastings, Factor there . . . 23rd July, 1716," in *Colonial Records of South Carolina, Indian Trade*, 89.

   1717—[Presents given by the English to the headman of Coweta, July 1717], in Mark F. Boyd, "Documents Describing the Second and Third Expeditions of Lieutenant Diego Peña to Apalachee and Apalachicolo in 1717 and 1718," *Florida Historical Quarterly* 31, no. 1 (1952): 118.

   1718—"A Table of Rates to barter by; viz., Quantity and Quality of Goods for Pounds of heavy drest Deer Skins [23 April 1718]," and "Agreement, for the Prices of the Goods under-mentioned, which might at any Time hereafter happen to be sold them [the Creeks] in their Towns . . . June the 3rd, 1718," in *Colonial Records of South Carolina, Indian Trade*, 269–81.

1720—"An acct. of Several things purches for Governor Nicholson to carry wth. him in order to make Presents to the head men of the Indians in Carolina [15 September 1720]," and "Invoice of a charge of Indian trading goods of abt. one thousand Pounds & for value, and must be sorted in Proportion for a greater or less value [15 September 1720]," Colonial Office, America and West Indies, CO 5/358, f. 30–31, Public Record Office, London [hereafter cited as CO].

1724—[Presents for head warriors of the Tallapoosas, for their service against the Yawmasees, 10 June 1724], in *Journal of the Commons House of Assembly of South Carolina, June 2, 1724–June 16, 1724*, ed. A. S. Salley (Columbia: General Assembly of South Carolina, 1944), 20.

1728—"Goods for the Indian Trade [from Virginia, November 1728]," in William Byrd, *Histories of the Dividing Line betwixt Virginia and North Carolina* (New York: Dover, 1967), 298.

1734—"Gift to be given to [the Creek Indian] Tallafolechee, brother of Skee, deceased, November 27, 1734," in *The Colonial Records of the State of Georgia*, ed. Kenneth Coleman and Milton Ready 30 vols. (Athens: University of Georgia Press, 1985), 29:48.

1738—"Presents for Indians, [sent to the colony of Georgia, May and August 1738]," in *Colonial Records of the State of Georgia*, 29:280 and 30:5, 13.

1739—"Presents for Indians [sent to the colony of Georgia, July and September 1739]," in *Colonial Records of the State of Georgia*, 30:56, 94.

1740—"Payment for Indian allies to St. Augustine, [4 February 1740]," in *The Colonial Records of South Carolina, Journal of the Commons House of Assembly, September 12, 1739–March 26, 1741*, ed. J. H. Easterby, 13 vols. (Columbia: Historical Commission of South Carolina, 1952), 2:177.

1742—"Indian Presents [sent to the colony of Georgia, March and July 1742]," in *Colonial Records of the State of Georgia*, 30:241, 248.

1743—"Indian Presents [sent to the colony of Georgia, September 1743]," in *Colonial Records of the State of Georgia*, 30:316–17.

1748–49—"Invoice of goods bought by Harmon Verelst for Indian Presents [for the colonies of South Carolina and Georgia, October 1748 to January 1749]," CO 5/389, f. 9–14, 18–41; and "An Account of the Distribution of His Majesty's Presents sent over for the Indians [i.e., Creeks, Cherokees, Chickasaws, Savannahs, Natchez, Choctaws, and Catawbas] Contiguous to and in Alliance with the Provinces of South Carolina and Georgia from 17th day of August to 21st December following 1749," CO 5/389, f. 177–90.

1751—"List of the Prices of Goods for the Cherokee Trade, November 1st, 1751," and "Presents given to the Cherokee Indians, 23 November, 1751 [Charleston, South Carolina]," in *Colonial Records of South Carolina, Documents Relating to Indian Affairs, May 21, 1750–August 7, 1754*, ed. William L. McDowell Jr. (Columbia, S. C.: South Carolina Archives Department, 1958), 146–47, 161–62.

1752a—"Memorandum of What we [traders from South Carolina at the Cherokee town of Cheowe] suffered by the Lower Creeks . . . May 2nd, 1752" in *Indian Affairs, 1750–1754*, 248.

1752b—"A List of sundry Goods delivered to the Catawba Indians at the Congaree Fort, 14 February, 1752," in *Indian Affairs, 1750–1754*, 217–18.

1755—"A List of Goods for Indian Presents . . . Feb. 3, 1755," and "A General Account of Indian Presents Distributed [to the Upper and Lower Creeks, Chickasaws, and Cherokees] by Order of His Excellency John Reynolds Esqr. Governor of Georgia from the 16th day of December 1755 to the 15th day of February 1757," in *Colonial Records of the State of Georgia*, 27:30–31, 80–84.

1756a—[Accounts of Sundries Disbursed to the Cherokees at Fort Loudoun, 6–8 August 1756], in *Colonial Records of South Carolina, Documents Relating to Indian Affairs, 1754–1765*, ed. William L. McDowell Jr. (Columbia, S. C.: South Carolina Department of Archives and History, 1970), 173–74.

1756b—"A List of Indian Presents to the Chickasaws delivered to Augusta [Georgia], June 15, 1756," in *Colonial Records of the State of Georgia*, ed. Coleman and Ready, 28 (part I):77–78.

1757a—"Account of Presents [sent from Charleston, South Carolina] to the Chickasaws of Breed Camp . . . August 26th, 1757," in *Indian Affairs, 1754–1765*, 445–46.

1757b—Edmond Atkin, "A List of Goods proper to be sent from England to Charlestown in South Carolina, to be given as Presents from his Majesty to the Indians in the Southern District, for the Service of the Year 1757," Loudoun Collection, LO 3517A, Huntington Library.

1758—"A List of Goods taken from the [South Carolina] Traders by Colonel Byrd for the Use of the [Cherokee] Indians [around Fort Prince George, 4 April–2 May 1758]," in *Indian Affairs, 1754–1765*, 456–58.

1759—"A Return of Indian Presents [to the Cherokees] . . . Fort Prince George, 14 April, 1759," in *Indian Affairs, 1754–1765*, 483.

1762—"Table of Goods and Prices for the Cherokee Indian Trade, Charles Town, July 19, 1762," and "Table of sundry (other) Wares and Merchandizes, with the respective Rates and Prices . . . to be bartered and sold at, to the [Cherokee] Indians, at the Factory at Fort Prince George, Keowee, . . . November 20th, 1762," in *Indian Affairs, 1754–1765*, 567–68, 576–79.

1763—"Major Farmar's Contingent Accounts [including "presents to the Indians"] for the Service of the Government at Mobille in Louisiana . . . 24th Octr 1763," in *Mississippi Provincial Archives, English Dominion, 1763–1766*, ed. Dunbar Rowland (Nashville: Brandon Printing Company, 1911), 69–71.

1765a—"Rates of Goods in the Upper & Lower Creek Nations . . . [for the "Province of West Florida"] 12th June 1765," and "Account of Presents delivered to the Indians at the Congress of Picolata November 15, 1765," in Peter J.

Hamilton, *Colonial Mobile*, rev. ed. (Boston: Houghton Mifflin, 1910), 539; *Mississippi Provincial Archives*, 215; James Covington, "English Gifts to the Indians: 1765–1766," *Florida Anthropologist* 13, nos. 2–3 (1960): 72–73; and *Colonial Records of the State of Georgia*, 28 (part II):118.

1765b—"[Schedule of] rates at which the Several Sorts of Goods are hereafter to be bartered for half dressed Deer Skins in [the Chickasaw and Choctaw] Country . . . 12th June 1765," in *Mississippi Provincial Archives*, 253–54.

1767–72—[George Galphin's Account Books on the Creek Indian Trade], George Galphin Papers, Manuscript Collection No. 269, Item 1: Account Book, December 1767–January 1768; Item 2: Account Book, October 1771–2 July 1772; Item 3: Account Book, 23 March–2 July 1772, Georgia Historical Society, Savannah.

1769—"Estimate of Presents & Provisions Annually Necessary for the Southern Department of Indian Affairs, exclusive of Several Meetings & Congresses, [1769]," and "Tariff, or, Rates which Goods are to be sold at, in the Country of the Indians, [1769]," CO 5/68, f. 128–29, 145.

1770a—"List of the effects which should be given . . . to the Nation of Pequeños Cados . . of the Post of Natchitoches . . New Orleans, January 22, 1770," in *Athanase de Mezieres and the Louisiana-Texas Frontier, 1768–1780*, 2 vols., ed. Herbert E. Bolton, (Cleveland: Arthur H. Clarke, 1914), 1: 133–34.

1770b—"List of Goods necessary for the annual Supply of the Village of the Grand Cadaux . . . Natchitoches, February 3, 1770," in *Athanase de Mezieres*, 1:143–44.

1770c—"Presents to the chiefs of the Comanchez, Taouaiazes, Tauacanas, Yscanis, Tancaoueys, and Quitseys . . . Natchitoches, May 20, 1770," in *Athanase de Mezieres*, 1:201–2.

1770d—"Tariff for Indian Trade in the Province of West Florida, 1770," in Daniel H. Usner Jr., *Indians, Settlers, and Slaves in a Frontier Exchange Economy: the Lower Mississippi Valley Before 1783* (Chapel Hill: University of North Carolina Press, 1992), 270.

1775—"Trade Prices at Rapides in Louisiana, 1775," in *Indians, Settlers, and Slaves*, 272.

1779—"Presents for Indians [at Natchitoches], March 21, 1779," in *Athanase de Mezieres*, 2:244–45.

1782—"Memorandum of the Goods [to be sent to John Fitzpatrick for the Indian trade at Manchac, [16 April 1782]," in *The Merchant of Manchac: The Letterbooks of John Fitzpatrick, 1768–1790*, ed. Margaret F. Dalrymple (Baton Rouge: Louisiana State University Press, 1978), 401–2.

1783—"Trade items and their value in skins, [Florida,] 1783," in Brent R. Weisman, *Like Beads on a String: A Culture History of the Seminole Indians in North Peninsular Florida* (Tuscaloosa: University of Alabama Press, 1989), 67.

1784—"Tariff arranged for the commerce of the Creek and Talapoosa nation in the general Congress celebrated in Pensacola the days of 31 May and 1 June 1784," in William S. Coker and Thomas D. Watson, *Indian Traders of the Southeastern Spanish Borderlands: Panton, Leslie & Company and John Forbes & Company, 1783–1847* (Pensacola: University of West Florida Press, 1986), 60.

1797—"Account of Andrew the Hunter, King of Cussatans, Bought at the U. States Factory, Fort Wilkinson, 3rd Aug. 1797," Creek Factory Records, Bureau of Indian Affairs, National Archives.

1798—"Inventory of Sundry Goods remaining on hand at the Tellico Factory the 18th May 1798 and turned over by James Byers Jr.[,] Factor[,] to his Succesor[,] John W. Hooker," Cherokee Factory Records (Tellico and Hiwassee), Miscellaneous Accounts, 1796–1810, Bureau of Indian Affairs, National Archives.

1799—"Journal of the Trading House at Fort Wilkinson, 22nd May 1799, Inventory taken by Matthew Hopkins," Creek Factory Records, Bureau of Indian Affairs, National Archives.

3. This sort of bead corresponds to type WIc in the Kidd and Kidd classification system; Kenneth E. Kidd and Martha Ann Kidd, "A Classification System for Glass Beads for the Use of Field Archaeologists," *Canadian Historic Sites: Occasional Papers in Archaeology and History* 1(1970): 45–89.

4. These beads correspond to type WIIc according to Kidd and Kidd, "Classification System for Glass Beads."

5. Waselkov, "French Colonial Trade," 39.

6. James Adair, *Adair's History of the American Indians*, ed. Samuel C. Williams (Johnson City, Tenn.: Watauga Press, 1930), 9.

7. *Indian Affairs, 1750–1754*, 436; *Athanase de Mezieres*, 1:144.

8. Adair, *History of the American Indians*, 7.

9. *Indian Affairs, 1750–1754*, 227.

10. For references to Indian slavery in the colonial Southeast, see Usner, *Indians, Settlers, and Slaves;* J. Leitch Wright Jr., *The Only Land They Knew: The Tragic Story of the American Indians in the Old South* (New York: Free Press, 1981); Peter H. Wood, "Indian Servitude in the Southeast," in *Handbook of North American Indians, vol. 4: History of Indian-White Relations*, ed. Wilcomb E. Washburn (Washington, D.C.: Smithsonian Institution, 1988), 4:407–9. See also Caleb Swan, "State of Arts and Manufactures, with the Creek Indians, in 1791," in *Information Respecting the History, Condition and Prospects of the Indian Tribes of the United States*, ed. Henry R. Schoolcraft, 6 vols. (Philadelphia: Lippincott, 1855), 5:692; Albert J. Pickett, *History of Alabama* (Charleston, S. C.: Walker and James, 1851), 422; and Tom Hatley, *The Dividing Paths: Cherokees and South Carolinians through the Era of Revolution* (Oxford: Oxford University Press, 1993), 32–33, 96–97.

11. Deerskins were classified by traders according to their weight and manner of preparation by the Indians. Traders distinguished between "heavy" and "light" skins, meaning those weighing more or less than two pounds. "Indian dressed" or "dressed" skins had been stretched, scraped on both sides, treated with deer brains, and smoked to produce a soft white leather that the Indians used for their own clothing and seldom traded. "Half-dressed" skins (also sometimes called "parchment"), scraped of both hair and flesh, were generally preferred by traders and by leathermakers in Europe. "Raw," "undressed," or "in the hair" skins were scraped on the flesh side only. Modern readers should be aware, though, that these terms were applied loosely and inconsistently by some traders. Since brain-tanned skins rarely found their way into the possession of traders after the first decade or so of the eighteenth century, they sometimes applied the term "dressed" to fully scraped but untanned skins. Likewise, "green" skins could be scraped on either one or both sides. The context of usage usually clarifies the intended meanings. See Waselkov, "French Colonial Trade," 37; Kathryn E. Braund, *Deerskins & Duffels: Creek Indian Trade with Anglo-America, 1685–1815* (Lincoln: University of Nebraska Press, 1993), 88. A letter of 24 April 1799 from Jonathan Harris, Keeper of U. S. Military Stores, to Edward Wright, Factor to the Creek Indians at Oconee, Georgia, described the treatment of deerskins after they had been obtained from Indian hunters.

> Deer Skins should have their Shanks and Pates cut off as soon as received & an account kept of the difference of Weight, which difference should be charged in the price per pound. Suppose it would average about 10 Per Cent; by taking off the shanks and pates, two good objects are in view, the one is to prevent the engendering Vermin which soon destroys the Pelt, the other is to decrease the Expence of transportation, which is considerable. During the warm Season your Peltries should be so arranged in your Skin House as to receive an airing and beating once a Week in the Shade, it is found on Experiment that to Sun Skins, will produce more Worms. If you pack the Furs bundled, care must be taken that the Beaver is placed as before mentioned & have coarser Skins, such as Bear, pelt out, put tightly round as Wrapping, and well lashed with strong Cords. Deer Skins should be as tightly packed as possible, and while the Bale is making, Whiskey or Spirits of any kind should be sprinkled among them, which will have a tendency to prevent the Worm from breeding. [Creek Factory Records, Bureau of Indian Affairs, National Archives.]

12. Jean-Bernard Bossu, *Travels in the Interior of North America, 1751–1762*, trans. and ed. Seymour Feiler (Norman: University of Oklahoma Press, 1962), 146; *The Colonial Records of the State of Georgia*, vol. 4 (1737–1740), ed. Allen D. Candler (Atlanta: Franklin Printing, 1906), 666; Verner W. Crane, *The Southern Frontier, 1670–1732* (New York: Norton, 1981), 118; Wright, *The Only Land They Knew,* 173; Richard White, *The Roots of Dependency: Subsistence, Environment, and Social Change among the Choctaws, Pawnees, and Navajos* (Lincoln: University of Nebraska Press, 1983), 9–13, 26–29, 92–93; Braund, *Deerskins & Duffels*, 69–70.

13. Peter H. Wood, "The Changing Population of the Colonial South: An Overview by Race and Region, 1685–1790," in *Powhatan's Mantle: Indians in the Colonial*

Southeast, ed. Peter H. Wood, Gregory A. Waselkov, and M. Thomas Hatley (Lincoln: University of Nebraska Press, 1989), 39.

14. Braund, *Deerskins & Duffels*, 70–72, 226–27; see also Nancy M. Miller Surrey, "The Commerce of Louisiana During the French Regime, 1699–1763," *Columbia University Studies in the Social Sciences* 167 (1916): 210–11, 217–18, 224, 351, 357; Paul Chrisler Phillips, *The Fur Trade*, 2 vols. (Norman: University of Oklahoma Press, 1961), 1:573, 2:198, 209; Converse D. Clowse, *Measuring Charleston's Overseas Commerce, 1717–1767: Statistics from the Port's Naval Lists* (Washington, D. C.: University Press of America, 1981), 54–56; White, *Roots of Dependency*, 58; Robert R. Rea, "British West Florida Trade and Commerce in the Customs Records," *Alabama Review* 37 (1984):146; Coker and Watson, *Indian Traders*, 35; Robin F. A. Fabel, *The Economy of British West Florida, 1763–1783* (Tuscaloosa: University of Alabama Press, 1988), 54, 57; Joel W. Martin, *Sacred Revolt: The Muskogee's Struggle for a New World* (Boston: Beacon Press, 1991), 60; Daniel H. Usner Jr., "The Deerskin Trade in French Louisiana," in *Proceedings of the Tenth Meeting of the French Colonial Historical Society, April 12–14, 1984*, ed. Philip P. Boucher (Lanham, Md.: University Press of America, 1985), 82, and Usner, *Indians, Settlers, and Slaves*, 246, 262–65.

15. William Bartram, *Travels Through North & South Carolina, Georgia, East & West Florida* (Philadelphia: James and Johnson, 1791), 214.

16. Crane, *Southern Frontier*, 112.

17. Phillips, *Fur Trade*, 2:185, 218; Charles Hudson, "Why the Southeastern Indians Slaughtered Deer," in *Indians, Animals, and the Fur Trade: A Critique of Keepers of the Game*, ed. Shepard Krech III (Athens: University of Georgia Press, 1981), 162–63; Richard White, *The Middle Ground: Indians, Empires, and Republics in the Great Lakes Region, 1650–1815* (Cambridge: Cambridge University Press, 1991), 523; Usner, *Indians, Settlers, and Slaves*, 273–75; Hatley, *Dividing Paths*, 163; Braund, *Deerskins & Duffels*, 72; Ian K. Steele, *Warpaths: Invasions of North America* (Oxford: Oxford University Press, 1994), 69.

18. Hudson, "Why the Southeastern Indians Slaughtered Deer"; for an overarching debate about the rationales for Indian overhunting promoted by the fur trade, see Calvin Martin, *Keepers of the Game: Indian-Animal Relationships and the Fur Trade* (Berkeley: University of California Press, 1978) and Shepard Krech III, ed., *Indians, Animals, and the Fur Trade: A Critique of Keepers of the Game* (Athens: University of Georgia Press, 1981).

19. For instance, see Arthur E. Bogan, "A Comparison of Late Prehistoric Dallas and Overhill Cherokee Subsistence Strategies in the Little Tennessee River Valley," (Ph.D. diss., Department of Anthropology, University of Tennessee, 1980), 162.

20. *The Colonial Records of the State of Georgia*, vol. 8 (1759–1762), ed. Allen D. Candler (Atlanta: Franklin-Turner, 1907), 311.

21. James Covington, "The British Meet the Seminoles: Negotiations Between British Authorities in East Florida and the Indians, 1763–68," *Contributions to the Florida State Museum, Social Sciences* 7 (1961): 27; Rowland, *Mississippi Provincial Archives*, 204.

22. Rowland, *Mississippi Provincial Archives*, 204.

23. Phillips, *Fur Trade*, 1:573.

24. Bernard Romans, *A Concise Natural History of East and West Florida* (New York, Printed for the Author, 1775), 104; Rea, "British West Florida Trade," 146–49.

25. Phillips, *Fur Trade*, 2:185; Braund, *Deerskins & Duffels*, 72.

26. Lawrence Kinnaird ed., "Spain in the Mississippi Valley, 1765–1794," three parts, *American Historical Association, Annual Report for 1945*, vols. 2–4 (Washington, D.C.: U.S. Government Printing Office, 1946–49), 4:293.

27. Benjamin Hawkins, *Letters, Journals and Writings of Benjamin Hawkins*, 2 vols., ed. C. L. Grant (Savannah: Beehive Press, 1980), 1:242.

28. Hawkins, *Letters, Journals and Writings*, 2:418.

29. Ibid., 2:440; see also 2:410–11.

30. Braund, *Deerskins & Duffels*, 72.

31. Hawkins, *Letters, Journals and Writings*, 2:778–79.

32. An authoritative reference on eighteenth-century cloth is Florence M. Montgomery, *Textiles in America, 1650–1870* (New York: W.W. Norton, 1984).

33. Charles E. Hanson Jr., "Printed Calicos for Indians," *Museum of the Fur Trade Quarterly* 24, no. 3 (1988): 1–11.

34. Charles E. Hanson Jr., "The Point Blanket," *Museum of the Fur Trade Quarterly* 12, no. 1 (1976): 5–10, and "Some Additional Notes on Trade Blankets," *Museum of the Fur Trade Quarterly* 24, no. 4 (1988): 5–11.

35. Charles E. Hanson Jr., "Trade Mirrors," *Museum of the Fur Trade Quarterly* 22, no. 4, (1986): 1–11.

36. Arthur Woodward, "Indian Trade Goods," *Oregon Archaeological Society Publication* 2 (1965).

37. *Colonial Records of South Carolina, Indian Trade*, 102; see also Charles E. Hanson Jr., "A Paper of Vermilion," *Museum of the Fur Trade Quarterly* 7, no. 3 (1971): 1–3.

38. Charles E. Hanson Jr., "Sheet Iron Kettles," *Museum of the Fur Trade Quarterly* 28, no. 1 (1992): 2–6.

39. Charles E. Hanson Jr., "Thread in the Fur Trade," *Museum of the Fur Trade Quarterly* 25 (1989): 9–13.

40. Charles E. Hanson Jr., "Tobacco in the Fur Trade," *Museum of the Fur Trade Quarterly* 24, no. 2 (1988): 2–11.

41. [The "Engages"], "More about Tobacco Boxes," *Museum of the Fur Trade Quarterly* 27, no. 4 (1991): 9–11.

42. John Lawson, *A New Voyage to Carolina*, ed. Hugh T. Lefler (Chapel Hill: University of North Carolina Press, 1967), 235.

43. *Colonial Records of the State of Georgia*, 28 (part II):116.

Ann Harper Fender [1]

Public versus Private Ownership: Saskatchewan Fur Trapping and Trading Legislation in the 1940s

Introduction

SASKATCHEWAN VOTERS in the early 1940s brought the Cooperative Commonwealth Federation (CCF) to provincial power. Many of the federation's "socialist" policies, such as its introduction of universal medical coverage, have been closely scrutinized.[2] The CCF's policies toward the fur trade have received less attention from political and economic commentators. Local contemporary managers in the fur trade paid more attention, as Hugh Ross indicated in his book, *The Manager's Tale*, about his many years with the Hudson's Bay Company. Between 1948 and 1957, he served as manager for the Saskatchewan district. He thus took over the district a few years after the Cooperative Commonwealth Federation became head of the provincial government in Saskatchewan. Among its many legislative actions the CCF set up the Saskatchewan Fur Marketing Service, holding its own auctions in the province's capital, Regina. The provincial government also set up its own stores, the Saskatchewan Government Trading Company, primarily to serve northern areas. Ross contended in his book that "Although the [fur trading] service was patronized by farmers and part-time southern trappers and by local fur dealers, the native and half-breed trappers in the north turned it hands down. . . ."[3]

The legislative actions that set up the agencies to which Ross refers include the 1944 amendments to Saskatchewan Act 251-252, which more stringently regulated the fur trapping and trading industry; the 1944 amendment to the Natural Resources Act; and the 1945 Natural Products Act. These actions effectively limited trapping to those licensed by the province to trap within a specified area and eventually created fur conservation areas in northern Saskatchewan. Legislation also created a crown corporation, the Saskatchewan Fur Marketing Service (SFMS), to buy furs from trappers and in turn to auction the furs at the new corporation's fur warehouse in Regina. Initially trappers had to sell particular furs such as beaver and muskrat to the provincial fur marketing service in order to receive trapping licenses, a requirement that was repealed by 1958.

Saskatchewan's movement into what had been private market activities in the fur trade partially reflected historical, social, political, and economic circumstances unique to Saskatchewan in the 1940s. Arguably this movement also reflected more general concerns about the effectiveness of private markets versus government agents in determining resource use and the distribution of its benefits. Microeconomists evaluate an economy by how effectively it uses resources to produce the goods and services that society demands and by how those goods and services are distributed among the people of the society. The first involves economic efficiency and the second, economic equity. Under neoclassical microeconomic theory, private markets can fail to perform effectively if these markets are not competitive. They also can fail when externalities exist. Both these conditions affect the distribution of benefits from economic activity, though equity issues arise even when markets are competitive and no externalities exist. In this chapter I examine whether market conditions warranted intervention by the government and whether the actions taken by the CCF significantly improved the efficiency and equity outcomes in the fur trade in Saskatchewan through its legislation in the early 1940s.[4] I conclude that the legislation had relatively little effect on fur prices and income, but might have affected conservation of fur species.

In the next section, I elaborate on the relevant legislation and compare it to related earlier legislation and conservation efforts. The third section considers the economic theory that underlies market failure due to monopoly and monopsony power; it also digresses briefly to consider how demand conditions can affect revenues to the producers and to the state from royalties. The fourth section looks at the economics of externalities. In the fifth section, I present data on fur returns and values for the decades of the 1930s, 1940s, and 1950s for Saskatchewan and for Canada. That section contains as well qualitative evidence via contemporary newspaper accounts and anecdotes on the effectiveness of Saskatchewan's policies toward the fur trade. The final section evaluates whether the policies that Saskatchewan legislators set into motion in the 1940s worked well in succeeding years to increase efficiency in the fur trade and to improve trappers' incomes.

Legislative Action and Prior Conservation Efforts

Part of the legislation in the 1940s seemed designed to encourage conservation, though these were not the first efforts of the province to discourage hunting of depleted species. As early as 1911, Saskatchewan had four salaried game guardians and numerous volunteers. According to Wayne Runge, posters summarizing the conditions of the 1914 Game Act were published in four languages and listed fines for hunting out of season. Fur dealers had to buy licenses by 1914.[5] In 1930, the federal government transferred control over provincial resources to Saskatchewan through the Natural Resources Transfer Agreement, thereby facilitating provincial action on resource management.[6] The provincial government had been limiting hunting and trapping, and the Natural Resources annual report for 1933 anticipated that "There can be no doubt that the present policy of the Department to lease trapping areas to bona fide trappers, will have a most important and beneficial influence on the fur trade of the Province."[7] Despite the policy and the optimism, the problem of resource depletion persisted into the 1940s and partially motivated further government involvement in the fur trade. The 1946 Federal-Provincial Fur Agreement provided federal funding and enabled the province to impose trapping regulations on treaty Indians. It designated northern Saskatchewan as a Fur Conservation Block and established approximately ninety-five Fur Conservation Areas within the block. The intent, as Runge describes the system, was to "bring about a recovery in the beaver population and to structure an orderly trapline management system that would reduce conflicts and maintain forest traplines as commercial entities."[8] The Fur Conservation Areas were further divided into zones and traplines, with the latter allotted to specific trappers.

Prior to formal government regulation, the Hudson's Bay Company had worried about depletion of fur resources in those regions that it controlled. Victor Lytwyn found in his study of the "Little North," a region north of Lake Superior and east of Lake Winnipeg, that the company attempted to limit the trade in beaver skins to allow the animals to flourish in the years following introduction of its retrenchment policy in 1810.[9] E. E. Rich described the company's Governing Committee in 1822 as advising that its Canadian traders should discourage Indians from hunting beaver and valuable fur animals in the summer because it prevented beaver from reproducing.[10] Again in 1823 the committee urged that particular regions be left unhunted so that animal populations could recover.[11]

In its legislative endeavors, the Saskatchewan government was concerned with how furs were marketed as well as with conservation. By establishing the Saskatchewan Fur Marketing Service, the CCF followed a pattern analogous to the establishment of marketing boards in other provinces and in the United States. Federal and provincial legislation in Canada provided for such boards. In Saskatchewan the Natural Resources Act of 1944 authorized the minister to "purchase and sell or otherwise dispose of or utilize any product of the resources of the province in lands, minerals, fur, game, fish, water, water powers or forests which are the property of the Crown."[12] The act additionally permitted the minister to require that any person licensed to trap on or after 1 October 1930 could be required to sell to the minister "whenever required by him to do so any product of such resources at the fair value thereof."[13]

British Columbia passed Canada's first marketing board scheme with its 1927 Produce Marketing Act. As M. W. Farrell describes such boards, they generally intend to supplement free market pricing by government-sponsored boards of grower representatives under a provincial marketing commissioner. These intentions can stem from the desire to use more orderly marketing to raise prices and farm incomes; they also can stem from compensating the sellers for the presumed market power of processors or distributors, "allegedly taking abnormal profits."[14] North American agricultural history includes anecdotal evidence of the buying power of larger purchasers of raw agricultural products and the bargaining disadvantage that individual farmers perceived when they dealt with the monopoly suppliers of transportation services and with monopsonistic (single buyer) purchasers of grain. Such perceptions influenced agricultural legislation in Canada and the United States. Similar motivations might have led legislators to protect isolated fur trappers.

Canada's courts ruled the British Columbia act unconstitutional in 1931. The federal government, however, passed the Natural Products Marketing Act in 1934, which provided that powers not held by the federal government could be assumed by the provincial governments.[15] John Black, writing in 1942, argues that the real objective of agricultural reformers in establishing marketing boards was "higher prices for farm products—not just a little higher farm prices, but big increases. . . ."[16] These higher prices could be obtained by exercising market control over the supply of a product, in effect cartelizing an industry to restrict quantity sold so as to drive up the product's price. If the demand for the product is price inelastic, the percentage increase in price is greater than the percentage decrease in quantity sold. When price increases, therefore, total revenue (which equals price times quantity) also rises.

Economics of Monopoly and Monopsony

Those economists who advocate a system of markets as an effective means of making and coordinating the economic decisions that scarcity of resources thrusts upon any society do so because they see competitive markets as protecting the buyers of products and the sellers of inputs from exploitation.[17] If one does not like the price or practices of one merchant, one is free to transact with another. Theoretically, the outcomes of the many independent decisions of buyers and sellers generate efficient outcomes. Allocatively efficient outcomes are those in which all voluntary, mutually beneficial transactions have occurred. In this situation of Pareto optimality, the only way to improve one person's economic situation is by worsening another's.[18] This theoretical outcome requires that all markets be competitive (no buyer or seller has market power), all participants be fully informed, and all costs and benefits of production, exchange, and consumption be purely private, with no spillover or external effects.

If instead of many sellers of a product there is only one, the result is monopoly. A monopoly maximizes profit, with price typically above the cost of producing an additional unit of output, the marginal cost. When price exceeds marginal cost, inefficiency occurs in the sense that the benefits to consumers of a lower price exceed the lost income to the producer of that lower price. Hypothetically, the consumers would gain enough from a price reduction to bribe the producer to lower it.

The parallel case of a single buyer of an input, such as raw fur for resale, is called monopsony. As the only purchaser, the monopsonist faces the industry supply curve of the commodity. Typically the amount that producers are willing to sell rises as price rises. In this scenario, the buyer induces the sellers to sell more by offering a higher price. Assume that the buyer seeks to maximize profits in its purchase of the input. To maximize profit, the buyer purchases an additional unit of the input as long as the cost of that additional unit is less than or equal to the additional revenue that unit is expected to generate. This additional cost, the marginal factor cost, depends upon market structure, that is, whether the buyer is one of many or whether it is a monopsonist. With many competitive buyers, no one buyer can affect the price of the input by choosing to buy more. Hence each assumes the additional cost to be equal to market price.

In contrast the monopsonist, as the only buyer, realizes that to buy more of the commodity in a fluid and repeated market raises the price not only on additional units purchased but also on all previous units purchased. Thus the additional cost of a unit of the input exceeds its supply curve price, as illustrated in figure 1, which shows supply, demand, and marginal factor cost curves and resulting prices in competition and monopsony. The competitive level of purchase would be 6 with price equal to $15. If instead of many small buyers of the resource or intermediate good there is a single buyer, that buyer's incentive to drive price down by restricting purchases leads to a profit-maximizing purchase level of 5 with price $12 paid to the seller. From a societal perspective, the monopsonistic market leads to a loss of economic welfare equal to the area of the triangle *abbc*. This loss occurs because the price paid to the competitive sellers is less than the benefits derived by the users of the resource. Those benefits are reflected by the demand curve for the resource. That demand results from the price final consumers are willing to pay for more of the product that the resource produces times the productivity of the resource in producing that final product. The monopsonist's ability to drive purchase price down by buying less leads to an inefficient social outcome. The efficient level of output occurs where the additional benefits of more output, as reflected by the demand curve, just equal the additional cost of more output, as reflected by the supply curve.

Numerous economic studies on agrarian discontent in the U.S. and Canadian Midwest in the late nineteenth and early twentieth centuries have examined the role of monopsonistic middlemen purchasers of grain. In the fur trade in northern Saskatchewan, the Hudson's Bay Company faced complaints about its power vis-à-vis the native trappers and sellers of fur. In those areas in which the company was the sole buyer of trappers' furs and the only seller of trade goods, it clearly had market power. Whether this power was sufficient to generate lower prices to the fur trapper is an empirical question that can be addressed by comparing the prices received by trappers in southern regions who had more access to competitive fur buyers with those received by trappers in more remote regions, making allowances for the higher costs of trading in remote locations. Arthur Ray, in his history of the post-confederation fur trade, described the Hudson's Bay Company's conservative reaction to modern transportation developments after World War I.[19] He contended that the new transportation technology created greater competition for the company. This reduced the company's monopoly power in selling trade goods and its obverse, monopsony power in buying furs. Supporting this picture of vigorous competition, Hugh Ross inevitably mentioned the opposition traders at almost each post in his description of his travels around the Saskatchewan district after World War II. For example, he wrote about the Buffalo Narrows area, where mink ranchers used the offal from the fish plant. Escaped ranch mink invariably interbred with local wild mink, leading to an amazing array of mink pelt colors. The wild mink commanded a higher price than the farm mink. Ross advised the company trader, "when in doubt, buy them as ranch mink and don't worry if you lose some of the crazier skins. Let the free trader buy those."[20] These anecdotal accounts suggest that the Hudson's Bay Company faced more competition after World War I than it had for many years previously, and that competition occurred both in the purchase of furs and in the retail trade. Runge reported that by 1895 Prince Albert, on the North Saskatchewan River roughly 250 miles north of Regina, had emerged as a center for conducting the fur business and that many independent traders operated along the forest fringe, some only for a season or two, some as specialists in one or two species. He also reported that 169 fur traders purchased licenses in 1914-15.[21]

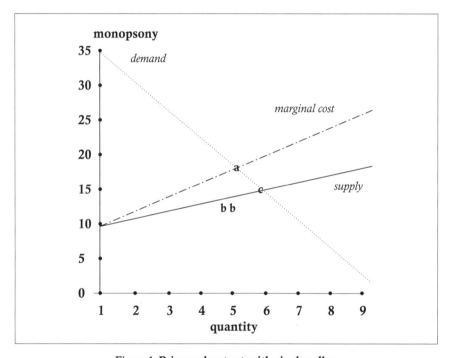

Figure 1. **Price and output with single seller.**

Externalities

In addition to its likely concerns about the market power of fur traders, the Saskatchewan government in the 1940s reacted to the depletion of fur resources that it found increasingly apparent. [22] In the 1934–35 *Report of Chief Clerk, Department of Natural Resources*, the report of the Game Commission noted:

> The fur trade is far from being satisfactory, and requires a complete reorganization from trapper to dealer. The present method of trapping is fast depleting the province of its fur, and present unethical methods of a percentage of the fur dealers warrants the conclusion that Government control

of all raw fur is essential if the province is to reap the benefit of its fur resources for any length of time.[23]

The economic concept of externalities clarifies why individual trappers seeking to maximize their individual real incomes would not conserve fur resources to guarantee future returns. Without property rights to a particular fur resource, any trapper who reduces current fur harvests to protect future production will find that others can reap the benefits of his conservation. Conservation therefore creates external benefits to those who do not partake in the decision to conserve or pay the cost of conserving. Similarly, harvesting all of the current stock provides benefits to the trapper, but some of the costs of this decision will be borne by others in the future who find the stock depleted. With external benefits and external costs, the decision-maker either does not receive the full benefits or bear the full costs of the decision. With externalities the private decision maker does not have an incentive to make socially desirable decisions, ones that take into account all benefits and costs.

Monopolies and monopsonies might offset the tendency for overexploitation of a resource to occur when external costs exist. The profit-maximizing monopoly produces less than its profit-maximizing competitive counterpart. A monopsonistic firm will purchase less of an input than will a competitive industry, because the monopsony has an incentive to reduce its input purchases so as to drive the price of the input down. There is nothing, however, in the market structure of monopoly or monopsony to suggest that the incentives to underproduce will just offset the external costs generated by production.

Traditional societies with small populations who strongly share a common value system might allocate hunting rights without formal distribution of common property. David Feeny, et al. hypothesized a continuum of rights structures for common property, ranging from open access to communal property to private property to state ownership and control. They argued that "successful exclusion under communal property is the rule rather than the exception . . ." and cited such cases as the Amerindian hunting and fishing lands in James Bay. Here, they found, "the communal property regime collapsed as a result of incursions by outsiders and recovered with the re-establishment of exclusion at least twice in the nineteenth century."[24] Modern polities think of limited property rights as being created by resource management agencies, but Berkes found that they can come into being by mutual agreement of individual users in "traditional" self-management.[25]

Even such groups apparently had difficulty preventing overhunting of scarce fur resources as the fur trade spread through eastern and central Canada in the eighteenth-century. In their recent study of the impact of the fur trade on beaver stocks in eighteenth-century Canada, Carlos and Lewis argued that competition between French and British fur trading companies led native trappers to overexploit fur resources, especially beaver.[26] Lytwyn concluded from Hudson's Bay Company documents for the Little North area that the retrenchment system of abandoning posts and establishing beaver quotas led to some Indians encroaching on the lands of others already living near the posts that remained open. Further, the Indians were not receptive to establishing family or band hunting territories. He cited James Sutherland, who wrote in 1815 that "the hunting grounds is common to the whole, and any stranger may come and enjoy the same privilege without molestation."[27]

After the Hudson's Bay Company merged with the North West Company in 1821, thereby gaining substantial control over the fur trade of the Canadian interior, the company had difficulty "closing" an area to hunting. Rich explained that a main effect of the HBC's attempts to allow an area to recuperate in the 1830s was that instead of an area being considered the traditional hunting grounds of one band, the whole district became considered a common ground. The natives moved into adjacent lands from which the company bought freely, overhunting that area.[28] These examples seem inconsistent with what is known about "the commons" in traditional societies. Peter Usher's examination of Inuit property rights looked for and found evidence of "property and tenure systems in Inuit social organization, ideology, and values."[29] Usher distinguished common property arrangements from communal property systems, with property rights under the latter arising from use and occupancy as evidenced by knowledge of the relevant territory. According to Usher, Inuit conceptions and corresponding responsibilities clearly influenced the conservation of resources. Open access to resources, he argued, "are characteristic of rapid economic change, unstable social institutions and the absence of local, community control. . . ."[30] Perhaps the behavior cited for Indians involved in the eighteenth- and nineteenth-century fur trade reflects, then, pressure on the resource because of "technological change or economic change . . . [that] may contribute to the breakdown of communal property mechanisms for exclusion. . . ."[31]

Assignment of property rights to the scarce resource gives the local decision maker, which can be a family, a firm, or a group rather than an individual, an incentive to examine all costs and benefits, future as well as present. For the resource of fur-bearing animals, however, assignment of property rights to land does not resolve the externalities problem if those animals are migratory. Under these circumstances, government can set quotas, then allocate licenses limited in catch to the preset quota.

Effects

The intent of Saskatchewan's fur legislation in the 1940s appears to have been threefold: to reduce the power of private fur traders and thereby raise incomes for trappers, to encourage conservation, and to generate revenues for the province. The department that administered the legislation published a pamphlet describing the marketing service as intended to generate surpluses that would be used to promote the fur industry and to finance increased social services. The service also aimed to secure the highest possible return for the trapper. J. L. Phelps, Minister of Natural Resources and Industrial Development, explained that the SFMS is "proof that the people of Saskatchewan can enjoy the benefits of orderly marketing. . . ."[32]

Thus, although the provincial government expressed interest in conservation of fur resources, it also was interested in the royalties it received on furs taken on provincial lands and also from license revenues. In his history of Saskatchewan, John Archer described various actions by the CCF to develop the resources of northern Saskatchewan; its "election platform had called for development of natural resources to provide revenue for social services."[33] If the government could control the flow of furs sufficiently and if fur demand were price inelastic, this control could lead to higher revenues for government and higher prices for trappers. The province simply did not have this much power over quantity and price on what was a world market and, realistically, fur revenues for the government were too limited to fund extensive programs. Provincial revenues from fur ranged from $66,000 in 1940–41 to $176,000 in 1949-50, while game license revenues varied from $37,000 to $153,000. Runge noted that this was the last period for which fur license revenues exceeded game license revenues.[34]

Other provinces had various trapping regulations in place by the mid-1940s, generally intended to preserve particular fur bearing species, but Saskatchewan with the SFMS had the only government-operated fur agency in Canada. If the differential legislation in Saskatchewan significantly affected fur totals and fur prices, at the least it should result in different patterns for output and price between the province and the country as a whole. Figure 2 shows the dollar value of beaver pelt sales in Canada and Saskatchewan between 1940–41 and 1959–60. Figure 3 shows similar total sales values for muskrat. Figures 4 and 5 compare the average value or average sales price for beaver and muskrat in Canada and in Saskatchewan between 1940 and 1959.

Data on fur prices and fur hunts provide aggregate information for the province and for the country. Disaggregated data from a sample for specific locations and trappers would permit clearer inferences about how changes in

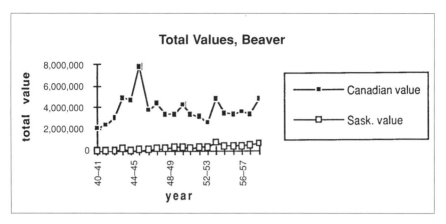

Figure 2. **Total beaver values, Saskatchewan and Canada.**

Source: Statistics Canada. Fur Production. Annual Reports; Wayne Runge, *A Century of Fur Harvesting in Saskatchewan* (Prince Albert, Saskatchewan: Saskatchewan Department of Environment and Resource Management, 1995).

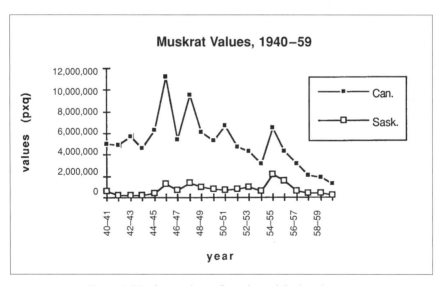

Figure 3. **Muskrat values, Canada and Saskatchewan.**

Source: Statistics Canada. Fur Production. Annual Reports; Wayne Runge, *A Century of Fur Harvesting in Saskatchewan* (Prince Albert, Saskatchewan: Saskatchewan Department of Environment and Resource Management, 1995).

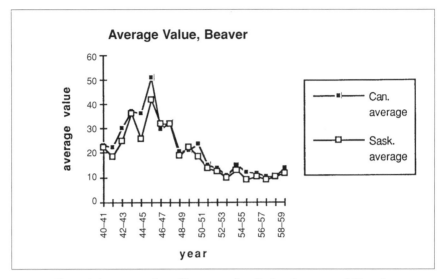

Figure 4. Average value of beaver pelts, Saskatchewan and Canada.

Source: Statistics Canada. Fur Production. Annual Reports; Wayne Runge, *A Century of Fur Harvesting in Saskatchewan* (Prince Albert, Saskatchewan: Saskatchewan Department of Environment and Resource Management, 1995).

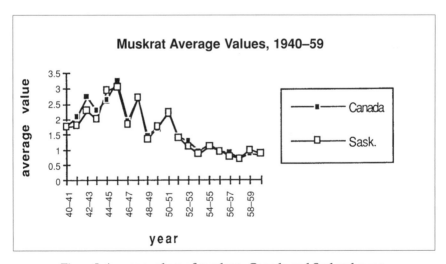

Figure 5. Average values of muskrat, Canada and Saskatchewan.

Source: Statistics Canada. Fur Production. Annual Reports; Wayne Runge, *A Century of Fur Harvesting in Saskatchewan* (Prince Albert: Saskatchewan Department of Environment and Resource Management, 1995).

institutions, the laws, and government services affected income and production. Even with disaggregated data, however, the problem remains that many factors influenced the production and prices of fur and it would be difficult to isolate the particular effect of any one factor. The natural cycle of animal populations, the weather and resulting water levels, and the condition of predators are outside the control of political agents. The vicissitudes of fashion and their effects on fur demand are only marginally more under the control of legislators. Further, even though Canada produced large quantities of furs relative to many other countries, Saskatchewan was typically the fifth largest producer among the country's provinces and territories, leaving it with little bargaining power As the various charts indicate, Saskatchewan's fur trade fortunes seemed to follow the national trend.

> By calculating correlation coefficients, we can test simply the viability of the visual impression conveyed by the data that Saskatchewan's legislation did not create outcomes different from those in the rest of Canada. A correlation coefficient measures the strength of the linear relationship between two variables without establishing whether that relationship is directly causal, indirectly causal, or the result of chance.[35] The calculated coefficient must lie between +1 and –1. A coefficient near +1 indicates a strong, positive relationship between the two variables, while a coefficient near –1 indicates a strong and negative relationship. Coefficients near zero suggest that the two variables are not linearly related. The correlation coefficient for average beaver prices between Canada and Saskatchewan for the years 1940-59 is .96; for the 1950s alone it is .885. For 1940-60, the correlation coefficient for the muskrat pelt values in Canada and in Saskatchewan is .979, while over the 1950s it is .982. These coefficients suggest a strong relationship between provincial and national fur prices. Interestingly, the correlation coefficient between total beaver sales for Canada and for Saskatchewan during these years is only .12. Total sales value results from price multiplied by quantity. The high correlation between prices and low correlation in revenue suggests that quantity of fur taken in the province followed a pattern somewhat different from that of the country as a whole.

In the agricultural sector, marketing boards have not been very successful in raising relative farm incomes or stemming the outflow of labor over the longer term unless coupled with prohibitive tariffs; many economists argue that these efforts to increase the prices of agricultural goods lead, at least in a static context, to considerable inefficiency. To the extent that the Saskatchewan Fur Marketing Board was designed to mimic the agricultural marketing boards, it seems likely to have created similar inefficiencies. If it, however, increased competition for furs, it could have led to increased efficiency by reducing monopsony power. Initially the province sought to increase the SFMS's power by virtually requiring licensees to use it.

Public choice theory suggests skepticism that a public monopoly or monopsony will behave more efficiently or benevolently than a private monopoly or monopsony. The SFMS seems never to have held an effective monopoly; at the very least, private fur traders such as the HBC continued to operate in Saskatchewan through the 1940s and 1950s.

The reaction of Indian trappers provides some insight into the effects of the legislation. The 1940s fur trade legislation affected northern trappers differently than southern trappers, partly because of the different role that trapping played in the livelihood of these two groups. In the north, trapping was the main source of income to supplement a subsistence livelihood for predominantly Indian (primarily Cree, with Chipewyan in the northwestern part of the province) and Métis trappers, whereas in the south the predominantly white trappers seemed to move in and out of the activity in response to market prices.[36] In his summary of the last one hundred years of fur harvesting in Saskatchewan, Wayne Runge finds that the number of total trapper license sales for the 1940s varied from 6,078 (1941–42) to 13,822 (1943–44); license sales reached a high of 26,108 in 1979–80, and fell to 3,240 by 1992–93. The influx of trappers in response to fur prices occurred primarily in southern Saskatchewan, where trappers were predominantly non-Indian; licensed trappers in the northern forests remained steady at 2,000-3,000, with about 1,400 of those Indian, 1,400 Métis , and 300 non-Indian.[37]

Hugh Ross, manager between 1948 and 1957 of the Saskatchewan district after eighteen years of previous experience with the HBC, primarily at northern posts, wrote that

> Dealing day-by-day with the native people, we understood how they felt about tomorrow. It might never come. If they were employed weekly, they were paid by the day. They might be dead tomorrow and money wouldn't be any good to them if they couldn't spend it. So the new CCF Fur Marketing Service was of no use to the northern trappers. They preferred the Company's system of giving them a trapping advance which they paid in full when they traded in their fur. And for the twenty years that the CCF party was in power, the two northern constituencies regularly returned Liberal representative.

J. L. (Joe) Phelps, Minister of Natural Resources and a rabid socialist simply could not understand their attitude and he regularly criticized what he called "the Hudson's Bay Company policy of keeping the natives enthralled in debt."[38]

Ross, as an old HBC man, would not be inclined to recall kind things about government regulation of the fur trade, though he did comment favorably on the government's investment in transportation systems and preventative health programs for the Indian population. His views on native attitudes also reflect some stereotypical responses, probably not unusual for the 1940s.[39] On a more sophisticated theoretical level, though, V. F. Valentine mirrors his analysis in describing the effects of the Saskatchewan Fur Marketing Service and the Block Conservation system on the Métis of northern Saskatchewan in the late 1940s.[40] Trappers marketing their furs through the SFMS could receive, if requested, an advance payment up to 50 percent of the appraised value upon depositing the furs with the service, but a charge of 6 percent per annum was made on the advance until the furs were sold. The service charged a 5 percent sales commission. Once the furs were sold at auction, relevant fees were deducted, and within ten days the Treasury Department issued checks for the net amount to trappers. Initially the legislation required trappers to sell their beaver and muskrat pelts to the SFMS.

This system effectively eliminated what Valentine viewed the Métis as needing most: credit. It meant that the trappers had to return frequently to settlements, because without credit they could not get a full season's provisions at one time. Valentine also noted that when Fur Marketing Service checks did arrive, they often were for smaller amounts than anticipated, leaving the trapper after "his long wait, broke, without credit, without a food supply, and in debt."[41]

According to Valentine, the Block Conservation System was designed to regulate, "by means of a defined area surrounding a particular settlement, the conservation of fur-bearing animals, and at the same time to put an end to their nomadic life by confining them to a settlement."[42] In concept, the conservation block system was democratic, with trappers in each area deciding how many furs could be taken, and with only the residents of a particular region eligible to purchase a trapping license. Valentine found instead that for the Métis in the late 1940s the system's rigidities encouraged overcrowding and consequent problems.

To an economist reading Valentine's article, it appears that the 1940s legislation, however well intended, established a partial system of individual property rights without any of the incentives that a full system would develop, but also without the informal controls of a traditional system. Given the inroads of the south into the north, disintegration of traditional controls likely would have resulted from changing political-economic conditions anyway. With a shift to a fully private property rights system, any improvements in the value of a given fur block area stemming from the licensee's efforts in constructing a trapper's shack or improved wildlife habitat or through conservation of a given nonmigratory species could accrue to the licensee by giving that person the right to sell the license. Such a limited property right also would give the licensee the right to increased (decreased) license value due to increased (falling) market prices for pelts, instead of such revenues potentially accruing to the provincial government. According to Runge, southern licensees can and do receive compensation for the improvements they have made on a particular license area, but the compensation is for physical capital in the form primarily of trappers' shacks. In the north, perhaps because the supply of fur zones and traplines is large relative to demand, traplines typically are not sold.[43]

Most of the articles in contemporary issues of the *Regina Leader Post* about the provincial fur marketing service and the conservation areas limited comments to factual developments. A 5 February 1947, editorial, however, observed approvingly the value of establishing exclusive trapping rights in particular areas to encourage conservation. The editorial did question the justification of the forced marketing policy. It noted government claims that this was essential to assure adherence to trapping quotas. It further noted, however, that private dealers who in the past had handled these pelts no longer could do so and that some already had exited the business. The editorial also noted that when muskrat pelts were taken from locations where no government funds had been spent, the government took 10 percent, and in developed areas where patrols were maintained, the government claimed 20 percent. The editorial writer considered both amounts excessive.[44] An earlier article describing the first fur auction stated that the Fur Marketing Service charged a sales commission of 5 percent of the sales price, and additionally charged for brokerage and packing. At that auction, about three-fourths of the furs were sold, with the unsold furs to await the next auction, about five weeks later, or to be sold by private deal.[45] A couple of 1947 headlines in the *Leader Post* suggested that Indians were irked by the conservation act's provisions, but the substance of the articles provide little support for believing there was widespread discontent; relatively few Indians resided in or about Regina, so the news account might not have reflected their perspective.

In elaborating on the role of credit in the fur trade, Hugh Ross explained in his book that each post manager "submitted a proposed list of trapping advances to be issued by him in the coming trapping season every summer . . ." based on post files that included for each trapper the following: marital status, family members, the trapper's record of fur sold over the past decade, whether each annual advance had been paid, and whether mitigating circumstances such as illness or weather had affected ability to repay the advance. Ross pointed out as well the importance of the post manager's understanding of each trader's character in assigning advances.[46] Private trading companies provided credit before furs were brought in; the SFMS provided no payment before the catch, and would only pay half of the estimated value of furs before they were sold.

The private traders not only provided trappers with credit; they also absorbed the risk of fluctuations in fur prices. In contrast, the provincial crown corporation paid trappers half the expected value of the pelt upon its receipt, then paid the remainder of the actual price received once the pelt had been sold. The trapper therefore could pocket large gains if the sales price of the fur was high, but also received less than anticipated if fur auction prices were less than anticipated. The HBC had a system in the 1940s and 1950s that gave to each post manager a share of the profits based on the success of his post in the fur trade and provisioning business; the bonus amounts varied between 10 and 25 percent of base salary, so were substantial relative to regular income. Hugh Ross observed that allocating company profits to posts was difficult when furs were shipped out only once or twice a year and all furs were sold in London. As furs began to be shipped to fur auctions in Montreal, Winnipeg, and New York, and were shipped more frequently, the link between the origin of a particular lot of furs and its auction price was clearer; this resulted in more precise attribution of revenues to a particular post. Overhead was allotted in proportion to sales revenue. A post with substantial number of unsold furs at the end of the accounting year had a large depreciation figure charged against its revenues.[47]

Under this system, fur trappers received a known price when they brought furs in (indeed, even in advance). Trappers did not receive the benefits if sales price for furs rose in the interval between the time they were paid and the actual sales of the furs, but they also did not suffer a loss if the sales price fell. Of course, the fur trading company likely built this risk into its price structure, resulting in lower prices paid to trappers for fur on average but with less dispersion of prices, especially in the short run, than the trapper could receive otherwise.

Conclusion

In today's climate of deregulation and downsizing of government, it is interesting to return to the enthusiasm of an era that sought through government intervention to improve the lives of ordinary folk. The fur-related legislation in Saskatchewan during the 1940s seems to have been a sincere effort to address the problems of low incomes from trapping and depletion of what were considered provincial fur resources. Did these efforts lead to improved economic efficiency and greater economic equity? The fragmentary economic evidence presented here, perhaps not surprisingly, does not yield an unambiguous answer. Even the goals of the program could be contradictory. If the rules succeed in reducing the hunts, trapper incomes are likely to fall unless demand is price inelastic.

Prices of fur followed a volatile pattern over the decades following Saskatchewan's fur legislation. Forces external to the province likely overwhelmed whatever effect the Saskatchewan Fur Marketing Service and provincial conservation rules could have had, and these likely were instituted well after the period of monopsony control over fur anyway. Because the Fur Marketing Service did not provide credit, among other reasons, it was not successful in controlling all fur sales within the province. In Canada, Saskatchewan is typically the fifth largest, among provinces, supplier of furs, so the service had relatively little control over national quantities.[48]

To the extent that Saskatchewan furs were marketed through the crown corporation, the province did gain an additional measure of control over the collection of furs and could attempt to use that control to enforce conservation measures. Initially the province used that control by forcing all muskrat and beaver to be marketed through the Saskatchewan Fur Marketing Service, but this regulation had disappeared by the mid-1950s.

Perhaps with ingenious timing, the province closed the service in 1982. Although fur prices and incomes hit highs in the early 1980s, with over 20,000 Saskatchewan trappers licensed between 1980 and 1983, prices, incomes, and the number of trappers declined rapidly afterward. In the 1992–93 season, only 3,240 trappers were licensed, and wildlife biologist Wayne Runge reported that "the bulk of active trappers are 55 years or older and recruitment of youth is minimal."[49] Over the longer term, prices of fur and incomes generated by trapping have responded to international economic conditions over which the province of Saskatchewan cannot exert effective control; in this area, the legislation did not have significant effect.

The number of fur-bearing animals in Saskatchewan appears currently to be at very high levels. Whether the provincial legislation caused this result is hard to ascertain, though stocks of muskrat and beaver were at low levels prior to the legislation of the 1940s. Wildlife managers now face the problem of wild animals whose populations are growing too rapidly to be diminished by the dwindling number of hunters and trappers, and which are creating nuisance problems for agricultural and urban populations.[50]

In summary, then, the Saskatchewan legislation has coincided with results more favorable to the "trappees" than the trappers. Whether this conservation result is coincidental or whether the legislation caused it is not answered clearly by the evidence.

Notes

1. I thank the editors of this volume for their very helpful comments about substance and style on earlier drafts of the paper. I also thank Professor Martha MacDonald of Saint Mary's University for her useful suggestions about economic analysis in the paper. Additionally, I appreciate the time, suggestions, and research results that Wayne Runge of the Saskatchewan Department of Environment and Resource Management kindly shared with me. They all did their best, and I am responsible for any errors that remain.

2. See, for example, Seymour Martin Lipset, *Agrarian Socialism: The Cooperative Commonwealth Federation in Saskatchewan, A Study in Political Sociology* (Berkeley: University of California Press, 1950). Professor Lipset revised and expanded his book for the 1971 edition, also published by University of California Press. The CCF was precursor to the contemporary New Democratic Party.

3. Hugh Mackay Ross, *The Manager's Tale* (Winnipeg, Manitoba: Watson and Dwyer Publishing Co., 1989), 119–20.

4. Because formal microeconomic analysis primarily uses static models to examine behavior, the interest of economists in how institutional arrangements affect economic behavior is not always apparent. Explicit focus on the importance of institutions, particularly the rules of the game including local custom, has become more important recently in application of economic theory to policy issues. For example, see Terry L. Anderson, ed., *Property Rights and Indian Economies* (Lanham, Md.: Rowman & Littlefield Publishers, 1992).

5. Wayne Runge, *A Century of Fur Harvesting in Saskatchewan* (Prince Albert: Saskatchewan Department of Environment and Resource Management, 1995), 8.

6. Ibid., 25.

7. *Saskatchewan Department of Natural Resources, Annual Reports, 1933* (Regina, Saskatchewan: Queen's Printers, 1933), 2.

8. Runge, *Century of Fur Harvesting*, 34.

9. Victor Lytwyn, *The Fur Trade of the Little North: Indians, Pedlars, and Englishmen East of Lake Winnipeg, 1760-1821* (Winnipeg, Manitoba: Rupert's Land Research Centre, University of Winnipeg, 1986), 161.

10. E. E. Rich, *Hudson's Bay Company 1670–1870, Vol. 2: 1763–1870* (London: Hudson's Bay Record Society, 1959), 471.

11. Ibid.

12. *Statutes of Saskatchewan, 1944, 1945, 1946* (Regina, Saskatchewan: Thos. H. McConica, King's Printer, 1946), 27.

13. Ibid.

14. M. W. Farrell, "Experience with Provincial Marketing Schemes in Canada," *Journal of Farm Economics* 31 (November 1949): 610.

15. Ibid., 611.

16. John D. Black, "Guideposts in the Development of a Marketing Program," *Journal of Farm Economics* 29 (August 1942): 616–31.

17. The ideas in this section reflect standard microeconomic analysis, such as that presented in Robert H. Frank, *Microeconomics and Behavior* (New York: McGraw-Hill, 1991).

18. David W. Pearce, ed., *The MIT Dictionary of Modern Economics* (Cambridge, Mass.: MIT Press, 1995), 324.

19. Arthur Ray, *The Canadian Fur Trade in the Industrial Age* (Toronto: University of Toronto Press, 1990), 177–221.

20. Ross, *The Manager's Tale*, 107–9.

21. Runge, *Century of Fur Harvesting*, 4, 8.

22. Many of the ideas in this section reflect standard microeconomic analysis of externalities, and further exposition can be found in such texts as Frank, *Microeconomics and Behavior*.

23. *Saskatchewan Department of Natural Resources, Annual Reports, 1935* (Regina, Saskatchewan: Queen's Printer, 1935), 35.

24. David Feeny, Fikert Berkes, Bonnie J. McCay, and James M. Acheson, "The Tragedy of the Commons: Twenty-Two Years Later," *Human Ecology* 18 (1990): 7.

25. Fikert Berkes, "The Common Property Resource Problem and the Creation of Limited Property Rights," *Human Ecology* 13 (1985): 188.

26. Ann Carlos and Frank Lewis, "Indians, the Beaver, and the Bay: The Economics of Depletion in the Lands of the Hudson's Bay Company, 1700–1763," *Journal of Economic History* 53 (September 1993): 465–94.

27. Lytwyn, *Fur Trade of the Little North*, 161–62.

28. Rich, Hudson's *Bay Company*, 472–74.

29. Peter Usher, "Property Rights as the Basis of Inuit Hunting Rights," in Terry L. Anderson, ed., *Property Rights and Indian Economies* (Lanham, Md.: Rowman & Littlefield, Publishers, 1992), 46.

30. Ibid., 51.

31. Feeny et al., "The Tragedy of the Commons," 7.

32. *Marketing Your Furs*, (Regina, Saskatchewan: Bureau of Publications, 194?).

33. John H. Archer, *Saskatchewan: A History* (Saskatoon, Saskatchewan: Western Producer Prairie Books, 1980), 271.

34. Runge, *Century of Fur Harvesting*, 35.

35. Pearce, *MIT Dictionary of Modern Economics*, 82.

36. The Métis are descendants of European or Canadian traders and Indian women.

37. Runge, *Century of Fur Harvesting*, 35, 63, 64, 74.

38. Ross, *The Manager's Tale*, 120.

39. Ibid., 119–120.

40. V. F. Valentine, "Some Problems of the Métis of Northern Saskatchewan," *Canadian Journal of Economics and Political Science* 20 (February 1954): 89–95.

41. Ibid., 92.

42. Ibid., 93.

43. Wayne Runge, interview with author, Prince Albert, Saskatchewan, 11 July 1995.

44. "Fur Conservation," editorial, *Regina Leader Post*, 5 February 1947.

45. "Fur Sales nets $5000 Profit," *Regina Leader Post*, 10 January 1945.

46. Ross, *The Manager's Tale*, 137.

47. Ibid., 138-39.

48. Runge, *Century of Fur Harvesting*, 83.

49. Ibid.

50. Ibid., 84.

SECTION 5

Old Faces, New Voices

Heather Devine[1]

Ambition versus Loyalty: Miles Macdonell and the Decline of the North West Company

Introduction

IN THE PAST, various fur trade monographs have focused on the social and cultural contexts that gave rise to the North West and Hudson's Bay companies. One topic that has attracted a great deal of scholarly interest has been the patriarchal nature of preindustrial social relations as exemplified in the organization of the seventeenth-century British communities and, more particularly, the "patriarchal household." Both Jennifer Brown and John Foster have argued that the patriarchal household model, which subsumed family members and servants under a hierarchical system of deferential, reciprocal patron-client relations, is a useful model for understanding fur trade social and structural relations.[2]

Unfortunately, the examination of patron-client relations in the fur trade has rarely ventured beyond the study of social relations within specific trading companies, or trading establishments. Another problem arises from the tendency to situate all studies of fur trade social relations squarely in the hinterland. This approach, however, tends to exclude important information about individuals' social and economic histories prior to their entry into the trade. In firms such as the North West Company, for example, it has been suggested that its corporate values, attitudes, and behaviors were based on prior socioeconomic relationships that employees brought with them into the company.[3] The nature and extent of this cultural transfer, however, remains poorly understood and requires additional study.

In a previous essay,[4] this writer investigated the American colonial roots of a number of Scottish expatriates, particularly those Scots who established new economic and social relationships under the auspices of Sir William Johnson, northern superintendent of the colonial Indian Department between 1755 to 1774. It was argued that Sir William Johnson's active participation in the fur trade of colonial New York, and the development of his vast frontier estates in the Mohawk Valley, served to instruct and inspire a number of Scots who were instrumental in founding the North West Company. Under Johnson's sponsorship the Scots were able to acquire the necessary skills to administer commercial enterprises of their own. As members of the Johnson "family"—either as tenants, as Indian Department officials, or as soldiers and militia—they were compelled to subsume their individual and clan-based interests. Their loyalties were transferred to Johnson, his immediate family, and to the British imperial system that had provided them with a new start in North America. These filial ties were maintained in the Loyalist communities of Upper and Lower Canada when Johnson's Scottish-American clients relocated northward after the American Revolution.

If one accepts the premise that the sociocultural roots of the North West Company lie in the communal and familial relationships transplanted to Loyalist Upper Canada from the Mohawk Valley, then it is possible that the decline of the North West Company as a commercial enterprise also had its origins in this milieu.

This chapter argues that the difficulties facing the North West Company in its later years were due, in part, to the firm's inability to evolve its corporate structure and its business practices away from those of the Loyalist oligarchy of Upper and Lower Canada. The company appeared unwilling to adapt its company hierarchy to reward innovative ideas and extraordinary achievements, or to accommodate personal ambition. Such innovation would have challenged the prevailing community standards for determining rank, mobility, and reward. Nor did the company *ethos* enable it to respond effectively when dealing with external threats to the enterprise, particularly when these attacks were deemed to have originated from its own extended society.

This chapter will explore the validity of these ideas by illustrating how one event in fur trade history—the establishment of Lord Selkirk's settlement on the Red River—epitomized the difficulties faced by the Nor'Westers when friends, relatives, and business associates engaged in activities deemed "disloyal." In particular, this study will focus on the career of Miles Macdonell, a member of a prominent Loyalist family associated with the North West Company. As Lord Selkirk's agent at Red River and as the first governor of Assiniboia (1811–15), Macdonell challenged the traditional allegiances of his family and his community in order to pursue his personal ambition—a course of action that was to have tragic consequences for the North West Company and, eventually, for Macdonell himself.

Lord Selkirk was a wealthy Scottish philanthropist who sought to alleviate the suffering of displaced Highland crofters by resettling them in North America. After unsuccessfully pursuing his goal through government auspices, Selkirk and his relatives purchased enough shares to acquire a controlling interest in the Hudson's Bay Company. The firm granted Selkirk approximately 300,000 square kilometers of land in the heart of North America, in an area that encompassed the Red River and its tributaries. Here Selkirk set out to establish an agricultural settlement, in territory also claimed by the North West Company and its Métis adherents. The founding of the settlement in 1812 brought the North West and Hudson's Bay Companies into immediate conflict, and resulted in years of violence and legal action that ended only with Selkirk's death in 1820 and the amalgamation of the two companies shortly thereafter.[5]

The historiography devoted to the Selkirk conflict is extensive, consisting of annotated collections of selected primary source documents created contemporaneously to the conflict; narrative accounts of events incorporating primary sources; biographical sketches of the principal participants; historiographical summaries of the literature; and more recent scholarly approaches to the controversy that have been used to illuminate specific aspects of pre-Confederation Canadian and eighteenth-century British social history.[6]

A great deal of additional information about the North West fur trade can be found in a source often neglected by fur trade scholars, the private correspondence of Loyalist families. In this chapter, the private correspondence of the "Scotus" branch of the Macdonell family will be utilized to gain additional insights into hitherto unknown aspects of the Selkirk controversy.

The Macdonell of Scotus correspondence consists of several collections of letters written by "Spanish John" Macdonell of Scotus;[7] his children John "LePretre" Macdonell (North West Company partner, farmer, and merchant); Miles Macdonell (Lord Selkirk's agent at Red River and the Hudson's Bay Company's appointed governor of Assiniboia); their sister Penelope Macdonell Beikie (wife of John Beikie, clerk of the Legislative Council of Upper Canada); and their youngest sibling, William Johnson Macdonell, a resident of Boston, Massachusetts. These letters document several decades in the life of the Scotus Macdonells as they discuss the fur trade and other commercial affairs, pursue political office, and nurture the relationships with family and friends necessary to maintaining their social and economic position.

Like many well-educated residents of eighteenth- and nineteenth-century Upper Canada, the Macdonells were prolific letter writers, and a great deal of their correspondence has survived to the present day in various repositories.

Much of the correspondence and other private papers of John "LePretre" Macdonell, now housed in the National Archives of Canada and the Archives of Ontario, were recovered by Father A. G. Morice, a Roman Catholic priest and historian of Western Canada who acquired these documents from private sources in the early part of the century. Some of Miles Macdonell's letters have survived in the previously mentioned correspondence, as well as in other archival collections, most notably the Selkirk Papers (MG 19-E1) at the National Archives of Canada.[8] A newly discovered collection of Macdonell correspondence, consisting of 37 letters written by John "LePretre" Macdonell, Miles Macdonell, Penelope and John Beikie, and William Johnson Macdonell was recently acquired by the Glengarry Historical Society of Williamstown, Ontario, in 1994. Additional collections of papers dealing with various branches of the Macdonell family exist in the Public Archives of Canada, the Archives of Ontario, and the diocesal archives of the Roman Catholic Church in Toronto and Kingston.[9]

The Loyalist Context of the North West Fur Trade

The Loyalists of Upper Canada lived in a preindustrial milieu where consanguinal relations governed most aspects of life. As historian Jane Errington notes, "an individual's community was confined to those in his or her family and to the few settlers he or she met occasionally at the mill, at work parties, or at social occasions. In this largely oral society, dependent on face-to-face communications, the individual defined him or herself not by social caste or rank but by location, by culture, by language, by religion, and by his or her place in the family. And this was reinforced by tradition and the rituals of life on the frontier."[10]

Errington notes that social relations in Loyalist Upper Canada were not class-based in the early years. The backbreaking labor required of all settlers to make their lands productive, and the overall lack of specie which made colonists land-rich but cash-poor, contributed to a degree of social leveling. Nonetheless, social distinctions did evolve. In a frontier society comprised of Loyalists to the British crown, it was demonstrated adherence to the ideology of loyalty, rather than material wealth, that became the benchmark for determining one's social status. The Loyalists of Upper Canada had a "garrison mentality" that stressed resistance to American republican ideals at all costs. To protect their British outpost on the continent, the Loyalist elite espoused an essentially antidemocratic social view, which sought to perpetuate rigid social hierarchies in order to maintain peace, order, good government, and further resistance to American incursions. Historians S. F. Wise and David Mills have argued that adherence to these ideas became the basis of political legitimacy and social acceptance in Upper Canada. People who challenged the prevailing sociopolitical order soon became outcasts, so those individuals and groups who wanted to succeed in Upper Canada usually found it expedient to find a place within the existing Loyalist patronage network.[11]

Military experience, particularly that gained in the Revolutionary War, was potent testimony to an individual's loyalty to community and family. Most Loyalist militias, like their American republican counterparts, were local brigades comprised of extended kin groups. When the members of Loyalist militia units were awarded military bounty lands in recognition of their service and as compensation for losses suffered in the American colonies, these familial units were kept together. The size and location of land allotments awarded to Loyalist refugees reflected their membership in particular militia units, their military rank at the conclusion of military service, their ethnic origins, and their religious faiths. An individual family's status in the community was determined by the simultaneous intersection of all of these variables.

Because of the lack of liquid assets and the relative slow progress of settlement, well-educated, well-connected Loyalists sought alternative professions that would provide them with additional status as well as a ready source of income. Some joined the military and sought military commissions. Others sought judicial appointments, such as sheriffalties, which would provide fees to augment income. Still others participated in the burgeoning commercial economy.

One attractive commercial alternative was the fur trade, because of the belief that a great deal of money could be made in a comparatively short time. However, it should be recognized that while the fur trade, and the fur country, were of financial importance to the employees of the North West Company, the interpersonal relations and the people that gave their lives meaning were, by and large, located in the Loyalist communities along the St. Lawrence. The fur trade was useful only to the degree that it could enhance life in Upper Canada, and was viewed as an economic extension of life in the settlements.

Several of the North West Company's directors, wintering partners, and clerks came from Glengarry Loyalist families that had established a tradition of service within the North West Company, such as the McKays, the Macleods, the McGillivrays, the McGillises, the Grants, the Camerons, the Frasers, and the Macdonalds. It is not surprising that members of the Macdonell family would also choose to participate in the fur trade.

Father A. G. Morice, in his biographical essay, "A Canadian Pioneer: Spanish John,"[12] describes the Scottish origins of the Macdonells of Skye, a staunchly Roman Catholic clan who were tacksmen[13] by birth and professional soldiers and adventurers by inclination. After the Battle of Culloden in 1746 and the subsequent disintegration of the clan system, various branches of the Macdonell family, seeking greener pastures, made the decision to emigrate to North America under the auspices of a distant Anglo-Irish relative, Sir William Johnson, northern superintendent of Indian affairs for British North America. They settled on Johnson's Mohawk Valley plantation in the colony of New York, where they remained until the Revolutionary War forced them to flee northward to Canada with their dependents.[14]

After the war, the Macdonells and other soldiers from disbanded militias settled in contiguous townships along the St. Lawrence River. The soldiers of the King's Royal Regiment of New York, including members of the various branches of the Macdonell family, settled in Glengarry and Stormont Counties in what is now Ontario on the substantial lands granted to them as a result of their military service. They were soon joined by other members of the family in a series of transatlantic migrations beginning in 1785,[15] and ending with the 1804 migration of the Glengarry Fencible Regiment under the leadership of their chaplain, the Rev. Alexander Macdonell.[16] Not surprisingly, Glengarry County became the unofficial seat of the Macdonell family in Canada.

Their well-earned reputation as military heroes, their genteel background as educated Highland tacksmen, and the numerical dominance of their family members and other dependents in Glengarry County enabled various male members of the Macdonell family to gain ready access to the land grants and the civil and military appointments that were the avenues to wealth and status in Upper Canada. Through the dispensation of patronage to friends and relatives, and public adherence to ideologically appropriate political, social, and religious practices, the Macdonells capitalized on their initial advantages as early Loyalists. They established a prominent[17] position for themselves in Upper Canada.

Occasionally, however, the professional aspirations of various Macdonell males came into conflict with those of other Macdonell kinsmen and associates. The North West Company, a concern that employed various Macdonells in prominent positions,[18] was to become the locus for the most sustained and destructive family conflicts. As traders in the Northwest during the precoalition period, the Macdonells became inextricably involved in a variety of hinterland disputes that created divisions with friends and kinsmen at home in

Glengarry. Perhaps the first of these was the conflict involving Sir Alexander Mackenzie and Simon McTavish, North West Company partners.

Like many other Scots Highlanders, Alexander Mackenzie migrated to North America with his family to settle in colonial New York State immediately prior to the American Revolution. During the Revolutionary War Alexander Mackenzie's father, Kenneth, and his uncle John joined the King's Royal Regiment of New York, the Loyalist militia unit raised by Sir John Johnson. While Kenneth and John Mackenzie served as lieutenant and captain, respectively, young Alexander traveled to the Mohawk Valley with his aunts, where he lived in Johnstown, the community at the heart of the Johnson estate, for two years. By 1778 Mackenzie had been sent to school in Montreal, while the remainder of the family migrated to Cataraqui, later called Kingston, and then to Glengarry County. He entered the service of the firm Finlay, Gregory, & Company (a firm later known as Gregory, Macleod & Company) in 1779. After years of spirited competition, Gregory, Macleod & Company merged with McTavish, Frobisher, & Company to become part of the North West Company in 1787.[19]

Not surprisingly, the Mackenzies and the Macdonells were old friends, linked by their common Highland ancestry, their tenure in the Mohawk Valley, their shared military ties to the King's Royal Regiment of New York, and their eventual residence in Glengarry County. When Alexander Mackenzie visited Glengarry County in 1797, one of his courtesy calls was to the home of "Spanish John" Macdonell of Scotus, who later wrote to his son, John "LePretre" Macdonell, a North West Company wintering partner, to convey Mackenzie's greetings.[20]

Such cordiality had vanished by 1800. Deteriorating relations between Alexander Mackenzie and Simon McTavish resulted in Mackenzie's departure and his involvement with another trading company, known variously as Sir Alexander Mackenzie and Company, the New North West Company, or, more colloquially, the XY Company.[21]

An early discussion of Mackenzie's rift with the North West Company appears in a letter from Penelope Beikie to William Johnson Macdonell dated 25 January 1801. She observed that

> John [Macdonell] is still in the North West and liked as well as ever, I am rather Concerned for him for the time to come as there is a formidable opposition against the Old Company who are joined by Alexander McKenzie one of the principle heads of the old Company, the reason he has deserted them is not known.[22]

In a July 1802 letter from Grand Portage, wintering partner John Macdonell provided these comments to his brother William:

> P.S. I set out for My wintering ground in a few days to fight against a Strong Opposition headed by our former Agent & copartner but now the new Created Knight Alexr. McKenzie a very ungratefull man who employs the money we helped him to amass to effect our destruction—But after three years trial their Share of the Trade is only 1/6 tho' they send half as many Goods, into the country as we do—we have this last year bought the lease of the King's posts of Tadousac below Quebec for the term of twenty years at 1025 pounds per annum. The bearer of this, Mr. Angus Shaw one of our proprietors goes down as our Agent to carry on the trade in that quarter & is to take up his residence in Quebec—We have now a Chain of Indian Trade which extends from the Atlantic to the Pacific Ocean for we have posts beyond the great Ridge calld' the Rocky Mountains which separate the waters that fall into both seas—Tadousac ports has communication with our posts up the *Cheneaux* of the 3 Rivers & the latter with those of River du Lievne and Temiscaming above which we have several posts all along the communication to the Sault of St. Marais then we have several posts along and Round the Lake Superior exclusive of Nipigon fond du Lac &c &c. We go to the South till we meet the Misisipi Traders and to the north till we intermix with those from Hudson's Bay—but due north we go far beyond the Limits of the HB. Compy so far that the Furrs traded in those distant regions only get here the Second year tho' every precaution is taken to facilitate their progress—
>
> > Dr. William
> > ever Your affectionate
> > Brother
> > John McDonell[23]

Despite Macdonell's dismissal of the threat from the XY competitors, the North West Company was forced to expend greater efforts to service their distant posts. In an 1803 letter to William Johnson Macdonell, brother-in-law John Beikie noted the following:

> Our affectionate Brother John encountered much difficulty, fatigue, and danger last winter on account of the opposition to the N.W.C. Being sent from the Grand Portage to a distant Post in the extensive Country of Athabasca, he & his party were stopped by the Ice one hundred Leagues from the place of their destination, were obliged to drag the Goods in Sledges upon the Snow & Ice and suffered incredible hardships of which hunger was not the least—being frequently reduced to eat Parchment leather boiled to glue in water, and sometimes roasted before the fire. Notwithstanding, he tells me his constitution is not in the least impaired by these severe trials, but I am convinced he will feel the effects of them at a more advanced period of life.[24]

Later that year John Beikie continued to report on John Macdonell's activities in the Athabasca Department:[25]

> We heard from John this Fall, but he is so far removed into the Indian Country this year that our Letters sent from here in March would not have reached him until the last of last September as that we shall have no answers until next Fall, his Letter is dated at Athabasca where he wintered last Winter. He says that the hunger cold and fatigue that he suffered last winter has entailed upon him a Rheumatism that will stick to him while he lives— think of this William, and consider us all easy and happy compared with this hard fate of your worthy Brother John, Heaven! so order it that he may live to come out of that barbarous Country—what will all his Riches be worth to him if he loses health—he says that during the summer he takes charge of Fort Chipéwéan—which is far Inland—he sent out this year from his Wintering Ground 300 Packs fine Peltry of Furr and 50 Kegs Castorum, and would have sent more had not his last summer's supply of Goods been prevented from reaching him in time by the Ice—The new Company of North West Merchants made but badly out in that quarter last Season, they only sent down 23 Packs & about 70 Castorum which was the returns of 9 North Canoes Manned with six men each exclusive of their proper officers.[26]

By 5 November 1804 an official agreement was signed between the old and new North West Companies[27] that ended the conflict and enabled the amalgamated firm to compete successfully against its long time rival, the Hudson's Bay Company.

Although the financial setbacks to the firm were initially overcome, the long-term damage to the North West Company could not be so easily repaired. Mackenzie had questioned his ranking in the North West Company hierarchy and demanded increased authority and compensation based on his exploits of discovery. When his demands were rebuffed he had quit the company to pursue his personal goals, a move that angered his friends and associates in Upper and Lower Canada.[28] Although Mackenzie was eventually welcomed back into the fold, he was excluded from any significant authority in the company. This exclusion, in turn, created a precedent for future defections, as Alexander Mackenzie left the firm for good and sought new partners to aid him in his trading ambitions.

The Selkirk Controversy

During the period that Alexander Mackenzie and his XY Company associates commanded the attention of the North West Company partners, another Highlander was laying the groundwork for his own plans for the North West, a settlement scheme that would eventually bring the Nor'Wester Macdonells into ruinous conflict with their close kinsmen.

Thomas Douglas, fifth Earl of Selkirk, was obsessed with the need to resettle displaced Scottish and Irish crofters in order to relieve the social misery brought by British government policies. His attention soon focused on North America's unsettled lands, and he set about to acquire the resources and the endorsements necessary to establish and maintain overseas settlements.[29]

Lord Selkirk had proposed a number of settlement schemes to the British government prior to 1802, including a proposed settlement at Red River. These were rejected as impractical. His new scheme of 1802 would establish a settlement between Lakes Huron and Superior. While Selkirk solicited government funds he approached Father Alexander Macdonell, then in Ireland, to participate in the scheme. He offered him £2,000 for his support. Father Macdonell flatly refused, citing the remoteness of the region and its location outside of Upper Canadian government jurisdiction. He noted that the settlement would "entirely destroy the North West Company," as it would sever communications between the winterers and Canada. Because many of the principal officers in the company were good friends he would not participate in a scheme that ran counter to their interests.[30]

His relative Miles Macdonell was less prescient. When Lord Selkirk traveled through Upper Canada in 1804, he first met Miles Macdonell at Osnabruck. Selkirk was so impressed by his qualities that he maintained contact with him until he was able to engage his services on a permanent basis. Miles had never been content to make his living as a simple farmer, and found it difficult to live within his means. He sought, with mixed success, the military appointments and political offices that would provide him with additional income and status.[31] Miles Macdonell was happy to be in the employ of Lord Selkirk, and performed a variety of services despite the opposition of various family members, including the influential Rev. Alexander Macdonell. In 1806 Father Macdonell lobbied the president and administrator of Upper Canada, Alexander Grant, to have Miles Macdonell appointed Sheriff of the Eastern District, perhaps as a means of preventing his cousin from entering Selkirk's service. Although the sheriffalty of the Eastern District was awarded to someone else, Miles Macdonell was given the sheriffalty of the Home District shortly thereafter.[32]

Future events and subsequent correspondence indicate that the Macdonells were unsuccessful in dissuading Miles from what they perceived as an unprofitable course of action. Despite having received the position of Sheriff of the Home District in April of 1807, an appointment that paid a comfortable £100 per annum, Miles remained Lord Selkirk's client and agent. He traveled to various Canadian and American cities to conduct business at

Lord Selkirk's request. Miles was not at liberty to divulge the full nature of his activities to his family, but he made oblique references to appointments and other favors that he was about to receive as a result of Lord Selkirk's largesse—benefits that would be enjoyed by all of the Macdonells.[33] In a letter written in June of 1807, barely two months into his appointment as sheriff of the Home District, Miles urged his brother William to move back to Canada, stating,

> I have a near prospect amounting almost to certainty of a Military appointment for myself which will enable me to resign the Sheriffalty in your favor. I have other views for you which I cannot explain in the compass of a letter to provide you to, should this not be agreeable. Let me entreat you not to lose any time in leaving Boston.[34]

Unfortunately, Miles's activities on Lord Selkirk's behalf did not bring more lucrative appointments or improve his financial situation. Despite his sheriff's salary, Miles continued to be burdened by debt as a result of the costs incurred to keep his daughters circulating in Montreal society, where they regularly attended the balls and evening parties hosted by the wife of Nor'Wester William McGillivray and other prominent socialites. Miles's only hope at relief was to borrow money from brother John Macdonell's North West Company account, in the hope that his daughters would eventually marry wealthy young men.[35] Not surprisingly, most of these suitors had strong North West Company connections.

> Catherine has foolishly rejected the addresses of Mr. John McDonald [of Garth], Mrs. McGillivray's brother, and has engaged herself to young Joseph Frobisher, a young man who has never owned anything for himself, & whose only prospect, is £5,000 of a legacy left to him by Mr. McTavish— a decent sum in the hands of a person with experience but may soon be exhausted without good management—there is nothing wanted but my consent which I have yet withheld—I received a vast deal of civility from Mr. McDonald—he even offered me money in the Most delicate manner—made presents of Furs to the Girls, in your name, to make it the most acceptable; paid us a friendly visit last week & staid a week. I thought him attentive to Amelia since Catherine discharged him.[36]

Despite Miles Macdonell's increased social ties to prominent Nor'westers, he continued to maintain his close friendship with Lord Selkirk. Unbeknownst to Macdonell, Selkirk was involved in activities that would eventually result in disaster for the North West Company. Over the summer of 1808 Selkirk had been approached by Sir Alexander Mackenzie in London, who apparently sought a partnership with the earl in order to purchase Hudson's Bay Company stock, which was seriously undervalued at the time due to increased operating costs and inaccessible markets.

According to historian J. M. Bumsted, Mackenzie wanted to use Lord Selkirk as a front in order to quietly accumulate shares in the firm without attracting undue attention. Mackenzie realized that although the Hudson's Bay Company was commercially moribund, it had a potentially lucrative royal charter over vast lands, and better transportation access to overseas markets. Buying undervalued shares while the company was vulnerable might enable Alexander Mackenzie to gain control over the firm. Bumsted states that it is unlikely that Lord Selkirk viewed Mackenzie's overtures as anything other than a speculative opportunity when he was first approached. But by 1809, Selkirk had disclosed his collaboration with Mackenzie to his brothers-in-law, John Halkett and Andrew Wedderburn. Both men recognized that Mackenzie was orchestrating a takeover bid for the Hudson's Bay Company and, recognizing the opportunity it offered for themselves, promptly began acquiring large amounts of stock. Lord Selkirk was quick to collaborate with his relations. His lobbying efforts with the British government had been largely unsuccessful. He was now determined to achieve his goal of a Red River settlement by working through the auspices of the Hudson's Bay Company rather than the British or colonial governments.[37]

Despite their six-year relationship, Miles Macdonell was not made privy to the true nature of Selkirk's London-based activities and their long-term implications. Miles's letters made veiled references to Lord Selkirk's lobbying efforts with the British government and continued to hint at prospects arising from their association, but Lord Selkirk's intentions for him remained clouded in mystery.[38]

> My patron & friend, the Earl of Selkirk, has asked me to go home to get a permanent situation from Government. What the Situation is, His Lordship does not mention—but from my knowledge of his cautious & upright character, I am convinced that he would never call for me at so great a distance without having something suitable and worthwhile in view.[39]

Meanwhile Miles's relatives, particularly Father Alexander Macdonell, became increasingly suspicious of Selkirk's intentions and their ramifications for Miles. In a letter from June of 1811, Father Macdonell expressed his concerns to his kinsmen John Macdonell. To wit:

> I have lately had letters from Miles, but not of a recent date. Lord Selkirk had not declosed [sic] then what situation he had in view for him, & his son Alexr Coll had not been yet appointed to a commission. I begin to entertain strong apprehensions that he will find himself much disappointed in the sanguine hope placed in his Lordship, & that it would have been more to his interest & to his credit to have remained at home in Scothouse & mind his own affairs than [to] dance attendance to the Earl of Selkirk & reduce himself to the disagreeable dilemma of either falling out with his Lordship (the

consequence of which would probably be the most complete disappointment of all his views, the loss of his time & of his trouble across the Atlantic ocean, besides the loss of his own affairs have suffered by his absence); or of entering, contrary to his own judgement & good sense into the fantastical scheme of his Lordship.

Mr. McGilvrey knows more of these schemes than I do, & I dare say he will satisfy you upon the subject if you wish it.[40]

What Father Macdonell did not know was that Lord Selkirk had presented a proposal to the Hudson's Bay Company for the establishment of a North American settlement in Hudson's Bay territory in February of 1811 that was approved in principle by the directors the month following. Furthermore, the grant had already been ratified by the company's shareholders at a stormy meeting on 30 May. In a futile effort to block the proposal, two minority shareholders with North West Company affiliations, Sir Alexander Mackenzie and Edward Ellice, presented a memorial stating the reasons why the establishment of a settlement in the wilderness would be disastrous for all concerned. The petitioning was to no avail. A large percentage of shareholders voted in favor of approving Selkirk's land grant, and, despite the desperate lobbying of North West Company agents to initiate negotiations to regulate the interior trade, arrangements for recruiting and transporting colonists were begun.[41]

Later Father Macdonell received a letter from Miles in which he described in detail his new role in Lord Selkirk's affairs as the agent responsible for settling the colony at the Red River, in the heart of the territory under Hudson's Bay Company control, known as Assiniboia.[42] Reverend Macdonell could not have been happy to receive this news. It confirmed his worst fears.

Although there are gaps in the Macdonell of Scotus correspondence during Miles Macdonell's tenure as governor of Assiniboia,[43] other sources discuss in detail the events that followed. During the first two years of the Red River experiment Miles Macdonell concentrated on securing adequate food supplies for the incoming settlers. Delays in migrating to the settlement had prevented the planting of a crop in 1812, which meant that other provisions had to be obtained locally. With this in mind he set about to establish good relations with the local fur trade companies and the Indians and Métis of the region. Macdonell benefitted from his extensive kin-based relations with various North West Company servants and partners in the Red River Department, who provided horses and provisions at his request. Miles's brother John Macdonell, a retired North West Company wintering partner, had previously been in charge of the Upper Red River Department. Duncan

Cameron,[44] another Macdonell relative, was proprietor of the post at Rainy Lake, the department adjacent to Red River. Alexander Greenfield Macdonell, Miles's brother-in-law and second cousin,[45] was in command of Fort Gibraltar near the forks of the Red and Assiniboine rivers. André Poitras, the father of John Macdonell's country wife Madeleine Poitras, continued in the service of the North West Company as a clerk in the Red River Department.

Tranquillity was brief, however. Miles mistakenly fostered good relations with the Nor'Westers while flouting Hudson's Bay Company policies in the region. He assumed, incorrectly, that the Red River Settlement was an autonomous entity administered independently of the Hudson's Bay Company. However, neither fur trading company shared this naive view. The Hudson's Bay Company expected Macdonell to purchase provisions through their firm, and felt that his activities were undermining the trade. The North West Company viewed the establishment of the colony as an opposition stratagem intended to establish a staging ground for moving into the lucrative Athabasca region. They also believed the colony's presence was designed to interfere with the free flow of provisions, primarily pemmican, to their own inland posts.

Efforts to keep incoming settlers adequately housed and fed were further complicated by North West Company employees who were instructed to discourage settlers from remaining at Red River. John Dugald Cameron,[46] North West Company partner in charge of the Lake Winnipeg Department, acted under orders from Montreal to persuade the the company's officers to turn against Miles Macdonell. The policy was effective. By April 1813 Miles Macdonell had ordered all dealings with the NWCo to stop.[47]

In January of 1814 dwindling food supplies had compelled Miles Macdonell to issue the "Pemmican Proclamation," which forbade the export of provisions of any kind outside of the boundaries of the colony without the governor's permission. This decree, followed by seizures of Northwest Company pemmican and harassment of their employees, served to further strain relations between the NorWesters, the local Métis, and the Hudson's Bay Company, particularly since it was not clear who had legal jurisdiction over the territory. Despite these provocations, the North West Company partners in charge of the Red River Department chose to be unusually conciliatory toward Miles Macdonell. Was it concern for the welfare of the colonists? Or did they still feel compelled to be civil to their kinsman? In any case, the partners agreed to Miles Macdonell's demand to provide the colonists with provisions over the winter, despite the fact that Macdonell already possessed substantial amounts of food previously seized from the Nor'Westers![48]

In the meantime, John McDonald of Garth, Nor'Wester wintering partner in charge of Fort George on the Columbia, had determined to retire from the fur trade. He joined a large brigade of voyageurs also intent on retiring to Canada, and traveled with them to Fort William. En route the brigade stopped at Red River, where McDonald encountered Miles Macdonell in fierce conflict with his North West Company colleagues. Perhaps out of loyalty to Miles Macdonell (whom John McDonald of Garth once viewed as a potential father-in-law), McDonald negotiated a truce between the Red River Nor'Westers and the Selkirk settlers.

The efforts to maintain good relations with Miles Macdonell were not appreciated by those directors gathered for the annual meeting of the North West Company partners at Fort William. The assembled partners excoriated their colleagues in the Red River Department who had surrendered pemmican to Miles Macdonell. The truce negotiated by John MacDonald of Garth was criticized by his associates and they angrily refused to recognize the agreement. The humiliated winterers returned to Red River with the understanding that they were to destroy the colony. MacDonald returned to Montreal, where he retired in November of 1814.[49]

By the summer of 1814 Miles Macdonell requested to relinquish his position as governor of Assiniboia, stating that "I find myself unequal to the task of reconciling so many different interests."[50] In August of 1814, Duncan Cameron and Alexander Greenfield Macdonell appeared in military dress at Red River, announcing to all that Cameron, and not Miles Macdonell, was the "Chief of this Country."[51] A few weeks later, Miles Macdonell suffered a nervous breakdown at York Factory,[52] an event that marked the beginning of his descent into the mental illness that was to plague him the rest of his life.

In the meantime, John Macdonell and his relatives in Glengarry County had been observing the conflicts at Red River with growing anxiety, particularly in regard to Miles's welfare. Rumors were circulating that Miles had been killed in a duel with his brother-in-law, Alexander Greenfield Macdonell. That story was later proven false.[53] Other gossip, fueled deliberately by local Nor'Westers and their sympathizers, also hinted that the Natives of Red River were planning to attack the settlement. In October of 1814 Colin Robertson, a disaffected former Nor'Wester in the employ of the Hudson's Bay Company, wrote to Lord Selkirk from Montreal. In his correspondence he enclosed a letter from John Macdonell indicating his willingness to provide assistance to his brother Miles if it would not jeopardize his North West Company interests.[54]

In a letter dated 8 June 1815 Lord Selkirk wrote to John Macdonell from London making reference to Macdonell's correspondence of October 1814, explaining how he had used the letter to lobby the British government for military protection for the colony. In his letter he was quick to assure Macdonell of his discretion, stating,

> In doing this I took every precaution to prevent your name being repeated; & I flatter myself there is no probability that Will McGillivray, or his associates, should learn of your testimony having been referred to—But if by my own accident this should come to their knowledge, I feel confident that they cannot succeed in any attempt to deprive you of your just share of the partnership.[55]

Selkirk concluded his letter by asking John Macdonell to move to Red River. He offered him a township of ten thousand acres in the settlement if he would set about to establish eight to ten families of settlers.

While Lord Selkirk endeavored to secure protection for his colony, Miles Macdonell continued to act as governor of Assiniboia, despite escalating opposition from Nor'Westers Duncan Cameron and Alexander Greenfield Macdonell, who offered inducements of free passage to Upper Canada for those colonists who wished to leave. In June of 1815, under the threat of imminent attack from freemen and mixed-bloods in the service of the North West Company, Miles Macdonell surrendered to North West Company representatives in order to protect the colonists from harm. He was later placed under arrest and taken to Montreal to stand trial for alleged crimes committed against the North West Company in the Northwest. Selkirk appointed Robert Semple, a Loyalist from Boston, to assume the post of governor of Assiniboia.

Selkirk intended to protect his colony. If the British government refused to provide military assistance he was determined to recruit his own army. To accomplish this goal, he approached John Macdonell once again. He asked Macdonell to write his brother William Johnson Macdonell, then employed in the Customs House in Boston, requesting that he make enquiries among the Irish Catholic immigrants to secure settlers for the colony at Red River. This scheme was also unsuccessful.[56]

The charges against Miles Macdonell did not proceed. He was released from custody on bail, after which he apparently traveled to England to spend the winter. In a letter to William Johnson Macdonell dated 23 May 1816, John Beikie noted the following:

> Miles arrived here on the 17th Instant in good health and has taken his departure for the Red River.—he saw his son Donald Aeneas[57] while in

England doing Duty at Windsor as Ensign in the King's Regt or 8th and had the pleasure before he left it of Seeing him Gazetted for a Lieutenancy in the 99th [sic] which Regt is at Halifax.[58]

Although Miles Macdonell was no longer governor of Assiniboia, he remained in the service of Lord Selkirk. While en route back to Red River in the spring of 1816, Miles Macdonell learned of the Battle at Seven Oaks, where twenty-one Selkirk colonists, including Governor Alexander Semple, were killed by a band of Métis led by Cuthbert Grant. Miles returned to Sault Ste Marie to warn Lord Selkirk, and wrote to his brother John regarding these events.[59] On 13 August 1816, Macdonell assisted Lord Selkirk in the capture of Fort William. Here William McGillivray and the North West Company partners were placed under arrest and sent to York to stand trial. In December of 1816 Miles Macdonell led a party of De Meuron mercenaries to recapture Fort Douglas at the heart of the Red River colony, a task completed on 10 January 1817. Macdonell resumed his tenure as governor of the colony for a few short months. He then returned to Montreal, where the Northwest Company officers were to stand trial for crimes committed in the Northwest.[60]

During this period of strife, correspondence between William Johnson Macdonell in Boston and his brothers appears to have broken off, until the spring of 1817, when a relieved William wrote to his brother John the following letter:

> My Dear Brother:
>
> Yours bearing date May 13th I duly received on the 9th inst. and which is the first from you for more than a year past I finally concluded you had gone to the N.W. in company with Miles and his Lordship & for whose safety I am somewhat alarmed and wish he was safe out of that part of the country and also out of his Lordship's employ, for I think he has kept him in hot water ever since.[61]

Miles Macdonell has been described as a man who "never understood his situation, or worse, refused to come to grips with it."[62] Perhaps it was in 1817, as the trial dates drew nearer, that Miles Macdonell began to reflect seriously for the first time upon the crisis that faced his kinsmen and himself. His initial thoughts may have turned to the fortunes of his brother, John Macdonell, who had supported him both financially and emotionally during the troubles at Red River. He was deeply in debt to his brother, and was aware that his actions may have implicated his brother in the eyes of the court. In a letter to John Macdonell, Miles soberly reflected upon his situation, stating,

> I would sacrifice all before you should be arrested in retaliation for the arrest of Mr. Gentron[63] [sic]—or Whatever I suffer I have in a manner brought it

upon myself in great measure but there is no use now in looking back—let us take care of the future. I am in a most forlorn state no residence which has partly been the cause of so much wandering. I have been here some time with my friend William—the consolations of religion is all that can be expected from him. The court of K.B. is at hand it sits at Cornwall in 30 instant—In a week afterwards at Brockville—I cannot think of being at variance with a kind brother to whom I owe so much.[64]

By 1818 the Selkirk trials at York were well underway, and Miles Macdonell sent letters to various friends and relatives regarding the progress of the proceedings.[65] In an effort to win the publicity war that was raging over the trial in Upper and Lower Canada, Miles expended considerable effort distributing copies of *The Memorial of Thomas Earl of Selkirk* (1818) and *A Sketch of the British Fur Trade*, both penned by Lord Selkirk.[66]

In retrospect, the outcome of the trial was inevitable. The oligarchy that ruled Upper and Lower Canada was prepared to bend the rules to accommodate local commercial interests over those of outsiders. Regardless of the magnitude of the crimes committed by agents of the North West Company, Lord Selkirk was unlikely to get a fair hearing in any Canadian court dominated by friends and relatives of the Nor'Westers. The person that Selkirk held responsible for the legal debacle that followed was John Beverley Robinson,[67] the prominent young lawyer hired on retainer by the North West Company in 1817 to represent them in litigation. Robinson had articled in the office of Nor'Wester Alexander Greenfield Macdonell's brother, Attorney-General John Greenfield Macdonell, in 1811 and had fought under his command at the battle of Queenston Heights during the War of 1812. Robinson had other important connections as well. His lifelong mentor was John Strachan, prominent member of the Executive Council of Upper Canada, and the husband of Nor'Wester Andrew McGill's widow. Robinson was also a protégé of William Dummer Powell, Chief Justice of Upper Canada, who had nurtured his rapid rise through the legal ranks.

Given Robinson's impeccable personal and professional credentials, it is not surprising that he was engaged by the North West Company. In 1818, however, he was forced to abruptly terminate his legal relationship with the firm due to his appointment to the post of attorney general of Upper Canada. Despite the formal severance of his North West Company ties, it was apparent that Robinson was operating in an obvious conflict of interest. He was now the official responsible for overseeing all prosecutions in criminal cases in Upper Canada, including those of the Selkirk trials. Given Robinson's prior affiliations, it is not surprising that he would have trouble maintaining his neutrality. Despite these concerns litigation proceeded. Perhaps in an attempt to give the trials the appearance of impartiality, Robinson initiated a series of charges and countercharges on behalf of both sides, which invariably faltered due to flimsy evidence. Unfortunately, the legal and political maneuvering served to extend the proceedings and permitted North West Company defendants, while free on bail, to escape into the interior.[68] Not surprisingly, both the North West Company and the Earl of Selkirk suffered crippling financial losses due to the trial.

By late fall of 1819, Miles Macdonell had resettled, reluctantly, at the Rivière au Raisin, home of his late father "Spanish John" Macdonell.[69] Miles could not have been happy at the prospect of moving back to Glengarry County. On all sides he was surrounded by retired Nor'Westers and their kinsmen. Many were fellow expatriates from the Mohawk Valley and had known him all of his life. They were now his bitter enemies.[70] Macdonell's erstwhile patron, Lord Selkirk, had left Canada and retired to France, where he died at Pau in April of 1820. His death served to clear the way for the amalgamation of the North West and Hudson's Bay Companies, which followed shortly thereafter.

By 1821 it became clear that events in the Northwest had scarred Miles Macdonell profoundly. The mental illness that had plagued him at York Factory returned. By early spring of 1821 Miles had moved once again, this time to Point Fortune, home of his brother John Macdonell. In a letter to William, John noted that "Miles is now with me, he is not himself, I wish he had never seen the Earl of S__." He went on to note in the same letter that he "thought Miles was to have had an annuity for life from the Earl of S__ but all that is blasted—he has nothing, and is moreover loaded with debt—He can hardly be said to be in his right mind, I shall use all my influence to keep him here with me, he has been hitherto very tractable—I fear he has Mrs. Beikie's complaint tho' as yet in a more moderate degree."[71]

Mental instability was not unknown in the Scotus family. The capture and sacking of York by the Americans during the War of 1812 saw John and Penelope Beikie's home invaded and ransacked. Penelope, the sister of John, Miles, and William, entered a state of mental illness from which she never recovered. To William Johnson Macdonell's horror, his favorite brother Miles seemed destined for the same fate.

> You alarm me much with regard to Miles, I hope in, and pray to God; it may not be his case, as is poor Penelope's, poor fellow, his life of "few days, has been full of trouble"—he mentioned her calamity to me when here, with a deal of affection, little did I then think that he had the least symptom similar—Were my circumstances as I could wish, how happy would I be to have him end his days with me here—tho in a land of strangers, there are many

noble hearted fellows here—I mentioned to Miles when here I wish you could be made British Consul for this State—his reply was "I can do anything with the aid of the Earl of Selkirk."[72]

By the summer of 1821 Miles Macdonell's illness was common knowledge in the fur trade community. On 13 June 1821, Nicholas Garry, deputy governor of the Hudson's Bay Company, had occasion to pass by the Long Sault during a trip from Lachine with William and Simon McGillivray. He noted in his journal that they had "landed at a small village where Mr. Miles Macdonald [sic] is living, now in a deranged state of mind."[73]

Miles's mental illness made it impossible for him to concentrate on work. His restlessness impelled him to travel constantly. He vacillated between periods of feverish activity and abject depression. Despite his obvious instability, his relatives continued to seek patronage appointments for Miles in a desperate attempt to keep him in one place. In a letter to John Macdonell, brother-in-law John Beikie, then in York, wrote:

> It goes to my heart to think that my much beloved Brother Miles should be in want of situations that yield so little, yet little as they are I have tried to get them for him namely the Offices of Sherriff and Registrar for the Ottawa District. I have seen Doctor Strachan on the subject. He seems much disposed to serve Miles, but that horrid Indictment against Miles he fears will stand in the way. However he says we will see what can be done with it. The Attorney General [John Beverley Robinson] seems also much inclined to serve Miles and perhaps we may get it set aside. . . .[74]

Given John Strachan's well-known opposition to Lord Selkirk's schemes, it is not surprising that his response to Beikie's request would be lukewarm. It was also unlikely that John Beverley Robinson, whose handling of the Selkirk trial was already controversial, would open himself up to further accusations of conflict of interest by promoting the interests of the Macdonell family.

In May of 1822 Father Alexander Macdonell wrote to his relative John Macdonell, asking:

> Is my friend Miles with You? Poor man, I wish he could be made to remain permanently in a proper key; he has had his share of the misfortunes of this life. What a pity he would not accept of them in the light they were intended by him who sent them, and sent them for the benefit of his soul?[75]

Later that year, John Macdonell reported on Miles's condition to his brother William, noting that "Miles, whom you inquire after is gone to York U.C. our Seat of Government and when I saw him last in May was recovering by degrees his composure of mind but has considerable progress Still to make to be himself, i.e. his Spirits were upon too high a key."[76]

A relatively tranquil period followed, and Miles conducted land transactions on behalf of his brother William. He continued to be plagued with financial problems, however, and noted that "I have not yet had settlement from the benefision [sic] of the late Earl of Selkirk which has left me not only bare but worse—in debt. I have certain means of leasing off all in a short time, I having something left to the good."[77]

Miles continued to lead an unsettled life. He spent the next two years in constant travel, visiting relatives, selling land in adjacent counties, and attempting to collect debts.[78] He also began taking remedies for real, or imagined, physical complaints.[79]

Unfortunately, Miles was unable to get permanent relief from the devils that haunted him. As A. G. Morice noted, "All ambition was now gone from him; he could now scarcely do more than seek solace and oblivion in means that were nocuous to body and soul alike, and linger on pending the inevitable."[80] Miles Macdonell died in the home of his brother John Macdonell on 28 June 1828, apparently of natural causes.

But was Miles's death natural? A rather curious exchange of correspondence concerning Miles Macdonell's demise hints otherwise. On 3 September 1828, over two months after Miles's death, a concerned and puzzled William Johnson Macdonell wrote the following letter from Boston to his brother John:

> Mr. McLean informed me that his friend had been to the news room to see some Canada papers, where he saw the death of poor brother Miles, which took place at your house on the 28th of June, which was the first intimation I had of it. This, I think, was on the 7th of July; since which I have had it confirmed from Lucy [William's daughter, resident in Brockville] . . . . I was in hopes you would inform me of his having performed his Easter duty, that I might have some Masses said for the repose of his soul. Please inform me in your next.[81]

John Macdonell had delayed in notifying William Macdonell of his brother's untimely death. A letter dated 13 August 1828 from John Macdonell to his brother William, preserved in the Macdonell of Scotus Correspondence, provides the first evidence of John Macdonell breaking the news to William. After a rather desultory discussion of debt repayment, land transactions, and transmission of mail, John *finally* dealt with the subject of Miles's death at the conclusion of his letter. To wit:

> I am very much concerned to inform you of the death of our poor brother Miles, who departed this life, <u>Suddenly</u>, in my House, on the 28th day of last June and I am afraid left his affairs in a very unsettled State, tho' I know little or nothing about them; He has a Son and Heir, Donald, a fine worthy fellow to look after them—I am more concerned for his dying without receiving

the Holy rites & Sacraments of our Holy religion than any thing else, (!) a dreadful warning to the living to employ well the precious time given them to work out their Salvation—With my best respects to your better half, whom I Shall ever love, and the boys; Believe me to be my dear brother,

> Ever yours affectionately,
> John Macdonell[82]

The letter above raises some interesting questions. Why did John Macdonell delay in informing his brother about Miles's death for six and a half weeks? This delay is curious, because in some of John Macdonell's previous letters to William Macdonell, deaths are discussed. Almost all of these letters were written within days of the demise. Also, the omission of any discussion of the *cause* of Miles's death is curious, given that in previous letters, John Macdonell did not hesitate to discuss the causes of death, and the disposition of the deceased prior to death. This failure on John Macdonell's part to even *speculate* on the cause of Miles's death is curious, given that he takes special pains to emphasize the word Suddenly in the correspondence by its capitalization and underlining in the original text. An additional feature of interest in the letter is John Macdonell's reference to Miles Macdonell's dying without receipt of the last rites, and the unsettled nature of his affairs, further reinforcing the sudden nature of the death. Do these disparate factors, considered together, imply that John Macdonell was using the phrase "departed this life, Suddenly" to denote *suicide*—a common euphemism that continues to be used today when discussing this sensitive subject?

Another letter from John Macdonell sheds additional light on the situation. In this letter, dated 17th 8 M 1828 (but, in all probability, written 17 October 1828), John Macdonell began by stating, "On receipt of yours of the 3rd/M last. . ."—an explicit reference to William's letter of 3 September 1828. He went on to respond specifically to William's expressed concerns about the state of Miles's soul, noting,

> I cannot assure you that poor Miles performed his Christian duty, last Easter term, I am afraid he did not, and as he was an inmate with me since October last, I think it would have come to My knowledge if he had—He was punctual in attending divine Service, whenever he could, kept fast days & was instructed in his religion, and full of faith. I pray daily for him, and heard Bishop Macdonell recommend him to the prayers of his congregation. I had him buried in the nearest Catholic cemetery of Sainte Madeleine de Rigaud, 7 Miles off—The aforesaid Bishop told me, that our countryMen, the Highlanders of Glengarry, talked Seriously of Coming in their Sleighs to convey his remains to repose among themselves—If they come they will Surely have the Bag Pipes!—I erected a conspicuous cross over his remains,

telling his time of death & age and caused a Service of 10$ to <u>be chaunted over his remains</u> for the repose of his Soul!!—[83]

This letter raises additional questions about Miles Macdonell's death and interment: why was Miles buried at Ste. Madeleine de Rigaud? Although John Macdonell points out that Ste. Madeleine de Rigaud, the nearest Catholic cemetery, was only seven miles away, it seems odd that Miles Macdonell would not have been buried at St. Andrew's alongside his father, "Spanish John" Macdonell. In fact, the letter above suggests that the Highlanders of Glengarry felt Miles's resting place was inappropriate as well, as John Macdonell stated that the residents of Glengarry considered collecting the remains to take back to St. Andrews, where they obviously felt they belonged.[84]

If Miles Macdonell committed suicide, it would explain the delay in notifying relatives and the discreet burial[85] in a French-Canadian parish in Quebec as opposed to a Scottish Catholic cemetery in Glengarry. One might argue, however, that a suicide victim would not be buried in a Catholic cemetery at all, as Roman Catholic canonical law of the period denied ecclesiastical burial to suicides. Exceptions were made, however, in cases where there was evidence that the victims were mentally ill.[86]

A suicide in a nineteenth-century Roman Catholic family was an embarrassing, shameful event, particularly in a family with prominent ecclesiastical connections such as those possessed by the Macdonell family. The odd behavior of Miles's close relatives in the matter of his death and interment is consistent with the concealment of a suicide in the family.[87]

Miles had become an embarrassment to the Macdonell family long before his death, however. His public opposition to the North West Company caused considerable dissension within the Macdonell family and within the Glengarry community itself. Because Miles Macdonell pursued his own personal goals in opposition to the collective goals of his family and community, he came to be viewed as something akin to a traitor. In a closely knit Upper Canadian community, whose very foundation was based upon an ethos of loyalty, Miles Macdonell found himself a permanent outcast. Miles Macdonell's constant travel in the years following the Selkirk controversy suggests that he felt uncomfortable spending any length of time at home in Glengarry. This is not surprising, given the region's strong North West Company connections. Even within the Scotus branch of the Macdonell family, which had been obliged to "close ranks" and support Miles publicly, there would have been a great deal of resentment over Miles's past behavior—a resentment of which he would have been keenly aware.

Suicidologists list four primary rationale for suicide. Suicide is committed for the sake of honor; to avoid the pain and ignominy attendant on disease, old age, and poverty; to be reunited with a dead spouse or children; and, finally, as a "sacrificial suicide," described as the "voluntary death of a man who thinks his own departure will advance his state, cause, party, or family."[88] Any one of these motives would have been apropos to the situation in which Miles Macdonell was to find himself. Miles's personal and professional reputation had been destroyed. His dreams of wealth and prestige had evaporated, and in their place remained a mountain of debt and shattered dreams. He had been widowed in each of his three marriages and was now alone. The final type of suicide, the sacrificial suicide undertaken to remove the stain of dishonor that his presence brought upon his family, might have been viewed as both appropriate and necessary to Miles Macdonell, a mentally unstable man who had lost his patron and his wealth, alienated his family, and felt himself alone.

Conclusion

The 1821 amalgamation of the North West and Hudson's Bay companies signaled more than an end to crippling competition in the wilderness. The merger brought with it a corporate restructuring, and in its wake the business practices influenced by kinship and community obligations fell into disrepute. The maturation of the fur trade into a modern commercial enterprise was not an anomaly. It reflected the beginnings of a world wide shift toward an industrialized economy where family-centred, patriarchal relations were obsolete, and where corporate loyalty took precedence.

Miles Macdonell was caught in the apex of this transformation. He had been raised to be a gentleman, and was unprepared and unwilling to make his living in the burgeoning commercial economy of Upper Canada. Miles had grown tired of the constant struggle to clear wilderness land and make it productive, and the dream of becoming a gentleman farmer faded quickly. The fur trade was arduous, and his family responsibilities limited his options. Instead, he chose what he thought was an easier, more palatable route to wealth and prestige as the client of Lord Selkirk.

Unfortunately, by shifting his personal allegiance to Lord Selkirk, Miles Macdonell violated community norms of loyalty. The tragic fate of Miles Macdonell would appear to confirm the idea that the residents of Glengarry County viewed the Northwest fur trade as an economic extension of their own community. Employment with, and support for, the North West Company was subsumed within the much larger hierarchy of patron-client relations that already dictated life in Loyalist Upper and Lower Canada.[89]

Although these close bonds of friendship and kinship offered distinct commercial advantages to the firm in its early years, the perceived or real betrayals of friends and of kin during the course of the company's operation contributed to its decline and eventual failure as a business enterprise. The long-standing consanguinal and business ties first initiated in colonial New York and transplanted to Upper Canada dictated the social and economic values, attitudes, and behaviors of the Nor'Westers. When a member of this "family" violated its collective norms of loyalty and challenged the established hierarchical structure to realize private ambition—as did Sir Alexander Mackenzie, and later, Miles Macdonell—the consequences reverberated throughout the Loyalist communities and within the North West Company itself.

Notes

1. I would like to acknowledge the financial support of the Social Sciences and Humanities Research Council of Canada during the research and writing of this paper. I am also indebted to Mr. Hugh MacMillan of Guelph, Ontario, and the Glengarry Historical Society, Williamstown, Ontario, for providing initial access to hitherto undocumented Macdonell of Scotus correspondence in their collections, and to Mr. Duncan MacDonald in Brockville, Ontario, for genealogical information. Dr. David Mills, of the Department of History and Classics at the University of Alberta, Dr. Jennifer S. H. Brown, Professor of History, University of Winnipeg, Dr. Lloyd Keith, Professor of History and Sociology at Shoreline Community College, Seattle, Washington, and Mr. David Anderson, past president, Glengarry Historical Society, provided comment on earlier versions of this paper and I thank them for their suggestions.

2. See Jennifer Brown, "Company Men and Native Families: Fur Trade Social and Domestic Relations in Canada's Old Northwest" (Ph.D. diss., University of Chicago, 1976), 92, 123–24, 240; and John E. Foster, "The Indian Trader in the Hudson's Bay Fur Trade Tradition" (Paper presented to the Second Canadian Ethnological Society Annual Conference, Winnipeg, 1975), 7–9. See Sylvia Van Kirk's discussion of these works in "Fur Trade Social History: Some Recent Trends," in *Old Trails and New Directions: Papers of the Third North American Fur Trade Conference*, ed. Carol M. Judd and Arthur J. Ray (Toronto: University of Toronto Press, 1980), 160–73.

3. See Brown, "Company Men and Native Families."

4. Heather Devine, "Roots in the Mohawk Valley: Sir William Johnson's Legacy in the North West Company," in *The Fur Trade Revisited: Selected Papers of the Sixth North American Fur Trade Conference, Mackinac Island, Michigan, 1991*, ed. Jennifer S. H. Brown, W. J. Eccles, and Donald P. Heldman (East Lansing: Michigan State University Press, 1994), 217–42.

5. J. M. Bumsted, "Red River Colony," in *The Canadian Encyclopedia*, Vol. 3., ed. James H. Marsh (Edmonton: Hurtig Publishers, 1985), 1553.

6. W. S. Wallace, "The Literature Relating to the Selkirk Controversy," Canadian *Historical Review* 13, no. 1 (March 1932): 45–50 for a listing and discussion of the primary documents generated at the time of the controversy. See also the introduction to both volumes of J. M. Bumsted, ed., *The Collected Writings of Lord Selkirk: Vol. One 1799–1809* (Winnipeg: Manitoba Record Society, 1984) and *The Collected Writings of Lord Selkirk: Vol. Two 1810–1820* (Winnipeg: Manitoba Record Society, 1988) for an excellent, detailed narrative of the Selkirk controversy as it unfolded, designed to place into context the annotated versions of documents, generated by Lord Selkirk, which are featured in this anthology. For narrative accounts of events incorporating primary sources see A. G. Morice, "A Canadian Pioneer: Spanish John," *Canadian Historical Review* 10, no. 3 (September 1929): 212–35; A. G. Morice, "Sidelights on the Careers of Miles Macdonell and His Brothers," *Canadian Historical Review* 10, no. 4 (December 1929): 308–32; and John Perry Pritchett and Murray Horowitz, "Five 'Selkirk' Letters," *Canadian Historical Review* 22, no. 2 (1941): 159–67. For biographical sketches of some of the key participants in the Selkirk controversy the reader is referred to volumes 5, 6, 7, and 9 of Francess Halpenny, ed., *The Dictionary of Canadian Biography* (hereinafter *DCB*) (Toronto: University of Toronto Press, 1983, 1987, 1988, and 1976, respectively) and J. G. Harkness, "Miles Macdonell," *Ontario History* 40 (1948): 77–83. For later examples of Selkirk historiography see F. L. Barron, "Victimizing His Lordship: Lord Selkirk and the Upper Canadian Courts," *Manitoba History* 7 (1984): 14–22; J. M. Bumsted, "A Tale of Three Settlements," *The Beaver* 72, no. 3 (June–July 1992): 33–41; and Gene M. Gressley, "Lord Selkirk and the Canadian Courts," in *Canadian History Before Confederation: Essays and Interpretations*, 2d ed., ed. J. M. Bumsted (Georgetown, Ontario: Irwin-Dorsey, 1979): 277–93.

7. Col. John Macdonell of Scotus a.k.a. "Spanish John" (b. 1728, d. 15 April 1810), migrated to Caughnawaga, Schoharie County, New York, at the invitation of Sir William Johnson, northern superintendent, Colonial Indian Department, in 1773. After the American Revolution he settled at St. Andrew's, near Cornwall, until his death. For a detailed discussion of Scotus' life, see Morice, "A Canadian Pioneer: Spanish John." See also "John McDonell" in *DCB*, 7:552–53.

8. More detailed information on the accession history of these collections is not available at this time. See Morice, "A Canadian Pioneer: Spanish John," 213, and Morice "Sidelights on the Careers of Miles Macdonell and His Brothers," 308.

9. For additional information on the location of Macdonell correspondence and other relevant documents see *DCB*, 7:439–40, 444–46, 543–44, 551–54, and 556.

10. See Jane Errington, *The Lion, The Eagle, and Upper Canada: A Developing Colonial Ideology* (Kingston and Montreal: McGill-Queen's University Press, 1987), 15.

11. S. F. Wise, "Upper Canada and the Conservative Tradition," in *God's Peculiar Peoples: Essays on Political Culture in Nineteenth-Century Canada*, ed. A. P. McKillop and Paul Romney (Ottawa: Carleton University Press, 1993), 169–84; and David

Mills, *The Concept of Loyalty in Upper Canada, 1784–1850* (Kingston and Montreal: McGill-Queen's University Press, 1988).

12. See Morice, "A Canadian Pioneer: Spanish John," 212–35.

13. Tacksmen were influential clan members who provide a Highland chief with military service in return for the privilege of managing land holdings.

14. See A. G. Morice, "A Canadian Pioneer: Spanish John," 213–23. See also Heather Devine, "Roots in the Mohawk Valley," 230–32.

15. For a detailed discussion of the Macdonell migrations to Glengarry County, see Marianne McLean, "Peopling Glengarry County: The Scottish Origins of a Canadian Community," in *Historical Essays on Upper Canada: New Perspectives*, ed. J. K. Johnson and Bruce G. Wilson (Ottawa: Carleton University Press, 1991), 151–73.

16. Alexander Macdonell (1762–1840), Roman Catholic Bishop of Kingston, was born in Scotland. He was the chaplain for the Glengarry Fencibles, a Highland regiment stationed in Ireland in 1798. In 1802, when the regiment disbanded, Macdonell obtained land grants in Glengarry County for the discharged soldiers. In 1812 he served as chaplain to the Glengarry Light Infantry, and in 1826 he was appointed the first Roman Catholic Bishop of Kingston. In 1831 he was appointed as a member of the Legislative Assembly of Upper Canada. See Hugh Joseph Somers, *The Life and Times of the Hon. and Rt. Rev. Alexander Macdonell, D.D. First Bishop of Upper Canada, 1762–1840* (Washington, D.C.: Catholic University of America, 1931); and J. E. Rea, "Alexander McDonell," *DCB*, 7:544–51. Bishop Macdonell should not be mistaken for another priest named Alexander Macdonell, Father Alexander "Scotus" Macdonell (1742–1803), uncle of "Spanish John" Macdonell (1728–1810). In 1786 Father Macdonell led a group of 604 Highlanders from Inverness-shire to Canada, some of whom disembarked at Prince Edward Island. The remainder proceeded on to Upper Canada, to the Rivière Raison four to five miles northeast of Williamstown, Ontario. Father Macdonell established St. Raphael's Church here and acted as parish priest until his death in 1803. See William Perkins Bull, *From Macdonell to McGuigan: The History of the Growth of the Roman Catholic Church in Upper Canada* (Toronto: Perkins Bull Foundation, 1939), 79–80.

17. How prominent were the Macdonells? J. K. Johnson uses the term *prominence* to denote "that the people so described enjoyed greater recognition and played more active roles in the affairs of their communities than did the majority of their contemporaries." In the biographical data comprising the appendix of *Becoming Prominent*, there are eleven separate references to Macdonells. See J. K. Johnson, *Becoming Prominent: Regional Leadership in Upper Canada, 1791–1841* (Kingston and Montreal: McGill-Queen's University Press, 1989), 9, 207–10.

18. Some members of the Macdonell family who entered the employ of the North West Company include Alexander Greenfield Macdonell (clerk, 1808–14; partner, 1814–20); Allan McDonell (XY Company, 1799–1804; clerk, NWCo, 1804–16; partner, NWCo, 1816–21), John Macdonell of Scotus (clerk, 1793; partner, 1796–1812), and Aeneas Macdonell (clerk, 1802–9).

19. W. K. Lamb, ed., *The Journals and Letters of Sir Alexander Mackenzie* (Toronto: Macmillan of Canada, 1970), 2–12.

20. See "Spanish John" Macdonell to John "LePretre" Macdonell, 4 April 1797, as cited in Morice, "A Canadian Pioneer: Spanish John," 228.

21. See R. H. Fleming, "The Origin of 'Sir Alexander Mackenzie and Company.'" *Canadian Historical Review* 9, no. 2 (June 1928): 137–55; and W. Stewart Wallace, "Alexander Mackenzie's Break with Simon McTavish," in W. Stewart Wallace, *The Pedlars From Quebec and Other Papers on the Nor'Westers*, (Toronto: Ryerson Press, 1954), 37–43; and Elaine Allen Mitchell, "New Evidence on the Mackenzie-McTavish Break," *Canadian Historical Review* 41, no. 1 (March 1960): 41–47.

22. Penelope Beikie to William Johnson Macdonell (hereinafter WJMcD), dated 25 January 1801. Macdonell of Scotus Correspondence (hereinafter McDSC), Glengarry Historical Society (GHS), Williamstown, Ontario.

23. John Macdonell to WJMcD, 13 July 1802, McDSC, GHS. See also Fr. Roderick Macdonell to John "LePretre" Macdonell, 25 April 1804. From Public Archives of Canada (PAC), MG 24, J 13 Macdonell Papers, as quoted by Morice in "A Canadian Pioneer: Spanish John," 233.

24. John Beikie to WJMcD, 3 October 1803, McDSC, GHS.

25. Until now it had been commonly believed that John Macdonell spent the bulk of his time, from 1799 to 1809, in the Upper Red River Department, after which he took charge of the Athabasca Department (see Herbert J. Mays, "John McDonell" in *DCB*, 7:552. It is clear from these letters, however, that John Macdonell was in Athabasca much earlier, as this correspondence indicates that he was stationed at a remote post in the Athabasca region during the winter of 1802, and that he took charge of Fort Chipewyan in the summer of 1803, if only for a brief time.

26. John Beikie to WJMcD, 17 November 1803, McDSC, GHS.

27. See Fleming, "The Origin of 'Sir Alexander Mackenzie and Company,'" 147. See also R. H. Fleming, "McTavish Frobisher and Company of Montreal," *Canadian Historical Review* 10, no. 2 (June 1929): 143–44.

28. See Wallace, "Alexander Mackenzie's Break with Simon McTavish," 38–42.

29. Lord Selkirk established three settlements in North America between 1803 and 1820; in Prince Edward Island; at Baldoon in Upper Canada; and at Red River in the North West Territory. As J. M. Bumsted has noted, Lord Selkirk was accustomed to hiring individuals to manage his business affairs, including the administration of his settlements. He was partial to hiring Scots, and members of the Macdonell family in particular, to undertake these tasks. The Macdonell kinsmen affiliated with the interests of Lord Selkirk included Alexander McDonell, sheriff and agent of the Red River colony (fl. 1815–23); Alexander McDonell (Collachie), agent of Lord Selkirk's Baldoon settlement ca. 1805–12; and Miles Macdonell, agent for Selkirk's settlement on the Red River and the first governor

of Assiniboia (ca. 1811–17). See J. M. Bumsted, "A Tale of Three Settlements," *The Beaver* 72, no. 3 (June-July 1992): 33–34.

30. Correspondence from the Macdonell Papers, PAC MG 24, J 13 as quoted in J. A. Rea, *Bishop Alexander Macdonell and the Politics of Upper Canada.* Research Publication No. 4 (Toronto: Ontario Historical Society): 13; See also Somers, *The Life and Times of the Hon. and Rt. Rev. Alexander Macdonell, D.D. First Bishop of Upper Canada, 1762–1840,* 27.

31. See Patrick C. T. White, *Lord Selkirk's Diary, 1803–1804* (Toronto: Champlain Society, 1958), 192–97; and Herbert J. Mays, "Miles Macdonell," *DCB,* 6:440–41.

32. As Penelope Beikie noted in a letter to brother William Johnson Macdonell in 1805,

> Poor Miles is now here, after his disappointment but he is not yet without hope, he tells me he wrote you from Albany but got no answer, at which he is not pleased, 'tho you are not to know this from me, I suppose he told you the purport of his journey, he was within half an hour of going to Boston when he heard from the Earl of Selkirk.

Possibly the "disappointment" is in reference to Miles losing the sheriffalty of the Eastern District. Penelope Beikie to William Johnson Macdonell, dated York, 1805. McDSC, GHS. The position was eventually rewarded to Capt. Neil McLean, who was known to Francis Gore, newly appointed lieutenant governor of Upper Canada. See Miles Macdonell to William Johnson Macdonell, dated 20 June 1807, McDSC, GHS. See also Rea, *Bishop Alexander Macdonell and the Politics of Upper Canada,* 21.

33. See Morice, "Sidelights on the Careers of Miles Macdonell and His Brothers," 310–12.

34. Miles Macdonell to William Johnson Macdonell, 20 June 1807, McDSC, GHS.

35. They [Miles's daughters] have ruined me in expenses; not me but you having been mentioned by Genl Drummond's Lady, Mrs. McGillivray & others, led them to considerable expenses in dress to attend balls, Bouls, & evening Parties given by these Ladies. W. McGillivray paid forrests acct for Boarding, Music, Drawing &c &c amounting to £64.15.3 for which I gave him a Draft on you. There is as yet an acct of upwards of £90 to pay to this Merchant for Dresses for which I trust you will enable me to discharge not wishing to draw for it without authority, to avoid any difficulty with W. McGillivray. . . .

See personal correspondence from Miles Macdonell to John Macdonell, 21 May 1809 in MS 821 John Macdonell Papers (hereinafter JMcDP), Archives of Ontario (AO).

36. Catherine and Amelia, his two eldest daughters by first wife Isabella MacDonald of Morar, had spent most of their childhood and young adulthood in a convent in Montreal after the death of their mother. Catherine's suitor, John MacDonald of Garth, wintering partner of the North West Company, had spent the winter of

1808 on furlough in Montreal living at the home of his sister Magdalen McGillivray, wife of William McGillivray. After Catherine's rejection he returned to the North West in the spring of 1809 to take charge of the Red River Department with John Wills. Catherine's new suitor, Joseph Frobisher, was one of the twelve children of Joseph Frobisher, a founder of McTavish Frobisher and Company. He was also a brother of Benjamin Frobisher, who was captured by Hudson's Bay Company men in 1819 during the course of the Selkirk conflict. See Miles Macdonell to John Macdonell, 21 May 1809, JMcDP, AO; Fernand Ouellet, "Joseph Frobisher" in *DCB*, 5:331–34; Fernand Ouellet, "Benjamin Joseph Frobisher" in *DCB*, 6:267–68; see also C. M. Livermore and N. Anick, "John McDonald (of Garth)" in *DCB*, 9:481–82.

37. See Bumsted, ed., introduction to *The Collected Writings of Lord Selkirk*, 2:xiv–xv.

38. See Harkness, "Miles Macdonell," 81–82.

39. Miles Macdonell to WJMcD, Quebec, 3 September 1810, McDSC, GHS.

40. Rev. Alexander Macdonell to John Macdonell, 14 June 1811. As quoted from the Macdonell Papers, PAC MG 24, J 13 by Morice, "Sidelights on the Careers of Miles Macdonell and His Brothers," 312. Father Macdonell enjoyed a very close friendship with William McGillivray, and the two were in constant communication over events in the Northwest. Macdonell was at McGillivray's bedside the night before the latter's death in London in 1825, and was left a small legacy in his will. See Rea, *Bishop Alexander Macdonell and the Politics of Upper Canada, 78–79. See also Marjorie Wilkins Campbell, Northwest to the Sea: A Biography of William McGillivray* (Toronto: Clarke, Irwin & Company, 1975), 221, 223

41. See Bumsted, introduction to *The Collected Writings of Lord Selkirk*, 2:xvi–xix.

42. Miles Macdonell to Rev. Alexander Macdonell, 7 June 1811. As quoted from the Macdonell Papers, PAC MG 24, J 13 by Morice, "Sidelights on the Careers of Miles Macdonell and His Brothers," 313.

43. Although the Macdonell of Scotus Correspondence held by the Glengarry Historical Society contains few letters from this period, the Selkirk Papers contain many of Miles Macdonell's letters, as well as additional letters written to William Johnson Macdonell. It is not clear how the letters to William Johnson Macdonell (which are included in the Selkirk Papers in a manuscript group known as the St. Mary's Isle collection) came to be separated from the letters now called the Macdonell of Scotus Correspondence, although undoubtedly they must have been part of this collection at one time. See Pritchett and Horowitz, "Five 'Selkirk' Letters," 159–67.

44. Duncan Cameron was the son of Alexander Cameron and Margaret Macdonell, Loyalists from the Mohawk Valley who later settled in Williamstown, Glengarry County, after the American Revolution. Duncan was a former ensign in the 1st Battalion of the King's Royal Regiment of New York, alongside his relative Miles Macdonell, who was also an ensign. Duncan would later come into conflict with his former comrade-in-arms after his appointment as bourgeois of the Red River Department ca. 1814–16. See W. S. Wallace, *Documents Relating to the North West*

Company (Toronto: Champlain Society, 1934), 429–30. See also E. A. Cruikshank, "The King's Royal Regiment of New York," in *Papers and Records—Ontario Historical Society*, vols. 27 (1931), 27: 320. See also Jennifer S. H. Brown, "Duncan Cameron," in *DCB*, 7:137–38.

45. Miles Macdonell was married to his second cousin Nancy Greenfield Macdonell, Alexander Greenfield Macdonell's sister. Nancy Macdonell died on 12 March 1806, but Miles and his brother-in-law continued to recognize their consanguineous ties. Alexander Macdonell made frequent observations regarding Miles Macdonell's ineptness at Red River, noting that, "from the moment Miles and his party arrived at Pembina, seldom or ever twenty-four hours passed without a call on my store for provisions; and it remains for them to say, whether I was then, or ever afterwards, deaf to their demands." Later, Miles Macdonell was to write a letter to the Montreal agents of the North West Company, requesting the removal of John Dugald Cameron and Alexander Greenfield Macdonell as wintering partners. See Alexander Greenfield Macdonell, *A Narrative of Transactions in the Red River Country; from the Commencement of the Operations of the Earl of Selkirk, Till the Summer of the Year 1816* (London: B. McMillan for Egerton, 1819), 4–6, 16.

46. Although the kin connections between John Dugald Cameron and Duncan Cameron are not clear, they were probably related, possibly cousins. When Duncan Cameron relinquished control of the Lake Winnipeg Department in 1811, he transferred responsibility directly to John Dugald Cameron. See Wallace, *Documents Relating to the North West Company*; see also Brown, "Duncan Cameron."

47. Mays, "Miles Macdonell," 441–43.

48. Bumsted, introduction to *Collected Writings of Lord Selkirk*, 2:xxxiv–xxxv.

49. Ibid. See Livermore and Anick, "John McDonald of Garth," 9:481–82; and John McDonald of Garth, "Autobiographical Notes—1791–1816," in *Les Bourgeois de la Compagnie du Nord-Ouest*, ed. L. R. Masson, 2 vols. (New York: Antiquarian Press, 1960), 2:53–56.

50. Miles Macdonell to Lord Selkirk, 14 July 1814, as quoted by Mays, "Miles Macdonell," 443.

51. Brown, "Duncan Cameron," 138.

52. Bumsted, "A Tale of Three Settlements," 40. See also Mays, "Miles Macdonell," 443.

53. ". . . Your letter by McMartin has set my mind at ease, because a Report prevailed for a great while here & which no one was able to contradict that Miles had fallen in a Duel with his Brother in Law Alexander (Greenfield). I always doubted the Report and am now happy you have dispersed the anxiety it occasioned— . . . ." John Beikie to John "LePretre" Macdonell, from York, U.C., 12 February 1815. In "John Beikie Correspondence" (Series A-1-6) JMcDP, AO. It is possible that Miles's nervous breakdown at York Factory in the fall of 1814 prevented his communicating with relatives in Upper Canada. See Mays, "Miles Macdonell," 443.

54. Colin Robertson to Lord Selkirk, 29 October 1814, Selkirk Papers (SP), Public Archives of Canada (PAC), 1252–65, as quoted by Bumsted, introduction to *The Collected Writings of Lord Selkirk*, 2:xxxvi, lxxxiii.

55. Lord Selkirk to John Macdonell, London, 8 June 1815, JMcDP, AO.

56. See personal correspondence from John Macdonell to William Johnson Macdonell, 16 November 1815; Lord Selkirk to William J. Macdonell, 1 December 1815 at Montreal; and William J. Macdonell to Lord Selkirk, Boston, 9 January 1816. As quoted by Pritchett and Horowitz, "Five 'Selkirk' Letters," 160–66.

57. Donald Aeneas Macdonell was born at Brockville, Ontario in July of 1794, the son of Miles Macdonell (Scotus) and Isabella Macdonell (Leek). Although a Roman Catholic, he attended John Strachan's school in Cornwall. During his life he held a series of military appointments (ensign, 8th regiment, 1813; lieutenant, 98th regiment, 29 November 1815; major, 1st regiment, Stormont Militia, 1822; lieutenant colonel, 1830; commander, militia, 1838) followed by political appointments (member of the house of assembly—Stormont, 1834–41). He was classed as a reformer. He married Mary Macdonell, daughter of Col. Archibald Macdonell of Leek. He died in March of 1879. See Johnson, *Becoming Prominent*, 208.

58. John Beikie to WJMcD, 23 May 1816, McDSC, GHS.

59. See Mays, "Miles Macdonell," 443. See also Miles Macdonell to John Macdonell from Sault Ste. Marie, 31 July 1816, as quoted by Morice, "Sidelights on the Careers of Miles Macdonell and His Brothers," 317–18.

60. Mays, "Miles Macdonell," 444.

61. William Johnson Macdonell to John Macdonell from Boston, 22 June 1817, JMcDP, AO.

62. Mays, "Miles Macdonell," 444.

63. Although not otherwise identified, "Mr. Gentron" possibly refers to either François or Louis Gendron, engagés with the North West Company. See table 1: "Genealogies of Red River Households, 1818–1870" for reference to François Gendron in D. N. Sprague and R. N. Frye, *The Genealogy of the First Métis Nation* (Winnipeg: Pemmican Publications, 1983). See also Masson, *Les Bourgeois de La Compagnie du Nord-Ouest*, 1:406 for a reference to Louis Gendron as an engagé in the Onion Lake Department, ca 1804.

64. Miles Macdonell to John Macdonell from Glengarry, 15 July 1817, JMcDP, AO.

65. Morice, "Sidelights on the Careers of Miles Macdonell and His Brothers,"319–20.

66. See Miles Macdonell to WJMcD, Montreal, 6 December 1818; and Miles Macdonell to WJMcD, 8 March 1819 at Cornwall, McDSC, GHS. Lord Selkirk's *Memorial* was intended to explain Selkirk's position regarding the troubles at Red River and was submitted to the Duke of Richmond before Selkirk's departure to England in 1818. Apparently the monograph, printed in Montreal in 1819, was meant for private circulation. See Wallace, "The Literature Relating to the Selkirk

Controversy," 45–50, and Bumsted, introduction to *The Collected Writings of Lord Selkirk*, 2:47–108, 110–230 for information regarding these publications.

67. See Robert E. Saunders, "Sir John Beverly Robinson," in *DCB*, 9:668–78.

68. The only person convicted of a serious crime, Charles De Reinhard, received a stay of execution and died of natural causes. See Barron, "Victimizing His Lordship: Lord Selkirk and the Upper Canadian Courts," 14–22;and *The Memorial of Thomas Earl of Selkirk in Bumsted*, introduction to *The Collected Writings of Lord Selkirk*, 2:110–197; Gressley, "Lord Selkirk and the Canadian Courts," 277–93; Wallace, "The Literature Relating to the Selkirk Controversy," 45–50.

69. John "LePretre" Macdonell, in a letter to his brother William, noted that "Our brother Miles has lately removed to the River Raison with his son Donald and Daughter Bella, and inhabits a very comfortable Domacile built near the Spot where the Worthy old commander's Scothouse stood." John Macdonell to WJMcD, 16 November 1819 at Point Fortune, McDSC, GHS.

70. Duncan Cameron, Miles's nemesis at Red River, settled at Williamstown, Glengarry County, in 1820. John Duncan Cameron, former Nor'Wester wintering partner who was captured with Benjamin Frobisher at the Grand Rapid in June of 1819, settled at Cornwall in 1821. Simon Fraser, former North West Company partner, retired to St. Andrews, near Cornwall, prior to 1820. Hugh McGillis, a North West Company partner arrested by Lord Selkirk in 1816, purchased Sir John Johnson's property at Williamstown, Glengarry County in 1816 and lived there until his death in 1848. John McGillivray, another North West Company partner arrested by Selkirk, settled at Williamstown, Glengarry County in 1818. Daniel McKenzie, a wintering partner arrested by Selkirk, retired at Brockville ca. 1818. Archibald McLellan, tried with Charles de Reinhard for murder, retired to Glengarry County ca. 1819. See Wallace, *Documents Relating to the North West Company*, 430, 431, 445, 468–69; 469–70; 476, 479–80.

71. John Macdonell to WJMcD, 10 April 1821 at Point Fortune, McDSC, GHS.

72. William Johnson Macdonell to John Macdonell from Boston, 15 July 1821, JMcDP, AO. It is possible that a hereditary strain of mental illness existed in the Macdonell family, given the considerable amount of intermarriage that took place between various cousins.

73. See Francis N. A. Garry, ed., "The Diary of Nicholas Garry, Deputy-Governor of the Hudson's Bay Company," in *Transactions of the Royal Society of Canada*, Volume V, Section II, 1900; (reprint, Toronto: Canadiana House, 1973), 28.

74. John Beikie to John Macdonell, 31 October 1821 at York, JMcDP, AO.

75. Father Alexander Macdonell to John Macdonell, 21 May 1822 at St. Raphael's. As quoted by Morice, "Sidelights on the Careers of Miles Macdonell and His Brothers," 321.

76. John Macdonell to WJMcD, 21 August 1822 at Point Fortune, McDSC, GHS.

77. Miles Macdonell to WJMcD, 20 September 1824 at Cornwall, McDSC, GHS.

78. Miles noted, "I have to go immediately to Montreal—a House has failed there

who got possession of some Money of mine which I much wanted—so much for broken Merchants—they bring down others in their fall." Miles Macdonell to WJMcD, 9 October 1826 at Brockville, Canada West, McDSC, GHS.

79. In a letter to William Johnson Macdonell, Miles noted, "I have used your specific remedy for all disorders, the Pearl Ash occasionally—I think it a good thing, tho' nauseous & repugnant to my taste—I shall endeavor to use it more frequently." Miles Macdonell to WJMcD, 9 October 1826 at Canada West, McDSC, GHS.

Pearl Ash is also known as potash—a crude form of Potassium Carbonate. In the past it has been used externally as a lotion to treat eczema and uticaria. It may have also been taken internally to ease stomach upsets. See Personal Communication, Patrick Crawford, PEINet - Sci.Med.Pharmacy Newsgroup to Heather Devine, via the Internet, Monday, 8 May 1995 re: *Historical Question— Pearl Ash*. However, another description of a medicinal substance appears in a letter written on 29 April 1822 to John Macdonell by a neighboring priest, Messire I. Félix, curé of Saint Benoiste, quoted in French by Morice, "Sidelights on the Careers of Miles Macdonell and His Brothers," 328. The priest provided a recipe for a pancake made of baked, pulverized oyster shells (which are comprised of calcium carbonate) mixed with eggs and fried in olive oil, to be eaten each morning on an empty stomach. It is probable that the pearl ash remedy to which Miles Macdonell refers is, in all likelihood, this concoction, which appears to have become a family "cure-all" in the Macdonell household.

80. Morice, "Sidelights on the Careers of Miles Macdonell and His Brothers," 324–25.

81. William Johnson Macdonell to John Macdonell, 3 September 1828, as quoted in Morice, "Sidelights on the Careers of Miles Macdonell and His Brothers," 325–26.

82. John Macdonell to WJMcD, 13 August 1828, McDSC, GHS.

83. John Macdonell to WJMcD, 17 October 1828 at Point Fortune, McDSC, GHS.

84. In fact, the remains of Miles Macdonell *were* eventually collected, and reinterred at St. Andrews sometime between 1828 and 1846, when his sister Penelope Beikie was buried. In a letter to William John Macdonell Jr., dated 6 April 1846, an elderly John Macdonell makes reference to "having deposited her remains in the burying ground of St. Andrew's Church where your Grandfather ['Spanish John' Macdonell] & Uncle Mile's were interred . . . " See John Macdonell to William John Macdonell, from Point Fortune, 6 April 1846, JMcDP, AO. J. G. Harkness, in his 1948 biography of Miles Macdonell, places Miles's grave site at St. Andrews, but makes no mention of the fact that Miles was first buried at Ste. Madeleine de Rigaud. See Harkness, "Miles Macdonell," 83.

85. None of Miles Macdonell's relatives appear to have been present at his burial, which took place three days after his death. According to the burial record entered in the parish register of Ste-Madeleine de Rigaud on July 1, 1828, only three individuals: Father H. Hudon, the parish priest, and two witnesses, François Séguin and Antoine Lalonde (possibly the gravediggers) are recorded as having witnessed

the interment. See Personal Correspondence, Lorraine Auerbach Chevrier, Point Fortune, Québec to Hugh MacMillan, Guelph, Ontario dated 23 June 1997.

86. See Doman Lum, *Responding to Suicidal Crisis: For Church and Community*. (Grand Rapids, Mich.: Eerdmans, 1974), 33.

87. John Macdonell's behavior in the event of Miles's death is a case in point. Not only did he delay in informing William Johnson Macdonell of the death, but his reference to the interment (i.e., "I had him buried . . .") is oddly impersonal. Also, John's final act—to have prayers chanted over Miles's remains for a fee—is quite common in cases where death is sudden and it is felt that the deceased has much to answer for. A second question—Did Bishop Macdonell officiate at the funeral of his own cousin? It is not clear from John Macdonell's correspondence of 17 October 1828 whether Bishop Macdonell performed the funeral mass or not. "Recommending him to the prayers of his congregation" is hardly the same as praying over his remains at a funeral!

88. See Henry Romilly Fedden, *Suicide: A Sociological and Historical Study* (London: Peter Davies, 1938): 50–53.

89. The biased nature of the legal proceedings in favor of the North West Company at the expense of Lord Selkirk is consistent with the tenor of behavior in Loyalist Upper Canada at that time. The political and legal system of Upper Canada was dominated by Scots Loyalists, their friends, and their business associates. The virtual dismissal of charges against Nor'Westers implicated of crimes in the Selkirk controversy was predictable, given the "localist" flavor of the Upper Canadian court system, which operated to maintain the status quo rather than the impartial rule of law. In this system, the courts favored the local mercantile community and "the larger needs of St. Lawrence commercialism," which included the interests of the North West Company. See Johnson's *Becoming Prominent*, 153, and elsewhere for a detailed demographic analysis of the social, economic, and political elites of Upper Canada. See also Wise, "Upper Canada and the Conservative Tradition," 169–84, for an explanation of the conservative ethos that governed social, economic, and political relations in Upper Canada.

Figure 1. **John Clarke.** *Courtesy of Museé du Château Ràmezay, Montreal.*

H. Lloyd Keith

The "Dried Spider" and the Gadfly: The James Keith - John Clarke Confrontation at Mingan, 1831–32

"Will you walk into my parlor?" said the Spider to the Fly,
" 'Tis the prettiest little parlor that ever you did spy;
The way into my parlor is up a winding stair,
And I've many curious things to show when you are there."
"Oh no, no," said the little Fly, "to ask me is in vain,
For who goes up your winding stair can ne'er come down again."

ABOUT THE TIME Mary Howitt sat down at her desk in England and first composed the lines to her famous poem, a living scenario of the "spider and the fly" was weaving itself out on the other side of the Atlantic. However, unlike the spider and the fly in her poem, the living spider was not particularly cunning nor was his foil silly and gullible, but for them as with the literary antagonists, the consequences were essentially the same. "He dragged her up his winding stair, into his dismal den, / Within his little parlor—but she ne'er came out again!" wrote Mary Howitt. This living "fly" did not meet such an immediately lethal fate but his career with the Hudson's Bay Company did terminate, as did the financial security that position provided. It was the end of a life as he had known it. The circumstances alluded to involved chief factors James Keith and John Clarke of the Hudson's Bay Company in the early 1830s at Mingan and Lachine in the British North American colony of Lower Canada.

Chief factor James Keith was in charge of the Hudson's Bay Company's Montréal Department between 1826 and 1843. As part of his responsibilities, he managed the affairs of the King's Posts and of the Isles-Mingan seigniory along the northern shore of the St. Lawrence estuary. On 4 June 1831, chief factor John Clarke, then in disfavor with George Simpson, North American governor of the Hudson's Bay Company, was appointed to the charge of the Mingan district under the superintendence of Keith, a man Clarke apparently despised. Clarke did not suffer well the indignity of his exile to such a remote and insignificant post. He took particular umbrage at serving under a man of equal rank whom he considered inferior in ability. Almost immediately, an acrimonious correspondence ensued between the two chief factors in which Clarke's intemperate language ultimately cost him his career. By 9 April 1834, John Clarke accepted the inevitable and acquiesced in what could be considered a "forced" retirement from the company's service.

Seldom do gadflies like John Clarke adjust well to the strictures of large-scale organizations. Their annoying self-absorption and constant criticisms of others are inimical to the cooperative management required by the organization. They are unwilling to subordinate personal concerns to corporate interests. Excitement and change, the very stuff of the provocative adventure they crave, are counterproductive to the careful and predictable routines of large, monopolistic companies whose interests lie in regularity and teamwork. Gadflies, such as John Clarke, thrive in times of turmoil but are merely unwanted pests in times of stability.

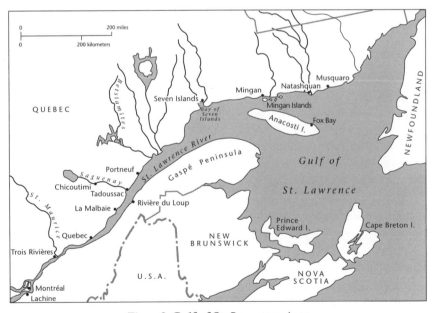

Figure 2. **Gulf of St. Lawrence Area.**

More in keeping with the requisites of the large international business concern is what William H. White called "The Organization Man." The organization man subordinates everything to the interests of the company. Men like James Keith not only work for the company, they *belong* to it as well. There is no separation of personal interests from the interests of the concern. Whatever small position they might hold, it is the common problems of collective work that dominate their attention. They believe the virtues of hard work, system, and thrift provide the basis for moral responsibility to the company. Only by acting consistently with those virtues can the company succeed in its competitive struggle in a hostile world. More than anything, the ethic of the organization man "rationalizes the company's demands for fealty and gives those who offer it wholeheartedly a sense of dedication in doing so."[1] The organization man is fully, almost obsessively, committed to promoting the welfare of the company. Whatever else he was, John Clarke was the antithesis of the organization man; James Keith, its prototype.

The modern organization man has his precedent in the dedicated, albeit unexciting, functionary in such nineteenth-century monopolies as the Hudson's Bay Company. This venerable company received its charter in 1670 under the elaborate appellation of "The Governor and Company of Adventurers of England tradeing into Hudsons Bay." When a vast wilderness needed exploration and discovery of its resources, adventuring gadflies were useful. When stiff competition threatened not only profits but the company itself, gadflies such as John Clarke served well in annoying the concern's adversaries. As the nineteenth century entered its second quarter, however, the Hudson's Bay Company faced few problems from an unknown wilderness and only trifling competition from mercantile rivals. The day of the gadfly had passed. Like the revolutionary zealot after the war is won, he found himself out of place in the new order of things.

Nevertheless, several of them lingered on past their time and struggled to find a niche where they might be needed and appreciated. Their penchant for an individualistic management style proved unsettling at a time when fitting in and conforming were called for. When the gadfly and the organization man found themselves in a power struggle within the company, the outcome was inevitable. Querulous John Clarke's confrontation in 1831 with the "dried spider" of Lachine, James Keith, resulted in the end of Clarke's career with the company three years later.

This essay will examine the circumstances and the correspondence, most of which is found in the Hudson's Bay Company Archives, that led to this confrontation and Clarke's premature retirement. In particular, ten previously unpublished letters, written by John Clarke and James Keith in 1831 and 1832, provide the corpus of this correspondence. The letters are central to understanding this power struggle in ways that mere organizational analysis cannot accomplish.

John Clarke

By 1831, John Clarke had long pursued a checkered career in the fur trade. Having been under the employ of the North West Company, the Pacific Fur Company, and the Hudson's Bay Company, he seemed to thrive during times of confrontation and conflict. He had developed a reputation as a bully, a braggart, and, at the same time, as a bold, dashing, and respected leader. Those who thought highly of John Clarke included young, impressionable clerks, voyageurs, and the few gentlemen with similar temperaments, while his more moderate peers and the senior clerks were often highly critical of his conduct.

Little is known of John Clarke's life prior to his entry into the fur trade. He was born in 1781 into a middle-class Montréal family. According to one of his critics, he was deficient in education although there is little evidence in his writing style or language use to betray such a deficiency. Clarke signed his first contract with the North West Company in 1800 as a nineteen-year-old apprentice clerk and served in the Athabasca, Mackenzie's River, and Peace River districts for the next ten years. His reputation for reckless bravado and assertiveness earned him the respect of his superiors and, by 1807, he had the charge of the Mackenzie River district. Two years later, he was placed in charge of Fort St. John on the Peace River.[2] Clarke assumed the management of that post for the next year and then, for some reason, determined to leave the employ of the North West Company and return to Canada.

It may have been the prospect of a flattering advancement in rank elsewhere that prompted him to resign his position. News of John Jacob Astor's new Pacific Fur Company had reached the Athabasca and beyond.[3] Clarke may have corresponded with Astor and, with skillful self-promotion, impressed the American with his leadership ability. Through a possible maternal link with Astor's family, an offer as a wintering partner in the new concern may have been greatly facilitated.[4] Astor had already raided the ranks of disgruntled Nor'Westers to provide the needed experience in his new company. It would not have been unlike him to do it again, particularly if the recruit was a distant family member. Whatever the circumstances, something tempted Clarke away from a promising career with the North West Company and he did not leave in an atmosphere of *bons amis*. In 1811, George Keith, brother of James and a senior clerk with the North West Company, characterized Clarke's behavior as reprehensible. "A little elevation," Keith observed, "is apt to dazzle and make us sometimes forget the previous footing we were on."[5] Even as a clerk, a rank he held with the North West Company in 1810, humility was a virtue totally alien to John Clarke.

John Jacob Astor enlisted Clarke as a wintering partner in the Pacific Fur Company, and of all the wintering partners, thought of him as "the brightest star in the Columbian Constellation."[6] Such faith in Clarke's abilities was not shared by at least one of the clerks who accompanied him on the voyage around Cape Horn to the Columbia River. Alfred Seton, twelve years Clarke's junior and related to the wife of Astor's biographer, Washington Irving, had little but criticism to say of John Clarke. His "bourgeois" was "not the Gentleman I expected to find him." Clarke tended toward "a certain selfishness," while "his conversations with one person is entirely about the bad qualities of another." In short, Seton felt that Clarke's "excessive weakness of character" rendered him unfit for command.[7]

While serving on the Columbia in May of 1813, Clarke's precipitous arrogance and reckless behavior won him the "general voice of disapprobation" from his Pacific Fur Company colleagues.[8] After leaving Spokane House late in May, Clarke and his party encamped at the mouth of the Palouse River on their way to Fort Astoria with the season's returns. During the night, a Native entered Clarke's tent and stole a silver goblet much valued by him. The next night the culprit was apprehended and, without thought of the consequences, was lynched in full view of the other Natives.[9] Rather than serving as a deterrent for future misbehavior on the part of the Natives, his rash actions provoked years of Indian hostility in the area. Clarke's recklessness was viewed as "extravagant" by those endangered by his behavior and left him, except for John Jacob Astor, with few friends in the Pacific Fur Company.[10]

Clarke left the Columbia in 1814, after the assets of the Pacific Fur Company were bought out by the Nor'Westers, and returned to Montréal. He was not long unemployed for, in May of 1815, Colin Robertson, special agent for the Hudson's Bay Company, reluctantly engaged Clarke to lead a probe into the Athabasca and Peace River country in opposition to the North West Company. Robertson thought of John Clarke as "a dashing young man," but one who "can only act as a second, or associate with a person of a graver cast of mind."[11] Nevertheless, Clarke was the only person available to Robertson of any experience to lead such an important mission.

Consequently, Clarke was placed in charge of the Hudson's Bay Company opposition of the Nor'Westers in the Peace River country. In the frequently bloody confrontations between the two rivals, Clarke's leadership abilities won the admiration of even his adversaries.[12] George Keith, Clarke's opponent on Lake Athabasca in 1817 (and critic of 1811), wrote, "To give the man his due, we must acknowledge he is an excellent leader. His men were kept in strict subordination without his appearing to be too severe, and he has a deal of influence with his clerks."[13] At the same time he wrote this, however, Keith expressed quite different sentiments to Roderick MacKenzie:

> Mr. Clarke brought in 10 canoes! Never did a set of men behave with such imbecility; I am sure they have ten thousand times regretted their engaging against us in His Lordship's [Lord Selkirk's] mad enterprise. The common engagés are, through necessity and ignorance, to be pitied, but I can hardly feel much for their leader.[14]

Even during these unsettled times, however, Clarke's love for a good fight earned him the censure of a young George Simpson, who wrote in his journal:

> The N. W. Co. are not to be put down by Prize fighting, but by persevering industry, Economy in the business arrangements, and a firm maintenance of our rights not by the fist but by more deadly weapons.[15]

It was clear to Simpson that Clarke's forte was not "persevering industry." He saw limited utility for Clarke's type of leadership in a peacetime Hudson's Bay Company and tried unsuccessfully to prevent him from becoming one of the chief factors at the time of the merging of the two rival companies in 1821.[16] He did not fit Simpson's idea of a desirable organization man. In the negotiations for the twenty-five chief factor positions that would be available after the merger, erstwhile Nor'Westers would obtain fifteen. While Clarke was not held in high esteem by Simpson, he was an even greater irritant to the "Gentlemen of the 2nd Part," as the Nor'Westers were sometimes called. Nevertheless, if the more notorious of the Nor'Westers were to be included, so, too, were the more notorious of the Bay men. Clarke, along with Robertson, would be among the chief factors, although Simpson would consider him "one of the company's worst bargains."[17] In any event, subsequent events proved Simpson right in his resistance to Clarke's appointment.

In 1823, Clarke was relieved of his charge at Red River for behaving in a manner the London Committee described as "unwarrantable . . . extremely imprudent . . . preposterous & indecorous."[18] His sense of self-importance had gotten him into trouble again. After the merger of the two companies, Clarke received the charge of the company's affairs at Fort Garry in the Red River Colony. In 1822, the company instructed its chief factors to prohibit anyone found in its territories from trading furs from the Natives.[19] Clearly, the intent was to discourage competition by free traders with the Americans.

However, in a challenge to the authority of Andrew Bulger, governor of the Red River Colony, chief factor Clarke chose to interpret the directive to apply not just to the free traders, but to the personal use of furs and dried leather for clothing by the settlers as well. In short, the settlers were to purchase all their necessaries at the company store and were not to treat with Natives.[20] In pursuing this policy, Clarke seized all furs and dressed leather he found in the possession of the Colonists. His preemptive conduct precipitated a confrontation with Andrew Bulger, who claimed that legal authority ran through his office and not the local factory of the Hudson's Bay Company. The company's directors agreed, admitting that "it was never the company's intention to prevent settlers from procuring skins for their own use." Clarke was condemned for "bringing into contempt the authority and privileges of the company and throwing the whole settlement into confusion."[21]

For the next six years, Clarke found himself posted "out of the way," at Lesser Slave Lake and at Fort Pelly in the Swan River District. Even here, trouble found him out. During his 1824 return to Lesser Slave Lake from York Factory, Clarke received a severe rebuke from George Simpson for neglecting the brigade under his command. It was Simpson's opinion that this neglect was caused by Clarke's undue attention to his "domestic affairs."[22] Clarke had gone on ahead of his brigade in a light canoe with his wife in order to make the passage more comfortable for her and, in his absence, a canoe had upset resulting in the loss of some of its trade goods. It was Simpson's view that had Clarke been present, the accident might not have happened. The chief factor failed to subordinate his personal concerns to the welfare of the company, a requisite of the organization man. As a result, the company's interests were damaged and Clarke's personal account with the company was charged with the loss. Clarke may have had extenuating circumstances, however, to which Simpson gave no recognition. If Clarke's spouse at this time was his Métis wife, Sophia Spence, she was suffering from an illness that would result in her death later that year.[23]

John Clarke's problems with Governor Simpson continued over the next several years. Sometime after 1826, Clarke apparently obtained a small herd of cattle from chief factor John Stuart that he maintained at company expense. Simpson, predictably, took extreme umbrage at such maneuverings when this unpropitious undertaking came to his attention. It was this bit of innovative capitalism that led Simpson to remark of Clarke that he was "A boasting, ignorant low fellow who rarely speaks the truth and is strongly suspected of dishonesty."[24]

During this time, Clarke's penchant for harping criticism toward his fellow officers was met with understandable reprobation. chief factor Allan McDonell opined that while John Clarke had maliciously slandered his name, "I smile with contempt at any thing he can say . . ." and advised others to do the same.[25] It seems that Clarke's slandering was directed more to the older, established gentlemen or to onetime Nor'Westers than it was to younger men in the service. By doing so, he ingratiated himself with the younger clerks whose favor he curried. Clerks like Thomas Simpson and his brother Alexander, step-cousins of Governor George Simpson and resentful of his authority, would find the brash, overbearing manner of a John Clarke seductively charming while the more staid, methodical manner of company functionaries, such as James Keith, would pale by comparison.[26]

This, then, was the reputation Clarke had earned for himself when the gadfly met the dried spider. By 1831, Simpson bragged to one of his friends, "I have had the Rod in a pickle for him these 2 years past [and] his appointment to Mingan will be the ruin & damnation of the fellow."[27] The governor's assessment of John Clarke was that "he is a vain silly idiot who will go to the dl in the end."[28] Simpson's judgment rarely failed him and, to insure the inevitability of his prophecy, Clarke was given superintendence of a small, insignificant post under the direction of chief factor James Keith.

James Keith

Like John Clarke, not much is known of James Keith's early life before he entered into the fur trade. He was born in rural Aberdeenshire, Scotland, to a middle-class farming family in 1782. He entered the fur trade about the same time as Clarke but, in contrast, followed a career productive of a secure if unexciting outcome, making him, at his retirement, one of the wealthiest men in Canada.[29] Apprenticing himself to a firm called the New North West or "XY" company in 1800, Keith entered the service of the "old" North West Company when the two firms merged in 1804. In 1821, he was one of the fifteen Nor'Westers appointed to the position of chief factor in the newly organized Hudson's Bay Company.

James Keith was made a partner in the North West Company in 1814 and served for five years at Fort George on the Columbia as the proprietor of that department. Alexander Ross, a clerk inherited from the Pacific Fur Company when that firm was purchased by the Nor'Westers, served under Keith for two seasons at Fort George. It is from his pen that the impression comes of Keith as a "punctilious but short-sighted" manager.[30] In the process of venting his spleen against the North West Company's management of affairs at Fort

George, Ross characterized Keith as one who "does everything by rule, and will hazard nothing."[31] This theme of the overly cautious, inactive proprietor whose timidity contributed to business losses has been echoed by historians such as John S. Galbraith, H. H. Bancroft, Arthur Morton, William Goetzmann, and Murray Morgan.[32] In all of these writings, the only authority for this judgment appears to be Alexander Ross, the somewhat pretentious clerk who never rose beyond that rank in the fur trade. Keith was, in fact, an efficient if somewhat austere administrator. Fort George on the Columbia was reasonably productive under his charge, given the circumstances under which he labored.[33]

Ross's judgment of Keith may have been close to the mark in some respects, judging from his subsequent career with the Hudson's Bay Company. Between 1826 and 1843, James Keith acted as the company's business agent in North America and superintendent in charge of the Montréal Department. In these roles, he acted more as an accountant than a fur trader, balancing debits and credits in both company and individual servants' accounts. Particular about detail and an obsessive record keeper, he was typecast for these duties. He had no private life to speak of, living only to serve the interests of the concern. This rather straitlaced and sanctimonious administrator insisted that everything be done with regularity, or "with a system," as he would have termed it. There is no better example of this than that provided by an apprentice clerk at Lachine House in 1831, Alexander Caulfield Anderson. Anderson had been enticed by John Clarke and Alexander Stewart, while they were on furlough in England in 1830, to begin his career as an apprentice clerk in the service of the Hudson's Bay Company. Anderson accepted their advice and arrived in Montréal in the spring of 1831 to serve his first year under the direction of chief factor James Keith. His year was spent in the routine duties of an apprentice clerk, and he may, in fact, have written the fair copies, or final drafts, of the letters in the Keith-Clarke correspondence. Despite the heavy duties imposed upon him, Anderson had occasion to characterize the attributes of his mentor. Of James Keith, Anderson wrote:

> our chief factor was the embodiment of regularity, almost to a caricature. Seated at dinner, a glass of Madeira invariably followed the soup, of Port accompanied the pudding, and so we regularly hob-nobbed. In the winter evenings, commencing at a stated [time], and terminating alike by rule, a single rubber of whist, never by any chance exceeded, played for six penny points, was the standard regulation.[34]

While Keith was not above the occasional conviviality, even it required a proper decorum:

> The occasional banquet in honor of visiting dignitaries while not exactly fast and furious, . . . presented at least a very warm contrast with the wonted frigidity of our every day's existence. Invariably, the next morning Keith would exclaim the inevitable "Now, gentlemen, these Saturnâ-âlia [sic] being concluded, we resume our duties."[35]

While his business sense, as well as his honesty, was highly respected by his colleagues, James Keith never seems to have won the admiration of those who served under him. To the contrary, they found him unapproachable and, as Thomas Simpson caustically remarked, the chief factor was as insipid as "a dried spider."[36] It appears that Keith's officiousness, at times, warranted this judgment. He insisted that his subordinates follow the rules to the letter but did not always inform them what the rules were; he assumed it was their responsibility to know. Sometimes a simple thing like reminding a subordinate of a change in accounting procedure or of an upcoming due date would have been appreciated. Chief Trader John Siveright's exasperation was evident when he wrote: "I have a great wish to take a turn to Scotland & said as much to Mr. Keith, but was told official application must be made a year before hand. If I knew when my rotation [was] coming (if at all) I would take advantage of it but do not like to be making application without some plea of actual necessity."[37] Unintended slights to subordinates such as this were the bane of James Keith throughout his career.

Young clerks had the harshest judgments of Keith. Perhaps this was because he was old and established while they were still young and aspiring. One clerk described him, in a carefully phrased understatement, as "a very cautious man, and not lavish of his praise."[38] Keith's aloofness revealed itself in other ways as well. Another clerk, Alexander Simpson, was banished from Lachine for excessive drinking and insolence, and held a grudge against old man Keith for the rest of his career.[39] Alexander Robertson, a clerk at Mingan, found himself suspended by Keith without pay for insubordination.[40] Robertson had chosen to follow orders given him by his immediate superior, John Clarke, that were in conflict with those issued by the superintendent of the Montréal Department, James Keith. In this case, even the London Committee found Keith's discipline a bit harsh and advised him to ease up a little so long as the clerk proved repentent.[41] While youthful subordinates were often uncompromising in their assessments of those in authority over them, Keith's superior, George Simpson, had much the same thing to say about him, albeit in gentler tones:

> very attentive to business in which he is regular & systematic, indeed both in business and private Life formal to a fault, his whole words and actions being governed by what he considers the strictest rules of propriety. . . .[42]

These, then, were the two personalities that came to loggerheads when Simpson, "taking his Rod out of the pickle," assigned John Clarke to Mingan Seigniory and, thence, subject to Keith's administrative authority. The arrogant, self-absorbed, yet frequently engaging personality of John Clarke was pitted against the deadened man of system, James Keith. John Clarke envisioned himself an indispensable officer whose services were required if the company was to prosper. He seemed oblivious to the contrary opinion held by his superiors as well as by those of equal rank. He assumed an air of superiority in his interaction with fellow officers reflecting his enormous conceit. He never considered subordinating his personal needs for the welfare of the company, considering, instead, that prerogative transcended the collective interest. James Keith, on the other hand, saw himself as an organization man, willing to submerge self-interest to the good of the whole, and he expected others to do the same. It is this contrasting view of the responsibility of the individual to the company that provided the basis of the clash between the dried spider and the gadfly. The ensuing battle of wills proved, as Simpson predicted, to "be the ruin & damnation of the fellow."

The Confrontation

"Sweet creature," said the Spider, "you're witty and you're wise,

How handsome are your gauzy wings, how brilliant are your eyes!

I have a little looking-glass upon my parlor shelf,

If you'll step in one moment, dear, you shall behold yourself."

"I thank you, gentle sir," she said, "for what you're pleased to say,

And bidding you good morning now, I'll call another day."

Like the spider in Mary Howitt's poem, Governor George Simpson appealed to the vanity inbred in Clarke's character to entice him away from any meaningful responsibility in the fur trade by promising him a post in the Montréal Department. Close to Canada's urban centers and the comforts they held, many posts in the Montréal Department were considered sinecures. Some, however, like Mingan, were as remote as those on the prairies or in the northern woodlands. Knowing this, Clarke, like the wary poetic fly, demurred from accepting Simpson's promise for a time, preferring to display his gauzy wings and brilliant eyes before the governor and committee in London, hoping to procure from them a lucrative retirement agreement. They were not impressed.

In April of 1831, after returning from his furlough to London, during which he tried unsuccessfully to convince the committee of his invaluable worth to the company, John Clarke arrived at Montréal to the news of his reassignment. Clarke had contemplated retirement and hoped that his negotiations with the governor and committee of the Hudson's Bay Company would provide a suitable settlement. He changed his mind when it became apparent that his conception of his value did not coincide with theirs. Short of a comfortable retirement, Clarke was willing to settle for a comfortable post in the Montréal Department. Previous to his sojourn to London, Clarke had the charge of the Swan River District, with headquarters at Fort Pelly on the Assiniboine River. From this relatively unimportant provisioning post, he was to be sent as far from any meaningful participation in the fur trade as the company's extensive domains would allow. Governor Simpson notified Clarke by letter of his appointment to Mingan Seigniory, located on Quebec's north shore of the Gulf of St. Lawrence and adjacent to Anticosti Island. Mingan was an isolated district and not significant as a fur-bearing area. In truth, Mingan served chiefly as a buffer to protect the more valuable Hudson's Bay preserves to the north from encroachment either by free traders or by Americans. It had not previously been considered worthy of the management of a chief factor, being left to the direction of lesser officers. Such a modest assignment was a humiliating affront to one who considered himself "in a great measure . . . responsible for the splendor & importance of their [the Hudson's Bay Company's] rank & standing in the great Commercial World."[43] Even more galling to Clarke was the expectation that he subject himself to the administrative authority of that "dried spider" at Lachine, James Keith.

From Montréal, Clarke journeyed down the St. Lawrence to Quebec but had yet to remove himself to Mingan by 6 June 1831, when Keith wrote a letter to him providing information and direction with respect to his new assignment. The two had already talked over the assignment previously in Lachine, but Keith added more detail and felt, no doubt, that it would be prudent to have it all in writing. This caution reflected that of Governor Simpson when he wrote Keith the previous August warning that Clarke might resist his subordination to Keith, and "it may be necessary to be a little more explicit with Mr. Clarke on the subject of his new appointment."[44] Keith informed the new manager of Mingan of some of the details concerning the newly acquired King's Posts, reminded him of the company's policies regarding wages and other housekeeping details, and advised him of the arrangements that had been made for transporting him to Mingan. Remembering, perhaps,

Simpson's stinging rebuke of Clarke's impropriety in taking his family to Lesser Slave Lake in 1824, Keith advised the chief factor that it might not be a good idea to take his family along with him to Mingan.

> In reference to what you stated verbally of your intention of taking with you to and afterwards supporting at Mingan your family, governess and other attendants I want merely to observe that only native and half breed women have heretofore resided at the company Establishment in this department who together with their families have been supported and fed at the expense of the person under whose protection they were by a certain deduction from the yearly wages which such persons would otherwise have been allowed in the event of his being single & unencumbered.[45]

Keith's purpose, no doubt, was to tactfully remind Clarke that any domestic expenses must be borne by him and that, in any case, his wife, Swiss-born Marianne Trustler, might not find Mingan agreeable to her comfort. Clarke's response to the effrontery of Keith's advice was to ignore it, a decision he would soon regret. Clarke and his household appeared in Quebec on 11 June with what the company agent there, James McKenzie, considered a mass of people and baggage worthy of Noah's Ark. Besides himself, his wife, three children, a governess, a maid servant, and two boy servants, Clarke's baggage included a brig, a coach, a horse, and an ass.[46] Room was found aboard the chartered schooner *Mary* for his entourage and baggage, and he left Quebec on 16 June, arriving in Mingan eight days later.[47] Within six weeks, personal tragedy struck the Clarke family. Sometime in mid-August, family members were out riding in the carriage when it upset and two of his children were killed. One was a daughter and the other a son, William, whose burial was witnessed by Captain Henry Bayfield of the Royal Navy on 21 August 1831.[48]

Writing to Keith on 9 August, just a few days previous to the accident, Clarke penned a letter quite critical of his predecessor, Joseph LaRocque. With his typical arrogance, he wrote:

> From the Information I have acquired added to my own observations since my arrival on this Coast I have reason to conceive Mingan Seigniory Susceptible to much improvement & beg to submit as a preliminary remark that the business of the Seigniory, hitherto, appears to have been conducted with little attention to system or economy and much want of Energy seems to have existed in the internal arrangements of the District.[49]

With this dismissal of his predecessor, Clarke then went into a detailed description of his plans for exploiting the commercial potential of the seigniory and surrounding territories. It is clear that Clarke had greater ambitions for Mingan than did Keith, Simpson, or the governor and committee. In Lesser

Slave Lake and Swan Lake Districts, Clarke had endeavored to attend to the company's interests by reducing dependence on imported provisions and by increasing the yield in the districts' returns. He set out to accomplish the same objectives at Mingan. However, from the very beginning of the seigniory's attachment with the Hudson's Bay Company, the objective had been merely to deflect competition from free traders and Americans so that they would pose no threat to the more valuable territory of Rupert's Land. As early as 1823, the London directorate informed the Montréal agents that "the great object in the management would be to keep the profits so low as to prevent any temptation to opposition."[50] This approach to business was totally foreign to John Clarke.

The fur trade, Clarke averred, might be expanded with profit up the coast as far as Labrador. The cod fishery might also yield a profitable return and, if a lease of Anticosti Island might be got at a reasonable cost, the foxes, martens, bears, and otters that abound on that island might be extracted to a great advantage. To help defray the expense of maintaining the additional personnel necessary to expanded operations, a company farm, once established, would provide most of the foodstuffs they would require.[51] Not privy to the master plan Simpson had in mind for the seigniories and the King's Posts, Clarke's ambitions for the district intended to render it economically viable, but were unrealistic in light of the overall objectives of the company.

Even had Clarke's designs been realistic, James Keith would, in all probability, have resisted their implementation. Keith, extremely conservative in new business ventures and not trusting Clarke in any case, would have found fault with any proposal involving anything more than a cursory alteration in customary procedure. His reputation as "a very cautious man who will hazard nothing" seems appropriate in the case of the reforms suggested by John Clarke. Some years later, Cuthbert Cumming, John Clarke's eventual successor, suggested to Keith some fundamental changes in the district that he thought would improve its profitability. Like those of John Clarke, his ideas were rejected out of hand.

> The new System now to be adopted I had in contemplation some time since and developed my views on the subject to our friend Mr. J. Keith but that Gentleman did not approve of such an extensive deviation from long established rules in the District & would not sanction any new arrangement having for its object such material alterations.[52]

Yet, the substance of Cumming's suggestions, as well as those of both his predecessors were eventually recommended by Keith, if not acted upon by the governor and committee.

However, the present reforms, suggested by John Clarke, were not to be subject to "more mature thought." True to form, in his letter of 7 October, Keith turned him back at every point. Faultless in its formality, Keith's tone nonetheless reflected an accountant's propensity to obstruction that must have infuriated Clarke. While condescending that Clarke must have taken into account "both sides of the question," Keith pointed out he may not have considered all possible contingencies in expressing his ideas for farming. The superintendent implied that Clarke must have overlooked the added cost of wages and subsistence, the cost of farm stock, building, and implements, the wear and tear on utensils, the loss incumbent on accident or weather, and the temptation that such activity would become more time consuming than the "main objects" of the company. After detailing the reasons why Clarke's farming reforms were not feasible, Keith made the mistake, for mistake it was to a character such as John Clarke, of offering the literary politeness of apologizing for "having so long dwelt on a subject which I confess myself very incompetent adequately to handle."[53] Of course, Clarke was not expected to take this expression literally, but in the moment of his public frustration and private anguish, he did just that.

Of course, Keith knew that without the farming operation it would not be economically feasible to sustain the added servants needed to carry out Clarke's other plans. This measured and logical response, Keith felt, would effectively thwart the designs that Clarke had in mind for Mingan.

John Clarke would not be so easily discouraged, especially by the likes of James Keith. To say that Clarke held Keith in contempt is only to draw attention to the blatant sarcasm in this reply of 27 October:

> The data upon which I formed my ideas of Farming is such as seldom disappoints me—my own observations. I purpose no agricultural speculation but merely intend converting the surplus time of the servants which for these some years back has been devoted to Drinking, Riot & debauchery, indispensable for the trade & fisheries to good Effect. However paradoxical farming on such a plan at Mingan may appear to you I feel confident it will be attended with important results to the general concern and I feel myself perfectly competent to get thro this without neglecting any of the other duties at Mingan.
>
> *I admire your candour in acknowledging your incompetency on this subject.* Leave those therefore who feel competent to follow the dictates of their own judgment. I have perfect confidence in the undertaking [emphasis added].[54]

Such a sneering disregard for a gentleman of the company was simply unheard of, at least in public and in official business correspondence. Perhaps Clarke had his own "rod in a pickle" for erstwhile Nor'Westers such as Keith and LaRocque. The fact that Keith was Clarke's superior only added to the temerity of this ill-advised retort. There is no question that Clarke was frustrated by Keith's obstructionism and felt that no matter how useful an idea might be, Keith would have reason not to act on it. In addition, it seemed that Keith was going out of his way to create problems for Clarke at Mingan. Every request Clarke made, from livestock to armament, was denied him. No doubt, in Clarke's mind, an administrator who would condescend to these measures warranted no respect, or even cursory consideration. Consequently, his language, which had formerly requested something, now demanded it. Keith was curtly directed to his own devices to ascertain the number of servants in the Mingan Seigniory. Of course, given the mood of the letter, it would have been difficult for Clarke to resist taking literally Keith's pro forma modesty with regard to his competency. Under ordinary circumstances, Clarke would have been out of place to write to a clerk in such a manner, much less a chief factor and his immediate superior.

Keith's reply, while delayed, was terse and quickly to the point:

> Herewith is letter to your address from Mr Secretary Smith dated 14th December 1831. Previous to receipt of which I was directed by the governor and committee to inform you "That they do not approve of your entering upon agricultural speculation at Mingan, as they consider that the People may be more profitably employed in the regular business of the concern."
>
> As a consequence of which we have not procured the two men on your requisition of last summer—Mr James McKenzie also lately informed me that he had used his endeavours, tho ineffectually to hire four young lads from 14 to 16 years of age as apprentices on the Terms you suggest in your letter, say for their food & clothing during a period of 5 to 7 years according to their age— [55]

Gone is the stylistic literary courtesy. There is nothing superfluous in this chilled and studied response to Clarke's intemperate letter of 27 October. Clarke was left with no room for argument. One did not argue with the governor and committee, although Clarke did try to plead his case in letters to them on 26 June and again on 28 July. The response came from London on 7 November 1832. The board left little doubt where Clarke stood in the matter:

> governor and committee having attentively considered not only the correspondence but your remarks thereon are of the opinion that you were not warranted in addressing Mr. Keith in the terms you did—that the expressions made use of in your communication with Mr. Keith were not only unprovoked and uncalled for but they were highly reprehensible, and the governor and committee entertaining the same feeling, which you have expressed in your letter of the 26th that the Mingan business can not possibly be transacted with satisfaction to either party whilst you remain at it, and

Mr. Keith as Superintendent of the Montreal Department (and to this the governor and committee would add with much benefit to the concern) have sent directions to Mr. Keith should he not already have placed some other [person] in charge of the District of Mingan to do so without delay.[56]

John Clarke appears to have been unaware that others did not share either the same sense of worth he felt for himself or the contempt he felt for Keith. To expect the board of directors of the Hudson's Bay Company to exonerate his behavior toward one of their most faithful and trustworthy proprietors would suggest total ignorance of his own reputation within the company's hierarchy as well as the esteem with which Mr. Keith was held by the committee in London.[57] Mr. Clarke had violated the most fastidiously held rules of propriety and then dared to suggest an "either he goes or I go" ultimatum in his letter to the governor and committee. Even the most naive would judge Clarke's career a terminal case. The chief factor gave up the management of Mingan Seigniory to Chief Trader Cumming in May of 1833 and proceeded to Montréal, where he and his household arrived on 3 June, taking up residence at the nearby village of Ste. Catherine's.[58]

Because Clarke could no longer remain in the Montréal Department, a place would have to be found for him elsewhere should he choose to remain in the company's service. Governor Simpson decided he was to be sent to the interior for the 1833/34 Outfit, should he not retire, and posted to Fort Good Hope on the Mackenzie River, where he could languish without the company of family or friends.[59] Keith had been instructed to provide him, should he miss the departure of the brigade, with "an extra canoe of voyageurs, canoe, provisions, and other usual appointments, suitable to Mr Clarke's ranking in the Service. . . ."[60] Even a gadfly with such a disagreeable reputation was not to be dishonored so long as he held rank as a chief factor in the service of the Hudson's Bay Company. However, Clarke declined his appointment to the interior, claiming ill health as his reason.[61]

John Clarke began negotiations with the governor and committee in October of 1833 for his retirement from the service. According to the Deed Poll, or the basic agreement between the company and its officers, upon retirement chief factors received one share equal to 1/84th of the profit on each outfit for seven years. The returns of an outfit included all the profits earned from the furs traded in a given fiscal year. Because these furs were not all sold at once but could be withheld from the market to be sold later, the actual income from an outfit frequently was not known for several years. Retired chief factors received one large payment in each of the seven years with adjustments added from time to time reflecting the sale of previously withheld furs. An estimate could be made of future profits, and earnings based on these estimates could be advanced to a retiring officer. Since such estimates were financially risky, the company was cautious in extending such a favor. Nevertheless, this is the line John Clarke pursued. He proposed the company buy out his retired interest but they declined, pointing out that the projected income from his retirement would not cover his present debts. Citing his delicate health, the chief factor asked the board to come "to a final adjustment of my Claims on them, and making immediate fair & honorable Proposals for my retired Interest to enable me to resign with close of outfit 1832."[62] The response must have been as shocking as it was disappointing for him:

> the governor and committee . . . do not admit you have any Claims on the company except the Interest you enjoy as a chief factor in the Fur Trade, and the way to insure to you the full value of that interest in retirement is to account to you for the Proceeds as they become due . . . and as any purchase founded in an anticipation of future profits must be uncertain and speculative, the governor and committee would much rather under the particular circumstances that have occurred, not become purchasers of your retired interest unless when you shall have retired you can show any way in which capital will be beneficial to you. Then, on your stating the Basis on which you are desirous to treat, the subject will be taken into consideration.[63]

Because Clarke was in the habit of overdrawing his account, the company had claims of *their own* on his active interest that had to be met before any negotiations for retirement could be entered into. However, they did agree to extend his leave of absence, originally granted only for 1833/34, for another year. Meanwhile, Mr. Clarke was told he had to await the full return on Outfit 1832 for any further consideration regarding his retirement, an inconvenience that could involve considerable delay. Finally, on 9 April 1834, the governor and committee did agree to accept Clarke's retirement from the service, but they did demur from purchasing his retired interest.[64]

Besides receiving the normal retirement allotment of 1/85 share in the profits for seven years, Clarke obtained a £1,500 loan from Governor Simpson at five percent interest per year using some railroad stocks he owned as collateral. With a positive balance finally showing in his account with them, the company now began paying some of Clarke's bills they had refused earlier to honor, most of which went to pay £1,000 to a single creditor.[65] Predictably, Clarke soon again faced cash flow problems and the company resumed denying him overdraft privileges.[66]

Rebuffed at every turn in his dealings with the company, John Clarke faced another setback of a personal nature in the summer of 1833. A carriage in which he was riding during an outing to his farm upset, injuring Clarke, his son, and the driver, and causing the death of his nephew.[67] This tragedy, coupled with the recent loss of two of his children and the setbacks he suffered in his business affairs, laid the groundwork for a series of misfortunes that haunted Clarke for the remaining twenty years of his life.

The Aftermath

The Spider turned him around about, and went into his den,

For well he knew the silly Fly would soon come back again:

So he wove a subtle web, in a little corner sly,

And set his table ready, to dine upon the Fly.

John Clarke had, indeed, been caught in that subtle web called Mingan where the master weaver, George Simpson, had drawn him into conflict with the dried spider in Lachine. Once into this "dismal den," Mary Howitt went on to write, "she ne'er came out again." Unlike Howitt's fly, Clarke did come out again but faced a life of forced retirement haunted by the specter of ever diminishing financial resources. The gadfly's end was to be a tortuous eighteen-year struggle for basic survival.

In the years after his retirement, John Clarke kept up a regular correspondence with the governor and committee in London, and with George Simpson, seeking redress for past claims on the fur trade, or asking for loans or extension of his credit on future earnings. His claims on the fur trade were found without merit and, with an exception here and there, his requests for loans and credit were denied. Lack of sufficient funds proved a continual and chronic millstone hanging around his neck. To his credit, in all his financial difficulties, Clarke did not neglect his children. In her paean-like memoir to her father, 74-year-old Adèle Clarke remembered nothing of these difficulties. To her, her childhood was filled with parties, high society, and affluence. There is nothing to belie the memory of a father who was brave, well-connected, and apparently well-off.[68]

Difficult as life was for Clarke after retirement, his chronic financial condition became acute after 1842 when his retirement income from the Hudson's Bay Company expired. At the close of accounts on 1 June 1842, John Clarke had a balance of £18.13.9ᵈ and he still owed a balance on a £500 loan earlier granted him by chief factor Angus Cameron.[69] The ensuing years saw Clarke requesting, begging, and even attempting to extort small loans from the now "Sir" George Simpson. The pathetic unraveling of the last ten years of John Clarke's life would suggest to the cynic that he lived too long.

Because of his chronic debt, Clarke lost his ploughing horses, horned cattle, and farm implements for want of £100 to pay a debt.[70] In 1846, when the mortgage holder on his farm, Beaver Lodge, threatened to foreclose for non-payment, Clarke asked Simpson to intercede, which he refused to do.[71] Clarke's son, Simon, requested of Simpson a small sum to enable him to take up his commission because his father had not the means.[72] By September of 1847, Clarke had been evicted from his home, Beaver Lodge, at Ste. Catherine's. The distraught Clarke wrote Simpson, blaming him for the "beggary of my family" as well as destroying all his prospects. In typical self-induced delusion, Clarke claimed responsibility for advancing Simpson "to the present position in society as well as the ample means that [he] now possess[es]."[73]

After such a recriminating letter, one would think Clarke would have done with Sir George. Humility, previously alien to Clarke's character, now served as his only recourse in his wretched life. Only a month after accusing Simpson of aiding and abetting his utter ruin, Clarke wrote once again, asking Sir George if he would intercede with the governor and committee in London in obtaining for him a small pension from the "Fund for the benefit of old retired Clerks."[74] For Clarke in 1831 in Mingan, to think of himself as a mere clerk would have been utterly mortifying. Now, sixteen years later and in complete destitution, it was all he had left. On 11 March 1848, Simpson wrote that he had met with success and that retired chief factor John Clarke would receive £50 per annum from the old retired clerks fund.[75] This would be Clarke's sole source of income until his death four and a half years later in 1852.

John Clarke's misery ended, for him, on 19 December 1852, but controversy followed him even into his grave. A Mrs. Brehant, who lived next door to the plot where Clarke was to be buried, objected to the proximity of the grave to her house. The remains had to be moved elsewhere.[76] Apparently, the first site was chosen to reduce the costs attendant to burial in the regular churchyard. Again Sir George was called upon, and in his final gesture to the man for whom he had his "rod in a pickle" for so long, the governor defrayed the expenses of his internment.[77] Clarke's widow, Marianne, who would be denied her request for a continuation of his pension, would survive him by 54 years.[78]

In a material sense, James Keith's subsequent career and retirement were as rewarding as John Clarke's were wanting. From his earliest days as an apprentice clerk in the fur trade, Keith had been an extremely prudent manager of his personal finances. Now that he had reached the upper echelon in the company, he was in a position to diversify his income by investing in stocks, debentures, and real estate. He had purchased £1,100 in Hudson's Bay Company stock in December of 1830 at 250 percent of its value. By 1835, the value of the stock had increased to 260 percent in addition to paying 12 to 15 percent in dividends and bonuses annually. With returns as handsome as this, Keith was induced to purchase £500 of additional stock in the company.[79] In addition to his Hudson's Bay Company stock, Keith invested in interest-paying personal loans, real estate, and stock in the Royal Steam Packet Company, the Canada Company, the Champlain and St. Lawrence Railway Company, and several Canadian banks.[80] Although never a spendthrift, the chief factor was able to afford a life of relative luxury. In 1834, he invested £2,189 of the company's money in the construction of a new headquarters at Lachine that doubled as his residence, for which he incurred no personal expense.[81] Keith was in the habit of ordering several hundred pounds worth of household items and clothing each year from London merchants and, in 1838, purchased a finely crafted British carriage and had it shipped to Lachine at his own expense for his personal use.[82] At the time of his retirement from the company in 1843, James Keith certainly earned his reputation as "about the most wealthy of the Gentlemen."[83]

With all his pecuniary success, James Keith's personal life was, in many ways, a contrast to that of John Clarke. Like Clarke, in 1831 Keith lost a daughter, Helen. She was the elder of Keith's two country children and, at the time of her death, had not yet reached her twentieth birthday, leaving behind three small children for her husband, Paul Pillon, to care for.[84] Although he was never close to Helen or her younger sister, Mary, James Keith nevertheless felt it his duty to provide for them. In 1827, Keith had purchased a farm for the Pillons and, after Helen's death, begrudgingly continued to provide financial support to Paul and the children up to the time of his retirement.[85] The younger daughter, Mary, was the recipient of Keith's attention throughout his life, although not with the same largesse as that given his Scottish relatives. Upon the marriage of Mary to Thomas Taylor, a postmaster in the service of the Hudson's Bay Company, Keith wrote the groom a letter of intended congratulations while emphasizing caution in expenditure and propriety in behavior. Thomas was informed that

> After such a union I would feel prompted both by duty & inclination to make you some immediate pecuniary accompaniment on account of my Daughter, but defer such pecuniary aid till you retire from the service or are in want of it, when it will be forthcoming[86]

By contrast, when Keith's Scottish niece married in 1839, he very generously sent her £1,000 as a wedding present.[87] Even though Keith felt legal responsibility for his two daughters and their children, he never seemed to receive the emotional satisfaction normally attendant to family ties.

James Keith's relationships with his colleagues in the fur trade continued unevenly. Along with the disagreeable correspondence with John Clarke, Keith exchanged unpleasantries with Alexander Fisher, Joseph LaRocque, François Antoine LaRocque, and even Governor George Simpson himself.[88] The difficulties with Simpson concerned the governor's cousin Alexander Simpson, who had been a clerk at Lachine since 1828. The causes of the friction between the chief factor and the impudent Alexander are not clear. In writing to his friend, chief factor J. G. McTavish at Moose Factory, Governor Simpson imputed the conflict as rooted in the young man looking "tenderly on one of the maid servants."[89] In none of Keith's letters to Governor Simpson, however, did he mention anything of the sort. The chief factor's complaints of Alexander included repeated intoxication, insolence, and assault on one of the company's servants; it did not include sexual advances.[90] Whatever the cause, in August of 1834, chief factor Keith sent young Simpson to Moose Factory, a transfer of which the governor did not approve. Keith was so upset he threatened to resign rather than endure the company of Alexander at Lachine. Alarmed that should the chief factor depart Lachine for any length of time the company's business would be impaired, Governor Simpson ordered Keith to send clerk George Gladman to Moose and instruct Alexander to proceed to Lachine without delay to take his place.[91] By April of 1835, however, Keith's pique had been mollified, and his threat to resign receded into the background. The emotionality of the affair left him depressed, and to relieve the anxiety over the near break with Governor Simpson, Keith decided to take a furlough to Europe for the ensuing year. His resolve concerning Alexander remained firm, however. Despite orders to the contrary, Keith did not order Alexander Simpson to Lachine but, instead, placed the company's affairs there in the hands of George Gladman.[92]

The enmity between James Keith and Alexander Simpson may not have been entirely due to impropriety on the part of the young clerk. Keith tended to wear his feelings on his sleeve and was easily offended at the mere hint of a slight or of a breach in etiquette. On at least one other occasion, the long friendship between Keith and Governor Simpson nearly terminated because of a perceived slight. When Keith retired in 1843, he returned to Scotland to settle down. He left a few odds and ends at Lachine on his departure that he requested be disposed of, including a carriage and harness for which he had paid £150 several years previous. His instructions were to dispose of the carriage and harness "at whatever price they may fetch." Simpson did his best to sell the items at auction, but the highest offer he got was £95, a figure he considered too low and so withdrew them. Keith considered this a flagrant disregard of his instructions and complained that it seemed to be a case of "out of sight, out of mind."[93] It was not the money, he claimed, but the idea that a trust he had placed in a supposed friend had been violated. The correspondence between Keith and the governor may have come to an end had not Simpson informed his friend a week after Keith's last indignant epistle that the retired chief factor was to receive a testimonial of silver plate subscribed to by 21 of his colleagues in the fur trade as a token of their thanks for his many years attending to their private accounts. Governor George Simpson had organized the subscription, which raised over £200, and was, himself, responsible for purchasing the plate.

Keith inherited from Governor Simpson the management of the private accounts of many officers and clerks in the Hudson's Bay Company. This "private agency" began in 1827 when Simpson received moneys from the estate of Thain, McGillivrays and company for settling accounts with past associates of the North West Company. Because the governor's demanding schedule took him away from Lachine for long periods of time, this management soon devolved upon chief factor James Keith. Keith insisted that his service in this regard be gratuitous to the point of taking umbrage if someone offered to pay. His investments in this private agency soon transcended those of the original beneficiaries, and he found himself engulfed with the time-consuming occupation of managing the affairs of over forty officers and clerks in the company. For this he sought only thanks, a payment he felt was rarely extended. It must have been especially gratifying, then, to receive the silver plate from about half of those who benefited from his services.[94]

James Keith was not mean-spirited nor particularly parsimonious. Although he had a penchant for rubbing people the wrong way, it was never intentional. The dourness so easily attributable to him and his petty peevishness may have been the result of congenital depression. He called it "dyspepsia," a complaint from which he suffered nearly his entire life.[95] The physical manifestation of his illness was an inability to digest food properly, a condition that occurred with increasing frequency toward the end of his life. The mental manifestation of his illness was depression. Throughout his personal correspondence (but *never* alluded to in business letters) mention is made of his suffering from the "blues." On one occasion, Keith's doctor prescribed blood letting and leeches on the abdomen, a treatment that was almost more lethal than the disease.[96] His marriage late in life provided a spark of happiness for a time, but his old complaints soon returned. On 27 January 1851, seven and a half years after his retirement from the service of the Hudson's Bay Company, James Keith died at his home at 101 Crown Street, Aberdeen, Scotland. "His physicians declared that he died of sheer debility—the consequence of his stomach absolutely refusing and nauseating all kinds of nourishing or strengthening food."[97]

Conclusion

Mary Howitt's poem "The Spider and the Fly" evokes only an imperfect metaphor of the Keith-Clarke confrontation. While John Clarke fell into a trap that ended his career with the Hudson's Bay Company, it was not one set by James Keith. Whatever his faults, Keith never connived to bring about the fall of chief factor John Clarke, nor would it have been in his character to have done so. He was simply the web by which the real spider in this episode, George Simpson, was able to induce John Clarke to become entangled.

Simpson had his "rod in a pickle" for Clarke from the beginning of their acquaintance. The governor did not suffer well those whose egos matched his own and Clarke's sense of self importance was exceeded by few in the fur trade. Simpson was the consummate organization man who insisted that those under his superintendence subordinate personal considerations to those of the company. The interests of the Hudson's Bay Company must always come first, a priority not always acceded to by John Clarke. Although his first impression was favorable, the governor's good opinion did not survive Clarke's willingness to provide for the comfort of his family at the expense of attending personally to company business, his abrasiveness with the governor and settlers of Red River, or his innovating venture into raising cattle at Swan River. It was this latter incident that prompted Simpson to initiate the plot that would lead to "the ruin & damnation of the fellow."

All his maneuvering would not have been necessary had George Simpson the freedom to act as he pleased. Had it been up to him, the governor would not have admitted John Clarke into the new Hudson's Bay Company in 1821 in the first place. Had he the prerogative, Simpson would have found reason to dismiss Clarke after 1821, but the Deed Poll, which served as the basic agreement between the company and its officers, limited his discretion. It made it extremely difficult to dismiss a chief factor or a chief trader even for good cause. Action could only be initiated against an officer by the governor in *Council*. Twelve chief factors must be present, two-thirds of whom must vote to expel. A final veto was held by the governor and committee in London.[98] No chief factor or chief trader was ever removed from the company's service under this provision of the 1821 Deed Poll.

One month before the governor and committee agreed to the conditions of John Clarke's retirement in 1834, a second Deed Poll was written in which provisions for removing a commissioned officer from the company's service were drastically liberalized. Instead of twelve chief factors, only three need be present at Council to consider removing a colleague from the concern. Only two need assent to it. In the 1821 Deed Poll, cause for charges of removal were restricted to intoxication or wanton misuse of the company's property. Under the 1834 rules, removal of an officer could be considered for misconduct or misbehavior that resulted in the injury of the trade in any manner. Certainly, many incidents in John Clarke's career would have easily fallen under this broad, vaguely worded provision. As a final coup de grâce, the Deed Poll of 1834 provided that the governor and committee would be at liberty at any time upon or after 1 June 1839 to place any chief factor or chief trader on the retirement list *without the necessity of stating cause*.[99] Never again would the company or its North American governor be saddled with the likes of a John Clarke.

Whether or not the checkered career of John Clarke had anything to do with the liberalized dismissal provisions of the 1834 Deed Poll can only be conjectured. It is not far-fetched, however, to assume that his case, so recently before the governor and committee, may have had some influence on their deliberations.

This series of events, then, provided the backdrop for the Keith-Clarke confrontation. In requesting an appointment to the Montréal Department, Clarke, no doubt, had in mind a sinecure much like that enjoyed by J. G. McTavish at Lake of Two Mountains. Instead, he found himself posted to the most remote and one of the less significant districts in the department. The governor knew this would offend Clarke's vanity, as would finding himself answerable to a company officer who was essentially a replica of George Simpson in miniature. The "ruin and damnation" of John Clarke was nearly two years in the making but, as Simpson anticipated, effectively removed him from the service of the Hudson's Bay Company. The spider had finally caught his fly.

Notes

1. William H. White Jr., *Organization Man* (Garden City, N. Y.: Doubleday Anchor, 1957), 3–7.

2. W. Kaye Lamb, ed., *Sixteen Years in the Indian Country: The Journal of Daniel Williams Harmon 1800–1816* (Toronto: Macmillan of Canada, 1957), 124. For reference to Clarke's lack of formal education, see Robert F. Jones, ed., *Astorian Adventure: The Journal of Alfred Seton 1811–1815* (New York: Fordham University Press, 1993), 83.

3. George Keith to Roderick MacKenzie, 21 January 1811, *Les bourgeois de la Compagnie du Nord-Ouest*, ed. L. R. Masson, 2 vols. (New York: Antiquarian Press, 1960), 2:93.

4. Two writers have suggested a possible family link between John Jacob Astor and John Clarke through the maternal line, although with no more apparent evidence than the identity of the mother's surname with the village from whence Astor originated. See W. Kaye Lamb, ed., *Journal of a Voyage on the North West Coast of North America during the Years 1811, 1812, 1813 and 1814 by Gabriel Franchère* (Toronto: Champlain Society, 1969), 112, and Jennifer S. H. Brown, "John Clarke," *Dictionary of Canadian Biography* [hereafter *DCB*] 13 vols. (Toronto: University of Toronto Press, 1985), 8:158.

5. George Keith to Roderick MacKenzie, 21 January 1811, Masson, *Les bourgeois*, 2:94.

6. Alexander Ross, *Adventures of the First Settlers on the Oregon or Columbia River, 1810–1813* (Lincoln: University of Nebraska Press, 1986), 195.

7. Jones, *Astorian Adventure*, 37, 71, 82.

8. Ross, *Adventures of the First Settlers*, 221.

9. Ross Cox, *Adventures on the Columbia River, Including the Narrative of a Residence of Six Years on the Western Side of the Rocky Mountains,* 2 vols. (London: Henry Colburn and Richard Bentley, 1831), 1:80–81.

10. If Adèle Clarke is to be believed, Astor thought so much of John Clarke after his return from the Columbia that he had a portrait painted of him and presented it to John's father. Adèle Clarke, *Old Montréal: John Clarke, his Adventures, Friends and Family* (Montréal: Herald Publishing, 1906), frontispiece. Colin Robertson engaged Clarke for the 1815 Athabasca campaign partly on Astor's good opinion of him. See E. E. Rich, ed., *Colin Robertson's Correspondence Book, September 1817 to September 1822* (London: Hudson's Bay Record Society, 1939), lxii–lxiii.

11. Rich, *Colin Robertson's Correspondence Book*, lxiii.

12. Arthur S. Morton, *A History of the Canadian West to 1870–71* (Toronto: Thomas Nelson and Sons, n.d.), 606.

13. George Keith to Thomas Thain, quoted in Morton, *A History*, 606.

14. George Keith to Roderick MacKenzie, 25 May 1817, Masson, *Les bourgeois*, 2:131.

15. E. E. Rich, ed., *Simpson's Athabasca Journal and Report, 1820–21* (London: Hudson's Bay Record Society, 1938), 324.

16. Glyndwr Williams, ed., *Hudson's Bay Miscellany, 1670–1870* (Winnipeg: Hudson's Bay Record Society, 1975), 172.

17. John S. Galbraith, *The Little Emperor: Governor Simpson of the Hudson's Bay Company* (Toronto: Macmillan of Canada, 1976), 40.

18. Winnipeg, Manitoba, Hudson's Bay Company Archives [hereafter HBCA], A.6/20, fo. 109.

19. Morton, *A History*, 629.

20. Ibid., 652–53.

21. Ibid., 655.

22. Frederick Merk, ed., *Fur Trade and Empire*, rev. ed. (Cambridge, Mass.: Harvard University Press, 1968), 11.

23. Galbraith, *Little Emperor*, 78.

24. Williams, *Miscellany*, 171–72.

25. Allan McDonell to James Hargrave, 22 April 1830, *The Hargrave Correspondence 1821–1843*, ed. G. P. de T. Glazebrook (Toronto: Champlain Society, 1938), 50.

26. Alexander Simpson, *The Life and Travels of Thomas Simpson, The Arctic Discoverer* (London: Richard Bentley, 1845), 84.

27. HBCA, B.135/c/2, fo. 73d.

28. Williams, *Miscellany*, 172.

29. Margaret A. McLeod, ed., *The Letters of Letitia Hargrave* (Toronto: Champlain Society, 1947), 156. Keith's relative wealth may have been overestimated by Letitia Hargrave. While he certainly was comfortably well-off, Keith's estate was valued at about £20,000 upon his death, far short of, say, George Simpson's, whose net worth exceeded £100,000. Galbraith, *Little Emperor*, 186.

30. Alexander Ross, *The Fur Hunters of the Far West*, Kenneth A. Spaulding, ed. (Norman: University of Oklahoma Press, 1956), 58, 61, 69–70, 77.

31. Ibid., 70.

32. Hubert Howe Bancroft, *History of the Northwest Coast*, 2 vols. (New York: Bancroft company, n.d.), 2:287; Morton, *A History*, 618; John S. Galbraith, *The Hudson's Bay Company as an Imperial Factor, 1821–1869* (Berkeley: University of California Press, 1957), 81; William H. Goetzmann, *Exploration and Empire* (New York: Vintage, 1966), 83–86; Murray Morgan, *Puget's Sound: A Narrative of Early Tacoma and the Southern Puget Sound* (Seattle: University of Washington Press, 1979), 19.

33. Keith increased the returns in beaver pelts in the Fort George area from 4,240 in 1816 to 5,592 in 1821. In addition, he diversified the company's activities along the coast by engaging in trade with the Russians and the Spanish. See H. Lloyd Keith, University of Winnipeg, Centre for Rupert's Land Studies, "The North West Company's 'Adventure to the Columbia:' A Reassessment of Financial Failure," December 1989, 13–14.

34. Alexander Caulfield Anderson, "Life at Lachine," Madge Wolfenden, ed., *The Beaver*, June 1952, 30.

35. Ibid., 31.

36. Simpson, *Life and Travels*, 84.

37. John Siveright to James Hargrave, 25 April 1832, in Glazebrook, *Hargrave Correspondence*, 91.

38. Ross, *Fur Hunters*, 84.

39. HBCA, B.135/c/2, fo. 138.

40. HBCA, A.6/22, fos. 280–82.

41. HBCA, A.6/22, fos. 301–2.

42. Williams, *Miscellany*, 177.

43. HBCA, B.135/c/2, fo. 69.

44. HBCA, A.6/22, fo. 234.

45. Keith to Clarke, 4 June 1831, HBCA, Copy No. 146.

46. HBCA, B.134/c/10, fo. 273; B.134/c/11, fo. 9. Clarke had left his son, Simon, in school in Montréal.

47. HBCA, B.134/c/10, fos. 283, 369. Besides Clarke, his family, servants, and baggage, space aboard the schooner had to be found for the missionary on his way to Mingan to attend to the spiritual needs of the Natives.

48. Ruth McKenzie, ed., *The St. Lawrence Survey Journals of Captain Henry Wolsey Bayfield 1829–1853* (Toronto: Champlain Society, 1984), 140. See also, Glazebrook, *Hargrave Correspondence*, 90.

49. Clarke to Keith, 9 August 1831, HBCA, Copy No. 146.

50. HBCA, B.134/c/1, fo. 13d.

51. Clarke to Keith, 9 August 1831, HBCA, Copy No. 146.

52. Cuthbert Cumming to James Hargrave, [1835], in Glazebrook, *Hargrave Correspondence*, 218.

53. Keith to Clarke, 7 October 1831, HBCA, Copy No. 146.

54. Clarke to Keith, 27 October 1831, HBCA, Copy No. 146.

55. Keith to Clarke, 7 May 1832, HBCA, Copy No. 146. See HBCA, B.134/c/12, fo. 226 for reference to Smith's letter.

56. HBCA, A.6/22, fos. 279–80.

57. In the midst of the controversy with chief factor John Clarke, the governor and committee in London found time to inform George Simpson that "We have been in such constant and regular communication with chief factor Keith on the affairs of the Montréal department, that we have little to say at present respecting them beyond the expression of our entire satisfaction with the measures that have been adopted bringing them into a well organized state." HBCA, A.6/23, fo. 129.

58. HBCA, B.134/c/18, fos. 243, 306.

59. HBCA, B.134/x/17, fos. 32–32d.

60. HBCA, A.6/22, fo. 301.

61. HBCA, A.6/23, fo. 55, 126.

62. HBCA, A.6/22, fos. 279–80.

63. Ibid.

64. HBCA, A.6/23, fos. 69–70, 126, 145.

65. Ibid., 148–49.

66. Ibid., 167, 200, 277–78. Although little is known of Clarke's financial affairs prior to 1821, he does appear to have been a poor manager of money throughout his career. One of the questionable assets of the bankrupt McGillivrays, Thain and company in 1825 was a note of an unspecified sum from John Clarke for which he had used real estate as collateral. HBCA, B.134/c/2, fo. 27. Among the list of debtors in a sketch of the Hudson's Bay Company's officers' balances in February of 1828, John Clarke is overdrawn for that outfit by some £120.__.5. HBCA, B.134/c/3, fo. 2.

67. J. D. Cameron to James Hargrave, 2 December 1833, in Glazebrook, *Hargrave Correspondence*, 116.

68. Clarke, *Old Montréal*, 9–47.

69. HBCA, A.11/28, fo. 129.

70. HBCA, D.5/15, fo. 421d.

71. HBCA, D.5/17, fos. 222–23.

72. HBCA, D.5/18, fos. 435–35d.

73. HBCA, D.5/20, fos. 243–44.

74. Ibid., 356–56d.

75. HBCA, D.4/37, fo. 44.

76. HBCA, D.5/35, fos. 351–51d, 352a–52b.

77. HBCA, A.6/30, fo. 97.

78. Clarke, *Old Montreal*, 14.

79. James Keith to Adam Macnider and Charles Tait, 16 December 1830, 18 December 1830, and James Keith to William Smith, 31 January 1835, Aberdeen, Scotland, University of Aberdeen [hereafter UA], Keith Papers, MSS (Davidson and Garden) 2769/I/57/3. James Keith to William Smith, 11 May 1835 and 30 July 1835, UA, Keith Papers, 2769/I/57/1, 19–20 of letterbook.

80. James Keith to William Smith, 13 February 1840, UA, Keith Papers, 2769/I/57/1, 46 of letterbook. "Stock represented by James Keith to 12 September 1843," UA, Keith Papers, 2769/I/57/3.

81. HBCA, D.4/127, fos. 23–24.

82. James Keith to Duncan Finlayson, 12 August 1838, UA, Keith Papers, 2769/I/57/1, 34 of letterbook.

83. McLeod, *Letitia Hargrave*, 156.

84. Ottawa, Ontario, National Archives of Canada [hereafter NAC], Keith Papers, Microfilm A–676, B–2: Memorandum of Correspondence, Private, 1806–50.

85. HBCA, D.5/24, fo. 455; NAC, Keith Papers, B–4: Private letterbook, 1828–1832.

86. James Keith to Thomas Taylor, 17 April 1831, UA, Keith Papers, 2769/I/57/4.

87. James Keith to William Smith, 9 September 1839 and James Keith to Mrs Dr Henry Milne, Lachine, 9 September 1839, UA, Keith Papers, 2769/I/57/1, 41 of letterbook.

88. James Keith to Joseph LaRocque, 12 March 1830; James Keith to Alexander Fisher, 16 March 1831 and 19 March 1832; James Keith to François Antoine LaRocque, 9 August 1832, UA, Keith Papers, 2769/I/57/4. Joseph LaRocque to George Simpson, April 1831, HBCA, D.4/125, fos. 50d–51.

89. HBCA, B.135/c/2, fo. 138. Judging from A. C. Anderson's description of the female servants at Lachine, the two "antiquated serving maids" were not likely to attract the amorous attention of any of the clerks. Anderson, "Life at Lachine," 30. Jennifer Brown, in her detailed study of fur trade company families found no reason to suggest sexual innuendo as reason for Alexander Simpson's banishment to Moose Factory. Jennifer S. H. Brown, *Strangers in Blood: Fur Trade Company Families in Indian Country* (Vancouver: University of British Columbia Press, 1980), 122–23.

90. James Keith to George Simpson, 7 August 1834, 18 November 1834, 20 April 1835, UA, Keith Papers, 2769/I/57/1, 8–9, 12–14, 16–17 of letterbook.

91. HBCA, D.4/21, fos. 39d–40.

92. James Keith to George Simpson, 20 April 1835, UA, Keith Papers, 2769/I/57/1, 16–17 of letterbook.

93. James Keith to George Simpson, 14 October 1844, HBCA, D.5/12, fos. 403–3d. James Keith to George Simpson, 22 October 1844, HBCA, D.5/12, fos. 406–8.

94. James Keith to George Simpson, Aberdeen, 29 October 1844, HBCA, D.5/12, fos. 423–23d; James Keith to William Smith, 3 August 1833 and James Keith to the governor and committee, 13 March 1834, UA, Keith Papers, 2769/I/57/1, 1–6 of letterbook. For a list of private accounts managed by James Keith to September of 1830, see NAC, Keith Papers, B–4: Private Letter Book, 1828–32. In a memorandum to the letter of thanks that Keith wrote to Governor Simpson, names of the first twenty subscribers were listed (one was added later) as well as four more who were solicited but failed to respond. James Keith to George Simpson, Aberdeen, 17 February 1845, UA, Keith Papers, 2769/I/57/2 and 2769/I/57/1, 109–10 of letterbook.

95. James Keith to George Simpson, 1 October 1850, HBCA, D.5/29, fos. 2–2d.

96. James Keith to George Simpson, 23 August 1849, HBCA, D.5/25, fos. 559–59d.

97. George Keith to Donald Ross, 6 March 1851, Public Archives of British Columbia, Add. MSS 635, A–E–R73–K26, File 70.

98. E. E. Rich, *The History of the Hudson's Bay Company 1670–1870* (London: Hudson's Bay Record Society, 1959), 407.

99. UA, Keith Papers, 2769/I/57/3.

Gwyneth Hoyle | # The Search for Silver: Johan Beetz and the Birth of the Fox-Breeding Industry

JOHAN BEETZ, a Belgian, came to the north shore of the St. Lawrence in 1897 for sport and chose to make it his home. His wealthy European background gave him an understanding of the value of furs, at a time when the market for luxury furs had increased dramatically. The peace and prosperity of the two decades at the turn of the twentieth century fueled the economies of Europe and North America. Consumer demand increased dramatically when a new style of fur coat was introduced in Paris in the 1890s. As an innovation, fur was handled as cloth, with the fur to the outside, and this created a surge in the market.[1] Luxury furs, such as silver fox, could no longer be supplied in sufficient quantities by the normal methods of trapping.[2] In response to the economic climate, Johan Beetz became a pioneer in the breeding of silver foxes.

Through his close association with the people of the area Johan Beetz had a brief but significant influence on the price of silver-fox pelts. In the short period that Beetz worked for Revillon Frères he raised the prices paid to trappers to reflect the higher European market values. The increased prices encouraged various attempts to breed these animals in captivity, and Beetz, because of his background in animal husbandry, was one of the more scientific fox breeders.

Silver is a rare but naturally occurring color phase of the common red fox, or *Vulpes vulpes*. Three color phases, red, black or silver, and cross—a mixture of black and red—can all occur in the same litter.[3] There is some black pigment in the color components of all common foxes. On red foxes it occurs on the legs, on the backs of the ears, and in a scattering of guard hairs on the back. The black guard hairs on the back of the cross fox are more pronounced and they extend across the shoulders in the form of a cross. Cross foxes constitute 20 to 44 percent of the red fox population. In the rarest color phase, black or silver, the fox is entirely black, except for a white tip on the tail, and this phase

315

forms 2 to 17 percent of the population.[4] White tips on the guard hairs give
the black fox a frosted or silver appearance which can vary from very dark to
very light. The relative rarity of black foxes combined with the beauty of the
markings determines the premium price that they command on the market.

Average Price of Silver Fox Pelts

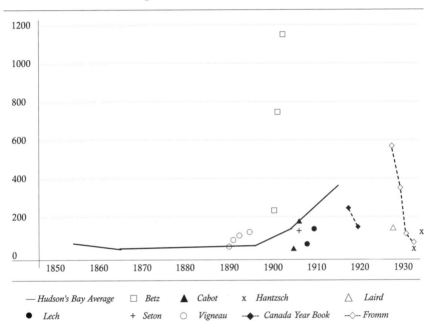

The Hudson's Bay Company's annual auction of pelts in London set the
tariff that guided the company's post managers in the prices they could pay
trappers the following year. The tariffs reflected the price on the world market but necessarily lagged behind by a year or more. Based on the average
price of each type of pelt, they did not take into account pelts of exceptional
quality or beauty of markings. William Brooks Cabot, the Labrador explorer,
has a story that illustrates the strict adherence to rules by the Hudson's Bay
post managers: "An Eskimo had brought a silver fox skin to Hopedale and
was offered $60. for it. He could get a good deal more at Davis Inlet . . .
begged hard to be allowed to sell it there. But he was not allowed to under
penalty of being cut off from all store privileges. At Nain they had 25 silvers
last year (1905) . . . one brought $180."[5] Other anecdotal evidence of the price

of silver-fox pelts from fur-traders' diaries, and writers such as Ernest Thompson Seton, show the prices paid to trappers to be well within the statistical limits of the average price, as illustrated in figure 1.[6] The prices paid by Johan Beetz on the north shore of the St. Lawrence in the early years of this century were the exception and were unusually high, as will be detailed later in this text.

While the north shore of the St. Lawrence is on the shipping route from Canada to Europe, it is also remote and isolated. The area consists of a narrow littoral, a low coastal plain rising in rounded, forested hills to as much as 2,000 feet as it reaches the Labrador Plateau.[7] The many turbulent rivers which flow out of this vast plateau form harbors wherever they pierce the

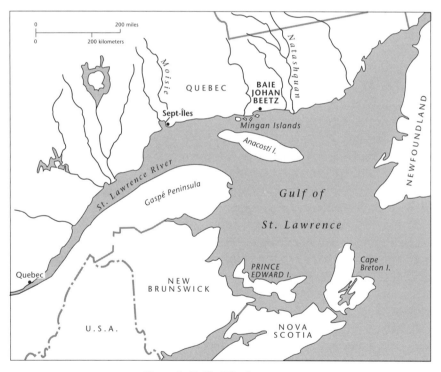

Figure 2. **Gulf of St. Lawrence.**

coastal plain. The area has long been home to the Innu people, also known as the Montagnais. Traditionally they wintered and hunted in small bands in the upland forests and on the plateau, coming down the rivers to gather in larger groups at the coast during the short summer. The arrival of Europeans and the establishment of trading posts, whether on the coast or in the interior, affected their seasonal migrations.[8]

Near the center of the region is the village of Mingan, more than 600 kilometers east of Quebec City. It was the headquarters of the original seigneury, the Terre-ferme de Mingan, granted to François Bissot in 1661. As the name implies it was closed to outside traders. The seigneury lay within the coastal plain, stretching from west of the mouth of the Moisie River east to Blanc Sablon. It contained an area of 800,000 arpents, or about 1,050 square miles, with poor soil for farming but rich in furs and fish. Small seasonal fishing stations operated along the shore with the only permanent settlement being at Blanc Sablon. The first seigneury, associated also with Louis Jolliet, was one of the oldest continuously operated trading posts in the country. It was leased in 1803 to the North West Company, and when that lease expired in 1825, to the Hudson's Bay Company, who operated there until the recent past.[9]

The seigneurial system was legislated out of existence in 1854. By then small fishing settlements had evolved at the mouths of the rivers, the spawning grounds for large schools of salmon. Some of the settlers turned to trapping on the slopes of the plateau to supplement their livelihoods.

Life at the Hudson's Bay post at Mingan was less isolated than at almost any other northern post. Ships of all sizes traveled along the coast, and ocean liners from Quebec City to Europe passed in the channel between Anticosti Island and the mainland. Small coastal boats and yachts, sailing in both directions, routinely called at Mingan, one of the best harbors on the coast. From the end of November to mid-April the port was closed to shipping, but there were monthly mail deliveries by dog team. After 1880 the telegraph line arrived, advancing forty miles farther down the coast each year.

The post journal from 1898–1910 recorded the pattern of seasonal life at Mingan. The breakup of the ice in the spring, the start of the shipping season, duck hunting on the Mingan Islands, the arrival of the salmon in the river, wild strawberry picking and haying on the islands, and the last flurry of shipping before winter set in were annual events. The Innu arrived from their hunting grounds throughout the spring and occupied houses built by the Hudson's Bay Company. They left for the interior uplands late in August, but returned at Christmas for a short time. While shipping brought the world to his wharf, the trader's life was confined to a ten-mile radius, west to Long

Point, north up the Mingan River, east to Eskimo Point, and south to the Mingan Islands. The salmon-fishing season attracted sportsmen, and for a few weeks the post manager hobnobbed with lords and judges:

> June 24. Mr. Fitch's yacht arrived from Gaspe to go to Romaine.
> Forty-six plus forty-four salmon taken.
>
> June 25. Watched Lord Stavordale fishing at the falls.
>
> June 26. Mr. Hills yacht is back.[10]

C. J. Black, the post manager in 1901, seemed to prefer these visitors to the Innu, and he consistently reported that the latter had poor returns from their traplines:

> August 31. Indians—all but two families—left. All feel discouraged as now impossible for them to reach their usual hunting grounds and will all be bunched together near the land-wash where fur-bearing animals are rare and provisions scarce. Glad to see them off—nothing but hard work and worry for me since April. With sick Indians, large advances and poor prospects, this has been the most wretched summer of my life.[11]

The problems of Mr. Black's wretched summer arose partially from the increasingly fierce competition for furs. With its relatively easy access to Quebec City, the Mingan post always had competition from individual free-traders:

> April 26. Boudreau, a trader from Moisie, arrived this a.m. anchoring along-side the Indian houses. It seems he is doing a little business. Some Indians are roaring drunk. I did not do much with Indians today although I offered good prices—the other fellow has apparently over bid me.[12]

In 1901 the competition escalated following the entry of Johan Beetz into the local fur trade. For a time Mr. Black, the Hudson's Bay manager, became a great deal more active, traveling along the coast in winter in both directions to collect furs when he had previously waited at the post for the furs to come to him. He summed up his discontent at the end of 1903:

> Dec. 31. The year is going out nicely but to me it has been the shabbiest year of my life, wife and family sick in hospital for almost 12 months, broke my collar bone and dislocated muscles of my right arm and shoulder. [This was on a fur-gathering trip when he fell from a cliff near the Romaine River.] Business was most contrary—large debts, poor hunts and furious competition.[13]

An unusual set of circumstances brought Johan Beetz to the north shore in 1897. The details of his life are taken from the biography written by two of his children.[14] Born in 1874 into a wealthy family in Belgium, he lived in a succession of châteaux, set in beautiful grounds with their own woods, where hunting parties were a regular feature of the social year. His father died when Johan was two years old, but his mother, trained as a lawyer, remarried an English major who encouraged Johan in all forms of sport, particularly hunting and fishing. His stepfather's hobby was fish-culture, his mother bred pedigree animals on their farm, and Johan became more and more interested in the development of this science. At the University of Louvain he studied natural science, chemistry, and medicine, both human and veterinary, with a special interest in anatomy. By the time he graduated at the age of 21, Beetz had been on a three-month safari in the Belgian Congo, and was engaged to be married to a childhood friend.

With the sudden death of his fiancée, Beetz was plunged into a deep depression and made plans to return to Africa for an entire year. While he was at Thomas Cook's travel agency finalizing these plans, his mother arranged for him to meet a man with property for sale on the north shore of the St. Lawrence. The property consisted of several acres and a small house and the price was only $500. For a Belgian in 1897, the location was almost as exotic as the Belgian Congo, the climate was healthier and it was a paradise for hunting and fishing. Very quickly Johan Beetz reversed his plans and within two weeks boarded a ship for Quebec to take possession of the property at Piastre Baie, just east of Mingan.

In the ship's dining room one of Beetz's table companions was a long-established Quebec furrier, Jean-Baptiste Laliberté, whose fur business still flourishes in Quebec City. These two became good shipboard friends, and on their arrival in Canada M. Laliberté was invaluable in providing Beetz with needed references at the bank and at customs. In addition, he introduced the sportsman and hunter to the commercial world of furs.

At Piastre Baie, with two guides, arranged by the previous owner of the property, Beetz threw himself into the sporting life. He admired the simplicity and resourcefulness of the local people and seems to have gained acceptance in the village. At the Tanguay home, which housed the general store, the post office, and the telegraph office, he was a frequent visitor. The young, recently bereaved bachelor found himself more and more attracted to the older daughter of the family. After eight months at Piastre Baie, he returned to Europe to discuss with his parents his forthcoming marriage to Adéla Tanguay and his intention to remain in Canada. He took with him a fine collection of furs he had trapped, which included fifteen black foxes, one of them beautifully marked with white on its four paws and half its tail. He also took furs that he had bought from trappers in the village, to seek a fair price for them on the European markets.

Beetz, from a society where furs were a consumer commodity, recognized that the North Shore trappers were getting only a fraction of the value of their pelts from the Hudson's Bay Company or itinerant free traders. Having been accepted into a local family, Beetz identified closely with the people of the village and had a stake in seeing that they received full value for their furs. Although the people had a good subsistence living from hunting and fishing, money was very scarce. For example, in 1898 the Hudson's Bay Company hired a laborer for $12 a month without board, and the following year hired a man and his wife for $162 a year with board.[15]

Beetz's marriage to Adéla took place on his return to Piastre Baie in the fall of 1898. The following year he replaced the small original house on the property with a large home, built on the smooth rock overlooking the harbor. Beetz decorated the house throughout with paintings and carvings of flora and fauna on the doors and wood paneling.[16] While building an active life on the North Shore, Johan Beetz maintained close connections to his home in Belgium. In 1900 he took Adéla to meet his family.

Visiting family and friends was not the only reason to return to Europe. Beetz had other plans, as was observed by the local lighthouse keeper. From his vantage point on Île au Perroquet, the outermost of the Mingan Islands, Placide Vigneau recorded all that was happening in the area in his daily journal.[17] In 1900 he commented:

> The intention of M. Johan Beetz is to buy the finest foxes that he can find for the Universal Exposition of Paris which takes place in the summer of 1900. All other buyers have been obliged to raise their prices, but in spite of that, they buy little. M. Johan Beetz has raised the prices and affected those of all the other fur-dealers in the same ratio. It is a veritable manna for the North Shore that finally the hunters receive the true value of their furs which they have such pains to procure. It would be a blessing of heaven if a man in the style of Mr. Beetz could come to make known also the price of fish and oil.[18]

While in Paris, Johan Beetz made contact with the French fur company of Revillon Frères, which was in the process of opening an office in Montreal. They had already opened a warehouse in Edmonton in 1899 in their first move into the Canadian fur trade. Their agent in Montreal, Paul d'Aigneaux, enlisted Johan Beetz as a fur buyer for Revillon on the North Shore. With a common bond in their aristocratic European background, Beetz and d'Aigneaux formed a life long friendship.[19] In 1902 Madame Marquise d'Aigneaux stayed at the Beetz home in Piastre Baie, waiting for her husband to return from a fur-buying trip farther down the coast.[20]

The prices paid for silver-fox pelts increased tenfold on the North Shore during the years 1900–1903. The journal entry of Placide Vigneau for 10 January 1900 foreshadowed the rising prices:

> Louis Cumming and William Lebrun, Eskimo Point have sold a silver fox pelt to Mr. Johan Beetz for the sum of $225. There has never been paid such a high price for a silver black fox. For a dozen years, some very beautiful foxes have been sold for $100 a pelt, but never more. The ordinary price for the finest silver black fox has always been from $60 to $80 a pelt, very rarely $90.[21]

Then on 27 February of the same year:

> It is known that Mr. Johan Beetz came to buy from Hippolyte Chavary at Natashquan post, a pelt of silver black fox for which he paid $720. It is one of the most beautiful foxes that has been taken on the North Shore, but it is also the most expensive.[22]

By 1903, Vigneau reported:

> Charles Maloney from Mingan took a magnificent silver fox which has been sold, January 6, 1903, to Mr. Black of the Hudson's Bay Company for $950. It is the highest price ever obtained for a fox pelt on the North Shore. Mr. Johan Beetz arrived the same day at Mingan and bought back this same pelt from Mr. Black for the sum of $1,150.[23]

The Hudson's Bay Company and Revillon Frères both took notice of the higher prices for furs. In 2 June 1903, Victor Revillon wrote to his father and uncles in Paris from Montreal: "D'Aigneaux and Beetz have paid prices veritably too high, given the risks that befall us in retailing the pelts directly." Anatole Revillon, one of the four brothers, writing from New York to Paris, 20 May 1903, stated that a New York employee confirmed his opinion that too high a price had been paid for the silver foxes sent down from Quebec: "I believe that it is dangerous for inexperienced men, as our young man in Canada, to buy merchandise at such a price, especially in lots of 10 to 12 pelts."[24]

The Hudson's Bay Company also had something to say on the subject, as M. R. Grahame at the Mingan post wrote to Fur Trade Commissioner C. Chipman:

> Beetz, chief buyer for Revillon from Mingan to St. Augustine, has encouraged storekeepers at small settlements along the coast to deal in furs both with Indians and Whites—he keeping them posted on tariffs by prices supplied from Revillon, Montreal. Merchants and traders from Sheldrake to Chateau Bay have paid excessively high prices. The buying of furs for cash at a profit (as before Revillon) has been ruined for the present.

In the same letter, he notes that by 1908 the situation had changed:

> Revillon's open opposition for the past winter has not been vigorous. In January, Beetz and the Chateau Bay agent received instructions from Montreal to stop buying for cash—Beetz told me this himself. Revillon have been paying senselessly high for the furs Beetz and agents have bought. Martens and otters were double the highest HBC prices at the London sales. Not good business. Beetz was not utilized as fur purchasing agent last winter.[25]

There was no further record of Johan Beetz working for Revillon Frères as a fur buyer.[26]

Such high prices for silver foxes, in particular, increased the incentive to try to breed these animals in captivity. In the beginning, live foxes trapped in the summer were kept in captivity until winter when their fur was prime. In 1901 Johan Beetz surprised his neighbors by spending $40,000, a huge sum at the time, for a large quantity of galvanized wire fencing.[27] After experimenting unsuccessfully for two years, he produced a litter that contained black or silver kits in the third year and began to raise foxes seriously in 1903 with sixteen pairs.[28] Revillon Frères had an interest in this operation, but by 1904 their report stated that the fox pens were the property of Johan Beetz and that they owned only four of the foxes.[29] Their interest in silver-fox farming did not continue,[30] but in 1929 the Hudson's Bay Company established a fox farm on one of the Mingan Islands.[31]

Interest in fox breeding was not confined to the North Shore. Johan Beetz was one of several silver-fox breeders in eastern Canada. On Prince Edward Island, Charles Dalton began attempts to raise and breed foxes as early as 1880. He finally obtained a litter of silvers around 1887, but they died before reaching maturity. Robert Oulton, another Island farmer, was experimenting with fox breeding about the same time. Around 1890, some say 1896, he and Dalton combined forces at a ranch near Tignish on Cherry Island (now Oulton Island), where their efforts were shielded from the eyes of the neighbors. Dalton built his own ranch at Tignish in 1898, while retaining a half interest in the Oulton ranch.[32] The prices for fox pelts were not exceptionally high at this time. The average price for a silver fox pelt at Hudson's Bay Company auction was $71.80 in the decade 1889–99, rising to $158.55 in the following decade. At the same time the German commercial agent, Emil Brass, recorded the prices paid for individual finest silver-black skins:[33]

1880	$ 632.70
1890	876.00
1900	2,822.66
1905	1,070.67
1906	1,557.33

This coincides with the rise in prices being paid by Johan Beetz on the north shore of the St. Lawrence.

The rise in price, along with the introduction of woven wire which made it possible to build enclosures for foxes, encouraged these men to continue experiments in fox breeding. Beetz claimed to have sold the first guaranteed pair of pure-bred silver foxes to Dalton and Oulton in 1905 for $25,000.[34] As Dalton and Oulton's success became known, farmers throughout Prince Edward Island began to erect fox pens. Before 1914 breeding pairs of five-month-old foxes were selling for from $12,000 to $16,000, while stock of proven fecundity could fetch as much as $35,000 a pair.[35] The physical geography of Prince Edward Island, the climate, the length of coastline in comparison to its area, the texture and structure of the soils, together with the predominantly agricultural population encouraged the growth of fox farming on a large scale.[36] By 1922, silver-fox ranching was closely regulated by the Canadian Silver Fox Breeders Association, based in Summerside, Prince Edward Island, which reported a total of 3,900 breeding establishments throughout nine provinces, 10 percent of the stock to be found in Quebec, as compared to 45 percent on Prince Edward Island.[37]

In 1912, there were eight hundred silver foxes in captivity in Canada, of which twenty were at Piastre Baie.[38] In 1914 Beetz had $100,000 worth of silver foxes in his enclosure. In 1920, in preparation for moving his family to Montreal, he bought Île de Vaudreuil, a low, wooded island, on the south side of the St. Lawrence River, west of Montreal, and moved his foxes there from Piastre Baie.

Because of the highly strung, nervous nature of foxes, breeding pens were shielded as much as possible from curious outsiders. The secretive nature of fox breeding makes it difficult to be certain of accurate information about the early breeders. Johan Beetz would like to be thought of as the first successful breeder in the country. In his treatise on fox breeding, the dates he used are ten years earlier than those given in the biography written by his children.[39] Some of the early dates mentioned actually predate his arrival in Canada.

Beetz was not the first successful breeder of silver foxes, but he was the most scientific, with a background in animal husbandry and some veterinary training. From the beginning he studied the natural habitat, noticing in the course of the semiannual hunting season, which ranged over a wide area, that the melanism that produced shades of black in a litter occurred more frequently near the course of certain rivers, and rarely on others. The rivers associated with the greater frequency had an especially high content of limestone and iron. Two pairs of the captured foxes consistently given water from the river near where they were trapped produced one and two silver kits, while two pairs not given special care produced only red kits. Experimenting further, he found that by adding iron to the water, the kits produced were a poor shade of brownish black.[40] Another interesting observation was the need of the foxes for salt water. During two distinct periods of the year, it was common to find foxes or their tracks in the bays or points where they could reach the water's edge. Beetz believed that the fur of foxes whose natural habitat was close to the sea was superior in thickness, color, and luster to that of those found inland.[41] This observation is borne out by the predominance of Prince Edward Island in the field of fox breeding.

An understanding of genetics, coupled with careful record keeping, was essential in producing a litter of silvers. Beetz reported digging out a den in which both parents were pure silver and the six kits were entirely red. His deduction was that both parents were first generation black, from red parents, and the area of the den was in an area deficient in limestone and iron.[42] Beetz continued his careful study of genetics and the selective breeding necessary to ensure regular litters of pure silver foxes.

With a scientific training that was unusual among farmers and trappers, and with a nature that combined intense curiosity with extreme energy, Johan Beetz pursued his interest in fox breeding with the same passion he brought to everything he tackled. The 1929 stock market crash nearly ruined the fox-farming industry. Appointed as director of the fur-breeding animal service by the provincial government, Beetz devoted himself to saving it. He closed his own fox farm, moved to Quebec City, and with his son as his assistant visited breeders throughout the province, grading pelts, performing autopsies on foxes, doing microscopic analyses, and advising on all aspects of fox farming. As part of this work he wrote a book of instruction for fox breeders. Published in 1931, it set out all that he had learned in nearly thirty-five years in the field.[43] This four hundred page book, *"L'Indispensable" à l'éleveur de renards argentés*, contains fifteen chapters covering every aspect of successful breeding: descriptions of the proper enclosures, the parts of the body, the different types of fur, hygiene, diet, mating procedures, bone structure, diseases, and much more. It is illustrated throughout by the author's own drawings and diagrams.

The University of Montreal, in conjunction with the Agricultural Institute at Oka, proposed to honor Johan Beetz with an honorary degree for his scientific and humanitarian work. He preferred to earn the degree by writing a doctoral thesis and defending it before a jury. He was awarded the degree of Doctor of Agricultural Science in 1936.

He had previously been honored by the people of his village when they had petitioned the government in 1910 to change the name of Piastre Baie to Johan Beetz Baie. Although he had moved his growing family to Montreal in 1922 for the sake of better schooling, Johan Beetz maintained his connections with the village through his wife's family. Their home, both on the North Shore and in Montreal, was noted for its liberal hospitality. Beetz was generous with everything he had. His rudimentary medical training was freely used to help the villagers without charge, using medicines brought in from a pharmacy in Quebec City. The village escaped the epidemic of Spanish influenza that ravaged Canada in 1918–19 by his single-handed efforts. Beetz personally boarded each boat arriving at the ports of Havre St. Pierre and Aguanish, took off letters and parcels, and disinfected himself before landing. Ottawa received complaints from passengers not allowed to land at Johan Beetz Baie,

Figure 3. Johan Beetz. *Damase Potvin*, Le Saint-Laurent et ses Îles, (*Québec: Editions Garneau, 1945*). Permission courtesy of M. Henry Beetz.

but there were no deaths from influenza. Ninety-two people died in the other two villages. He was eventually praised for his stand.[44]

For his pioneering work as a fox breeder and his generous financial help to his fellow citizens during a quarter century on the North Shore, King Albert I of Belgium named him Chevalier of the Order of Leopold II. The king remembered Johan Beetz from their youth in Belgium, when they lived in neighboring châteaux.

Johan Beetz was not the first in the field, but he is recognized as a highly successful pioneer silver-fox breeder. His close identification with the people of the North Shore led to their receiving higher prices for their furs, prices which reflected the higher prices on world markets. This in turn boosted the incentive to breed silver foxes. Fox breeding was only a part of Beetz's legacy. He is likewise recognized for his scientific and artistic work, now housed in Quebec's provincial museums.

Notes

1. References to the use of fur as a fabric occur in Georgina O'Hara, ed., *The Encyclopedia of Fashion*, (New York: Harry N. Abrams, 1986), 94; R. Turner Wilcox, ed., *The Dictionary of Costume*, (New York: Charles Scribner's Sons, 1969), 115; and Marcel Sexé, *Two Centuries of Fur-Trading 1723–1923: Romance of the Revillon Family* (Paris: Revillon Frères, 1923), 28.

2. For a discussion of the effect of the economic climate on the fur trade see Arthur J. Ray, *The Canadian Fur Trade in the Industrial Age* (Toronto: University of Toronto, 1990), chap. 3 and H. A. Innis, *The Fur-Trade of Canada* (Toronto: Oxford University Press, 1927), chap. 2.

3. A. P. Low of the Geological Survey reported finding a litter of 7 kits, 2 red, 3 cross, and 2 black or silver on the Moose River in 1887. (Mammals, Labrador Peninsula, GSC, 1896, p. 314L) from Ernest Thompson Seton, *Lives of Game Animals*, vol. 1, part 2 (Boston: Charles T. Branford, 1953), 470.

4. A. W. F. Banfield, *The Mammals of Canada* (Toronto: National Museum of Natural Sciences, National Museums of Canada, published by University of Toronto, 1974), 298–99.

5. William Brooks Cabot, *Labrador* (Boston: Small, Maynard and Co., 1920), 217.

6. The average price up to 1914 is based on the Hudson's Bay Company fur sales as recorded in J. Walter Jones, *Fur-Farming in Canada* (Ottawa: Commission of Conservation, 1914), 203–8. Additional data come from *Canada Year Book* (Ottawa: Dominion Bureau of Statistics, 1921), 313; and Kathrene Pinkerton, writing about the Fromm brothers of Wisconsin, who dominated the market by

1928, in *Bright with Silver* (New York, William Sloane, 1947). Because silver foxes in the wild are so uncommon, writers sometimes mention the price which trappers received for them: Ernest Thompson Seton, *Arctic Prairies* (1911; rev. ed., New York: Harper Colophon, 1981), appendix F, p. 353, wrote that a silver fox pelt fetched $150, pre-1907, Slave River; Cyril Lech, in personal, unpublished diary entries made in Fort Hope, Ontario, 1908–9: "Dec. 1, 1908 . . . Bought a silver fox for $80 . . . Dec. 16, 1908 . . . Johnny and Akis in from Kaganagami with another silver fox for $150."; Wally Laird, Revillon fur trader, 1924–28, in a personal letter to the author, 13 March 1994: "Re silver foxes—they were very rare where I traded and prices were high—at today's rate as high as $1,500 [this would translate to $150, using a factor of one-tenth as seen from the context of his letter]. I can only recall one good one being traded at Stanley." [1925]; Bernard Hantzsch, "Extreme North-eastern Labrador," The *Canadian Field Naturalist* 46 (1932): 11.

7. Vaino Tanner, *Outlines of the Geography, Life and Customs of Newfoundland-Labrador* (Helsinki: Acta Geographia 8[1], 1944), 127.

8. For a brief history of the Innu or Montagnais people see E. S. Rogers and Eleanor Leacock in *Handbook of North American Indians, The Subarctic, Volume 6*, ed. June Helm (Washington, D.C.: Smithsonian Institution, 1978), 169–89; see also Francis Harper, *The Friendly Montagnais and Their Neighbors in the Ungava Peninsula* (Lawrence: University of Kansas Press, 1964). For descriptions of Montagnais seasonal migration see Henry Yule Hind, *Explorations in the Interior of the Labrador Peninsula*, 2 vols. (London: Longman, 1863); Mathieu Mestokosho, *Chroniques de chasse d'un Montagnais de Mingan* (Québec: Ministère des Affaires culturelles du Québec, 1977).

9. Ernest Voorhis, *Historic Forts and Trading Posts of the French Regime and of the English Fur Trading Companies* (Ottawa: Department of the Interior, 1930), 114–15; Mario Lalancette, "Exploitation of the Gulf of St. Lawrence," in *Historical Atlas of Canada*, ed. R. C. Harris (Toronto: University of Toronto Press, 1987), 1: plate 54; for notes on the Bissot and Jolliet families see Nive Voisine, "Bissot, François-Joseph" and C. J. Russ, "Jolliet de Mingan, Jean-Baptiste" in *Dictionary of Canadian Biography*, ed. David Hayne, vol. 2 (Toronto: University of Toronto Press, 1969); Damase Potvin, *Le Saint-Laurent et ses Îles* (Québec: Editions Garneau, 1945), 295–312.

10. Hudson's Bay Company Archives (hereafter HBCA), B 132 a8. Post records, Mingan, 1898–1910, entries 24–26 June 1901.

11. Ibid., 31 August 1901.

12. Ibid., 26 April 1901. (In the journal the date is 1900, but on 3 June the writer recognized his error and changed the date to 1901.)

13. Ibid., 31 December 1903.

14. The life of Johan Beetz is detailed in a biography by two of his children, Jeanette and Henry Beetz, *La merveilleuse aventure de Johan Beetz* (Montreal: Lemeac, 1977). Where possible, archival sources have been used to verify events.

15. HBCA, B 132 a8. Post records, Mingan, 1898–1910, 31 October 1898 and 1 May 1899.

16. This house is now a museum, which is open to the public from the beginning of May to mid-October.

17. Potvin, *Le Saint-Laurent et ses Îles*, 324.

18. This is a translation of "The Journal of Placide Vigneau," as quoted in Beetz and Beetz, *La merveilleuse aventure de Johan Beetz*, 96–97. Vigneau's daily journal for the years 1857–1926 is contained in Tome 46, *Rapport des Archives du Quebec*, 1968, Roch Lefebvre, Editeur Officiel du Québec, but this particular quotation is not in the edited version.

19. D'Aigneaux wrote a foreword to the family biography of Johan Beetz.

20. The movements of Beetz and d'Aigneaux are reported regularly by Placide Vigneau and by the Hudson's Bay Company post manager.

21. Beetz and Beetz, *La merveilleuse aventure de Johan Beetz*, 96–97; Vigneau's journal, 176–77.

22. Ibid.

23. Ibid.

24. Revillon Archives, Paris, on microfilm, Reel F-1580 at the Public Archives of Canada (PAC), Ottawa. This item is from the section entitled Montreal correspondence, 1902–10.

25. HBCA, A.12/FT.217/2, section entitled "Competition in the Bay, 1902–09, Revillon Brothers and others," 8 October 1908.

26. There is no direct reference in any of the literature to Beetz's break with Revillon Frères. Beetz acted as an agent on behalf of the company through his connection with Paul d'Aigneaux. D'Aigneaux's relations with the company were strained following his mishandling of the voyage of the *Eldorado*, see L. F. S. Upton, "The Wreck of the Eldorado," *The Beaver*, autumn 1968, 27–31, and he left Revillon's employ by 1905. The correspondence relating to this is in the Revillon Archives, Reel F–1580.

27. Blaise Gagnon, "Phidelem Harvey (1913–1995) de Baie-Johan-Beetz," in *La revue d'histoire de la Côte-Nord*, no. 21 (November 1995): 26.

28. Johan Beetz, "La fourrure du renard argenté dans le Québec," extract of doctoral thesis, in *Revue de l'institut Agricole d'Oka*, 10, no. 1 (1936): 10 and 104–8.

29. Revillon Archives. PAC Reel F–1580, Property Titles, 18 January 1904.

30. Jones, *Fur-Farming in Canada*, 13.

31. J. Eric Love, "Raising Foxes for Fur," *The Beaver*, June 1931, 223–25.

32. The story of the origins of fox farming on Prince Edward Island can be found in Jones, *Fur-Farming in Canada*, 15–19; R. Allan Rankin, "Fox Farming on Prince Edward Island," in *Exploring Island History*, ed. Harry Baglole (Belfast, P. E. I.:

Ragweed Press, 1977), 165–68; "A History of the Silver Fox Breeding Industry," in *Canadian National Record for Foxes* (Ottawa: Canadian Silver Fox Breeders Assoc., 1922), 1: xxv–xxxiii.

33. Jones, *Fur-Farming in Canada*, 215.

34. Beetz and Beetz, *La merveilleuse aventure de Johan Beetz*, 111, and Beetz, "La four-rure du renard," 103. This information is recorded only in Beetz material and is not recorded by Jones or Rankin.

35. *Canada Year Book* (Ottawa: Dominion Bureau of Statistics Office, 1916–17), 35.

36. F. A. Stilgenbauer, "Geographic Aspects of the Prince Edward Island Fur Industry," in *Economic Geography*, 1927, 3: 110–25.

37. *Canadian National Record for Foxes*, 1:xxv.

38. Jones, *Fur-Farming in Canada*, 53.

39. Beetz in *"La fourrure du renard,"* 103.

40. Ibid., 104. This information is difficult to confirm. It is known by discussion with wild-life biologists and in a survey of the literature that black kits are not found in all parts of the country. The substance that causes pigmentation—both in humans and in animals—is called melanin. Phaeomelanin produces hairs that are yellow to red, eumelanin produces black, according to A. Searle, *Comparative Genetics of Coat Colour in Mammals* (London: Logos Press, 1968), 69. The genes determine the choice of melanin. A recessive "non-agouti" gene will choose eumelanin. Eumelanin is found to have a high content of heavy metals, particularly iron. Calcium and barium are also often present. This information is from A. Needham, *The Significance of Zoochromes* (New York: Springer-Verlag, 1974), 62.

41. Johan Beetz, *"L'Indispensable" à l'éleveur de renards argentés* (Montreal: Librairie Beauchemin Ltée., 1931), 259–60.

42. Ibid., 105.

43. Beetz and Beetz, *La merveilleuse aventure de Johan Beetz*, chap. 23.

44. Ibid., chap. 13, quoting from *L'information medicale de Montréal*, 20 May 1958.

Harry W. Duckworth | Halifax as a Cradle of the Post-
✺ | Conquest Fur Trade in Canada

THE CONQUEST of Canada by the armies of Britain in 1759–60 suddenly threw open to British merchants a new economic opportunity. The colony itself contained perhaps 70,000 French-speaking inhabitants, whose requirements for manufactured goods would now be satisfied from Britain. Beyond the farms was the vast northern forest, still largely unknown to Europeans, that long had given New France its major export, the produce of the fur trade. The London business community already was anticipating the arrival of the Canada furs. At least two prize cargoes of furs, taken in the holds of French ships as they tried to run the blockade of naval vessels and privateers in 1758, had been sold at auction in London.[1] One important meeting place for London merchants trading to the American colonies, the New York Coffee House behind the Royal Exchange, had already celebrated the conquest of Louisbourg in 1758 by changing its name to the "New York and Cape Breton" Coffee House. With the news of Wolfe's victory on the Plains of Abraham, the further sobriquet "and Quebec" had been added to the New York's sign boards. There was more to these name changes than patriotic fervor. Edward Clarke, the coffee house keeper, was offering his establishment as the natural meeting place for the anticipated Canada trade.[2]

Like all the colonial trades, the money needed to finance a British trade with Canada would be raised in London by commission merchants, the capitalists of the trade. These men sometimes began their careers in the colonies, but once established in London they seldom visited America again, depending for the safety of their capital on trusted agents, often family members. The business of the London commission merchant consisted of purchasing and shipping British manufactured goods and then receiving and marketing the returns, which the colonies could remit in payment for the debts incurred. In the case of Canada, furs would be the most valuable remittance, on a value-to-weight basis, though other, bulkier commodities, such as deerskins, lumber, grain, and potash, would also be shipped.

Once the Conquest was complete, the merchants of New France did their best to locate new merchants in London who could replace the severed links with La Rochelle, but these new arrangements were not long-lasting.[3] The most important post-Conquest business arrangements in Canada were completely new, and were made by the first London commission merchants to turn their attention to the newly acquired colony. As might be expected, these men already had experience trading with the American colonies. One of the most successful commission merchants trading to Canada, John Strettell, had learned the rudiments of his trade in Pennsylvania, where he had gained an understanding of the Indian trade through contracts to provide trade goods to the Indian Trade Commissioners of that colony.[4] Another early London commission merchant interested in Canada was Charles Crokatt, whose father, James Crokatt, had been one of the most important traders to South Carolina.[5]

A particularly influential role was played by merchants who had cut their teeth in the American trade at Halifax. Halifax was a special place. Purpose-built in 1749 as a citadel and naval base to answer the French base at Louisbourg, it provided excellent wartime opportunities for businessmen interested in selling to the military. The harbor had no economic hinterland, however, and at the end of the Seven Years War Halifax lost its boom town character. Moneymaking opportunities became more limited. Merchants with Halifax interests who craved wider fields of operation, and also those less entrenched in the local economy, now looked to Canada. This chapter concerns two Halifax merchants who took the opportunity of the Conquest of Canada to become London commission merchants concerned in the Canada trade. Dealing with Canada meant dealing in furs, and this chapter will concentrate on the direct contributions that these two merchants, Robert Grant and Robert Hunter, made to the post-Conquest fur trade.

Robert Grant

Robert Grant, a Highlander from Strathspey, was living at Halifax by July 1752; a newspaper advertisement describes him as a retail merchant in October of the following year. He was already more than thirty years old, but nothing is known about his prior business career.[6] He must have had good connections to government, for he quickly obtained a contract for victualling the Navy in the port, and in 1755, after determined string pulling by his London friends, the Lords of Trade recommended that Grant be appointed to the Executive Council of Nova Scotia.[7] Grant's fellow clansman and London supplier, Sir Alexander Grant, who had orchestrated the appointment and doubtless also the naval contract, wrote in a family letter that Grant

> has of late been in a verry Thriving way and is now worth some money if his Accots were once passed at the Board on which he depends, his office is Lucrative which has drawn much envy on him, so that he Requir'd great Interest to support him in his Place, which Nevertheless I have been able to bestow on him, and I have now got him to be appointed one of the Council of the Country wherein he lives which being one of the Chief Posts in the Government, will let him above the reach of many who gave him disturbance.[8]

Grant's own relations were surprised. One of them wrote to another, "I wish he may behave well on his preferrment, its an honour I never expected to see him have & that few of our Country are trusted with but if he show any of that plotting disposition I am affraid he has formerly been Justly bleamed for it may be the worst thing that Could happen him."[9]

Robert Grant needed protection, for his handling of his naval contract was not giving satisfaction. According to the governor of Nova Scotia, Charles Lawrence, who quickly came to detest Grant, in the year 1757 Admiral Holburne "turned [him] out of his employment for practices that the whole Fleet declared were infamous, and for which Mr Holburne spoke of him in the presence of Lord Loudon and fifty other Land and Sea Officers as a disgrace to the Council of Nova Scotia." The following year, during the siege of Louisbourg, Governor Lawrence was disgusted to find Grant, a member of his Executive Council, selling "Liquors and other articles to the Troops in common with other Pedlars upon the Beach."[10]

After spending the summer of 1758 thus profitably at Louisbourg, Robert Grant went directly to England, evidently to solidify some business arrangements. In the fall of 1759 he was again found peddling to the troops, this time to Wolfe's army before Quebec.[11] He had not appeared in Halifax for well over a year, and Governor Lawrence took the opportunity of the long absence to have Grant removed from the council. Back in England the following winter, Grant pleaded to the Lords of Trade to be reinstated, but in the last letter that Governor Lawrence wrote to the Lords before his own death in October 1760, Lawrence bitterly opposed this.[12]

Robert Grant did not regain his seat on the Executive Council of Nova Scotia, but evidently he already had what he wanted from Halifax—enough money to develop his own business interests with London as a base.[13] No information has been found as to how rich he really was at this point in his life, but his new independence is shown by the fact that in 1761 he broke with his old supplier, Sir Alexander Grant. Soon after, he formed the partnership of Alexander, Robert and William Grant, to ship goods to Canada.[14] The partners' main customers were other clansmen—another William Grant, later known as William Grant "of St. Roch," and Charles Grant of Quebec.[15]

William Grant of St. Roch was apparently sent to Quebec in 1759, just after the surrender of the city, when he was only fifteen years old, to collect some debts for Robert's firm. There was little cash in the colony during the next few years. Many of the newly arrived British and American merchants were still trying to establish themselves and were short of capital. In such an environment William Grant, by splashing Robert's money about, buying seigneuries and other property, moved quickly to a position of influence in the colony. In the spring of 1766, still only twenty-two, he sent a frisson of alarm through the Canadian fur trading community when it was learned that he had purchased from the last governor-general of New France, Pierre de Rigaud de Vaudreuil de Cavagnial, what purported to be the exclusive right to trade at Michilimackinac and La Baye, for a stated price of 160,000 livres. The title to this trade, based on alleged ownership of property at Green Bay, astride the major canoe route to the Mississippi, was not accepted by the British authorities, but the episode remains an interesting example of what real money could do in Canada, in the first few years after the Conquest. The relationship between Robert Grant and William Grant of St. Roch broke up in quarrels about what had happened to Robert's money in William's hands—about £80,000 sterling, a vast sum in the small Canadian economy of the time.[16] William went on to play a sustained and influential role in the colony, as his biographer, David Roberts, has explained.[17]

When the firm of Alexander, Robert and William Grant of London was wound up, probably in the winter of 1766–67, its customers were apparently transferred to John Strettell, who was fast becoming one of the most successful of the London merchants trading to Canada. The most important of these customers was probably the firm of Paterson and Grant of Quebec, outfitters for the fur trade from the mid 1760s onward. It was through their family connections that such North West Company partners as William Holmes and the brothers Robert and Cuthbert Grant (senior) entered the fur trade.[18]

Robert Grant, former Halifax merchant and member of the Council of Nova Scotia, continued to hold on to naval victualling contracts well into the 1770s. In the year 1783, now over sixty years old, he purchased the Highland estate of Wester Elchies, Carron, and Knockando. He was known as Robert Grant of Elchies until his death at eighty-five in 1805. His legacy to the fur trade of Canada was an infusion of capital in the first few years after the Conquest, on which other men built their fortunes and then were able to send trade goods further and further into the Northwest. His legacy to Canada reached well beyond the fur trade. The network of Strathspey Grants and their relations, a network that Robert Grant of Elchies first introduced to Canada, long continued its search for opportunities for its bright young men in different parts of the Empire, and was still casting up such business geniuses as Donald Smith and George Stephen a century later.[19]

Robert Hunter

Robert Hunter, the second of the Halifax merchants who made early contributions to the Canada trade, was probably a Lowland Scotsman, very likely from Kilmarnock in Ayrshire. His firm of Robert Hunter and Alexander Miller, merchants, was in existence in London by 1759.[20] Legal suits that they brought in the Halifax Court of Common Pleas during the next few years show that the firm shipped dry goods to retail shopkeepers at Halifax.[21] Miller soon died, and once the war with France was over, commercial involvement in Nova Scotia led Hunter to Canada. In 1763 and 1764 a partnership including Hunter, William Berry, and the Halifax merchant Brook Watson sent their brigantine, the *Ranger*, with cargoes to Quebec.[22] Over the next few years Hunter's growing importance in the Canada trade is shown by his signature on some of the petitions and addresses to government. He was one of the trustees of the fund set up in London to relieve the sufferers from the Montreal fire of 1765.[23] He was one of the regular correspondents of the lawyer Fowler Walker, who had been retained by Canadian mercantile interests to lobby government for various purposes in 1767 and 1768.[24] By this time Hunter had another business partner, one Baily, and the firm of Hunter and Baily was prominent in the Canada trade until 1772, after which Hunter continued on his own.[25] Nothing has been discovered about Baily; Hunter was clearly the driving force.

During most of his career, Hunter's major business was to supply British manufactured goods for the retail trade within the province of Quebec. He was probably responsible for introducing to Canada a number of businessmen from Kilmarnock, his own hometown.[26] The first and most important of these was John Lymburner, who, along with the Halifax merchant Brook Watson and others, obtained a grant of a seal fishery along the north shore of the St. Lawrence as early as 1761. During the next ten years Lymburner was among the Quebec merchants who lobbied on behalf of the fishing industry

in the Gulf of St. Lawrence, received large shipments of British manufactured goods, and invested in the timber trade. His disappearance at sea in
1772, during one of his several trans-Atlantic voyages, must have been a considerable shock to the colonial trade.[27] Other Canada merchants and traders
whose introduction to the colony was probably due to Robert Hunter included the elder William Lindsay, John McKindlay, and William, Robert, and
James Aird.[28]

Regardless of his main business interests, Hunter had to deal in furs, simply because Canadian merchants so often remitted payments to England in
furs, but he had a specific, intense interest in the fur trade in the period 1767-
70. This arose out of the circumstances by which two entrepreneurial individuals came together in the summer of 1767 at Michilimackinac, the cockpit of
the Canada fur trade. One was that well-known and deeply controversial figure, Major Robert Rogers, former military hero of the French and Indian War,
commander of Rogers's Rangers, and now, having charmed certain influential
figures in England, the commandant at Michilimackinac Fort. [29] The other
was a young Scotsman, Alexander Baxter, a representative of English
investors who were looking for some kind of money making opportunity
around the Upper Great Lakes. Baxter's investors included those who had got
Major Rogers his post at Michilimackinac, and the two men were certainly
helping one another in some way.[30] By the following year, Rogers's enemies
had him locked up and charged with treason (he was eventually acquitted,
though his days at Michilimackinac were over), while Baxter's investors had
decided that what they wanted was a mining monopoly around Lake
Superior. In the summer of 1767, though, Robert Rogers was riding high,
Alexander Baxter was in league with him more than the local traders realized,
and the business in which they chose to collaborate was the obvious one for
Michilimackinac, the fur trade.

Rogers arrived at Michilimackinac in 1766, and among his first actions
was the dispatch of two parties to the upper Mississippi. These were to
explore far to the Northwest, and if possible discover the mythical Oregon
River that would lead effortlessly to the Pacific Ocean.[31] Exploration was the
official purpose, but the expeditions carried trade goods with them. Rogers's
plan was a way of circumventing the severely restrictive fur trade policy still
in force in that year, which required the traders to wait for their Indian customers at the great posts of Detroit and Michilimackinac rather than wintering among them in the fur country itself.

The two exploring parties sent out in the fall of 1766 got no farther than
the upper Mississippi, where their trade goods were expended as presents to

the Indians. This route to the Northwest was a difficult one. It had probably been chosen because the traditional route, over Grand Portage and through the chain of lakes to Rainy Lake, Lake of the Woods, and the Winnipeg River, was known to be blocked by the Rainy Lake Ojibway. Two recent attempts had been made to get trade goods into the Northwest by way of Grand Portage, but the Ojibway astride the route had insisted that any goods that came to their country must satisfy their own needs, long deferred since the disruption of trade by the French and Indian War.[32]

In the summer of 1767 Rogers assembled a large outfit of Indian trade goods to supplement what he described as inadequate supplies of Indian presents at the post, by purchasing them from the Michilimackinac traders. In payment Rogers gave bills of exchange drawn on Sir William Johnson, the superintendent of indian affairs—bills that would never be paid.[33] Nonetheless, for the moment Rogers was well positioned to enter the Northwest fur trade for himself, if only he could disguise his participation. The expedition he would send might get past Rainy Lake if a generous portion of the outfit was actually left at a post there, thus satisfying the Ojibway at the lake, who then would permit the rest of the canoes to go beyond. The Indian Commissary at Michilimackinac who issued the trade licences, Benjamin Roberts, was not on good terms with Rogers. Soon they would be enemies. This must be why it was Alexander Baxter who sponsored six of the nine canoes licensed to leave Michilimackinac "for the North West" on 7 July 1767—Baxter was acting, it is likely, as a cat's paw for Robert Rogers himself.[34] These six canoes, the largest trading adventure licensed at Michilimackinac for any destination that summer, were in the care of an experienced old voyageur named François Leblanc, and were licensed to go to Fort Dauphin and Fort la Prairie, the most westerly posts known to the French. Two more canoes were licensed to Maurice Blondeau, another veteran trader, for Fort Dauphin and Fort la Reine. One more canoe was licensed for Lac la Pluie and Lac du Bois. This last was surely to buy the cooperation of the gatekeepers of the Northwest trade, the Ojibway of Rainy Lake.[35]

The plan succeeded. Seventeen years later, the Frobisher brothers cited it as the first penetration of trading canoes from Canada to the Northwest after the Conquest. Hudson's Bay Company journals testify that François Leblanc wintered on the lower Saskatchewan, as he had intended, in 1767–68.[36] This pivotal event is well known to fur trade historians; what seems not to have been noticed is that it was planned and executed by the celebrated Major Robert Rogers. His contributions to the exploration of the Northwest were therefore not as nugatory as his biographers have judged.[37]

What does this have to do with Robert Hunter, the London commission merchant with an interest in the trade of Canada? The connection emerges the next year in London, in the spring of 1768. By this time Alexander Baxter had returned from Canada, and he, his father, and a few Canadian adventurers had joined a consortium of London merchants and members of Parliament in a plan to obtain a monopoly of mines and minerals around Lake Superior.[38] Among the stockholders in this would-be mining enterprise was Robert Hunter. Hunter appears to have been the man who established credit for Alexander Baxter during his attempts, in the next few years, to get a working mine under way.[39]

Hunter was more deeply involved than this. In the summer of 1768, François Leblanc and his canoemen returned to Michilimackinac with the first post-Conquest harvest of Northwest furs. Alexander Baxter was not yet back in Canada, and Major Rogers was in Montreal, preparing to stand trial for treason. Leblanc's success was to be repeated in the ensuing season by another Michilimackinac trader, James Finlay, who wintered on the Saskatchewan in 1768–69. Finlay cheekily offered to hire away the Hudson's Bay Company servants whom he encountered at his Saskatchewan River post, and told them, if they were interested, "You will Direct your Letters to Mr. James Finley, Merchant in Montreal; To the Care of Messrs Hunter & Baily, Merchants in London."[40] The fact that Finlay was poised to take more goods into the new Saskatchewan River post when Leblanc came out shows that this first post-Conquest Northwest enterprise survived the fall of Robert Rogers. Robert Hunter was the common factor.

Finlay spent only the one winter on the Saskatchewan. In 1769 he came out with a rich cargo of furs, which he took directly to England. It was probably Robert Hunter who obtained an interview for Finlay with Lord Hillsborough, secretary of state, perhaps hoping that Finlay would reinforce in Hillsborough's mind the importance of the explorations being carried out by fur traders in the northwestern parts of North America. Finlay was said to have cut a poor figure as an explorer, however. Voyageur guides had taken him to the Saskatchewan, but he himself seemed to Hillsborough "an illitterate person entirely unacquainted with Geography or perhaps the common points of the Compass could give but little light to his Lordship of the Country he was in."[41] The reestablished trade to the Saskatchewan faltered badly in the next two seasons. Difficulties again were encountered getting canoe loads past the Rainy Lake Ojibway. Perhaps Rogers's solution of committing goods to them was being neglected. When the route again became secure, the Northwest trade had fallen into other hands.[42]

The Lake Superior Mining Company struggled along until the end of the winter of 1772–73, when Alexander Baxter was recalled to England. One of the principal London speculators committed suicide, and the whole business collapsed amid recriminations.[43] The failure of the mines probably made little difference to Robert Hunter, who prospered in the Canada retail trade until at least the early 1790s. He was evidently a leader of the London merchants interested in Canada, for he wrote many of the letters by which those merchants endeavored to influence government policy in the colony.[44] One particular aspect of his interests came to prominence when Hunter's junior partner, Caleb Blanchard, was sent to Canada in 1785 to recover the debts of their insolvent Canadian customers in the aftermath of the Revolutionary War. Hunter's son, Robert junior, accompanied Blanchard as a tourist, and recorded his experiences in a diary. Innocent but not entirely naive, young Robert Hunter recorded the cordiality with which the Airds, Hunter's most troubled customers, treated him, as Caleb Blanchard inexorably tightened the noose.[45]

This chapter adds another dimension to our understanding of the Canada fur trade. If we confine our inquiries within the colony, we will remain puzzled by trends and events that are comprehensible only if we know where the actors had come from, and what business forces were moving behind them in the mother country. The establishment of Halifax in 1749, bringing with it the demands of the newly settled military and civilian populations for British manufactured goods, provided a brief opportunity for enterprising retail merchants to make a lot of money. The most successful were able to establish themselves as commission merchants in London, and when Canada fell to British conquest, these merchants were well placed to transfer their attentions to Quebec and Montreal. The Halifax trade of the 1750s was not the only source of investors in the newly conquered Canada, but it was especially important in the early years after the Conquest.[46] The endless supply of cash available to a teenaged William Grant in the early 1760s, or the concentration of capital at Michilimackinac by which the Grand Portage route to the Northwest was reopened in 1767, are phenomena that make sense only when we study the London investors who made them possible. That London had so much influence on the Canadian economy in the late eighteenth century is just a measure of the immaturity of that economy. As the economy expanded, the figures that had sustained its infancy became remote, irrelevant, and quaint.

Notes

1. The furs and skins from the cargo of the *Sauvage*, "a French Prize from Canada, taken by the City of Cork Privateer," were sold by a consortium of London brokers at Garraway's Coffee House on 22 June, 20 July, and 17 August 1758. Those from the cargo of the Marie Anne, "a French Prize, from Canada, taken by the Charming Nancy Privateer, William Snow, Commander," were sold by some of the same brokers on 17 August and 19 October. The fur cargo of the *Belliqueux*, "from Canada, taken by the Antelope Man of War, Capt. Saumarez," were similarly sold on 10 May 1759 (see notices in the London *Public Advertiser* of those dates). The inventories of these prize cargoes as they are described in the press notices, and the prices at which the different furs sold at Hudson's Bay Company auctions at the same period, allow us to calculate that these prize cargoes contributed furs and skins to the London market on a scale comparable to the Hudson's Bay Company's own sales. Thus, these sales clearly foreshadowed the impact that the capture of Canada would have on the London fur market.

2. The history of the New York Coffee House as the center for the Canada trade in London is outlined in Harry W. Duckworth, "Selling Canadian Furs in London, 1760-1821," in I. McLaren, M. Payne, and H. Rollason, eds. *Papers of the 1994 Rupert's Land Colloquium* (Winnipeg: Centre for Rupert's Land Studies, 1997), 10-25.

3. J. E. Igartua, "Étienne Augé," in *Dictionary of Canadian Biography* (hereafter *DCB*, 12 vols. to date)(Toronto: University of Toronto Press, 1979), 4:35; J. E. Igartua, "Jacques-Joseph Lemoine Despins," in *DCB*, 4:461; R. Dumais, "Pierre-Joseph Gamelin," in *DCB*, 4:286; G. Joannette and C. Joron, "Pierre Guy," in *DCB*, 5:345–46. These articles point out the success of their subjects in establishing London contacts in the first years after the Conquest, but do not make clear how short-lived the new arrangements were.

4. Harry W. Duckworth, "British Capital in the Fur Trade: John Strettell and John Fraser," in Jennifer S. H. Brown, W. J. Eccles, and Donald P. Heldman, eds., *The Fur Trade Revisited. Selected Papers of the Sixth North American Fur Trade Conference, Mackinac Island, Michigan, 1991* (East Lansing/Mackinac Island: Michigan State University Press and Mackinac State Historic Parks, 1994), 39–56.

5. For James Crokatt and Charles Crokatt, see K. A. Kellock, "London Merchants and the pre-1776 American Debts," *Guildhall Studies in London History* (London: Guildhall Library, 1974), 1:109–49.

6. Grant's father was collector of customs for the Isle of Man: for a brief account of the family see "Grant of Carron formerly of Elchies," in *Burke's Landed Gentry*, 17th ed. (London: Burke's Peerage Ltd., 1952), 1051–52. Robert Grant is listed as an inhabitant of the town of Halifax, with a total household of six, in the census of heads of families taken in July 1752 (T. B. Akins, "History of Halifax City," appendix F, in *Collections of the Nova Scotia Historical Society for the Years 1892–94* (Halifax, N. S.: Morning Herald Printing and Publishing Co., 1895), 8:254. Grant's advertisement of a cargo for retail sale, chiefly dry goods, is in the *Halifax Gazette* for 20 October 1753.

7. For Grant's appointment to the council see Calendar of State Papers relating to Nova Scotia, in *Report on Canadian Archives for the Year 1894* (Ottawa: S. E. Dawson), 207; the Royal Warrant making the appointment was dated 31 December 1755, Provincial Archives of Nova Scotia (hereafter PANS), RG1 vol. 347, no. 13. A useful source of information on Robert Grant's activities is the family letters in the Grant of Tammore Papers, British Library (hereafter BL), Add. 25,411 to 25,413.

8. Sir Alexander Grant to "Mr. William Grant Mercht in Aberdeen," London, 3 August 1756 (copy), in Grant of Tammore Papers, BL, Add. 25,411, f. 183.

9. William Grant to his father, Robert Grant of Tammore, Aberdeen, 12 August 1756, BL, Add. 25,411, ff. 188–89.

10. PANS, RG1 36, doc. 50, Lawrence to Lords of Trade, 1 September 1760.

11. PANS, RG1 36, doc. 50; BL, Add. 25,412, ff. 36–37; *Journal of the Commissioners for Trade and Plantations, Jan 1764–Dec 1767* (London: HMSO, 1933), 432–33; National Archives of Canada (hereafter NAC), MG19 A2 ser. 3, vol. 61, nos. 66–68, 74.

12. PANS, RG1 36, doc. 50; *Journal of the Commissioners for Trade and Plantations*, Jan *1759–Dec 1763* (London, HMSO, 1935), 95–96, 105; *Report on Canadian Archives, 1894*, 221–22.

13. The influence of the Grants at Halifax was briefly maintained after Robert's departure, for Alexander Grant, presumably the man of this name who was to become a partner with Robert in the firm of Alexander, Robert and William Grant, was appointed to the Executive Council in 1761 (PANS, RG1 vol. 347, no. 23). Earlier the same year, when the acting governor went ahead with plans to set up the Indian trade in the colony as a government monopoly, Alexander Grant obtained the contract to supply the goods; the monopoly was forbidden by the Lords of Trade before the end of 1761, but Grant had already advanced goods and money in excess of £7,000 (PANS, RG1 vol. 37, nos. 5, 7, 11; *Report on Canadian Archives, 1894*, 246, 261, 266). He probably left the colony about 1765, became a merchant in London, and died in 1783 (*Kent's Directory* [of London] *for the Year 1771* (London: H. Kent, 1771), and later years; *Gentleman's Magazine*, 1783, 94).

14. BL, Add. Ms. 25,412, ff. 100, 103, 118, 118b, 120, 152, 164, 164b.

15. "William & John Grant are both here from North America, William deales largely with us, he is partner with Stuart & Gray & in a thriveing way" (Robert Grant [of London] to Robert Grant [of Tammore], London, 4 November 1762, BL, Add. 25,412, ff. 164, 164b). For Charles Grant, see William Grant to Robert Grant of Tammore, Montreal, 27 May 1768 (this letter has been separated into two parts; the first part is Add. 25,412, ff. 288–89 and the remainder is Add. 25,413, ff. 190–92).

16. BL, Add. 25,412, f. 288b.

17. D. Roberts, "William Grant," in *DCB*, 5:367–76.

18. For the relationship of Paterson and Grant with Strettell, see Duckworth, "British Capital in the Fur Trade," 43. For the connections of Holmes and the Grant brothers with this firm, see W. S. Wallace, *Documents Relating to the North West Company* (Toronto: Champlain Society, 1934), 449, 451, 458.

19. The connection between Robert Grant of Elchies and Donald Smith (Lord Strathcona) is as follows. The firm of Paterson & Grant, Robert Grant's customers, introduced another Robert Grant (1752–1801, from Lethendry in Strathspey) into the Northwest fur trade, and this Robert became a partner in the North West Company. One of the clerks whom Robert Grant brought into his company was his cousin John Stuart (1779–1847), also from Strathspey. Stuart became a chief factor in the Hudson's Bay Company after the union of the companies in 1821, and his nephew, Donald Smith (1820–1914), began his career in Canada as a Hudson's Bay Company clerk, eventually rising to become governor of the company. He is best known as the main financial backer of the Canadian Pacific Railway.

20. Hunter's connection with Kilmarnock is suggested by the fact that several of his Canadian customers, such as the Lymburners and John McKindlay, came from there (see endnotes 27 and 28, below); the name Hunter is common in the town, but careful genealogical research would be needed to identify Robert and his family in Kilmarnock records. Hunter and Miller are first listed in Kent's *Directory of London* for 1759, as merchants in Paternoster-row; in 1761 they were in Dean's-court, St. Martin's-le-Grand (Kent's *Directory*, 1761).

21. Suit, Inferior Court of Common Pleas for Halifax, March 1763, Hunter vs. Treleaven, PANS, RG37, Halifax County, Box 15; and Suit, Slayter & Watson vs. Rider, March 1763, PANS, RG37, Halifax Company, boxes 13 & 14.

22. NAC, RG4 A3 vol. 1, pp. 3, 127. William Berry was Hunter's partner at the time: Hunter and Berry are listed as merchants in Lothbury, in Kent's *Directory of London* for 1763, but not in the next few *Directories*, which give Robert Hunter on his own. The heavy involvement of this brief partnership in Canadian business is illustrated by the fact that William Berry held 49,753 livres in Canadian paper money in January 1765 (NAC, MG 5 A 1 vol. 467, f. 66, pp. 195–98).

23. Memorial to the King from the Merchants and Traders of the City of London, *London Gazette*, 18 May, and *Gazetteer & London Daily Advertiser*, 23 May 1763; list of trustees of the subscription for the relief of the sufferers in the Montreal fire, *London Gazetteer & New Daily Advertiser*, Wed. 8 January 1766; letter of London merchants concerned in the Canada trade to Board of Trade, 19 April 1765, printed in the *Quebec Gazette* 4 July 1765.

24. BL, Add. 31,915.

25. The firm of Hunter & Baily is listed at No. 54, Lothbury, in Kent's *Directories* from 1767 to 1770, and then at No. 12, Coleman Street, in 1771 and 1772; the earliest *Directory* in which Robert Hunter appears on his own is *The London Directory for the Year 1772* (London: T. Lowndes, 1772). He continued at the Coleman Street address up to 1780, and then the *Directories* show him at the prestigious location of No. 7, King's Arms Yard, where he remained for the rest of his business career.

26. See A. J. H. Richardson, "William Finlay," *DCB*, 6:254, for a clear statement of the linkages among the Lowland Scots merchants trading to Canada: "Consisting principally of Hunters, Patersons, Parkers, Robertsons, and Dunlops in London, Glasgow, Kilmarnock, and Greenock. . . ." Richardson realized the importance of this grouping, but did not go so far as to place Robert Hunter of London as the center of it.

27. For John Lymburner's involvement in the dispute over fishing rights in the gulf with the governor of Newfoundland, see Public Record Office (hereafter PRO), CO42 vol. 25, pp. 37–38 (microfilm at NAC); Hardwicke Papers, BL, Add. 31,195, f. 72 (copy at NAC). For large shipments consigned to him under the bale marks ILymburner and IL in 1763 and 1764, see NAC, RG4 A3 vol. 1, pp. 6, 171–81. For his involvement in the timber trade, see Copy of Agreement dated 6 August 1771 between Lymburner, Udney Hay, and James Glenny, all of Quebec, to ship barrel staves from Canada to London, in W. D. Powell Papers (Metropolitan Toronto Reference Library [MTRL], Baldwin Room, L16, B.70, p. 4); Lymburner provided the working capital for this enterprise. John Lymburner's younger brother Adam is better known because of his efforts on behalf of responsible government in the late 1780s (D. Roberts, "Adam Lymburner," in *DCB*, 7:522–25); there was also a third brother, Matthew, in Canada. All three brothers matriculated at the University of Glasgow. Their parentage is given in the University records (W. Innes Addison, *The Matriculation Albums of the University of Glasgow from 1728 to 1858* [Glasgow: James Maclehose & Sons, 1913], 43, 82, 96); and these in turn lead to baptismal entries in the Kilmarnock Old Parochial Register.

28. Y. Thériault, "William Lindsay," in *DCB*, 6:400–402; D. S. MacMillan, "John McKindlay," in *DCB*, 6:471-73. R. R. Gilman's article "James Aird," in *DCB*, 5:9–10, has no information about his brother William, a Montreal merchant, but considerable data are available in various primary sources. See in particular invoices of goods sent by Hunter under the bale mark WA to William Aird in 1776 (Ermatinger Papers, Accounts, NAC, MG19 A2 Ser. 3, vol. 65, nos. 476–479) and 1781 (NAC, MG23 G III 17).

29. For Robert Rogers, see C. P. Stacey's brief but comprehensive account in *DCB*, 4:679–83.

30. See Rogers to Captain Tute, Michilimackinac, 20 July 1767, "Mr. Baxter the gentleman that I wrote you is a going to England on my account emediately," (J. Parker, ed., [St. Paul: Minnesota Historical Society Press, 1976], 199).

31. Documents relating to these expeditions sent off by Rogers are conveniently brought together in Parker (1976).

32. An unnamed "adventurer" tried to take goods beyond Rainy Lake in 1765 and again in 1766, but "the Indians of Lake La Pluye having then been long destitute of Goods, stop'd and plundered his Canoes, and would not suffer him to proceed further" (B. and J. Frobisher to General Haldimand, 4 October 1784, in Wallace, *Documents*, 70). This unnamed adventurer may have been Maurice Blondeau, who participated in the successful expedition of 1767.

33. The list of Michilimackinac traders who contributed goods to Rogers and signed a document stating that they were concerned that the Indian presents provided through official channels would not be adequate for the season, is provided by D. A. Armour, ed. *Treason? at Michilimackinac: The Proceedings of a General Court Martial Held at Montreal in October 1768 for the Trial of Major Robert Rogers* (Mackinac Island: Mackinac State Historic Parks, 1967), 88–89. For examples of correspondence with Sir William Johnson from Montreal merchants, when it was emerging that Johnson would not honor Rogers's bills on him, see A. C. Flick, ed., *The Papers of Sir William Johnson* 13 vols. (Albany: The University of the State of New York, 1928–), 6:427–28, 441.

34. Roberts seems to have had no idea that Baxter and Rogers were working together—in a report to Sir William Johnson at the end of the summer, Roberts reported that Baxter had been sent to Michilimackinac by the English parliamentarians, Charles Townshend and Samuel Touchet, and "some people think he is concerned to the NW" (Roberts to Johnson, Michilimackinac 31 [sic] September 1767, in Flick, *Papers of Sir William Johnson*, 5:712). The English politician Charles Townshend was the patron who had made it possible for Robert Rogers to get his appointment at Michilimackinac. Two surviving letters from Rogers to James Tute, commander of one of the exploring parties of 1766, show that Baxter was working with Rogers, and that the fur trade adventure under François Leblanc, including the idea of placing a post at Rainy Lake to satisfy the Indians there, was Rogers's idea, (Armour, *Treason*, 54–55).

35. C. E. Lart, "Fur-Trade Returns, 1767," *Canadian Historical Review* 3 (1922): 351–58. Of the posts mentioned, Fort Dauphin and Fort la Reine (now Portage la Prairie) were in the present Manitoba; Fort des Prairies was a general name for posts on the Saskatchewan River; and Lac la Pluie and Lac du Bois are Rainy Lake and Lake of the Woods, respectively.

36. Wallace, *Documents*, 70; J. B. Tyrrell, ed., *Journals of Samuel Hearne and Philip Turnor* (Toronto: Champlain Society, 1934), 7–8.

37. E.g., C. P. Stacey, "Robert Rogers," in *DCB*, 4:681, speaking of the explorations sent off in 1766: "Nothing important came of these efforts."

38. For the list of stockholders in the Lake Superior Mining Company, see documents in Flick, *Papers of Sir William Johnson*, 6:242–47.

39. Ermatinger to Hunter and Baily, Montreal, 26 July 1770, Ermatinger Letterbook, NAC MG19, A2 (microfilm C-4556), pp. 4, 7.

40. York Factory journal, 19 June 1769, quoted by W. S. Wallace, *The Pedlars from Quebec* (Toronto: Ryerson Press, 1954), 8. James Finlay was in Canada as early as the winter of 1764–65 (*Quebec Gazette*, 15 November 1764, 31 March 1768); *Bulletin des Recherches Historiques*, 39 (1933):158; John Porteous Diary, in *Ontario Historical Society Papers & Records*, 33:78. In 1767, Finlay acted as security on licenses issued at Michilimackinac to traders going to various points on Lake Michigan and the Mississippi (Lart, "Fur-Trade Returns, 1767," 353, 354, 356). His name, like Hunter, is common in Ayrshire, and he may be another example of a Scotsman who was introduced to Canada by Robert Hunter.

41. Daniel Claus's journal of a visit to Canada in September 1770, in Flick, *Papers of Sir William Johnson*, 7:953; Tyrrell, *Journals of Samuel Hearne and Philip Turnor*, 10; Todd to Rinkin & Edgar, Michilimackinac, 8 September 1769, Edgar Papers (photostats), NAC, MG19 A1, pp. 227–30; and Finlay's license to leave the province, 28 October 1769, NAC, RG4 B28, vol. 4.

42. For the reduced activity of Canadian fur traders on the Saskatchewan in 1769 and 1770, see Wallace, *The Pedlars*, 9. After 1770 the trade beyond Grand Portage was largely in the hands of Isaac Todd, James McGill, and the Frobisher brothers, an alliance that developed into the first North West Company.

43. A charter for the Mining Company was not obtained until 1772; for a summary of the London end of the business and the suicide of Samuel Touchet, one of the organizers, see L. B. Namier, "Samuel Touchet," in L. B. Namier and J. Brooke, eds., *The History of Parliament. The House of Commons 1754–1790* 3 vols. (London, HMSO, 1964), 3:535-36. Much other information on the mines is to be found in Flick, *Papers of Sir William Johnson*. Alexander Baxter seems to have remained in England after this; he is probably the "—Baxter, Esq. late of Canada" who was married in London in 1774 (*London Daily Advertiser*, 18 November 1774).

44. For letters from Robert Hunter to officials concerned with Canada, see, for instance, *The Manuscripts of the Earl of Dartmouth. Vol. 2. American Papers. 14th Report of the Historical Manuscripts Commission, Appendix Part 10* (London, HMSO, 1895), 241–42, 394–95, 577–78; and Haldimand Papers, BL, Add. 21,697, f. 95; 21,732 ff. 247, 351, 373, 432; 21,733 f. 62; 21,734 ff. 93, 375; 21,735 ff. 44, 409; 21,736 ff. 55, 61. It appears that he is the Robert Hunter who died at his country house at Kew, near London, in 1812 (L. B. Wright and M. Tinling, eds., *Quebec to Carolina in 1785–1786. Being the Travel Diary and Observations of Robert Hunter, Jr., a Young Merchant of London* [San Marino, Calif.: Huntington Library, 1943], 312–13), though more research would be needed to establish this for certain.

45. Wright and Tinling, *Quebec to Carolina*, 31–32, 37–38, 48; *Quebec Gazette*, 28 July 1785; Deed of Assignment in Étude E. W. Gray, Archives Nationales de Québec, Montreal Regional Archive, CN1-184, 1 October 1785.

46. The best known of the Halifax merchants involved in the post-Conquest trade to Canada, Brook Watson, has been the subject of considerable published work, and it seemed superfluous to recapitulate that here. For a brief but comprehensive biography of Watson, see L. F. S. Upton, "Sir Brook Watson," in *DCB*, 4:842–44.

Contributors

About the Contributors

Janet E. Chute received her doctorate in anthropology from McMaster University, Hamilton, Ontario. She has taught Native American studies, anthropology, and sociology and is associated with graduate faculties at Dalhousie University. She also conducts studies into the cultural history of, and is actively involved in claims for Mi'kmaq First Nations in Nova Scotia, and Ojibwa First Nations north of Lakes Huron and Superior in Ontario.

Peter Cook is currently writing a doctoral dissertation at McGill University on the symbolic and institutional aspects of French-Native diplomacy in the seventeenth-century Northeast. He has published "New France's Agents of Intercultural Diplomacy: The Western Frontier, 1703–1725," in *Proceedings of the Twentieth Meeting of the French Colonial Historical Society* (1996), as well as several biographies in the *Biographical Dictionary of American and Canadian Naturalists and Environmentalists* (1996).

Bruce Alden Cox has lived for years in Ottawa, where many of the events recounted in his recent article, "Whitemen Servants of Greed: Foreigners, Indians, and Canada's Northwest Game Act of 1917," took place. He teaches anthropology at Ottawa's Carleton University. He has written and edited books and articles on aboriginal studies and indian-white relations. *Los Indios del Canada* is his most recent book.

Heather Devine is currently a doctoral candidate in history at the University of Alberta. She has published and presented several articles in the fields of fur trade social history and cultural heritage education. Heather's article, "Roots in the Mohawk Valley: Sir William Johnson's Legacy in the North West Company," appeared in *The Fur Trade Revisited*.

Harry W. Duckworth is professor of chemistry at the University of Manitoba. Inspired by the presence of the Hudson's Bay Company Archives in Winnipeg, his home city, he chose to pursue a scholarly interest in the fur trade. His article, "British Capital in the Fur Trade: John Strettell and John Fraser" appeared in *The Fur Trade Revisited*.

Gerhard J. Ens is an associate professor of history at the University of Alberta, Edmonton, Alberta. His research interests include Métis and fur trade history, and he has served as a research consultant on Métis land claims cases. The University of Toronto had recently published his book *Homeland to Hinterland: The Changing World of the Red River Métis in the Nineteenth Century* in 1996.

Ann Harper Fender received her Ph.D. in economics from Johns Hopkins University and is a faculty member at Gettysburg College. Her publications include, "Discouraging the Use of a Common Resource: The Crees of Saskatchewan," *Journal of Economic History*, "Market Power and Locational Decision: The Hudson's Bay Company, circa 1800," in *Essays in Economic and Business History*, and "A Transactions-Cost Analysis of the Hudson's Bay Company, " in *Le Casto Fait Tout: Selected Papers of the Fifth North American Fur Trade Conference, 1985*. Ann has also published *Location of the U.S. Iron and Steel Industry, 1879–1919*; and "Sex Role Stereotyping in Economics and Business Administration," in *Sex Bias in Academe: A Symposium*.

Jo-Anne Fiske is an associate professor at the University of Northern British Columbia, where she teaches women's studies. She holds a Ph.D. in anthropology. She has published numerous articles in the areas of ethnohistory and cultural relations of First Nations in Central British Columbia. Her work has appeared in *Feminist Studies, Ethnohistory, American Indian Journal of Culture and Research*, and *B.C. Studies*.

Gwyneth Hoyle is presently a research associate with the graduate program at Trent University's Frost Center of Canadian Heritage and Development Studies. Gwyneth's research in northern travel literature led to her sustained interest in the firm of Revillon Frères, a French fur trade company. Gwyneth has coauthored with Bruce Hodgins *Canoeing North into the Unknown*, a historical record of travel on Canada's northern rivers.

H. Lloyd Keith is professor of history and sociology at Shoreline Community College in Seattle, Washington. He holds a Ph.D. in sociology and higher education from the University of Washington. He currently teaches Northwest and Canadian history and is actively engaged in research in the

Canadian fur trade. Presently, he is working on a documentary history of the early fur trade in the Mackenzie River Basin.

Caroline Mufford is a long-time resident of central British Columbia who has been active in working with First Nations and involved in recording both oral histories and community histories. She is presently a graduate student in First Nations studies at the University of Northern British Columbia.

Laura Peers is an ethnohistorian who specializes in Ojibwa and northern Cree history from the Great Lakes to Saskatchewan. She is the author of *The Ojibwa of Western Canada, 1780–1870* and a number of other publications. She is currently a SSHRC Postdoctoral Fellow at the University of Winnipeg.

Carolyn Podruchny is a graduate student at the University of Toronto. She is writing a dissertation that explores work, play, gender, race, and culture among French Canadian laborers in the Montreal fur trade from 1780 to 1821.

Susan Sleeper-Smith is currently an assistant professor in the Department of History at Michigan State University, Susan received her Ph.D. from the University of Michigan in 1994. She teaches early American, Native American, and environmental history. Her research interests focus on women in the western Great Lakes and Mississippi River Valley fur trade. She has published in the *American Indian Journal of Culture and Research*, and on H-Net, Humanities-On-Line.

Gregory A. Waselkov has directed archaeological excavations at French colonial and historic Creek Indian sites. He is presently an associate professor of anthropology at the University of South Alabama. He recently coedited *William Bartram on the Southeastern Indians* in 1995, and is currently writing a book on archaeology at Old Mobile, the original capital of French colonial Louisiana.

Bruce M. White holds a Ph.D. in anthropology from the University of Minnesota and an M.A. in history from McGill University. He has conducted extensive research on the fur trade and has written numerous articles pertaining to social and economic relationships between people who participated in the trade. His article, "The Fear of Pillaging: Economic Folktales of the Great Lakes Fur Trade" appeared in *The Fur Trade Revisited*.

William Wicken is an assistant professor in the Department of History at York University in Toronto. Formerly a research associate at the Gorsebrook Institute, Bill served on the Program Committee of the Seventh North American Fur Trade Conference in Halifax.

Index

A

Ainsse, Joseph, Louis, 34, 188
Alec, Janet, 13, 16, 17
Alec, Lashaway, 13
Alexis, Adanas, 21
Allouez, Father, 55
Anderson, Alexander Caulfield, 291
Anderson, Thomas G., 165
Askin, John, Jr., 162
Askin, John, Sr., 161, 162
Assiniboia. *See* Red River settlement
Astor, John Jacob, 286, 287, 308n.10
Auldjo, Alexander, 35

B

Bachelor's Club, the, 33, 48n.11
balance sheet, in determining fur trade profitability, 184-88
Baxter, Alexander, 336, 337, 338, 339, 344n.34
beads, as trade good, 200-201
Beaver Club, the: appropriation of laborers' heroic experiences, 32, 37-38, 43, 44, 45; and the aristocracy, 38; calumet in functions of, 35-36, 44; consumption of alcohol in functions of, 36, 42, 43-44; dinners of, 35-36, 42-43, 44; dress codes of, 43; emphasis on male heroic ideal, 32, 36, 41, 42, 45, 46; emphasis on merits over birthright, 39; entrance requirements for, 40; ethnic and religious affiliations within, 39-40, 41; exclusion of fur trade laborers from, 37; founding of, 31; ideals of, 39; importance in transition from frontier to polite society, 41, 47n.2; intermarriage among members of, 39; membership of, 31, 34-35, 38, 39, 40; motto of, 45; organizational structure of, 40; political and economic power of members of, 35; role in development of gender and class identities of members, 36, 37-39; role in reminiscing in, 32, 44-45; ties to the North West Company, 34-35, 48n.16; ties with freemasonry, 34; toasts of, 40-41
beaver: importance of to Carrier nations, 17, 27n.7; pelt values, Saskatchewan and Canada, 233, 234
Beetz, Johan, *326*; breeding of silver foxes, 323, 324-25; early interest in animal breeding, 320; early life of, 319-20; education of, 320, 325; employment by Revillon Frères, 321-23, 329n.26; high prices paid for pelts by, 317, 321-23; marriage of, 320; move to Canada of, 320; and Spanish influenza epidemic, 326-27
Beikie, John, 249, 266
Beikie, Penelope Macdonnell, 249, 265
Berry, William, 335, 342n.22
Black, C. J., 319
Blanchard, Caleb, 339
Block Conservation System, the, 225, 237